MAKE THE SCORE...
GET THE JOB!!!

Free Live Support

The Job

Choosing the right study guide is one of the most important decisions you will ever make. Effective test preparation is the key.

The Score

Your goal is to achieve the highest possible score. To succeed on this difficult and rigidly timed exam, you must master the incredible speed demanded and learn skills that you've never even dreamed of.

Postal Exam Quick Course

This course offers complete test preparation in less than 12 hours. It is designed to be as quick and easy as possible, but nothing is left out. You get it all in one economical package ... full details on the exam, six up-to-date practice exams, free live support, and much more.

T. W. Parnell ... Best Selling Test Prep Author

Mr. Parnell's study guides are consistently ranked national bestsellers. Postal exam applicants praise his realistic practice tests and his simple yet effective test taking strategies. Customers say that his guides are easier to use and offer more test prep value. Mr. Parnell can help you jump-start your Postal career just like he has for thousands of others!

Just listen to what others have to say about Mr. Parnell's study guides ...

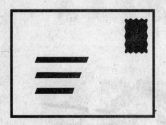

I used your book and got a job. I am living proof that at age 47 you can do it with good instruction and proper strategies. - J. G., Virginia

Buying your book was the best money I ever spent. Your book is easy to understand and has awesome strategies. The Postmaster offered me a job the very day I got my score in the mail. - J. D., Arkansas

*I still can't believe that I got a score of 100! When people ask how I did it, I tell them to go buy your book. Your practice tests are **EXACTLY** like the real thing, and your test taking tips are an absolute lifesaver. - J. B., New Hampshire*

After purchasing your course and another book, I realized that your course was much easier to use. I received a score of 100! Your book made all the difference in the world. - K. I., Missouri

I didn't even get the book until the day before the exam, and I still scored a 95.4. This book is a must for anyone who wants to score high enough to really get a job. - S. S., Michigan

Postal Exam Quick Course

Exams 470 & 460

Complete Test Preparation in Less than 12 Hours

The material in this book is believed to be current and accurate as of the publish date to the best of the author's knowledge. The information presented herein is based upon the author's experience, observations of Postal procedures, comments from Postal employees, and comments from experienced Postal exam applicants.

Code 470460-006499

Mr. Parnell welcomes feedback from his customers.

Send us your score. Let us know how well the Postal Exam Quick Course worked for you.

E-mail address: info@pathfinderdc.com • *Postal address: P.O. Box 1368, Pinehurst, TX 77362-1368.*

To the love of my life ... Rebecca

A message from the author ...

With over 800,000 employees at more than 38,000 facilities, the U.S. Postal Service is the nation's largest non-military employer. **Postal jobs offer great wages, unbeatable job security, and a complete benefits package** that includes excellent health insurance, a generous retirement program, and more. As of the publish date of this book, starting wages for the fulltime jobs filled from exam 470 were $13.61 - $16.72 per hour.

The Postal Service offers **career opportunities without demanding specialized education or work experience.** A high school diploma is not even required. The only real requirements are that you must be a U.S. citizen or a permanent resident and you must be between the ages of 18 and 65. Of course, there will be the usual background check and drug screen.

Sounds almost too good to be true? It is ... sort of. Not the facts about Postal jobs - those are all true. The frustrating part, the major obstacle, is that **there is an extremely difficult employment exam between you and one of these jobs.**

Postal authorities advise that **over 70% of all applicants fail the exam** and that the average score of those who manage to pass is only a 76. The highest possible score (without veterans preference points) is 100, and 70 is passing. Experts agree that a score in the high 90's is needed to be called in for employment within a reasonable period of time.

What can you do to overcome the odds? If everyone else performs so poorly, what can you do to assure success? The answer is a formula frequently quoted by professional athletes. This is your secret to success as well.

TRAINING + COMMITMENT = SUCCESS

This guide provides your training needs - the instruction and the practice tools. You must provide the commitment. **If you commit yourself to the simple test prep schedule outlined in this course, success will follow.**

For the most effective use of this guide, **just follow the step-by-step instructions.** You will first learn about the circumstances surrounding the test and about exam content. Then you will learn about critically needed test taking strategies. Finally you will master the required skills and speed as you take a series of six realistic and up-to-date practice tests.

You have purchased the best Postal test prep tools available. **You have the opportunity to turn your dreams into reality.** The key now is commitment - your commitment. Do not let this opportunity escape for lack of effort! Show the initiative. Muster the effort. Go forth and conquer!

T. W. Parnell

TABLE OF CONTENTS

Continued on next page …

HOW TO USE THE POSTAL EXAM QUICK COURSE

Yes, you can effectively prepare for Postal exams 470 and 460 in less than 12 hours. You can indeed excel on the exam without spending five years (pardon my exaggeration) working through one of those 500 page books. All you have to do is complete this simple step-by-step course.

You can spread the 12 hours (or less) out over whatever number of days you like. To prepare leisurely, you can work less than an hour per day over a couple of weeks. If you happen to wait until the last minute, like so many of us do, that's OK too. You can do all the test prep work in only a few days. I know of applicants who, even though they did not even buy my book until the day before the test, scored very well after doing all their preparation in a single day. I certainly do not recommend waiting until the last day, but this demonstrates the flexibility and success of the course.

This course is totally flexible and can be arranged to fit anyone's schedule. You do not have to complete each session in a single sitting. The individual sessions can be broken down however you like. As detailed in the instructions, each major session can be broken down into shorter sessions.

The Postal Exam Quick Course offers you three different ways to prepare for the exam. You can use the book by itself for basic preparation. For more detailed instruction, we offer the book with three audio CD's. For computer assisted instruction, we offer the book with a CD-ROM. If you do not already have the audio CD's or the CD-ROM, visit our website *www.PostalExam.com* or see the order form at the back of the book for details. These CD's are tremendous test prep tools that greatly enhance your preparation and make your practice work absolutely realistic and convenient.

In the Test Preparation portion of the course, you will learn all about the exam and about the all-important test taking strategies. Three different sets of Test Preparation instructions are provided on the following page. One set of instructions is for individuals preparing with the book only. A second set of instructions is for individuals preparing with the book and audio CD's. The third set of instructions is for individuals preparing with the book and CD-ROM. Choose the instructions that apply to you, and simply follow the step-by-step directions.

In the Practice Exams portion of the course, you will master the necessary skills and speed as you take six complete practice exams. As before, three different sets of Practice Exam instructions are provided … one set for individuals preparing with the book only, one set for the book with audio CD's, and one set for the book with CD-ROM. On this type of exam, knowledge is of little value without practicing to master what you have learned.

Now, relax and stop worrying. Test taking anxiety can hinder your performance and lower your score. **We're going to make your test preparation and the actual exam as easy and painless as possible.** I am quite serious about asking you to relax and stop worrying. I am also serious when saying that we're going to make your test preparation and the exam as easy and painless as possible. As you progress through this course, you will become confident in your newly acquired abilities. This confidence will greatly improve your performance and your score.

I take the responsibility of preparing you for the exam most seriously. I realize that test preparation includes more than strategies and practice tests. **By the time you complete this course, you will be fully prepared in every possible way - including psychologically and emotionally.**

Enough of this rousing pep talk. Let's get started …

Test Preparation

For most people, this portion of the course should take 3 hours or less as detailed below. This portion of the course can be broken down into several shorter sessions as detailed below.

Book Only	Book with Audio CD's	Book with CD-ROM
• Read and study the first 60 pages of the book. • Per the table of contents, these pages are broken down into a number of sections that cover various topics including general exam and job info, scoring formulas, specific sections of the exam, test taking strategies, etc. • You can complete this segment in one sitting or break it down into as many shorter sessions as you like using the table of contents as a guide. To prepare leisurely, spend a short period of time studying each day over a period of several days. • It will probably take you less than 3 hours to review these pages. The 3 hours allowed for this segment is very generous.	• Follow along in the book as you listen to the detailed instruction and examples on the Postal Exam Training Course CD. • The CD is broken down into 10 tracks. Per the CD label, each track covers a particular topic. • You can complete the CD in one sitting or break it down into several shorter sessions using the 10 tracks as your guide. To prepare leisurely, complete a few tracks each day over a period of several days. • As you go through the CD, you will be asked to take Complete Practice Test #1 section by section. It will be easier to understand the strategies and information presented if you have already experienced the particular section of the exam being discussed. • It will probably take you less than 3 hours to complete the CD. The 3 hours allowed is generous.	• Follow along in the book as you complete the 6 test prep classes on the CD-ROM. Each class covers particular topics. • You can complete the 6 test prep classes in one sitting or break them down into 6 shorter sessions - one session for each class. To prepare leisurely, complete one class each day over a period of several days. • As you go through the 6 test prep classes, you will be asked to take Complete Practice Test #1 section by section. It will be easier to understand the strategies and information presented if you have already experienced the particular section of the exam being discussed. • More detailed instruction is presented on the CD-ROM than on the audio CD because more data can be stored on a CD-ROM. • Since more detailed instruction is presented on the CD-ROM, it will probably take you the full 3 hours to complete the 6 test prep classes. It may take some people a little more than 3 hours.

By the time you finish the Test Preparation portion, you will have a clear picture of what to expect on the exam and of the test taking strategies that make the exam manageable. In the Practice Exams portion, you will do the practice work necessary to master the required skills and speed.

Practice Exams

For most people, this portion of the course should take 6 to 9 hours as detailed below.
This portion of the course can be broken down into several shorter sessions as detailed below.

Book Only	Book with Audio CD's	Book with CD-ROM
• Take Practice Exams 1, 2, 3, 4, 5, and 6.	• Take Practice Exams 2, 3, 4, 5, and 6. Skip Practice Exam 1 since you took it while working through the Postal Exam Training Course CD. (However, if you were naughty and did not really take Practice Exam 1 as instructed while working through the Postal Exam Training Course CD, take it first and then proceed with Practice Exams 2, 3, 4, 5, and 6.)	• Take Practice Exams 2, 3, 4, 5, and 6. Skip Practice Exam 1 since you took it while working through the six test prep classes on the CD-ROM. (However, if you were naughty and did not really take Practice Exam 1 as instructed while working through the six test prep classes on the CD-ROM, take it first and then proceed with Practice Exams 2, 3, 4, 5, and 6.)
• Our schedule allows 90 minutes for each exam. There is only 68 minutes of real testing time in each exam. You will likely finish in less than 90 minutes.	• Our schedule allows 90 minutes for each exam. There is only 68 minutes of real testing time in each exam. You will likely finish in less than 90 minutes.	• Our schedule allows 90 minutes for each exam. There is only 68 minutes of real testing time in each exam. You will likely finish in less than 90 minutes.
• You can take each exam in one sitting or break them down into shorter sessions. Each exam consists of four sections, so you can easily break each exam down into two, three, or four shorter sessions. To prepare leisurely, spread the practice work out over a period of several days.	• You can take each exam in one sitting or break them down into shorter sessions. Each exam consists of four sections, so you can easily break each exam down into two, three, or four shorter sessions. To prepare leisurely, spread the practice work out over a period of several days.	• You can take each exam in one sitting or break them down into shorter sessions. Each exam consists of four sections, so you can easily break each exam down into two, three, or four shorter sessions. To prepare leisurely, spread the practice work out over a period of several days.
• Score each section of each exam as you complete it to measure your performance and progress.	• Score each section of each exam as you complete it to measure your performance and progress.	• Score each section of each exam as you complete it to measure your performance and progress.
• Practice Exam 1 is your first real exposure to the exam, and you have not yet mastered the necessary skills and speed. Do not be discouraged with your performance. Every one blows it the first time around. Practice Exam 1 simply teaches you what to expect and is the first step in a building process.		
• Your performance will improve with each practice exam. After completing all six, you will be prepared for the actual exam. (Note: If you feel the need for extra practice, see page 60.)	• Your performance will improve with each practice exam. After completing all six, you will be prepared for the actual exam. (Note: If you feel the need for extra practice, see page 60.)	• Your performance will improve with each practice exam. After completing all six, you will be prepared for the actual exam. (Note: If you feel the need for extra practice, see page 60.)

GENERAL ENTRANCE TEST BATTERY 470

The 470 exam is a phenomenally popular test used to fill all entry-level processing, distribution, and delivery career positions - over 90% of all fulltime jobs. Thousands of people typically apply when it is offered. A Postal Exam Specialist in Chicago advised that over 169,000 people applied on one occasion when the 470 exam was offered there. What this means to you is that the competition is fierce and that you must make the highest possible score while you have the chance.

The 470 exam is identical in content to the Rural Carrier Associate Exam 460. Even though these two exams are identical, they have different names and are given on different occasions because the 470 exam is used to fill fulltime jobs, and the 460 exam is used to fill a particular part-time job. We will first discuss the 470 exam, and then take a look at the 460 exam.

There are five entry-level jobs filled from the 470 exam. All upper-level processing, distribution, and delivery career positions (the bulk of all fulltime jobs) are filled by individuals who started in one of these entry-level positions and worked their way up. When you are first hired into one of these entry-level jobs, you start out in a Part-Time Flexible (PTF) probationary position. This PTF title will be discussed in detail later. Below are job descriptions with starting wages for these entry-level jobs. Details on fulltime Postal benefits are provided on the next page.

Clerk	Clerks process incoming and outgoing mail in both plant and Post Office facilities using automated mail processing equipment or manual methods of sorting and distribution. Some Clerks work at the front counter selling stamps and serving the public in a number of ways. The work involves continuous standing, stretching, and reaching.
Starting Wages	$15.68 per hour ($31,106 per year) as of late 2003

City Carrier	City Carriers travel planned routes to deliver and collect mail. City Carriers typically cover their route on foot or by vehicle. They must work outdoors in all kinds of weather, have a valid state driver's license, a safe driving record, and at least two years of documented driving experience.
Starting Wages	$16.72 per hour ($33,217 per year) as of late 2003

Mail Handler	Mail Handlers load and unload containers of mail. Mail Handlers transport mail and empty equipment throughout the building. They also open and empty sacks of mail. This position requires heavy lifting.
Starting Wages	$13.61 per hour ($29,967 per year) as of late 2003

Mark-Up Clerk	Mark-Up Clerks type change of address data into a computer and generate labels used to forward mail. Mark-Up Clerks must have good data entry skills and pass a typing test.
Starting Wages	$14.89 per hour ($29,508 per year) as of late 2003

Flat Sorting Machine Operator	Flat Sorting Machine Operators key data into a machine, from memory or by zip code, to distribute large flat pieces of mail. Flat Sorting Machine Operators must have an ability to maintain close visual attention for long periods of time.
Starting Wages	$15.68 per hour ($31,106 per year) as of late 2003

Fulltime Postal Benefits

The five jobs filled from the 470 exam are entry-level career positions. Like all fulltime Postal jobs, they come with the below complete package of benefits (accurate as of late 2003).

Salary Adjustments
Regular salary increases, overtime pay, night shift differential, and Sunday premium pay.

Health Insurance
Postal employees are eligible for the Federal Employees Health Benefits Program, which provides excellent coverage with most of the cost paid by the Postal Service.

Retirement
Postal employees are eligible for the federal retirement program, which provides a defined benefit annuity at normal retirement age as well as disability coverage.

Thrift Savings Plan
Career Postal employees may contribute to the Thrift Savings Plan, which is similar to 401(k) retirement savings plans.

Life Insurance
Postal employees are eligible for the Federal Employees' Group Life Insurance Program. Basic coverage is paid for by the Postal Service, with the option to purchase additional coverage through payroll deduction.

Flexible Spending Accounts
Career Postal employees are eligible for the Flexible Spending Accounts Program after one year of service. Tax-free FSA contributions can be used to cover most out-of-pocket health care and dependent/day care expenses.

Leave
Career Postal employees are eligible for a generous leave program to that includes vacation leave and sick leave.

Holidays
The Postal Service observes 10 holidays each year.

Explanation of the Part-Time Flexible (PTF) Title

It is absolutely imperative that you understand the Part-Time Flexible (PTF) title. When you are first hired into one of the five entry-level jobs filled from the 470 exam, **you start out as a probationary PTF employee.** You will work in this probationary position for a period of time before being converted into to an accredited career employee. You will generally work fulltime hours and receive appropriate wages, but you will not be entitled to benefits until being converted to a career employee.

The Postal Service starts new employees in this probationary position so any that don't seem to be working out can be more easily discharged. We have all heard stories about how difficult it is to fire a career federal civil service employee, and this job security is one of the attractive aspects of Postal jobs. Since it is so difficult to discharge a career employee, **the Postal Service uses this opportunity to weed out undesirables.** However, you should not be overly alarmed by this policy. It takes a real disaster to be considered undesirable.

Fulltime Job in Highest Demand

As of late 2003, **the job in greatest demand is City Carrier**. The Postal Service has more need to hire City Carriers than any other job. Consider the below quote from a recent Postal publication:

> *"The number of delivery points increases by 1.7 million each year. This increase results in … 4,800 new carriers."*

Basically, this means that **the Postal Service must hire at least 4,800 new City Carriers each year** just to satisfy expanding demand. And this doesn't include the large number of City Carriers that must be hired each year to replace employees that leave due to normal reasons. The Postal Service experiences more employee turnover in City Carrier positions than in any other jobs. Plus, Postal authorities say that fewer individuals are applying for City Carrier positions in recent years. The bottom line is that, while there is more demand for City Carriers due to expansion and employee turnover, fewer people are applying for these jobs.

As a matter of fact, **many Postal districts have begun testing frequently - as often as twice a year - just to fill City Carrier Positions.** This is amazing in view of the fact that individual districts usually only offer the 470 Battery exam once every few years.

To recruit more applicants for City Carrier jobs, **the Postal Service significantly increased starting wages for this position.** As of late 2003, City Carriers started out at $16.72 per hour … the highest starting wages for any entry-level Processing and Distribution job.

What more could we ask for? Unless you simply refuse to work as a City Carrier, this is the job to apply for. Even if you don't love the idea of being a City Carrier, it could be a great way to get your foot in the door and then transfer to another type position at the first opportunity.

RURAL CARRIER ASSOCIATE EXAM 460

The 460 exam is given more frequently than any other Postal exam. Most districts give the 460 exam twice a year, and many districts accept applications for the 460 exam year-round. **The 460 exam is used to fill part-time relief Rural Carrier Associate (RCA) jobs.** RCA's fill in for fulltime Rural Carriers when the fulltime Rural Carrier is out due to days off, vacation leave, sick leave, etc.

For those seeking fulltime career Postal jobs, the RCA job can be a stepping stone toward success. When a fulltime Rural Carrier job becomes available, it is offered to the senior RCA at that location. Most Postal employees will tell you that a fulltime Rural Carrier position is the best job that the Post Office has to offer. You work in relaxed rural environment with very little supervision. It's almost like being self-employed.

The 460 exam is identical in content to the General Entrance Test Battery 470. Even though these two exams are identical, they have different names and are given on different occasions because the 460 exam is used to fill part-time RCA positions, and the 470 exam is used to fill fulltime jobs. The 470 exam was discussed earlier in the book. Since the 460 and 470 exams are identical, this one book will prepare you for either.

Even if you are not seriously interested in an RCA position, taking the 460 exam for the practice value as you prepare for the 470 exam is an excellent idea. Since the 460 is given much more frequently than the 470, it is quite possible that you will be able to apply for the 460 and actually take it before being scheduled for the 470. There is tremendous value in experiencing a real exam. Of the various benefits such an experience offers, one of the greatest is the confidence you will feel when you later take the 470. This psychological boost can contribute significantly to your performance on the 470. Most individuals taking the 470 enter the test site full of apprehension, which is certainly detrimental to their performance. This, of course, is one of the reasons you are preparing for your exam. Adding the experience of taking an actual Postal exam to your preparation efforts will contribute greatly to your success.

Below is the RCA job description with starting wages. As a part-time position, the RCA job does not come with benefits. Of course, when a senior RCA converts to a fulltime Rural Carrier position, he or she receives the full package of Postal benefits.

Rural Carrier Associate	Rural Carrier Associates are non-career employees who serve on a rural route. They sort, deliver, and collect all classes of mail up to 70 pounds along a rural route using a vehicle. Rural Carrier Associates provide customers on the route with a variety of services, including selling stamp supplies and money orders. They must generally provide and maintain their own vehicle, but are given an equipment maintenance allowance. Applicants must have a valid state driver's license, a safe driving record, and at least two years of documented driving experience. Rural Carrier Associate positions may lead to a career position as a regular Rural Carrier. When a regular Rural Carrier vacancy exists, the Rural Carrier Associate in the office with the longest period of continuous service may elect to be converted to the career position.
Starting Wages	$15.00 - $16.00 per hour depending upon the location as of late 2003

Employment Eligibility Requirements

Postal employment eligibility requirements are generous. Almost anyone can qualify. Specifics follow.

Education
There is no education requirement. A high school diploma is not even required.

Age
Anyone between the ages of 18 (16 with a high school diploma) and 65 at the time of employment is qualified.

Citizenship
Must be a U.S. citizen or permanent resident alien.

Language
Basic competency in English.

Selective Service Registration
Males born after 12/ 31/ 59 must be registered with the Selective Service.

Employment History
Must provide current and 10 year (if applicable) employment history.

Military Service
Veterans must provide Copy 4 of the DD Form 214 and Certificate of Release or Discharge from Active Duty.

Background Check
A local criminal history check is required prior to employment, and a more extensive criminal history check is completed at employment.

Drug Screen
A qualification for employment is to be drug free and is determined through a drug screen.

Medical Assessment
A medical assessment is conducted to provide information about an applicant's ability to physically or mentally perform in a specific position.

Safe Driving Record
A safe driving record is required for employees who drive at work.

EXAM APPLICATION PROCESS & TEST DATES

With the Postal Service, you don't apply for a job - you apply to take an exam. You don't get to fill out an employment application unless you score high enough on the exam. How to apply is easy. Finding out when you can apply is the difficult part.

Obstacles

Erratic Testing Schedules
Exams are given by individual Postal districts and/or sub-districts on an as-needed basis. There are many Postal districts across the U.S., and most of them are divided up into a number of sub-districts. The net result is hundreds of individual testing locations scattered across the U.S., each of which does its own testing when, where, and how it chooses. Since exams are given on an as-needed basis, the frequency with which they are offered varies widely from one location to another. For instance, some locations may give the 470 exam as often as twice a year, while other locations may offer it only once every few years. There's simply no such thing as regularly scheduled exams.

Application Dates
When a location decides to give an exam, they first announce an application period that can be as short as one week or as long as several months. The length of the application period varies greatly from location to location. The important point is that you can only apply during the specified application dates. Therefore, the most important topic for you right now is the application dates, not a test date.

Announcement Numbers
Another important topic is the announcement number. The Postal Service assigns an individual announcement number for each testing event. In order to identify the particular exam you want to take, you must have the proper announcement number when you apply. Your application cannot be processed without this number, and the number is only valid during the specified application dates.

Test Dates
On the average across the U.S., applicants are usually scheduled to take the test about four to six weeks after applying. But this can vary greatly. There have been some cases where the test was not given until several months afterwards.

There may be two reasons for delayed test dates. First, they usually wait until after the application period ends before giving the test. In cases where the application period is open for several weeks or even months, there may be a significant delay for those who applied early on. However, in other cases where the application period is open for several months, they may give the test several times during the application period as sufficient numbers of applications are accumulated. Secondly, after all the applications are received, they have plan the logistics required to give the exam. And, since thousands of applicants may respond, arranging to test all of them takes a great deal of planning.

They will notify you of your test date by sending you a scheduling notice by mail. Most applicants receive their scheduling notices about two weeks before the scheduled test date. You are supposed to receive the scheduling notice at least one week before your test date. It is not possible to find out anything about your test date until you receive the scheduling notice.

How to Find Application Dates & Announcement Numbers

Your most pressing need is to find application dates and announcement numbers. This is also the most challenging part of the process. Described below are ways you can find this critically needed info.

Finding Application Dates & Announcement Numbers Online

The Postal Service now publishes exam application dates and announcement numbers online at *http://uspsapps.hr-services.org/usmapdetail.asp.* This is one of the best Postal testing developments in years. Information on testing opportunities anywhere in the U.S. is now only a click away! (Note: This web address was valid as of the publish date of this book. However, it is possible that future website revisions may render this address invalid. If this address does not work when you try it, go to their home page *www.usps.com* and search for job or employment related pages.)

When visiting this page, you will first need to select which type of announcements you wish to see - "Examinations", "Casual/Temporary", or "Show Both". Select "Examinations" to see info on open exams. Next you will find a map of the U.S. and a dropdown window with all the states listed. Simply click on the map or use the dropdown window to choose a state. Then, all open exams in that state will be displayed by locality along with announcement numbers.

Each announcement number, by the way, is a link to the online application for its particular exam. The announcement numbers are underlined and are in blue font to identify them as hyperlinks. The quickest way to apply from this point is to simply click on the announcement number, and you will be taken to an online application form for that particular exam.

Below is a sample of what you will see on the announcement page followed by explanations.

City/State	Announcement Number	Exam Number	Exam Title	Opening Date	Closing Date
DOVER, DE	<u>67235</u>	470	Processing, Distribution and Delivery Positions	07/11/2003	07/26/2003
DOVER, DE	<u>62452</u>	460	Rural Carrier Associate	06/02/2003	11/28/2003

The **City/State** is the location of the key Post Office for the testing event. Usually, this Post Office is responsible for a larger area surrounding it.

The **Announcement Number**, **Exam Number**, and **Exam Title** are self-explanatory.

The **Opening Date** is the date that the application period begins for that particular exam … the first date that you can apply. It is not possible to apply before this date. As a matter of fact, the exam will not be listed on the online announcement page until this date.

The **Closing Date** is the date that the application period ends for that particular exam … the last date that you can apply. It is not possible to apply after this date. As a matter of fact, the exam will no longer be listed on the online announcement page after this date.

The **Test Date** is not given because it is not available until after all the applications are in and until after arrangements are made for a testing facility.

Online announcements greatly simplify the application process. But, there is a catch - exam info is displayed only during the application period. If you don't happen to check the online announcement page during those dates, you may miss out on the opportunity altogether. Thankfully, it is not unusual nowadays for application periods to remain open for several weeks ... or even several months in some cases. However, one and two week application periods are still very common. To avoid missing out on a testing event, you should check back at this site regularly. We suggest that you check back at least once a week until the test you want to take is finally announced.

Inquiring about Application Dates & Announcement Numbers by Phone

Wouldn't it be great if we could just simply ask by phone for exam info? In fact, you can ... that is, you can if you know how to reach someone who really has answers. You see, the Postal Service does not publish their internal phone numbers. They may not, but we do!

Having been in the Postal test prep business since 1982, Pathfinder has collected over 270 phone numbers for key hiring and testing offices nationwide. These numbers, which ring directly into the very human resources and testing departments you need to talk to, are listed in the Postal phone directory at the back of this book. Just pick a number for the location nearest you and give them a call. Be sure to identify the city and state where you would like to take an exam. The nearest office to you is usually the one to talk to, but some districts have strange geographic boundaries, and in such a case you may be referred to another office that is over your area.

Other Ways to Find Application Dates & Announcement Numbers

In many localities, the Postal Service has what they call a "Hiring & Testing Hotline". This is a phone number that rings into a recorded announcement of open employment and testing opportunities. You can call this number 24/7 to hear recorded info. Unfortunately, this number is almost never published in the local phone book. What good is a Hotline if nobody knows it exists? Well, maybe no one else knows, but you do! All their Hiring & Testing Hotline numbers nationwide are listed in the Postal phone directory at the back of this book.

These Hotline phone numbers are great, but just like online announcements, there's a catch. The catch, again, is that the recorded info is usually available only during the application period. If you don't happen to call the Hotline during the application dates, you may miss out on the opportunity altogether. As before, to avoid missing the opportunity, we suggest that you call at least once a week until the test you want to take is finally announced.

When the Postal Service decides to give an exam, they post notices with the application dates and announcement number in the lobbies of all Postal facilities in the area being tested. However, how many of us make a habit of checking out the notices on the bulletin board in the local Post Office when we go in? For that matter, when is the last time you actually stopped by your local Post Office?

Sometimes, but certainly not always, they run an ad with the application dates and announcement number in the local newspaper. Due to a limited budget, it seems that they more often do ***not*** advertise in the paper. And, if they do run an ad, it is usually there for only one weekend or maybe even for only one day. If you don't happen to look at the paper on the particular day the ad is there ... and look at the particular page the ad is on ... you will never find out about the testing event.

How to Apply

As detailed below, there are two ways to apply - online or by phone. The Postal Service no longer uses paper exam application forms. As discussed previously, applying is easy once you have found the critically needed application dates and announcement numbers.

Applying Online

To apply online, go to *http://uspsapps.hr-services.org/beginapp.asp.* When applying online, the very first thing they ask for is an announcement number. Once you enter a valid announcement number, you will be taken to a second screen that asks for your name, social security number, mailing address, phone number, and e-mail address. That's the only info they want. As discussed before, you're only applying to take a test ... you're not applying for a job. You won't be asked to fill out one of those long employment applications unless you score high enough on the exam to be offered a job. Then, about two weeks before your test date, you will receive a scheduling notice instructing where and when to report for the exam. (Note: This web address was valid as of the publish date of this book. However, it is possible that future website revisions may render this address invalid. If this address does not work when you try it, go to their home page *www.usps.com* and search for job or employment related pages.)

Another way to apply online was discussed in the section about online exam announcements. In this section, we discussed the fact that the online announcement number is actually a hyperlink to an online application form. In fact, if you click on the announcement number link, you will be taken to the very online application form mentioned in the above paragraph. The only difference is that the announcement number will already be filled in on the application for you when you link your way to it.

Applying by Phone

To apply by phone, use a touch-tone phone to call the toll-free application number 1-866-999-8777. You will be asked to provide the same info mentioned above (except for the e-mail address) using the touch-tone keypad and by speaking slowly and clearly. Just like applying online, the very first thing they ask for is an announcement number. Once you enter a valid announcement number, you will be asked for the rest of your info. Then, about two weeks before your test date, you will receive a scheduling notice instructing where and when to report for the exam. (Note: This phone number was valid as of the publish date of this course. However, it is possible that future changes by the Postal Service may render this number invalid. If this number does not work when you try it, pick the location nearest you from the Postal phone directory in this book, and give them a call to find out the number you should use.)

HIRING PROCESS

Revolutionary New Hiring Program Makes It Easier to Get A Job

The Postal Service plans to have a new hiring program in place sometime in 2004 that will make it far easier to get a Post Office job anywhere in the U.S. This new program will call for more participation by the applicant, but the extra effort is well worth it. As of the publish date of this book, a pilot of this program was being tested in nine districts.

Depending upon when and where you take the exam, it is possible that you could be hired under the old program. According to contacts within the Postal Service, there is almost a 100% certainty that the new program will indeed be adopted. But, there is a remote possibility that the new program could be abandoned. Just to be safe, we will review highlights of both the old and new programs.

Old Hiring Program

Under the old program, when you apply to take an exam, you are applying for jobs only in the local area. When taking a test, a list of local facilities is provided, and you are usually allowed to mark up to three locations where you would like to work. Similarly, when taking the 470 exam, you are asked to mark which of the entry-level jobs you are willing to accept. Assuming that you score high enough, you will only be offered the jobs and locations you marked.

After the exam is given, the names of all applicants that pass are placed on a local hiring register, which is simply a list of names ranked in order by score. In essence, if you pass the exam, you have automatically applied for the jobs and locations you marked. As job openings become available, the highest names (scores) on the register are called in for interviews. Eventually, they offer the exam again and build a new register from the results of the new exam.

Unless you refuse to accept particular jobs or locations, we encourage applicants to mark the maximum number of choices. This greatly increases your potential employment opportunities. If you accept a less than ideal job or location, later transfers are always a possibility. And, you are not forced to accept any offers. You have the right to refuse an offer and request that your name remain active on the register. This way, you will still be considered the next time a job opening becomes available.

New Hiring Program

Under the new program you still have to take an exam, but that's where the usual part ends. You use one exam score to go online, check for posted job openings, and apply for jobs anywhere in the U.S. that are filled from that particular exam. You can apply for posted jobs all across the country with your one exam score! Following are tentative details on the new program. This information was valid as of the publish date of this book, but it is possible that parts of the program could be revised by the time it is instituted nationally. When you take an exam, you will be given full current details.

Here's where your participation is needed … Under the new program, you are not automatically considered for any jobs. To be considered for a job, you must find its online posting and apply. During the pilot program, only involved applicants can apply in this fashion. Once the program is functioning nationally, all applicants will be given details on how to use it. But, anyone can visit the website to check it out. The address is *http://jobsearch.usajobs.opm.gov/a9usps.asp*. This is the Postal job postings page on the USA Jobs website. (Note: The above web address was valid as of the publish date of this course. If this address does not work for you, go to the Postal Service homepage *www.usps.com* or to the USA Jobs homepage *http://www.usajobs.opm.gov/* for help.)

On this site, first choose the job title(s) and location(s) for your search, and then all jobs fitting your choices are displayed. Along with other details, an opening date, closing date, and job announcement number are given for each job posting. You can only apply during the posted application dates. Job openings are only posted during their specified application dates, so you must check back frequently to assure that you don't miss any opportunities. Those who apply will be considered based upon their test scores. As always, your exam score is the most important part of getting a Postal job.

You can also use your one exam score to apply for jobs by phone under the new program. Just use a touch-tone phone to call the toll free application number 1-888-880-0415. But, when applying for a job by phone, you can only apply during its specified application dates, and you must have the job announcement number. This is the same challenge we faced when discussing how to apply for exams ... How do you find application dates and announcement numbers? You find job application dates and announcement numbers the very same ways that you found exam application dates and announcement numbers - online, by phone, Hotlines, postings in Post Office lobbies, etc. Review the section on how to find exam application dates and announcement numbers for details. (Note: This phone number was valid as of the publish date of this course. However, future changes render this number invalid. If this number does not work for you, pick the location nearest you from the Postal phone directory in this book, and give them a call to find out the number you should use.)

According to our contacts, once the new program is fully functioning, individuals who took an earlier exam will probably be merged into the program in some fashion. This will enable everyone, regardless on when they took an exam, to apply under the new program once it is fully in place.

In addition to the obvious benefits of this new program, there is an absolutely fabulous benefit hidden just below the surface. Under the old hiring program, what happened if you took an exam in your hometown but scored poorly because you did not prepare well? What happened was that you didn't get a job, and you had to wait up to several years before the exam was offered again.

But ... Under the new program, all you have to do is wait for the test to be given again anywhere within traveling distance. It doesn't have to be in your hometown. If you are willing to drive a few hours to take the exam again and to improve your score, just keep your eyes open for testing events elsewhere in your state and in neighboring states. The exam may be offered somewhere within driving distance in only a few months ... or maybe even in only a few weeks.

So, this time you (1) diligently prepare with our course, (2) drive a few hours to take the exam again, (3) make a great score, and (4) use the great score to apply for openings anywhere in the U.S. - including in your hometown. So what if you have to drive a few hours to take the exam again. It's worth it to go from zero chance to a real chance for a Postal career!

You can take exams anytime and anywhere they are offered. But remember this ... In every case they will keep your newer score and toss the older score. So if you retake an exam to improve your score, be very serious about your test preparation. It would be heartbreaking to retake an exam only to make a lower score the second time.

The USA Jobs website, by the way, is operated by the U.S. Office of Personnel Management for the purpose of posting federal job openings to the public. You may want to visit their homepage at *http://www.usajobs.opm.gov/* to check out all types of federal job postings, not just Postal jobs.

Employment Interview

The most important element of the hiring process is your score. Without a high enough score, nothing else matters. But, there is another important step - the employment interview. As with any other potential employer, you must go through the interviewing process, and **the interview can make you or break you**. There are many publications available about how to present yourself in an interview. You may want to review one in preparation for your interview. Below are points to consider and/or to be prepared for:

- Arrive early. Do not be late!
- Remember - first impressions are lasting.
- Your personal appearance, grooming, attitude, and behavior are being examined.
- Establish eye contact with the interviewer. Failure to do so leaves a poor impression.
- Be attentive and interested. Ask relevant questions.
- Try to relax. Speak clearly and in a normal tone of voice.
- Don't respond too quickly. Pause to think before answering.
- Be prepared to answer honestly about past work experiences and work relationships.
- Do not make excuses for past mistakes. Show that you have learned from them.
- Be prepared to discuss why you want a Postal career and what you can contribute.
- Thank the interviewer for his/her time. Make his/her last impression of you favorable.

There is one question you can expect for sure if you interview for the position of City Carrier. They always seem to ask how you would react if faced with a bad dog when attempting to make a delivery. Various customers have shared their responses to this question with us, but there is one response that seems to be the best. (Please bear in mind that this is an opinion, and that it is only an opinion.) The best response we have heard is, if the dog is particularly aggressive, to postpone delivery until supervisory advice can be obtained in order to avoid an on-the-job injury or incident.

Special Hiring & Testing Benefits for Military Veterans

Eligible veterans may qualify for special testing, scoring, and hiring benefits. The following benefits and requirements are quoted from various publications. However, these requirements are revised from time to time, particularly as U.S. military personnel become involved in armed conflicts.

To take advantage of these special benefits, or for additional information, veterans should call the nearest Postal facility listed in the phone directory at the back of this book.

Rather than waiting for the next public exam to be given, honorably discharged veterans may apply within 120 days (before or after) of their discharge date for any exam that was offered to the public during the period they were in the military.

Rather than waiting for the next public exam to be given, eligible 10 point veterans may apply once at any time for any or all exams at any or all installations. In some cases for some jobs, an eligible 10 point veteran must be hired before a non-veteran even if the non-veteran has a higher exam score.

Eligible veterans may qualify to have 5 or 10 preference points added to their raw test scores. It is possible for an eligible veteran to score over 100 on an exam after adding preference points. The following explanation of preference points was excerpted from a Postal Service publication.

5 Points (Tentative)
May be awarded to a former member of the Armed Forces who was separated with an honorable discharge (or under honorable conditions), is not disabled, and who meets one or more of the following criteria:

- Served on active duty in a pre-World War II campaign or during World War II (12/7/41 - 4/28/52).
- Served on active duty during the period beginning 4/28/52 and ending 7/1/55.
- Served on active duty for more than 180 consecutive days, other than for training, any part of which occurred between 2/1/55 and 10/14/76.
- Began active duty after 10/14/76 and before 9/8/80 and served in a campaign or expedition for which a campaign badge is authorized.
- Enlisted after 9/7/80 or entered on active duty through means other than enlistment after 10/14/82 and completed 24 months of continuous service or the full period for which called to active duty and served in a campaign or expedition for which a campaign badge is authorized.
- Enlisted after 9/7/80 or entered on active duty through means other than enlistment after 10/14/82 and completed 24 months of continuous service or the full period for which called to active duty and served active duty during the period beginning 8/2/90 and ending 1/2/92.
- Served in a campaign or expedition for which a campaign badge is authorized and was discharged early under 10 U.S.C. 1171 or for hardship under 10 U.S.C. 1173.

10 Points - Compensable (Less than 30%)
May be awarded to a former member of the Armed Forces who was separated with an honorable discharge (or under honorable conditions) and has a service-connected disability that is at least 10% but less than 30% compensable.

10 Points - Compensable (30% or More)

May be awarded to a former member of the Armed Forces who was separated with an honorable discharge (or under honorable conditions) and has a service-connected disability that is 30% or more compensable.

10 Points (Other)

May be awarded to:

- Veterans who were awarded the Purple Heart.
- Veterans who receive compensation or pension from the Department of Veterans Affairs or disability retired pay from the Armed Forces.
- Veterans who have a service-connected disability that is not compensable or that is less that 10% compensable.
- The unremarried widow or widower of a honorably separated veteran, provided the deceased veteran served in active duty during a war, or the veteran died while in the Armed Forces.
- Spouses of certain veterans with a service-connected disability.
- Mothers of certain deceased or disabled veterans.

What's on the Exam?

The twin 460 and 470 exams consist of the below four sections.

The **Address Checking Section** has 95 questions, each of which consists of a pair of addresses. In this section you will are given only six minutes to compare the address pairs in all 95 questions and to answer if they are exactly alike in every way or if they are different in any way at all.

The **Address Memory Section** requires you to memorize 25 addresses found in five boxes. You will have several three and five minute timed segments during which you are to memorize the locations of these addresses and/or to complete related practice exercises. During the final segment, you are given only five minutes to answer 88 questions from memory about the locations of these addresses. This is by far the hardest part of the exam.

The **Number Series Section** gives you 20 minutes to answer 24 math questions. Each question consists of a series of numbers whose elements follow one or more sequences. You are to figure out the sequences involved and calculate what two numbers would logically follow in the series.

The **Following Oral Instructions Section** has 31 questions and lasts as long as it takes for the questions to be presented verbally either by the test administrator or by a recording. Each question is a set of instructions that prompts you to make certain marks in your test booklet and then to darken the correct answer(s) on the answer sheet.

Answers for all four sections of the exam are marked on an **Answer Sheet**. The answer sheet is broken into four sections, one for each of the above four sections of the exam. All questions on the exam are multiple choice. To answer each question, you darken an oval on the answer sheet that contains the proper answer (A, B, C, D, or E) for that question. In this book, the answer sheets are necessarily printed with black ink. However, **on real exams, answer sheets are printed in various colors**. Depending upon which exam you take, the answers sheet may be printed with pink ink, blue ink, etc. This should not present any problems, but we wanted to forewarn you so that you are not taken by surprise. Unexpected surprises can be distracting and may affect your performance.

Scoring Formulas

Each individual section of the exam is scrored separately. Then the scores for the individual sections are combined to create the overall exam score. Details follow. (Don't blame me, by the way, for the goofy formulas and/or the lack of information. I'm just the messenger. The Postal Service made up these scoring formulas and decided what information should be made available to the public, not me.)

To score the **Address Checking Section**, count your number of correct answers and your number of wrong answers. Then subtract the number of wrong answers from the number of correct answers. The result is your score.

> **Address Checking Example:** Let's say that, out of the 95 questions in the Address Checking section, I managed to answer 85 in the time allowed. And, of the 85 that I answered, 75 were correct, and 10 were wrong. To score myself, I subtract 10 (the number of wrong answers) from 75 (the number of correct answers). My score is a 65.

To score the **Address Memory Section**, count your number of correct answers and your number of wrong answers. Then subtract ¼ of the number of wrong answers from the number of correct answers. The result is your score.

> **Address Memory Example:** Let's say that, out of the 88 questions in the Address Memory section, I managed to answer 76 in the time allowed. And, of the 76 that I answered, 60 were correct, and 16 were wrong. To score myself, I subtract 4 (¼ of the 16 of wrong answers) from 60 (the number of correct answers). My score is a 56. When figuring ¼ of the number of wrong answers, the result will rarely be a whole number ... as in ¼ of 16 = 4. So, you will frequently need to round off. For instance, if you had 11 wrong answers, ¼ of 11 = 2.75. In this case, you round 2.75 off to the whole number 3.

To score the **Number Series Section**, simply count your number of correct answers, and that is your score.

> **Number Series Example:** Let's say that, out of the 24 questions in the Number Series section, I managed to answer 22 in the time allowed. And, of the 22 that I answered, 20 were correct, and 2 were wrong. My score is simply a 20 ... the number of correct answers. Wrong answers do not figure into the formula for this section.

To score the **Following Oral Instructions Section,** simply count your number of correct answers, and that is your score.

> **Following Oral Instructions Example:** Let's say that, out of the 31 questions in the Following Oral Instructions section, I managed to answer 30. And, of the 30 that I answered, 27 were correct, and 3 were wrong. My score is simply a 27 ... the number of correct answers. Wrong answers do not figure into the formula for this section.

When it comes to the overall exam score, things get even more complicated. The Postal Service will not release formulas for calculating final overall exam scores for fear of "compromising the integrity of the testing process". We know how they score the individual sections, but not how they mix those individual scores together to come up with a final score.

From experience though, **we do know a few things about the final exam score.** We know that the highest possible score (without veterans' preference points) is 100, and that 70 is passing. We know that there are 238 questions on the exam. Therefore, if you answered every question correctly within the time allowed, you would accumulate 238 points. We know also that you do not have to answer every question correctly and capture all 238 of the possible points in order to score a perfect 100. We have learned that you can still score a perfect 100 even after losing about 12 points whether by answering questions incorrectly or by leaving them blank. And, we know that you can score a 96 or 97 even after losing about 24 points whether by answering questions incorrectly or by leaving them blank. However, every point you miss after the first twelve, whether by answering incorrectly or by leaving the question blank, hurts your final score. We know as well that the score is not a percentage. You cannot say that your score will be a 90 just because you captured 90% of the points.

It is important that you **score every practice test you take** in order to measure your progress and to determine how much more effort is needed and/or where it is needed. However, measuring your progress can be difficult if you do not have the proper tools (scoring formulas) for measuring it. Sure, you can score the individual sections, but if anyone claims that they can tell you how the individual section scores convert into an overall exam score, they are telling you an untruth. Our best advice is simply to never be satisfied with any score you make. Score each practice test for the sole purpose of beating that score next time. Always strive to improve your performance on the next practice test. Your goal should be to capture every possible point - to achieve your highest possible score. Applicants are called in for employment on the basis of scores, so your objective is to be as close to the top of the list as you possibly can be!

How do unanswered questions (blank answers) affect your score? Unanswered questions are not mentioned in the scoring formulas. But, do not mistakenly assume that this means they are acceptable. Just the opposite, unanswered questions severely hurt your exam score. Consider this … As mentioned previously, there are 238 questions on the exam. Therefore, if you answered every question correctly, you would accumulate 238 points. To make a high score, you need to capture as many of these points as possible. Every point you fail to capture, whether by leaving a question unanswered or by answering it incorrectly, reduces your final score. Obviously, it is to your advantage to correctly answer as many questions as possible and to leave the fewest possible questions blank.

To confuse matters more, **applicants usually receive two different scores from a single test when taking the 470 exam**. As noted earlier, there are five entry-level career positions filled from the 470 exam. The Postal Service uses one scoring formula to create a score for three of these positions - Clerk, City Carrier, and Flat Sorting Machine Operator. They use another scoring formula to create a score for the other two positions - Mail Handler and Mark-Up Clerk. (This is the historic grouping of positions and scores, but it is possible that the grouping could be revised at some point.) So, you end up with two different scores from a single test.

When the 470 exam is given, it is usually for the purpose of filling all five of the previously discussed entry-level jobs. However, there are occasions when it is given to fill not all of these jobs, but instead only one or a few of them. On such occasions, if there is only one type of job to be filled, or if the few jobs to be filled are within the same grouping, you will receive only one score.

Since exam 460 is used to fill only one particular job, applicants get only a single score when taking this test. It is unknown whether the scoring formula used for the 460 exam is the same as or different from the 470 scoring formulas.

Should You Guess on the Exam?

You should not guess on the Address Checking or Address Memory sections. As noted in the their scoring formulas, you are penalized for incorrect answers on these sections. Therefore, guesses are more likely to hurt you than help you.

However, **guesses are acceptable on the Number Series and Following Oral Instructions sections** due to their particular scoring formulas. On these two sections, if you guess and get the correct answer, you picked up an extra point. And if you guess wrong, you simply missed a point that you were not going to capture anyway. If you do make a guess, go with your first choice - don't sit and debate between two or three possible answers. Psychological tests have shown that your first choice is usually the best one. Obviously, however, guessing in any form should be a last resort.

Are You Allowed to Make Marks or Notes during the Exam?

During the Address Checking and Address Memory sections, you are absolutely not allowed to make marks or notes of any kind in the question booklet. The only type of marking you are allowed to do during these sections is darkening your answers on the answer sheet. Making marks or notes of any kind in the question booklet during the Address Checking or Address Memory sections will result in disqualification.

However, **during the Number Series and Following Oral Instructions sections, you are specifically instructed to make certain marks, notes, and calculations in the question booklet** in order to find the correct answers. During these sections, not only is it is acceptable to make marks or notes in the question booklet; it is even required.

Preparation before the Exam

On this type of exam, **knowledge is of absolutely no use without sufficient practice** to develop the skills, strategies, and speed necessary to succeed. This calls for consistent study and practice. <u>Cramming the night before will not work!</u> Following are several tips for your advance preparation:

- **Study all of the material in this book and take all the practice exams before your test date.** Do not wait until the day before the exam to start studying! On the other hand, do not complete all your practice work months before the exam date either. Natural memory loss will cause you to lose some of the skills and speed that you worked so hard to master. Follow our performance proven test prep schedule for the best results.

- It is very important that you **take the practice tests under conditions as similar as possible to the real exam.** Find a quiet setting where you will not be disturbed while taking the practice tests. Timing yourself cannot be stressed enough during the practice tests. It is impossible to master the extreme rate of speed required without being precisely timed and experiencing the immense pressure of time. To conveniently and precisely time yourself, use either our Timed Practice Test CD or our Test Prep CD-ROM. Visit our website *www.PostalExam.com* or see the order form in the back of the book for details. Use the answer keys in the back of the book to score each practice exercise as you complete it. This will enable you to identify any areas of weakness and concentrate more on them.

- A psychological term called the **"practice effect"** applies to all sections of the exam. The practice effect occurs when a person repeatedly takes an exam a number of times during a brief period of time. For most people, exam scores will be higher the more often you take the test because of increasing familiarity with the material. This trend should become evident as you score your practice exams. Your score on the second exam should be higher than on the first, the third should be even higher, and so on.

- As you learn to **pace yourself for speed and accuracy**, your scores should increase. For example, let's say that at first you were only able to finish half the questions on a practice test during the time allowed. This may be discouraging, but at least you answered most of them correctly - you only missed a few. You should be proud of this score, right? No, wrong --- *very wrong!* You are putting way too much emphasis on accuracy and not nearly enough on speed. To solve this, you must push yourself and practice to develop more speed. Or, let's say you finish an entire practice exam within the required time period, but half of your answers are wrong. It should be obvious that you are placing too much emphasis on speed and not enough attention on accuracy. To solve this, simply slow down and check your answers more carefully. The key is to find a happy medium between speed and accuracy.

- This book gives you **simple short-cut strategies** that will greatly enhance your test-taking ability and your score. It is critically important that you understand and master these strategies so that you can make the highest possible score.

Scheduling Notice

As previously discussed, about two weeks before your test date, you will receive a scheduling notice advising when and where to report for the exam. Below are details on the scheduling notice and explanations for some of the confusing information it contains.

The scheduling package is a 12 page booklet. In addition to the date, time, and location for your test, it contains general information about the testing process and a few sample questions for each section of the exam.

The scheduling package instructs you to tear page 1 off the booklet and to bring page 1, a picture ID, and two #2 pencils with you in order to be admitted. Page 1, the page that you tore off the booklet, serves as your pass to enter the exam site.

The **sample questions in the package** are provided simply to make unprepared applicants aware of exam content. Altogether, these few sample questions do not represent even 10% of a complete practice test, and they provide no real practice value.

Note, however, that **the format of the few sample questions in the package confirms that the exam format in this book is accurate and up-to-date**. Do not be confused by conflicting formats that may be presented in other books.

The scheduling package repeatedly states "You will not be expected to be able to answer all the questions in the time allowed." This is certainly true of the general public, most of who completely fail their exams. But, **this does not mean that failing to answer all the questions is acceptable.** As discussed earlier in the scoring formula section, you need to capture every possible point, and every point you lose - whether by answering incorrectly or by leaving questions unanswered - hurts you final score. After completing this course, you however, will be prepared to achieve your highest possible score. You will have mastered the skills and speed necessary to succeed.

Note as well that **the Address Memory sample questions confirm the accuracy of the repeating elements and of the Second Digit Strategy to be discussed later in this book.**

Also, the package mentions that you will have "three practice exercises" in the Address Memory Section. This is indeed true. But, for some reason, they do not mention that you will have an introductory exercise and two study periods as well before the final segment. **Be assured that the Address Memory format of seven segments presented in this book is exactly right.**

Test Day

Once your scheduled test date arrives, here are a few pointers that will help out:

- **Get a good night's rest, and have a light, nutritious meal**.

- **Do not drink too many liquids before the test**. Do visit the restroom before starting your test. This may sound trivial, but it may literally make the difference between success and failure. The test will last over two hours, and applicants are not allowed to leave the exam room during the test for any reason whatsoever. You surely will not perform well if forced to take the exam under uncomfortable and distracting conditions.

- **Dress in layers so that you can comfortably tolerate extreme temperatures in the exam room.** I have gone to testing events during the heat of summer dressed in light clothing only to freeze due a supercharged air conditioning system. I have gone to testing events during the cold of winter dressed in warm clothing only to be roasted in the exam room due to a supercharged heating system. The exam is usually given in a large rented facility. The Postal employees administering the exam have no more knowledge of the heating and cooling system or ability to control the temperature than you do. Dress so that you can add or remove layers of clothing to accommodate whatever environment is encountered in the exam room.

- **Leave home early, and plan to arrive at the test site early**. Allow time for any conceivable delays (auto problems, traffic congestion, etc.) that you can possibly imagine. If your notice says that the test is scheduled for 9:00 AM, the doors will be literally locked at precisely 9:00 AM. It doesn't matter whether you are 30 seconds or 30 minutes late - you are late period, and you will not be admitted. The rules are absolutely rigid on this matter. Also, due to the large number of exam applicants, there is always a long line of people at the exam site waiting to be processed and seated. I have witnessed a few cases where there were simply not enough seats to accommodate all the applicants. It is a very good idea to arrive early so that you won't have to stand in line forever and to assure that you don't get turned away.

- Another reason to arrive early is to have a chance to **familiarize yourself with the examination room**. Applicants who have acquainted themselves with their surroundings are more comfortable and tend to perform better.

- **Bring page 1 from the scheduling package that you received by mail and a picture I.D.** You will be checked at the door for both these items, and you will not be admitted into the test site or allowed to take the exam if you do not have them.

- **Bring pencils** as instructed in your scheduling packet. Usually there are plenty of extra pencils made available at the test site, but don't automatically assume that such will be true. If you don't bring your own pencils, and if they don't provide any for you, how can you take the test?

- **Work diligently on each section of the test until you are instructed to stop**. Every second counts. If you finish before time is called, go back to check your answers in that section, but only in that section. Do not ever open your test booklet to a section other than the one you are supposed to be working on at that point. Turning to a section other than the one you are supposed to be working on is grounds for disqualification.

- On a related topic, **do not ever open your test booklets or pick up your pencil until your are instructed to do so.** Likewise, immediately stop working, close your test booklets, and put down your pencil upon being instructed to do so. Failure to comply may look like an attempt to cheat and may cause you to be disqualified. It would be heartbreaking to be disqualified because you innocently doodled with your pencil or because you absentmindedly opened your test booklet when you were not supposed to. An excellent training tool to help avoid such catastrophes is our Timed Practice Test CD described in the order form at the back of the book and on our website *www.PostalExam.com.* In addition to precisely timing you as you take your practice tests, this CD reviews the instructions for you section by section and emphatically directs you exactly when to open or close your booklet and when to pick up or put down your pencil.

- **If you finish all the questions in one section before time is called, can you go back to other sections to finish questions there that you did not have time complete?** No, absolutely not. You will be specifically instructed to open your test booklet only to the section you are taking at that moment, and then to close it immediately when time is called. Opening your booklet to another section is grounds for disqualification.

- **If you finish one section with extra time left over, can you go back to re-darken answers in previous sections that may not appear to be darkened well enough?** No, absolutely not. Again, you will be specifically instructed to mark answers on the answer sheet only for the section you are supposed to be taking at that time. Marking answers in another section of the answer sheet may appear to be an attempt to cheat and may lead to your disqualification.

- **I feel compelled to emphasize the possibility of being disqualified.** You can be disqualified for failure to follow instructions or for doing anything that might be interpreted as an attempt to cheat. There are monitors continually wandering around the room to assure that applicants follow instructions and do not cheat. If an applicant appears to be doing something unacceptable, he or she can be disqualified without even knowing it. The monitor may silently make a note of the person's name, and then arrange for that person to receive an ineligible (failure) rating. That person might have performed wonderfully and might have deserved a great score, but the record will reflect an ineligible rating due to some type of improper conduct. Or, the person who appears to be acting improperly might be physically escorted from the room and rated ineligible. I don't want to make you paranoid, and I have never heard of a circumstance where an individual actually was disqualified. But, it is a very real possibility. When taking your exam, actions that can lead to disqualification will be stringently discussed by the exam administrator. I simply want to impress this possibility upon you in order to assure that it will not happen to you.

- **Mark the answer sheet clearly.** If you erase, do it completely. The machine scoring your answer sheet is not able to distinguish between intentional marks and accidental marks or changes.

- **Pace yourself.** Find a happy medium between speed and accuracy. Do not spend too much time on any one question.

- **Try not to let other people or noises distract you** - and there will be distractions and noises no matter how hard the test administrator and monitors try to avoid it. As a matter of fact, the monitors can create distractions themselves. I have personally experienced situations where two or three monitors stopped for a chat … right beside me … and during the test!

EXAM CONTENT AND TEST TAKING STRATEGIES

There are four elements essential to successful test preparation - knowledge of exam content, test taking strategies, practice tests, and commitment. This book provides information on exam content, effective strategies, and authentic practice tests. The only element we cannot provide is commitment. Thorough and complete test preparation demands dedication and a drive to succeed.

Following are important points of which you should be aware as you begin your preparation:

- When you take the real exam, and likewise when you take the practice tests in your book, in every case **you will be working with two 8-1/2" X 11" booklets** or pages - the very size of this book. One will be the test booklet containing the questions. The other will be the answer sheet booklet where you mark your answers.

- **The questions are all multiple choice, and the answers are always in the form of a letter – A, B, C, D, or E.** The way you mark answers on the answer sheet is to darken the oval containing the correct answer or letter.

Success is virtually impossible without effective test taking strategies. Following are strategies that apply to the test as a whole. Later we will learn about strategies for each individual section.

Exam Strategy #1 We will use the military strategy "**Divide and Conquer**". If we master each section individually, we cannot help but succeed on the exam as a whole.

Exam Strategy #2 During the first three sections of the exam, **check frequently to assure that the number of the question you are answering matches the number of the answer sheet item you are marking.** Marking answers in the wrong answer sheet spots can be disastrous. If you get out of order on question 3 and don't discover it until you are on question 53, it is entirely possible that you have just blown 50 questions. Recovery from such a disaster is almost impossible.

Exam Strategy #3 To increase your speed and to avoid getting out of order as described above, **the test booklet and answer sheet should be placed as close together as possible** at all times. If both booklets are fully opened, you are working on at least 11" X 34" of paper spread out on top of your table, as pictured in the below illustration. The questions and answer spots are so far apart that errors are likely to happen.

Your first strategy to avoid this problem is to **fold the booklets in half at the stapled seams and place the folded booklets next to each other**. This one step cuts the distance between questions and answers by half. Flip the folded booklets over as needed and as you progress through the exam.

Then, depending on the positions of the questions and answers, **you can usually even lay one booklet partially on top the other**, as pictured in the below illustration. Now the questions and answers may be only a few inches apart. These strategies can bring the questions and answer spots very close together indeed for greater speed and accuracy.

Exam Strategy #4 | Another strategy to avoid getting out of order is to **use one of your spare pencils, the side of your hand, or your finger(s) to guide your eyes** back and forth between the test booklet and the answer sheet. In essence, you are using one of these items to mark your spot and track your progress as you race through the test so that you don't accidentally skip a question and get out of order. But, <u>do not</u> use any thing else (like a ruler or a piece of paper) for a guide as you practice at home. It may be easier, but you will not have access to anything like that on the actual test. During the exam, the only items you are allowed to have with you are the ones you were instructed to bring - which include only yourself (complete with all parts of your body) and your pencils. Becoming dependent on a tool that will not be available at the real exam can have disastrous results.

Exam Strategy #5 | **If you somehow get out of order despite efforts to the contrary, all may not be lost**. The best plan to salvage such a predicament is to skip ahead to the next question and continue - being cautious to mark answers in the correct spot. Then, when you finish and if sufficient time remains, you can try to find where you got off track and attempt corrections.

Exam Strategy #6 | **Each strategy presented offers value in terms of points earned** on the test. Some strategies enable you to capture many points, and others only a few. The sum total is what is important to you. To achieve your highest possible score, you should master all these strategies through practice - do not ignore the ones that may seem less valuable. Any tool that can add any points at all to your score is incredibly valuable.

Exam Strategy #7 | The first three sections of the exam are rigidly timed. In each section you are asked to complete more questions in a limited period of time than a most people could ever hope to accomplish without some kind of help. This book is your help. Your goals are to [1] learn about the contents of the exam; [2] study the strategies given; and [3] master the necessary skills, strategies, and speed as you take the six complete practice exams. **On this type of exam, knowledge is of little value without practicing to master what you have learned.** As previously mentioned, our Timed Practice Test CD described on the order form in the back of the book and on our website *www.PostalExam.com* is a convenient tool for practicing realistically and for timing yourself precisely in order to master the needed speed.

Exam Strategy #8 | **Once you master the necessary level of speed, you will notice that you develop a certain pace** - not unlike a runner competing in a race. What happens to a runner who stumbles or stops in the middle of a race? Not only does the runner lose time while he or she is stopped, the runner also loses time as he/she strives to regain the original pace - the runner is not moving as rapidly until his or her maximum pace is again achieved. The runner would have performed much better if he or she had not stopped.

The same principle holds true on the Address Checking and Address Memory sections of this exam where speed is the most critical element. As you race through these sections marking answers at maximum speed, **do not stop to make a correction if you suddenly realize that you have answered a question incorrectly**. Like the runner, you would be giving yourself a double whammy - you lose time while you're stopped, plus you work more slowly (answer fewer questions) as you rebuild your pace. Think of the seconds lost as you attempt the following steps to make a correction:

1. Stop writing.
2. Raise your pencil away from the paper.
3. Reverse the position of your pencil so that the eraser is facing the paper.
4. Erase the wrong answer.
5. Raise your pencil away from the paper again.
6. Reverse the position of your pencil again so that the lead is facing the paper.
7. Brush away the bits of rubber that were ground off your eraser as you used it.
8. Invariably, you see that part of the mark remains, so you decide to erase again.
9. So, you raise your pencil away from the paper again.
10. Reverse your pencil again so that the eraser is facing the paper.
11. Erase the remaining marks.
12. Raise your pencil away from the paper again.
13. Reverse the position of your pencil again so that the lead is facing the paper.
14. Brush away the bits of rubber again.
15. Look closely to assure that you really did erase all of the mark this time.
16. Mark the correct answer.
17. Attempt to rebuild you original pace as you answer the next several questions.

Most people go through these 17 counterproductive and time consuming steps every time they stop to make a correction. A better idea would be to pause just long enough to make a tiny dot next to the incorrect answer. Then, when you finish all the questions in that section (and most people are able to finish all of them all after completing this course), go back to correct the answers where you made the tiny dots. This strategy enables you to make the best use of the limited time available.

Exam Strategy #9 | As you are beginning to see, and will shortly see even more, this exam is not like any other test you've ever taken before. In many cases, the information and strategies presented will be understood better and will be appreciated more after experiencing a practice test. Accordingly, you are encouraged to **review the instructions and strategies again after completing each of your practice exams.**

ADDRESS CHECKING SECTION

In this section, there are 95 questions, each consisting of a pair of addresses, that must be answered in only 6 minutes. Your are to determine whether the two addresses in each question are exactly alike in every way or if they or different in any way. If they are alike, you mark the answer "A" for Alike. If they are different, you mark the answer "D" for Different. On this section, you have only two answer choices - A or D. For a clearer picture, review the two samples below:

Sample 1.   5432 Lassiter Rd   5432 Lassiter Rd   Ⓐ Ⓓ

The two addresses in this sample are exactly alike, so you would darken the oval with the letter "A".

Sample 2.   Susquehanna, PA   Susquehana, PA   Ⓐ Ⓓ

These two addresses are different. The letter "n" appears twice in the city name to the left, but only once in the spelling on the right. So, you would darken the oval with the letter "D".

This section is truly a speed test. **Comparing addresses is not terribly difficult, but doing so accurately at the pace demanded is next to impossible without the right strategies and a great deal of practice.** This section is important for several reasons, not the least of which is the fact that it offers the most potential points - it has more questions, meaning more points you can capture, than any other section. Following are the strategies needed to master this section:

Address Checking Strategy #1   **Push yourself for speed.** Force yourself to practice at pace beyond your level of comfort. When you become comfortable at that faster speed, push yourself yet again to an even faster pace beyond your newly acquired level of comfort. Repeat the cycle over and over as you continually increase your ability and tolerance for speed. All of us learned in school to place most our emphasis on accuracy and little, if any, on speed. The result is that most of us have a speed/accuracy imbalance - at least in terms of this exam. The challenge is, via practice, to learn to place a little more emphasis on speed and a little less on accuracy. This may sound odd, but consider this … How good a score should you expect if every question you answered was correct, but you were only fast enough to answer half the questions in the time allowed? You will score far better if you answer all the questions within the time allowed, even if you answer a few incorrectly because you were working so fast!

Address Checking Strategy #2   **Distributive Practice** is what athletes do … consistent practice over a period of time. Considering the extreme speed, subtle muscle control, and level of eye/hand coordination demanded, the Address Checking section is quite similar to an athletic event. Approach your practice as though you were training for the Postal Olympics rather than a Postal exam.

Address Checking Strategy #3   On every section of the test, the exam administrator will briefly explain the instructions, advise you to open your booklets, direct you to pick up your pencil, and finally tell you to begin. The vast majority of exam applicants do not know what to expect, but **your preparation will give you a particular advantage** on the Address Checking section. Unlike the others who are hanging on the administrator's every word and therefore have a delayed reaction time, you (1) should have your finger on the edge of your booklet before the administrator says the first word; (2) immediately flip it open as the administrator begins to utter the words "Open your test booklet"; (3) as the administrator gives further instructions, answer the first few questions in your mind; and (4) when the administrator says to pick up your pencil, immediately mark those first few answers that you did in your mind. You did not cheat, but you did pick up an advantage of a few points on everybody else by using your foreknowledge and common sense.

Address Checking Strategy #4   **Scan the addresses ... Do not read them.** You don't have time to read and digest every number and letter in the addresses. Simply scan them looking for differences.

Address Checking Strategy #5 Train yourself to **scan over the shorter or easier address pairs only once, and the longer or more difficult address pairs only twice.** *NEVER MAKE A THIRD PASS!* There is simply not enough time. With practice, this can be accomplished.

Address Checking Strategy #6   **What if you find that, near the end of the time allowed, you do not have time to complete the final few questions at your present pace?** In such a case, speed through the final questions allowing only one scan per question no matter how difficult the addresses look. The odds are in your favor that you will get more right than wrong. The resulting score should be better than if you had not answered the final few questions at all.

Address Checking Strategy #7   **As you move your eyes back and forth from the test booklet to the answer sheet and back again, use this back and forth motion to do your scans.** When reading, you must go from left to right. But, in this case, you are scanning, not reading. Scanning from left to right seems more natural. However, with practice, you should be able to scan the letters and numbers in the addresses for differences from right to left (backwards) just as easily. This way, you don't waste the time it takes to move your eyes all the way back over to the left side of the addresses before beginning your next scan.

Address Checking Strategy #8   If you finish before time is called, you should obviously **check you answers**. But ... Should you check all of them? Should you check only the ones marked "A" for alike? Or, should you check only the ones marked "D" for different? You do not have time to check all the answers. Check only the ones marked "A" for alike. Our studies indicate that most of the answers you marked "D" for different are probably correct - you marked "D" because you really saw a difference between the addresses. Mistakes occur when you miss a subtle difference because you are working so fast, and you mark the answer "A" for alike rather than "D" for different.

Address Checking Strategy #9   Once you find a difference between the two addresses in a question, immediately mark the answer "D", and move on to the next question. **Do not continue looking for more differences.** One difference makes the two addresses just as different as ten would.

Address Checking Strategy #10   **Do not guess on the Address Checking section**. Due to the scoring formula, wrong answers count against you. On this section, there is more risk of harm than good when guessing blindly.

Address Checking Strategy #11   **You cannot make notes or marks of any kind** in the test booklet during the Address Checking Section. The only marks you are allowed to make are the answers you darken on the answer sheet.

Address Checking Strategy #12   **Practice is the key to performance.** If you are not satisfied with your Address Checking scores after completing all six practice exams in the book, you may want to do extra practice work to improve your performance. We provide free extra Address Checking practice tests for this very purpose. See page 60 for details.

ADDRESS MEMORY SECTION

This section is important due to the number of potential points available - second only to the Address Checking section. The scored portion of the Address Memory section has 88 questions to be answered in five minutes. Turn to the Address Memory section of one of your practice exams in this book to see how the section is structured and what the questions look like.

This is by far the hardest part of the exam. Without the right strategies, the speed is formidable, and the memorization is virtually impossible. This section is the biggest reason so many people fail. The Address Memory strategies in some books are so complicated and technical that they do more harm than good. **Of the many benefits provided by this book, perhaps the greatest is the simple yet phenomenally successful Address Memory strategies you are about to learn.**

On this section, you are to memorize 25 addresses in five boxes as displayed in the sample below.

A	B	C	D	E
4700-5599 Camp Ishee 5600-6499 Sarah Kaytham 4400-4699 Lang	6800-6999 Camp Hunter 6500-6799 Sarah Island 5600-6499 Lang	5600-6499 Camp Dearman 6800-6999 Sarah Carlton 6500-6799 Lang	6500-6799 Camp Norwalk 4400-4699 Sarah Nultey 4700-5599 Lang	4400-4699 Camp Plank 4700-5599 Sarah Airline 6800-6999 Lang

The boxes are labeled A, B, C, D, and E. **Your goal is to remember which box each address is located in.** Each question in this section is an address from one of the boxes. To answer, darken the letter of the box the address came from - A, B, C, D, or E.

In each box, at the top is an address with a number, the next one down is a word address without numbers, in the middle spot another number address, then another word address, and finally at the bottom a number address again. **This is the exact format you will see on the actual exam.**

The addresses are very repetitive. The repeating addresses make memorization far more difficult. Looking at all five boxes horizontally, we notice that the top number addresses all contain the same street name "Camp". Viewed horizontally again, the middle number address in each box contains the street name "Sarah", and the bottom number addresses all contain the street name "Lang". Each street name is repeated five times horizontally. Looking at the top address in Box A, we see the number 4700-5599. In our sample, 4700-5599 repeats at the bottom of Box D and in the middle of Box E. Most the numbers repeat two or three times at various locations in the different boxes. Again, **you will see these very types of repeating formats on the actual exam.**

The Address Memory section is broken into seven timed segments, as listed below in their proper order. This segmented format adds even more confusion to an already bewildering task:

1. A simple three minute exercise consisting of only a few questions with the boxes shown. This segment's purpose is simply to demonstrate how to answer the questions. The boxes and addresses shown are the same ones that will be used throughout all seven segments.

2. A three minute segment during which you are to study and memorize the locations of the 25 addresses. There are no questions in this segment. You are provided only with the five boxes to be studied and memorized.

3. A three minute exercise during which you are asked to answer 88 questions from memory if possible, but the boxes are available if you need to refer to them. This is a practice exercise. It is not scored and will not effect your exam score.

4. A three minute exercise during which you are asked to answer 88 questions from memory. You are not given the boxes to use - you must work from memory. Thankfully, this is another practice exercise that is not scored and that will not effect your exam score.

5. Another study period like Segment 2 with the same boxes and addresses, but five minutes long instead of three minutes.

6. An 88 question exercise similar to Segment 3, but five minutes long instead of three. You are asked to answer from memory if possible, but the boxes are shown for your use if needed.

7. **This final segment is the one and only part of the Address Memory section that is scored**. Your score on this segment is your score for the Address Memory section, and it does effect your overall exam score. Presumably, the prior segments of the Address Memory section were there to help you remember the addresses for this final scored segment. Most people, however, find the strange format and broken periods of concentration to be more confusing that helpful. On this final segment, you are given 88 questions to answer in only five minutes, and you must answer from memory - the boxes are not displayed.

Following are the strategies needed to master the Address Memory section. These strategies should enable you to vastly reduce the volume of material to be memorized, to more easily memorize the remaining material, and to answer the 88 questions within the five minutes allowed.

| Address Memory Strategy #1 | **Memorize the addresses horizontally across the page**, not vertically down the page. Most people find horizontal memorization to be more manageable.

| Address Memory Strategy #2 | **Memorize only the first four boxes - Boxes A, B, C, and D**. Ignore Box E - the fifth box. As you take the test, mark the addresses appropriately that you recognize as having come from Boxes A, B, C, or D. By the process of elimination, where did any address come from that you don't recognize? Necessarily, from Box E - the one you did not memorize. So, mark every address you don't recognize with the answer "E". Using this strategy, you can correctly answer every question dealing with Box E even though you intentionally did not memorize any of the addresses in Box E. This one simple, common sense strategy alone reduces the material to be memorized by 20%!

| Address Memory Strategy #3 | **Use imagery and/or association to horizontally memorize the word addresses** in Boxes A, B, C, and D. Simply put, tie the words together to form an image, mental picture, phrase, or concept which you can relate to and that you can therefore remember more easily. It helps to form an image or association where the words are imagined to interact with each other in some way. The more realistic, lifelike, and/or graphic your image or association - the better you can remember it. Each person will see a different image or association in the word addresses based upon his or her individual personality, experiences, likes, dislikes, etc. It may take a little thought, but you should eventually be able to find an image or association in almost any series of words. It becomes easier with practice. A vivid imagination contributes to your effort. The words must be tied together and memorized in the same order as they appear from left to right.

Using the five boxes given earlier as samples, let's try out this strategy. The word addresses in these sample boxes, by the way, are actual addresses from real exams I have taken.

- The first horizontal row of word addresses from the Boxes A, B, C, and D read as follows. Remember, we are only concentrating on the first four boxes. We will ignore Box E.

Ishee Hunter Dearman Norwalk

As an outdoorsman, I immediately saw something I could relate to when looking at these words. I used parts of the words to create the sentence:

"I hunt deer now."

Notice the highlighted parts of the words:

Ishee Hunter Dearman Norwalk

I took liberty with the word "dear" out of "Dearman" and used it to refer to animal "deer". Also, I played with the sequence of the letters in the word "Norwalk" to come up with the word "now". Being a hunter, I can very easily remember this sentence. Let's say I used to hunt ducks but wanted to try something different - so… "I hunt deer now".

How does this association help? If I see any of the words Ishee, Hunter, Dearman, or Norwalk in a question as I take the test, I silently recite to myself the memorized association/sentence "I hunt deer now." If the word in the question is Ishee, which relates to "I" (the first element of my memorized sentence), the answer is A. Why? Because (1) we memorized the words in horizontal order from left to right; (2) therefore, the first word in my memorized sentence necessarily came from the first box - Box A; and (3) the word in the question relates to the first word in my sentence which relates to the first box - Box A. If the word in the question is Hunter, the answer will be Box B - second word in my memorized sentence…second box…Box B. If the word in the question is Dearman, the answer is Box C - third word…third box…Box C. And of course, the word Norwalk will relate to my fourth word "now" so the answer would be Box D - the fourth box. In each case, I silently recite my sentence which immediately tells me the answer by the position of the word in my sentence - first/A, second/B, third/C, or fourth/D.

- Now let's look at the other horizontal row of word addresses from Boxes A, B, C, and D:

Kaytham Island Carlton Nultey

When taking a real exam, I again immediately saw something in the words that related to me. You see, my wife has a friend named Kay who is a real car nut. She always seems to be trading in her current car for a new one, only to do it again several months later. Here's what I saw:

"Kay is (a) car nut."

Notice the highlighted parts of these words:

Kaytham Island Carlton Nultey

As in the previous example, I used parts of words and did a little rearranging of the letters in the word "Nultey". In this case, as I silently recite my sentence, I sort of mumble and play down the "a" in my sentence to emphasize that it is not a key word. It is only an aid to help me make sense of the key words that relate to Boxes A, B, C, and D. Just like before, when I see one of the words Kaytham, Island, Carlton, or Nultey in a question - I silently recite my sentence, and the position of the word in my sentence tells me what box the address came from. First word…first box…Box A; second word…second box…Box B; etc.

- The situation I am about to suggest has not actually happened to me, but it is a possibility, so we must be prepared. The two word address examples we just discussed came from different exams. But, what if they had been on the same test? Here's the problem - there are two "i" words: "Ishee" in the first sample from Box A and "Island" in the second sample from Box B. This would cause confusion if I use my sentences as they are. If I discovered this type of duplication, I would go back to the first sentence and use "She" from "Ishee" instead of "I" to make the sentence "She hunts deer now". No problem - my wife occasionally hunts with me. So, "she hunts deer now" rather than ducks.

- What if you recite the wrong phrase/sentence? What if you recite the one that is supposed to go with the other horizontal row of word addresses? No problem! The word address in the question should prompt you to recite the proper phrase/sentence. But even if you recite the wrong one, don't worry. There's only two of them. If the first one doesn't fit, recite the other one. What if the word address in the question doesn't fit either of your memorized sentences? That's OK too. Some of them are not supposed to - the ones from Box E, which you purposely did not memorize. As reiterated below, you will be able to correctly answer all Box E questions by the process of elimination even though you did not memorize any of the addresses in Box E.

- How do we answer questions we don't recognize? We simply mark the answer E. This is part of our plan. By the process of elimination, any word address we don't recognize necessarily came from Box E. So, we mark all unrecognized word addresses as "E" and get every one of them right without even trying to really memorize them!

Address Memory Strategy #4   **Use the "Second Digit Strategy" to memorize the number addresses.** Here's how it works:

Look at the top row of number addresses across the sample boxes horizontally from left to right as shown below. We see at least 65 characters that we must memorize:

Box A	Box B	Box C	Box D	Box E
4700-5599 Camp	6800-6999 Camp	5600-6499 Camp	6500-6799 Camp	4400-4699 Camp

By ignoring Box E as previously discussed, we can reduce the number to something over 50, but that's still a lot. What if we could identify a single key character from each box and memorize only that one item. This would cut the material to be memorized by over 90%. But with all the repetition from box to box, is there a key non-repeating element? Let's analyze the addresses to see if anything does not repeat…

We can rule out the street names - in our sample boxes, the street names Camp, Sarah, and Lang that accompany the number addresses repeat horizontally across all five boxes. What about the numbers themselves? Let's look at the top numbers from all five boxes:

Box A	Box B	Box C	Box D	Box E
4700-5599	6800-6999	5600-6499	6500-6799	4400-4699

Look at the first digits from each address in order horizontally as highlighted above. The character in the first digit location of Box A is the number "4", in Box B it is a "6", in Box C it is a "5", in Box D a "6", and in Box E a "4". The first digits won't help us because of the repetition. The first digit in both Boxes A and E is a "4". Also, the number "6" repeats as the first digit location of both Boxes B and D.

What about the other digits? The third digit in each box is a 0. Same for the fourth digit. In the fifth digit location, the number 6 repeats three times - in Boxes B, C, and D. The number 9 appears in both the seventh and eighth digit locations of all five boxes. As you see, the numbers repeat all across the board. This is true for all the number addresses in all the boxes.

But, what about the second digit numbers? We didn't try them. Let's try our sample and see:

Box A	Box B	Box C	Box D	Box E
4700-5599	6800-6999	5600-6499	6500-6799	4400-4699

The second digit characters in order horizontally, as highlighted above, are the numbers 7, 8, 6, 5, and 4. *They don't repeat!* Here is our key non-repeating element. But, how do we use it? First, remember we only memorize the first four boxes - A, B, C, and D. Using our Second Digit Strategy, the only elements we will memorize are the second digit numbers from each address followed by the street name, which means all we want to memorize from this sample is "7 8 6 5 Camp" - or in a condensed form "7865 Camp" - which sounds and looks like a single address itself. This is something you can remember easily … "7865 Camp". Close the book and silently recite it. See, you've already got it memorized! This is tremendously easier than trying to memorize over 65 characters.

So, we've memorized "7865 Camp". What do we do now? As you take the test, any time you see a question with the street name Camp, look at the number in the second digit location of the question. Look only at the second digit - ignore all the other numbers. Let's say that the address in the question is "4700-5599 Camp". We look at the second digit in the question and see that it is a "7". Now, we silently recite what we memorized - "7865 Camp". The second digit in the question (the number 7) matches the first number in the series we memorized. So the answer is "A" - the question relates to the first number we memorized which relates to the first box - Box A. If the second digit of the question matched the fourth number in the series we memorized, the answer would be "D" - the question relates to the fourth number in our series which relates to the fourth box - Box D. And so on.

Using the Second Digit Strategy on the other horizontal rows of number addresses in our sample boxes, we would memorize "6584 Sarah" and "4657 Lang". When taking the test, if you find a question with the address "6500-6799 Sarah", the answer is automatically "B". The second digit in the question matches the second number in the series we memorized for Sarah, which relates to the second box - Box B. If the question is "6500-6799 Lang", we silently recite "4657 Lang" and quickly discover that the answer is "C". The second digit in the question is the number "5", which is the third number in the series we memorized for Lang. So, the answer is "C" - the question relates to the third number in our series which relates to the third box - Box C. With practice, this strategy becomes second nature and phenomenally increases your Address Memory speed and accuracy.

Some people, by the way, find it easier to remember the numbers to be memorized if they associate the numbers with (or picture the numbers in their minds as) sports scores, test scores, dates, temperatures, years, etc. Try this strategy to see if it works for you.

And, some people find it easier to remember if they memorize the street name first followed by the numbers. To memorize in this fashion, you would remember "Camp 7865" instead of "7865 Camp". Then, when you see the street name "Camp" in a question, you would silently recite "Camp 7865" instead of "7865 Camp".

Some people prefer to memorize in pairs rather than all four numbers at once. To do so, spend the first three 3 minute study periods (a total of 9 minutes) memorizing the first two numbers for each - **78** Camp, **65** Sarah, and **46** Lang. Then, spend the final two study periods (a total of 10 minutes) memorizing the last two numbers for each to complete the job - 78**65** Camp, 65**84** Sarah, and 46**57** Lang. Smaller, manageable tasks can be easier.

What if the second digit in the question doesn't match any of the numbers we memorized? No problem - it means that the address in the question necessarily came from Box E. Remember, we intentionally did not memorize any addresses from Box E. So, we mark the answer "E" for any address we don't recognize and correctly answer all Box E questions by the process of elimination.

The only location we did not consider was the sixth digit location, which, like the second digit, also does not repeat. If necessary, you can use the sixth digit in the same fashion, but the second digit is in a more convenient location to work with.

The pattern just discussed has appeared on every exam of which we have knowledge since the new 460 and 470 exams were created in 1993. We send representatives out to take exams as often as possible, and they confirm in every case that this pattern holds true. We hear daily from customers nationwide who confirm that it continues to hold true. However, in the highly improbable (almost impossible) case that you find the second and/or sixth digits to repeat on your exam, simply look for a another digit that does not repeat and use the same strategy for that particular digit.

To allay the fears of anxiety prone applicants, there is one other strategy you can use as a back-up in the highly improbable (almost impossible) case that you find the second and/or sixth digits to repeat. This back-up strategy is much more difficult to use, but is easier than trying to remember all the characters. With this strategy, you again ignore Box E. For Boxes A, B, C, and D, you memorize the first two numbers followed by the street name. For instance, you would either memorize them all together as a single group "47 68 56 65 Camp", or you would memorize them as four separate items "47 Camp", "68 Camp", "56 Camp", and "65 Camp". You can immediately tell that either method would be most difficult. By the way, this is the strategy that most study guides tell you to use.

These first four strategies alone have transformed the Address Memory section into a manageable task. We have reduced the memorization into the below brief items.

7865 Camp
She hunts deer now.
6584 Sarah
Kay is (a) car nut.
4657 Lang

And, there are even more helpful Address Memory strategies yet to come …

Address Memory Strategy #5 Refer back to explanation of the seven timed segments in the Address Memory section. Notice that segment 1 and 3 each give you three minutes to do practice exercises with the boxes shown for your use. Segment 6 is a similar five-minute exercise with the boxes shown. In all three of these segments, you are asked to mark answers, but these segments are not scored. Since they are not scored, it doesn't matter what answers you mark. Wouldn't it be great if you could use these three segments for **extra minutes of study and memorization time** instead of marking answers? Well, you can - but with care. When given instructions during the exam, you are expected to follow them, but there is a way around it in this case. Here's how…

- In segment 1, you are given the five boxes and asked to answer several sample questions in three minutes, but again this exercise will not be scored. The purpose of this exercise is simply to acquaint test takers with the format of the Address Memory section - but you already know all about the format. So, take a few seconds to mark random answers (it doesn't matter what you mark because they will not be scored), and then spend the rest of the time memorizing.

- Likewise, in segment 3 you are given three minutes to do an 88 question exercise with the boxes shown - but again, it will not be scored, and you are certainly not expected to answer all 88 questions. From past experience, they know you will only be able to answer a small portion of that number, and with very little accuracy at that. So, take a few seconds to make a handful of random marks on the answer sheet, and then spend the rest of the time memorizing.

- The same is true for segment 6, but you are allowed five minutes. Again, the boxes are shown. And again, you make a handful of random marks and spend the rest of the time memorizing. Since this exercise will not be scored, there is no reason to make a sincere attempt.

You just picked up an extra eleven minutes for memorization! You now have five study periods, three at 3 minutes each and two at 5 minutes each, for a total of 19 minutes to memorize.

Address Memory Strategy #6   **Answer the 88 questions in order.** Do not attempt to go through the test twice - answering only the word address questions first and the number address questions later. Unfortunately, *you simply do not have enough time to take the test twice!* And that is exactly what you would be doing. Answering 88 questions in five minutes is challenging enough. To attempt going though the test twice in five minutes is all but impossible.

The above strategy about answering the 88 questions in order is indeed a valid one that is the best method for 99% of the people. However, from time to time I run into a customer who may benefit from doing just the opposite. The odds that you personally are such an individual are quite small.

Allow me to explain … Almost everyone has more trouble with the number addresses than the word addresses. But, there are a very few people who have a huge problem with the number addresses. Trying to answer the number addresses questions slows these people down so much that they don't have the opportunity to attempt answering all the word address questions - the questions that they could easily handle if they just had the chance to try them.

For these people who have a huge problem with the number addresses, I suggest that they **do** answer the word address questions first and then go back to answer as many of the number address questions as they can in the remaining time. I recently helped one applicant who had such a problem with the number addresses that the best she could score was in the 30's or 40's. When she tried this alternate method, her score went up to the 50's and 60's. Your goal, of course, should be to score much better than this. But given her limitations, she was happy to have improved that much.

Let me give you two warnings about this method. First, if you believe that you are one of the few people with huge number address problems, try both methods to see which works best for you. Most people are surprised to find that answering the 88 questions in order works better for them after all. Secondly, be very, very careful that you mark your answers in the correct spots on the answer sheet. When skipping all around from question to question rather than answering the questions in order, there is an excellent chance that you will mark answers in the wrong answer sheet spots and end up failing for sure!

Address Memory Strategy #7   **You cannot make notes or marks of any kind in the test booklet during the Address Memory Section.** The only marks you are allowed to make are the answers you darken on the answer sheet. Sure, it would make things much easier if you could make notes or write down your memorized numbers and/or words, but if you do, they are sure to catch it and fail you.

Address Memory Strategy #8   **Do not guess on the Address Memory section.** Due to the scoring formula, wrong answers count against you. On this section, there is more risk of harm than good when guessing blindly.

Address Memory Strategy #9   **Practice is the key to performance.** Speed is just as important as memorization. If you memorize all the addresses perfectly but can only answer half the questions in the time allowed, you have gained nothing at all. Practice is absolutely essential to develop the skills and speed required. As mentioned previously, our Timed Practice Test CD is the most convenient way to practice realistically and time yourself precisely. Plus, this CD repeats the instructions for you section by section. This really helps on the Address Memory section with its confusing format of seven segments. You can check out this CD on our website *www.PostalExam.com* or in the order form at the back of the book.

If you are not satisfied with your Address Memory scores after completing all six practice exams in the book, you may want to do extra practice work to improve your performance. We provide free extra Address Memory practice tests for this very purpose. See page 60 for details.

Address Memory Strategy #10   **Try to complete and stop your Address Memory practice work at least one day before your scheduled test date for the real exam.** Do not continue doing Address Memory practice work all the way up to the night before. Otherwise, the addresses from your practice tests may still be lingering in your mind as you attempt to take the actual exam. Do not let this happen to you. The end result could be failure.

NUMBER SERIES SECTION

In the Number Series section you are given 20 minutes to answer 24 mathematical questions - just under one minute per question. Each question consists of a series of numbers followed by two blanks. Turn to the Number Series section in one of your practice exams to see what the questions look like. Within each series of numbers are one or more sequences. **Your job is to identify the sequences and to calculate, based upon the sequences you identified, what two numbers would logically follow in the series**. Again, these are multiple choice questions. You will have five possible answers from which to choose - A, B, C, D, and E. Each possible answer consists of a pair of numbers, but only one contains the correct pair of numbers in the proper order. You will encounter several types of sequences. Each will be discussed in detail as we examine Strategy #1 - Circles and Squares. The strategies needed to master the Number Series section follow:

| Number Series Strategy #1 | First let's review the types of sequences found in these mathematical questions. Then we will discuss the **Circles and Squares Strategy** used to solve the more difficult types of sequences. Simple mathematical principles rather than a particular strategy are used to solve the first two types of sequences.

- **NUMBER SERIES - ADDITION:** Below are examples of series where the relationship between the numbers is one of simple addition. This is the simplest type of series. It can usually be identified and solved with a quick examination.

    Sample 1:   21   25   29   33   37   41   45   ____   ____

    A quick examination shows this is an addition sequence increasing by 4. (21 + 4 = 25; 25 + 4 = 29; 29 + 4 = 33; and so on.) We can now go to the last shown number of 45 and calculate that the correct answers are 49 and 53. (45 + 4 = 49; 49 + 4 = 53)

    Sample 2:   21   42   63   84   105   126   147   ____   ____

    This one may appear a little more difficult, but upon examination it proves to be another fairly simple addition sequence increasing by 21. (21 + 21 = 42; 42 + 21 = 63; 63 + 21= 84; and so on.) We can now go to the last shown number of 147 and calculate that the answers are 168 and 189. (147 + 21 = 168; 168 + 21 = 189)

- **NUMBER SERIES - SUBTRACTION:** This is a similar type of sequence, but the relationship between the numbers involved is one of simple subtraction. Examples follow.

    Sample 1:   23   20   17   14   11   8   ____   ____

    This sample is a subtraction series decreasing by 3. (23 – 3 = 20; 20 – 3 = 17; 17 – 3 = 14; and so on.) By applying the subtraction sequence to the last shown number of 8, we find that the answers are 5 and 2. (8 – 3 = 5; 5 – 3 = 2)

    Sample 2:   60   53   46   39   32   25   ____   ____

    This sample is a subtraction series decreasing by 7. (60 – 7 = 53; 53 – 7 = 46; 46 – 7 = 39; and so on.) We apply this sequence to the last shown number and find the answers to be 18 and 11. (25 – 7 = 18; 18 – 7 = 11)

- **NUMBER SERIES - ALTERNATING ADDITION:** Now we find the series becoming more difficult. There will be two separate addition sequences in a single series. Here is where we learn the benefits of a simple yet effective strategy called Circles and Squares. Examples follow:

Sample 1:   2   1   4   2   6   3   8   ___   ___

This appears to be a confusing series indeed. To solve the series, we must identify and separate the sequences involved using the Circles and Squares strategy. Here's how it works... First, draw a circle around any numbers you see that seem obviously related. In this case, I see the sequence 2, 4, 6, and 8; so I put circles around these numbers like so:

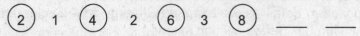

Next, I draw squares around any remaining numbers that don't appear to be related to the circled sequence - yielding a series that looks like this:

Now we need to determine where the blanks fit into our sequences by following the pattern of circles and squares. It is easy to see that we are alternating a circle, then a square, then another circle, and another square. Following this pattern, the first blank will obviously be a square, and the second blank will be a circle. Now our series with the circle and square patterns looks like this:

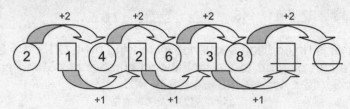

Finally, we find our answers by following the numbers in the two separate patterns. Following the circles, we quickly see an addition sequence increasing by 2. By adding 2 to the last shown number in the circle pattern, which is an 8, we find that the answer to the second blank with a circle around it will be a 10. Following the square pattern, we see an addition sequence increasing by 1. We add 1 to the last shown square pattern number, which is a 3, and find that the answer to the first blank with a square around it will be a 4. We have our answers --- 4 and 10.

Sample 2:   22   7   9   23   11   13   24   ___   ___

This is another case of two separate addition sequences within one series. Again, let's look for some numbers that obviously go together. Right away, I notice that the 22, 23, and 24 follow a pattern, so I'll put circles around them. Then, I'll put squares around any remaining numbers. The result should look like this:

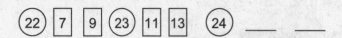

We've identified the two patterns/sequences, but what pattern will the blanks fit into? Looking at our circles and squares, we see a pattern of one circle and then two squares, one circle and then two squares, and so on. Applying this pattern to our blanks, we see that they will both be squares and will look like this:

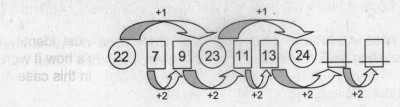

We have learned that the circle pattern can be ignored because both answers fit into the square pattern only. If we solve the square pattern, we will have found our answers. The square pattern is obviously an addition sequence increasing by 2. (7 + 2 = 9; 9 + 2 = 11; 11 + 2 = 13) Now, we can apply this sequence to the last shown square pattern number of 13 to find that our answers are 15 and 17. (13 + 2 = 15; 15 + 2 = 17)

- **NUMBER SERIES - ALTERNATING SUBTRACTION:** These problems are similar to those above, but the two sequences involved deal with subtraction. Examples follow:

Sample 1.   42   41   40   21   20   39   38   ____   ____

Right away, I see some related numbers - 42, 41, 40, 39, and 38. I will put circles around those numbers and squares around anything remaining as displayed below:

42 41 40 21 20 39 38 ____ ____

Now, following the patterns of three circles, two squares, and so on; we see that the first blank will be a circle and that the second blank will be a square - like this:

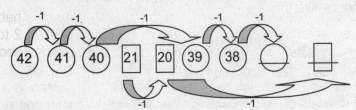

The circle pattern is decreasing by one. So, we apply this pattern to the last shown circle number of 38 and find that the first blank will be a 37. The square pattern is also decreasing by one. We likewise apply this pattern to the last shown square number of 20 and find that the second blank will be a 19. We have the answers - 37 and 19.

Sample 2.   90   80   12   70   60   12   50   ____   ____

Again, at least one pattern is readily visible - 90, 80, 70, 60, and 50 - so we circle these numbers and put a square around any remaining numbers.

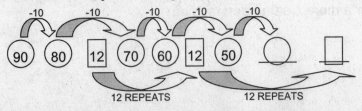

49

Now, by following the pattern of two circles, one square, two circles, one square, and so on; we can see that the first blank will be a circle and that the second blank will be a square. Let's solve the circles first - they are decreasing by 10 each time. We apply this pattern to the last shown circle and find that the first blank will be a 40. The square pattern is simply the number 12 repeating over and over - so the second blank will be a 12. We have the answers - 40 and 12.

- **NUMBER SERIES - ALTERNATING ADDITION AND SUBTRACTION:** One of the sequences within the series this time will be addition, and the other will be subtraction. Examples follow:

Sample 1.   13   12   3   5   11   10   7   ____   ____

The first related numbers I see are 13, 12, 11, and 10 - so I put a circle around them and a square around any remaining numbers - like this:

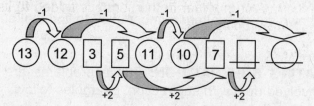

Following the pattern of two circles, two squares, and so on; we see that the first blank will be a square and that the second blank will be a circle. Looking at the circle pattern, which is decreasing by 1 each time, we find that the second blank will be a 9. Looking at the square pattern, which is increasing by 2 each time, we find that the first blank will be a 9 also. We have the answers - 9 and 9.

Sample 2.   50   26   24   55   22   20   60   ____   ____

The first pattern I see is the 50, 55, and 60. So, I will put circles around these numbers and squares around any remaining numbers – like this:

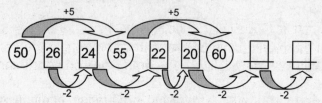

Following the pattern of one circle, two squares, and so on; we see that both blanks will be squares. We can ignore the circle pattern and find our answers by solving the square pattern only. The square pattern is decreasing by 2 each time. By applying this to the last shown square number of 20, we find that our answers will be 18 and 16.

- **NUMBER SERIES - GRADUATING ADDITION AND/OR SUBTRACTION:** The final type of series we will examine have graduating sequences. In this type of sequence, the addition and/or subtraction factors increase or decrease systematically rather than remaining constant. Review the following examples for a more clear understanding.

Sample 1.   2   3   5   8   12   17   _____   _____

This is a graduating addition series where the addition factor begins as a "1" but then increases by "1" each time it is used as displayed below:

$$+1 \quad +2 \quad +3 \quad +4 \quad +5 \quad +6 \quad +7$$
$$2 \quad 3 \quad 5 \quad 8 \quad 12 \quad 17 \quad \_\_\_ \quad \_\_\_$$

Following this graduating sequence, we can see that the answers will be 23 and 30. (17 + 6 = 23; 23 + 7 = 30)

Sample 2.   1   2   4   8   16   32   _____   _____

In this graduating addition sequence, each number in the series is added to itself to create the next number as displayed in the following diagram:

$$(1+1) \quad (2+2) \quad (4+4) \quad (8+8) \quad (16+16) \quad (32+32)$$
$$1 \quad 2 \quad 4 \quad 8 \quad 16 \quad 32 \quad \_\_\_ \quad \_\_\_$$

By following the sequence, we see that the answers will be 64 and 128. (32 + 32 = 64; 64 + 64 = 128)

Sample 3.   5   8   13   21   34   _____   _____

In this graduating addition sequence, each number is added to the number before it in order to create the next number in the series. Note the following diagram:

$$5+8=13 \quad 8+13=21 \quad 13+21=34 \quad 21+34=55 \quad 34+55=89$$
$$5 \quad 8 \quad 13 \quad 21 \quad 34 \quad \_\_\_ \quad \_\_\_$$

By following the sequence, we see that the answers will be 55 and 89.

The above three examples are all of Graduating Addition Series. Graduating Subtraction Series would obviously be similar, but the relationship between the elements in the series would be one of subtraction rather than of addition. You will likely see both types on your exam.

You will also find alternating series questions involving graduating addition and/or subtraction sequences. In fact, you should expect to experience questions where all the different types of sequences are mixed together in various fashions. Likewise, the Number Series practice tests in your book contain questions with all types of intermingled sequences. Remember to use the Circles and Squares Strategy to solve any type of alternating series where two or more sequences are mixed together.

| Number Series Strategy #2 | Fairly simple examples were intentionally used in the previous samples. The intent is to more easily demonstrate the strategies given. The use of more challenging sequences would only serve to confuse you and divert your attention away from the strategies being presented. There will be some simple problems on your actual exam, but there will definitely be more difficult ones than easy ones. This also holds true for the practice tests in this book. **With practice, you will learn to knock out the easier ones quickly so that you will have more time to solve the difficult one by applying your strategies.**

Number Series Strategy #3 **On this section, you should attempt to answer the easier looking questions first and then go back to work on the harder looking ones**. They are all worth exactly one point, no more and no less, whether they are easy or difficult. Look at it this way … What if you used up the final remaining few minutes of the test trying to work on a very difficult question - say number 21. As you close your test booklet, you glance over questions 22, 23, and 24 (that you never even got to try because you were still working on number 21) and see that they look incredibly easy. You mentally kick yourself and think "If I would have just skipped number 21 and gone on to 22, 23, and 24 - I would have picked up those three points easily. Instead, I lost all four points by wasting the last few minutes on number 21." You have an average of just under one minute per question. If you quickly answer the easy ones first, you will have more than one minute each left for the harder ones.

Number Series Strategy #4 **They will make ingenious attempts to confuse you.** There may be two, three, or maybe even four different sequences within a single series. There will be unrelated numbers mixed in just to throw you off. There will cases where the same number repeats over and over within the series. (See NUMBER SERIES – ALTERNATING SUBTRACTION sample number 2). The secret is to remain calm and to use your strategies to Divide and Conquer. Don't get flustered. Remember, there are two basic rules for solving all number series problems: [1] find the pattern or patterns, and [2] apply the pattern or patterns to determine what two numbers would logically follow in the series.

Number Series Strategy #5 **Do not leave any questions blank - blind guesses are acceptable.** This section is scored by simply counting the number of correct answers. So, if time is about to be called and you have not finished the last few questions, guess blindly. It cannot hurt you, and you just may get one or two right - which means one or two extra points.

Number Series Strategy #6 **If you can solve one pattern but not the other, choose the answer by the process of elimination.** You will have five answer choices, each consisting of a pair of numbers. If you are sure that the answer in the first blank should be the number 67 but cannot figure out what number should be in the second blank, look over the answer choices. If only one of the choices has the number 67 in the first blank location, you have found the correct answer no matter what the other number is. If more than one answer choice shows the number 67 in the first blank location, make your best educated guess.

Number Series Strategy #7 **Solutions for all the Number Series problems are given in the back of the book.** For a better understanding of the problems that you missed, closely review their solutions. This should enable you to correctly answer such questions the next time you encounter them. Number Lines, like those used to diagram the solutions in the back of the book, can be used as another tool to solve problems on the test. Most people find the Circles and Squares Strategy to be quicker and easier. However, if number lines are easier for you - especially on more difficult problems - you should certainly use them.

Number Series Strategy #8 **You can make marks, notes, etc. the test booklet during the Number Series Section.** In order to answer the questions, you must do your calculations somewhere. You will be instructed to do your calculations in the spaces between the questions, in the margins, and in other blank spaces found in the Number Series Section of the test booklet. But, the only marks you can make in the Answer Sheet booklet are the actual answers that you darken.

Number Series Strategy #9 **Practice is the key to performance** … the key to mastering your strategies and to recognizing sequences. And again, our Timed Practice Test CD is the best tool for practicing realistically. See our website *www.PostalExam.com* or the order form in the back of the book for details.

FOLLOWING ORAL INSTRUCTIONS SECTION

In this section, a number questions are presented verbally either by the Exam Administrator or on a recording. By following the verbal instructions given for each question, you will create the correct answer, which you will then mark on your answer sheet. This section is very difficult for many until they fully understand it. We have been told that over 60% of all test takers fail this section entirely. This is because **many people never really comprehend how to answer the questions correctly**. But, once it is understood, this section becomes the easiest for many test takers.

When taking this part of the test, there are no questions to read. Instead, there will be a page in the test booklet containing circles, squares, lines, words, numbers, letters, etc. The verbal questions are actually instructions that direct you to select or mark certain items on the page. The selections/marks you make, coupled with the instructions you hear, will lead you to the correct answer. Note the below examples:

Sample 1. _____ A _____ B _____ C _____ D _____ E

For a question like this on the actual exam, you may be told to write the number "67" on the line beside the third letter from the left, and then to mark on your answer sheet the number-letter combination you just created. Accordingly, you would write the number "67" beside the letter "C", which is the third letter from the left. Then you would darken item "67-C" on your answer sheet.

Sample 2. [__ 45] [__ 14] [__ 73] [__ 57] [__ 38]

On this question, you may be instructed to write the letter "D" on the line inside the box with the largest number, and then to mark the number-letter combination you just made on your answer sheet. So, you would write the letter "D" on the line inside the box containing the number "73", which is the largest number. The number-letter combination you created by writing the letter "D" beside the number "73" is "73-D". Accordingly, you should darken item "73-D" on your answer sheet.

If you are a normal and at least partially sane human being, these samples probably only confused you even more. The following strategies should give you a better understanding of the Following Oral Instructions section and provide the test taking tips needed to master this section:

| Following Oral Instructions Strategy #1 | **Number-Letter Combination.** A clear understanding of this term is essential for answering correctly. Most of the verbal questions/instructions cause you to create a number-letter combination, which is simply a number and a letter paired together. For instance, a particular question may instruct you to write the letter B beside the number 18 and then to mark the resulting number-letter combination on your answer sheet. The number letter combination you have just created is 18-B. The answer to this question is 18-B. To mark the answer, go to number 18 on the answer sheet and darken letter B.

The problem is that you may be answering question number 3, yet you are marking an answer at item number 18 on the answer sheet. This goes against everything we have ever learned about taking a test. Up until this very point in our lives, we have always marked the answer to question 3 at item number 3 on the answer sheet, and marked the answer to question 18 at answer sheet item 18, and so on. Herein lies the problem. For this section of the exam, we must unlearn our orderly approach toward test taking.

On the Following Oral Instructions section, the number of the question will have nothing whatsoever to do with where you mark your answer. The one and only thing that dictates where you mark your answer is the number-letter combination. If the number-letter combination for question 13 is 77-D, you mark the letter D at item number 77 on the answer sheet. The fact that this is question number 13 does not matter at all. If the number-letter combination for question number 25 is 4-C, you mark the letter C at item number 4 on the answer sheet.

Occasionally, you will be instructed to simply darken a certain letter at a particular item number on the answer sheet without having first created a number-letter combination. For instance, for question number 23 you may simply be told to darken the letter A at item number 6 on the answer sheet. There was no number-letter combination involved. But, for the most part, a number-letter combination will be involved and will dictate where you mark your answer.

Following Oral Instructions Strategy #2   **Multiple Answers.** There will be instructions that cause you to create several number-letter combinations for a single question. This causes incredible confusion for most individuals when they are told to mark their answers. Being orderly test takers, we expect only one answer for each question and only want to mark one answer for each question. Again, we must unlearn our orderly approach. Be aware that there will indeed be questions that have multiple answers and that you are indeed expected to mark all of them.

Following Oral instructions Strategy #3   **Timing.** The questions/instructions will be read to you at a rather slow and deliberate rate of approximately 75 words per minute. The will be a pause of about five seconds between each question for you to mark your answers. Do so rapidly and be ready to listen to the next question. If the question has multiple answers, mark them quickly so that you will be ready for the next question. The verbal questions will start again in about five seconds whether you are ready or not. And, how can you possibly answer the next question correctly if you do not hear the complete question?

Following Oral Instructions Strategy #4   **If you become confused on a particular question**, should you [1] continue worrying with it and trying to salvage it while the Exam Administrator (or recording) moves on and begins reading the next question or [2] **skip it and be ready to listen to the next question**? If you didn't get it, then you didn't get it. Let it go. Why miss the next question (maybe even the next two or three questions) worrying over the one you already lost. It makes much more sense to let it go and be prepared to capture the next point(s).

Following Oral Instructions Strategy #5   **You _can_ mark in the question booklet during this section** of the exam. As a matter of fact, the questions specifically direct you to do so.

Following Oral Instructions Strategy #6   **Guessing, where possible, on this section is acceptable**. Like the Number series section, this one is scored by simply counting your correct answers. So, why not guess? You may pick up a few extra points. But, there are two problems with guessing in this section. First, where do you guess? Since the number of the question has nothing to do with where you mark you answer, how do you know where to mark your guess? You cannot guess unless you understood at least enough of the question to know where to make a guess. Secondly, there are only about 31 questions, but there are 88 answer spots on the answer sheet. Again, where do you guess? Same answer. You can only guess if you understood the question well enough to know where to make a guess (A, B, C, D, or E) on the answer sheet.

Following Oral Instructions Strategy #7   The key to success is to **listen closely and to follow the instructions explicitly.** The questions will intentionally sound confusing. You cannot allow you mind to wander or to try to make some type of rational sense out of what you are hearing. Simply listen, and do everything you are told to do exactly as you are told to do it.

Following Oral Instructions Strategy #8   **The majority rules!** Several questions will instruct you to mark a certain answer if a particular item of information read to you as part of the question is true/accurate. The Exam Administrator (or recording) will then follow up by instructing you to mark a different answer if that particular item of information is not true/accurate. For instance, a question might read: "If 82 is greater than 55 and 14 is less than 18, mark the number-letter combination 77-B on your answer sheet. If not, mark the number-letter combination 25-D." In this case, the information read to you is accurate, so you would mark 77-B. Bear in mind however, that most such questions will more challenging than this rather simple example.

It can be beneficial to pay attention to the other test takers (there will likely be hundreds of them) around you when answering such questions. Let's assume, for instance, that you are in the middle of a two-part question like the sample in the above paragraph. Let's assume further that you feel that the first item of information given is not true/accurate, so you choose not to mark the first answer offered. Instead, you plan to mark the second answer choice that is about to be offered. But, during the pause as you wait to be given the second answer choice, you hear a great deal of scribbling noises from throughout the room as the majority of your neighbors mark the first answer choice on their answer sheets. What's more, with your peripheral vision, you notice a great deal of frantic movement as your neighbors mark the first answer.

Stop and think … Is it more likely that you are the only one who properly understood the question and that all your neighbors are complete idiots? Or, is it perhaps more probable that the majority of your neighbors understood the question better than you did and that you are about to answer incorrectly? I propose that the majority understood better than you did and that you will be ahead of the game to follow their lead. *The majority rules!*

Just the opposite, if you begin marking the first answer choice but notice that no one around you is marking anything on their answer sheets, again I suggest that you stop and think. It would likely be best to choose the second answer choice as the majority of your neighbors seem to have done.

In the introduction to this section, it was mentioned that many applicants completely fail this section of the exam. However, just because most of your neighbors do not understand how and where to correctly mark their answers (number-letter combinations), this does not necessarily mean that they do not know what the correct answers are. It is most unlikely that they are all morons who are ignorant of the basic principles of math, social studies, etc. For the most part, they are probably intelligent individuals who simply failed to grasp the strange instructions for this illogical and irrational part of the exam.

Following Oral Instructions Strategy #9   **Make notes.** When you looked at one of the Following Oral Instructions practice tests in the back of your book, you probably noticed that the sample test booklet page contains a number of questions consisting of rows of items - shapes (circles, squares, rectangles, boxes), numbers, letters, lines, etc. Frequently, the instructions you hear will provide identifying information about the items in the row. Such a question may sound and look something like the following sample.

"Look at the five boxes in question number 8. Starting from the left side, the first box has mail for Jackson and Canton. The second box has mail for Greenville and Glendale. The third box has mail for Kingsville and San Marcos. The fourth box has mail for Houston and Dallas. The fifth box has mail for Lawerenceburg and Auburn. Write the letter "D" as in dog on the blank line beside the number in the box that has mail for Greenville and Glendale. Write the letter "A" as in apple on the line beside the number in the box that has mail for Houston and Dallas. Now, mark the number-letter combinations you have made on your answer sheet."

8. | ____ 49 | | ____ 18 | | ____ 62 | | ____ 14 | | ____ 87 |

By the time you have listened to this long and confusing question in its entirety, how in the world are you supposed to recall which box is which in order to mark the correct answer? The solution is for you to make brief notes as you hear the question. Remember, you <u>can</u> mark in your test booklet on this section of the exam. So, as you hear identifying information about particular items, make notes accordingly. In this case, you would write the respective city names (probably in an abbreviated form) beside each box for later recognition.

| Following Oral Instructions Strategy #10 | **Converting time of day into numbers.** Several questions will instruct you to convert a time of day into a number. You may be told to find the first two numbers of the time of 5:30 PM on the answer sheet and then to darken the letter B. The first two numbers in the time of 5:30 PM are a 5 and a 3. Put together, they make the number 53. So, we would find number 53 on the answer sheet and darken the letter B. Or, you may be told to find the last two numbers of this time and to darken the letter A. So, you would find the number 30 and darken the letter A. If you were told to find the first number, it would be the number 5. As previously discussed, simply do as you are instructed. Don't waste time trying to make sense of it.

| Following Oral Instructions Strategy #11 | To **practice realistically**, you must either [1] have a friend or relative read all the practice tests to you or [2] listen to the practice tests on my Oral Instructions Practice Tests CD. *Do not read the questions yourself as you take the practice tests!* This would be cheating yourself because you most certainly will not be able to read the questions yourself when taking the real exam. On the real exam, you must answer exclusively based upon what you hear. If you want to succeed on the actual test, you absolutely must practice the same way - by having the questions read to you with the proper pace, diction, and pauses.

Unfortunately, we do not all have a friend or relative conveniently at hand to read the questions to us at a moment's notice and at any hour of the day or night. In response to recurring requests, we produced an **Oral Directions Practice Tests CD** containing the complete Following Oral Instructions sections from all six practice tests in your book. This CD presents the questions professionally and realistically at the proper pace and with proper diction and pauses. The CD makes practicing the Following Oral Directions section convenient anytime and anywhere you choose - you are no longer dependent on someone else's schedule or whims. For more details, see the order form at the back of your book or visit our website *www.PostalExam.com.*

| Following Oral Instructions Strategy #12 | **Practice is the key to performance** ... the key to mastering your strategies, to developing the talent of listening attentively, and to train yourself to simply follow instructions without attempting to rationalize what you hear.

SPEED MARKING

A Revolutionary Breakthrough in Test Taking Technology

Science and common sense combine to create a breakthrough in test taking technology - the "Speed Marking System." Research indicates that this system, which combines unique strategies with a specially designed test-taking pencil, can more than double your marking speed.

As you should have discovered by now, speed means everything on the Postal exam. You have been encouraged to sacrifice a measure of accuracy in favor of speed. It has been proven that knowledge is of no value without sufficient speed to answer all the questions within the allotted time period. You have been instructed to practice zealously to develop the level of speed required. Most of the strategies suggested serve a single purpose - to increase your speed.

What if you were offered a magic tool that would more than double your speed at marking answers? Imagine the extra time you would have to answer more questions - to make more points - to achieve the highest possible score! Sure, we're only talking about saving a second or two per question. But, those seconds add up to minutes, which add up to points, which add up to exam scores, which make or break Postal careers. That's what this book is all about - adding points to your exam score to increase your chance of success. To quote a point made earlier in the book: "Any tool that adds points to your score is incredibly valuable." So, how does this magic system work? Like this ...

| Speed Marking Strategy #1 | **Use the ergonomically designed "Speed Pencil"** A few years ago, I discovered a phenomenal new pencil ideal for taking standardized tests.   Since this uncommon new pencil, which we have nicknamed the "Speed Pencil," is not readily available at traditional retail outlets, Pathfinder Distributing Company has obtained a distributorship and has made it available to Postal exam applicants as part of a Speed Marking System. See the order form at the back of the book for details. Features of this revolutionary new test-taking tool include:

- An *oversize tripod grip with ergonomically designed contact points.* Benefits include relaxed hand posture, efficient muscle action, more comfort, enhanced control, and less fatigue. The Speed Pencil feels more like an extension of your hand rather than a burdensome writing implement.

- *A larger diameter number 2 graphite lead nearly double the size of regular pencils.* The broader marking surface enables you to darken answers more than twice as fast.

- *Triangular longitudinal design to avoid roll-away's.* Nothing is more frustrating than chasing roll-away pencils under tables and across floors when you are supposed to be answering questions on a rigidly timed test. Normal pencils with their more rounded construction seem to roll away at every chance. This benefit may sound trivial at first, but it can literally make the difference between success and failure. I'm embarrassed to admit that this roll-away disaster has happened to me. Once, before discovering the Speed Pencil, I was taking the exam with standard pencils. As insurance, I had four pencils with me. In the middle of the exam, I accidentally dropped the pencil I was using. Not only did this pencil roll off the table, in the process it bumped into my spare pencils, and they rolled off as well. So, off I go literally chasing pencils under tables and across floors while everyone else was marking answers. Had I been serious about getting a Postal job, such an incident would have resulted in certain failure. Since discovering the Speed Pencil, this roll-away disaster has not happened to me again - nor do I expect it to.

Speed Marking Strategy #2 **Use a dulled pencil.** The scheduling packet sent to you will instruct you to bring two number 2 lead pencils. What condition will you want these pencils to be in? Sharp, of course! Frequently, they have extra pencils available at the test site for applicants who forget their own pencils or for applicants who break the lead on their own pencils. What condition will these extra pencils be in? Sharp, of course! We have always been taught to use a freshly sharpened pencil, and we prefer to use a freshly sharpened pencil. So, we will naturally bring sharp pencils with us to the test. If offered extras at the test site from a box of loose pencils, which will we choose? The sharpest ones we can find, of course.

This is precisely the opposite of what we should do. Picture in your mind a fine point ink pen and a broad tipped marker. If you wanted to darken a large circle in a hurry, which would you use? Which would enable you to darken a given area faster? The broad tipped marker, of course, because of its larger marking surface. It would take forever to darken a large circle with a fine point pen. The same principle holds true for pencils. Picture a freshly sharpened pencil and one with a dulled and blunted lead. Which one has a broader marking surface? Which one will darken a circle quicker? Which one will mark answers faster on your exam? The one with the dulled and blunted lead, of course. This is your second Speed Marking Strategy - **make sure your pencil, preferably your "Speed Marking Pencil", has a dulled and blunted point.** If offered extras, choose dulled ones. If only sharpened pencils are available, immediately dull them. A sharp pencil is you worst enemy.

Speed Marking Strategy #3 **Use an enhanced pencil position and grasp.** The following two techniques can significantly increase your speed. Most people find these techniques to be lifesavers. With practice, these techniques will become second nature for you.

- **The first strategy is to hold the pencil in a more horizontal than vertical position** as displayed in the below illustration. This dramatically increases your speed by enabling you to use the larger and broader side of the pencil lead, rather than the point, as your marking surface. Experiment with different angles of contact to find which works best for you. Holding your pencil in this fashion will feel awkward and unnatural at first. But stick with it. With sufficient practice, most people feel very comfortable using the pencil in this fashion.

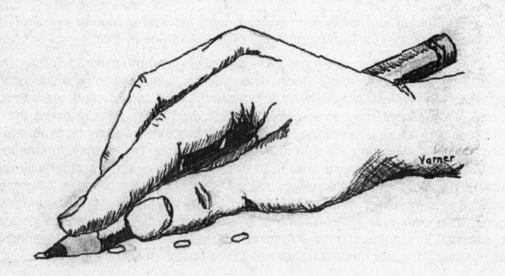

- **The second strategy is to grasp the pencil each time you pick it up so that your thumb (or forefinger) is always touching the side with the printing on it** - usually the manufacturer's name and/or logo. Pick it up and hold it the very same way each time so that you consistently use the same broad and flattened edge as your contact surface. When laying the pencil down, always place it with the printed side facing up so that you can more easily grasp it properly when picking it up again. Most people rotate the pencil within their grasp as they write with it, which tends preserve the lead's conical point. In a normal writing situation, this is logical. However, there is nothing normal or logical about this test. By consistently holding the pencil in the same position all the time, you maintain the integrity of the dulled and flattened contact point, and you even improve and broaden the contact surface by constant contact with the paper at the same point.

Speed Marking Strategy #4   **Use only two to three revolutions of your pencil to darken each answer.** With the speed pencil, you may be able to do it in only one or two revolutions. With practice and by using the above strategies, this is indeed possible. What's more - it is necessary in order to answer all the questions within the time allowed. You do not have time to endlessly scribble around and around inside the circle to assure that you have darkened every nook and cranny. Your goal is to darken 80% to 90% of the circle. The scanner that scores your test will register an answer that is 80% to 90% darkened. The extra time and effort to try for 100% is not necessary. But, an answer darkened only 50% to 60% may not register. Your goal should be 80% to 90%.

Speed Marking Strategy #5   As you have learned, **speed is particularly critical on the Address Checking and Address Memory sections**. You will want to use your speed marking strategies on these two sections for sure. Speed is important, but not quite as imperative, on the Number Series and the Following Oral Instructions sections. As a matter of fact, the marking you do on the latter two sections is closer to normal writing than it is on the first two. Accordingly, on the Number Series and the Following Oral Instructions sections, it will probably be to your benefit to hold your pencil in a more normal grasp.

To check out or order the "Speed Marking System", visit our website *www.PostalExam.com* or see the order form at the back of the book.

FREE EXTRA PRACTICE TESTS

Postal exam applicants can be grouped into three basic categories as detailed below.

Group 1 (the vast majority of applicants) make no effort to prepare. Either they are not aware that test prep tools exist, or they are not motivated enough to prepare. Of course, most of them fail.

Group 2 applicants have good intentions, but they do not have commitment. They buy a study guide, but they do little (if any) practice work ... and their scores reflect their lack of preparation.

Group 3 applicants are truly committed. These are people who are motivated enough to complete the practice work in their study guides, and these are the people who make the top scores. The best of Group 3 applicants, the ones who really excel on the exam and who get the first jobs, are the ones who are willing to invest extra time and effort to achieve the highest possible score. These are the people who score each practice test and then seek out extra practice work for the sections of the exam where they need improvement. The one and only key to improving performance is practice.

For these applicants, we have provided **extra Address Memory and Address Checking practice tests as free downloads from the web.** The most difficult section of the exam is the Address Memory section, followed by the Address Checking section. If an applicant feels the need for more practice work, it will always be for one of these sections ... or perhaps for both. After taking all six complete practice exams in the book, if you are not satisfied with your performance on one or both of these sections, simply download, print, and take the free extra practice tests. To download the extra Address Memory practice tests, go to *http://www.PostalExam.com/pages/test/address_memory*. Go to *http://www.PostalExam.com/pages/test/address_checking* to download the extra Address Checking practice tests. If you want extra practice tests but do not have access to the internet (or if you would rather not have to download and print them), printed copies are available for a nominal fee. For details, see the order form at the back of the book or visit our website *www.PostalExam.com*.

There is no such thing as too much practice. If you feel the need for even more practice, you can retake the practice tests again and again. By the time you complete all the practice work once, you will have dealt with thousands of individual addresses, and it is unlikely that you will remember any particular address. Each time you retake a test, it should seem like a new one. It is up to you to choose how much or how little time to invest in additional practice.

TEST PREP SUPPORT

The instructions, strategies, and concepts discussed in this guide are presented as simply as possible to assure full understanding. If a subject seems confusing, reading over that section again will usually clear it up. You may want to review the subject more than once - perhaps after each practice test. Experiencing the subject on a practice test is frequently the best way to grasp it. For assistance with urgent matters, our Test Prep Support Group is available Monday through Friday (except holidays) from 8:00 AM to 5:00 PM CST. Contact info for the Test Prep Support Group is provided below. When requesting test prep assistance, you must confirm your status as a Pathfinder customer by providing the code number found at the bottom of page 3 in your book.

Test Prep Support e-mail address: support@pathfinderdc.com
Test Prep Support phone number: 281-259-2302

COMPLETE PRACTICE EXAM #1

This complete practice exam contains all four sections of the actual exam. The instructions given are similar to those on the actual exam. The format of this practice exam is identical to the actual exam.

It is imperative that you take the practice exam in as realistic a fashion as possible. **Your practice will have no value unless it is done realistically.** Therefore, you must precisely time yourself on the Address Checking, Address Memory, and Number Series sections. Our Timed Practice Test CD is a convenient way to practice realistically and time yourself precisely. Also, you must listen to the Following Oral Instructions questions on our Oral Instructions Practice Tests CD or have someone read them to you - *do not read the questions yourself!* The Following Oral Instructions questions can be found in the back of your book if someone will be reading them to you.

When taking a practice exam, first turn to the back of your book and tear out one of the **Complete Practice Exam Answer Sheets.** Mark the answers to the scored segments of the exam on this answer sheet. Remember, of the seven segments on the Address Memory Section, only the final one is scored. Accordingly, you should mark answers for only the final Address Memory segment on your Complete Practice Exam Answer Sheet. The other segments of the Address Memory Section that call for answers have their own sample answer sheets where you should mark answers.

Answer keys are provided in the back of your book. Immediately upon completing each section of a practice exam, **it is imperative that you score yourself** using the formulas given in the Scoring Formulas section of the book. Scoring is necessary in order to gauge your progress and to identify your individual areas of weakness that may need extra attention.

After completing and scoring each practice exam, move on to the next. **After finishing all six exams, you should be prepared for the actual exam.** If you feel the need for more practice after completing six practice exams, see page 60 for details on our free extra practice tests.

Do not look over the practice exam questions until you are ready to start - usually meaning either until (1) you have started the Timed Practice Test CD or the Oral Instructions Practice Tests CD or (2) you have set a timer for the allotted period of time. Similarly, after completing one section of the practice test, do not look over the next one until your are ready to start it. Likewise, stop working and put down your pencil immediately when the allotted period of time has expired. As has been emphasized before but cannot be emphasized enough, your practice is of absolutely no value unless it is done realistically. Also, you must train yourself (1) to not open your test booklet or pick up your pencil until instructed to do so and (2) to close your booklet and put down your pencil immediately upon being so instructed. The Postal Service has zero tolerance on these matters. Any variance may be viewed as cheating and may result in your disqualification.

COMPLETE PRACTICE EXAM #1
Part A – Address Checking

Directions

In the Address Checking section, you are to decide whether two addresses are alike or different. You have 6 minutes to answer 95 questions. Each question consists of a pair of addresses. If the two addresses in the pair are exactly alike in every way, darken the oval with the letter "A" for _Alike_. If the two addresses are different in any way, darken the oval with the letter "D" for _Different_. Mark your answers on the Complete Practice Exam Answer Sheet in the section entitled Address Checking. Begin when you are prepared to time yourself for precisely 6 minutes.

Notes:
- _You will notice that the questions on this section of your practice exam are spread across two pages. This is the exact format of the Address Checking section on the real exam. To save printing costs, some study guides condense the two pages of this section down to only one. Other study guides, for reasons we cannot even begin to guess, stretch the Address Checking section out over several pages._
- _You will also notice that the Address Checking questions are presented in a font, or type of print, that is different from the rest of the book. This font closely matches the type of print used on the real exam, and - as you will see - it makes this section even more challenging._
- _It is imperative that you practice realistically and that you become acquainted with the actual format of the test. We have therefore formatted the page layout and the font of the Address Checking section on this practice exam realistically for your benefit._

Part A – Address Checking

1.	5643 52nd St., Monongahela, PA	5643 53rd St., Monongahela, PA
2.	1111 Liegh Dr.	1111 Liegh Dr.
3.	Oak Ridge, Mn. 44777	Oak Ridge, Mn. 44477
4.	832 Rich Ave. NW Suite 2344-A	832 Rich Ave. NW Suite 2344-A
5.	232 Sunset Blvd.	323 Sunset Blvd.
6.	7463 Washington Cir.	7464 Washington Cir.
7.	Pearl, Ms. 39573-9834	Pearl, Ms. 39573-9834
8.	4532 Pecan Village Apt.	4532 Pecan Village Apt.
9.	9356 Main Drive West	9356 Main Drive East
10.	601 W Oklahoma Fairfax KS	601 W Oklahoma Fairfax KS
11.	Lake Falls, Nev. 98007	Lake Falls, Nev. 98007
12.	Newton, W. Va.	Newton, W. Va.
13.	8729 East Randall St. Apt. #E-963	8792 East Randall St. Apt. #E-963
14.	877 39th Ave.	877 39th Ave.
15.	218 Pinelawn NW	218 Pinlawn NW
16.	1940 Dewey Cir., Washington, DC	1940 Dewey Cir., Washington, DC
17.	Rolling Fork, S.D. 44532	Rolling Fork, S.D. 44532
18.	3022 Thomas Jefferson St.	3202 Thomas Jefferson St.
19.	10013 Fire Tower Bridge Rd.	10013 Fire Tower Bridge Rd.
20.	7113 Raggio Lane	7113 Raggio Lane
21.	1009 Lynn Ave.	1009 Lyne Ave.
22.	768 Vandanburg Naval Air Station NW	768 Vandanburg Naval Air Station NW
23.	Marshal, Tex. 70043	Marshal, Tex. 70034
24.	204-A Fechet Dr.	204-A Fechet Dr.
25.	324 Harmon Circle	323 Harmin Circle
26.	Twin Oaks, Ark. 70054-8545	Twin Oaks, Ark. 70054-8545
27.	305 Parkview Dr.	305 Parkview Dr.
28.	205-B Bay Springs Lane	205-B Bay Sprins Lane
29.	Porter, Pa. 22087-3216	Porter, Pa. 22087-3216
30.	1335 Lafayette Dr.	1335 Lafayette Dr.
31.	6212 North St.	6212 North St.
32.	211 Brynmawr Av. Pascagolua MS	211 Brymnawr Av. Pascagolua MS
33.	5908 Gulf Stream	5980 Gulf Stream
34.	Anderson, Ala. 46477	Anderson, Alk. 46477
35.	787 St. George Cathedral Square	787 St. George Cathedral Square
36.	Beauvoir Manor Apt. SW	Beauvoir Manor Apt. SE
37.	Lee, Ind. 77889-1563	Lee, Ind. 77889-1563
38.	100 Van Buren Ave.	100 Van Buren Ave.
39.	2234 Bilmarsan Dr.	2234 Bilmaran Dr.
40.	212 Mocking Bird Rd. at 51st St.	212 Mocking Bird Rd. at 51st St.
41.	1343 West 9th Ave.	1434 West 9th Ave.
42.	209 Jeff Davis Ave.	209 Jeff Savis Ave.
43.	4934 Running Brook Farms	4934 Running Brook Farms
44.	New Haven, Conn. 06515-2226	New Haven, Conn. 06515-2226
45.	7449 53rd St. NW	7449 53rd St. SW
46.	Normal, Ala. 35762-8911	Normal, Ala. 34567-8911
47.	4408 W. Railroad St.	4408 W. Railroad St.
48.	97883 North 15th St.	97883 North 15th St.

49.	3323 Court House Rd., Hot Coffee, GA	3232 Court House Rd., Hot Coffee, GA
50.	Mt. St. Helen NE	Mt. St. Helen NW
51.	454 Maple Grove Blvd.	454 Maple Grove Blvd.
52.	Shakopee, Minn. 47484-5640	Shakopee, Minn. 47494-5640
53.	#1 Shell Square	#1 Shell Squares
54.	8583 Northridge Office Annex	3583 Northridge Office Annex
55.	101 McGoey SE	101 McGoey SE
56.	Rolling Hills, Wyo. 23785-1842	Rolling Hills, Wyo. 32785-1842
57.	2004 West Brooklyn Ave.	2804 West Brooklyn Ave.
58.	672 Beatline	673 Beatline
59.	5944 Millroad St.	5944 Millroad SW
60.	212 Klondyke Rd., Aleutia, AK	212 Klondyke Dr., Aleutia, AK
61.	4767 Rushing Wave	4767 Rushing Wave
62.	66672 Wekls	66627 Wekls
63.	Rainbow Inn South, Room 3346	Rainbow End South, Room 3346
64.	3424 Cook Drive	3424 Cook Drive
65.	8823 Railway	8823 Railway
66.	Milkwaukee, Wis. 45376-6518	Milkwaukee, Wis. 45376-6518
67.	1422 North Gate S	1422 North Gate N
68.	2345 97th Ave.	2435 97th Ave.
69.	8456 Alabama St.	8436 Alabama St.
70.	Sunnydale, MO 65339-1492	Sunnydale, MI 65339-1492
71.	0672 Rich Lane	672 Rich Mane
72.	1234 Rosewood	1234 Rosewood
73.	98 Dogg Cove, Lake Conroe, TX	889 Dogg Cove, Lake Conroe, TX
74.	Pearl Center SSW	Pearl Center SWS
75.	7455 John Galloway Office Park	7455 John Galloway Office Park
76.	433 Old Pass Rd.	433 Old Pass Rd.
77.	1111 Gardendale	11111 Gardendale
78.	3573 St. Charles Ave.	3573 Charles Ave.
79.	San Cosa del Ray, CA 97566-4500	San Coas del Ray, CA 97566-4500
80.	6340 Alexander Rd.	6340 Alexander Rd.
81.	411 Porche SW	411 Porche SW
82.	Bloomington NW	Bloomington N
83.	3332 Wishing Dr.	3332 Wishing Dr.
84.	Waveland, OR 96643-5353	Waveland, OR 96643-5353
85.	6632 Taylor	3212 Taylor
86.	5598 Longview Rd.	5598 Lonview Rd.
87.	213 Bilmarsan Dr., Haut St. Marie, MI	213 Bilmarsan Dr., Haut St. Marie, MI
88.	6244 Yorkshire Lane	6422 Yorkshire Lande
89.	225 Acacia Av	225 Acacia Av
90.	Rustwood, Mass. 24665-4566	Rustwood, Mass. 24665-4566
91.	739 Nixon Rd.	739 Mixon Rd.
92.	8654 Lakelawn Blvd	8654 Lakelawn Blvd
93.	11000 Tucker rd, Bumpershoot, LA	1100 Tucker rd, Bumpershoot, LA
94.	1686 Bilglade	1686 Bilglade
95.	14 Back Bay	14 Black Bay

COMPLETE PRACTICE EXAM #1
Part B – Address Memory

Directions

In the Address Memory section, you are to memorize the locations of 25 addresses in five boxes. During this section, you will have several study periods and practice exercises to help you memorize the location of the addresses shown in the five boxes. Answer the questions by darkening the oval containing the letter (A, B, C, D, E) of the box the address came from - Box A, Box B, Box C, Box D, or Box E. At the end of each segment, you will be given instructions on how and where to continue. After completing six preliminary segments, the actual test will be given as segment #7.

Turn the page to begin Segment #1 of the Address Memory section.

Note: You will notice in this practice exam that segments 3, 4, and 6 of the Address Memory section are spread across two pages. The five boxes, the 88 questions, and the sample answer sheet in these segments are spread across two facing pages. This is the exact same format that you will experience on Address Memory segments 3, 4, and 6 of the actual exam. To save printing costs, other study guides frequently condense these segments down from two pages to only one. However, it is imperative that you practice realistically and that you become acquainted with the actual format of the test. We have therefore formatted the Address Memory section on this practice exam realistically for your benefit.

COMPLETE PRACTICE EXAM #1
Part B – Address Memory – Segment #1

The purpose of this small exercise is to acquaint you with the format of the Address Memory section. The first two questions are answered for you. You are to spend three minutes studying this page and answering sample questions 3, 4, and 5. After completing Segment #1, turn to Segment #2 for further instructions. Begin when you are prepared to time yourself for precisely three minutes.

A	B	C	D	E
4700-5599 Camp Oak	6800-6999 Camp Broad	5600-6499 Camp State	6500-6799 Camp Orchid	4400-4699 Camp Forest
5600-6499 Sarah Magnolia	6500-6799 Sarah Dearman	6800-6999 Sarah Cox	4400-4699 Sarah Ocean	4700-5599 Sarah Pittman
4400-4699 Lang	5600-6499 Lang	6500-6799 Lang	4700-5599 Lang	6800-6999 Lang

1. 4400-4699 Sarah ⒶⒷⒸ●Ⓔ
   This address came from Box D, so we sill darken the oval with the letter D.

2. Dearman Ⓐ●ⒸⒹⒺ
   This address came from Box B, so we will darken the oval with the letter B.

3. Oak ⒶⒷⒸⒹⒺ
   Now that you know how to answer, you do questions 3, 4, and 5.

4. 6500-6799 Camp ⒶⒷⒸⒹⒺ

5. 5600-6499 Camp ⒶⒷⒸⒹⒺ

The correct answers are D, B, A, D, and C.

COMPLETE PRACTICE EXAM #1
Part B – Address Memory – Segment #2

In this segment, you are given three minutes to study and memorize the addresses. There are no questions to answer in this segment - it is a study period only. However, on the actual exam, the boxes are not reprinted for your use. Instead, you are instructed to turn back to Address Memory Segment #1 and to spend three minutes studying the boxes displayed there. So, we will do the very same on this practice exam. After studying for three minutes, turn to Segment #3 for directions on how to continue the Address Memory Section of the exam. Begin studying when you are prepared to time yourself for precisely three minutes.

COMPLETE PRACTICE EXAM #1
Part B – Address Memory – Segment #3

You have three minutes to answer 88 questions. Try to answer from memory, but the boxes are shown if you need to refer to them. Mark your answers on the sample answer sheet at the bottom of the pages. After completing this segment, turn to Segment #4 for further instructions. Begin when you are prepared to time yourself for precisely three minutes.

A	B	C
4700-5599 Camp Oak 5600-6499 Sarah Magnolia 4400-4699 Lang	6800-6999 Camp Broad 6500-6799 Sarah Dearman 5600-6499 Lang	5600-6499 Camp State 6800-6999 Sarah Cox 6500-6799 Lang

1. 5600-6499 Lang
2. Forest
3. State
4. 4400-4699 Sarah
5. 4700-5599 Lang
6. Magnolia
7. Broad
8. 4400-4699 Lang

9. 4400-4699 Camp
10. 4700-5599 Camp
11. Pittman
12. 6800-6999 Lang
13. 6500-6799 Camp
14. Ocean
15. Cox
16. 4700-5599 Sarah

17. Oak
18. 5600-6499 Camp
19. 5600-6499 Sarah
20. Orchid
21. 6800-6999 Camp
22. 4400-4699 Sarah
23. 6500-6799 Sarah
24. 5600-6499 Lang

25. Oak
26. Forest
27. 5600-6499 Camp
28. Broad
29. 5600-6499 Sarah
30. Dearman
31. 6500-6799 Lang
32. Pittman

33. 4700-5599 Sarah
34. 5600-6499 Lang
35. Magnolia
36. Cox
37. 6800-6999 Lang
38. 6500-6799 Camp
39. 4400-4699 Camp
40. 6800-6999 Sarah

41. 4700-5599 Camp
42. Forest
43. Cox
44. Dearman
45. 5600-6499 Camp
46. State
47. 4400-4699 Lang
48. Magnolia

1 Ⓐ Ⓑ Ⓒ Ⓓ Ⓔ
2 Ⓐ Ⓑ Ⓒ Ⓓ Ⓔ
3 Ⓐ Ⓑ Ⓒ Ⓓ Ⓔ
4 Ⓐ Ⓑ Ⓒ Ⓓ Ⓔ
5 Ⓐ Ⓑ Ⓒ Ⓓ Ⓔ
6 Ⓐ Ⓑ Ⓒ Ⓓ Ⓔ
7 Ⓐ Ⓑ Ⓒ Ⓓ Ⓔ
8 Ⓐ Ⓑ Ⓒ Ⓓ Ⓔ

9 Ⓐ Ⓑ Ⓒ Ⓓ Ⓔ
10 Ⓐ Ⓑ Ⓒ Ⓓ Ⓔ
11 Ⓐ Ⓑ Ⓒ Ⓓ Ⓔ
12 Ⓐ Ⓑ Ⓒ Ⓓ Ⓔ
13 Ⓐ Ⓑ Ⓒ Ⓓ Ⓔ
14 Ⓐ Ⓑ Ⓒ Ⓓ Ⓔ
15 Ⓐ Ⓑ Ⓒ Ⓓ Ⓔ
16 Ⓐ Ⓑ Ⓒ Ⓓ Ⓔ

17 Ⓐ Ⓑ Ⓒ Ⓓ Ⓔ
18 Ⓐ Ⓑ Ⓒ Ⓓ Ⓔ
19 Ⓐ Ⓑ Ⓒ Ⓓ Ⓔ
20 Ⓐ Ⓑ Ⓒ Ⓓ Ⓔ
21 Ⓐ Ⓑ Ⓒ Ⓓ Ⓔ
22 Ⓐ Ⓑ Ⓒ Ⓓ Ⓔ
23 Ⓐ Ⓑ Ⓒ Ⓓ Ⓔ
24 Ⓐ Ⓑ Ⓒ Ⓓ Ⓔ

25 Ⓐ Ⓑ Ⓒ Ⓓ Ⓔ
26 Ⓐ Ⓑ Ⓒ Ⓓ Ⓔ
27 Ⓐ Ⓑ Ⓒ Ⓓ Ⓔ
28 Ⓐ Ⓑ Ⓒ Ⓓ Ⓔ
29 Ⓐ Ⓑ Ⓒ Ⓓ Ⓔ
30 Ⓐ Ⓑ Ⓒ Ⓓ Ⓔ
31 Ⓐ Ⓑ Ⓒ Ⓓ Ⓔ
32 Ⓐ Ⓑ Ⓒ Ⓓ Ⓔ

33 Ⓐ Ⓑ Ⓒ Ⓓ Ⓔ
34 Ⓐ Ⓑ Ⓒ Ⓓ Ⓔ
35 Ⓐ Ⓑ Ⓒ Ⓓ Ⓔ
36 Ⓐ Ⓑ Ⓒ Ⓓ Ⓔ
37 Ⓐ Ⓑ Ⓒ Ⓓ Ⓔ
38 Ⓐ Ⓑ Ⓒ Ⓓ Ⓔ
39 Ⓐ Ⓑ Ⓒ Ⓓ Ⓔ
40 Ⓐ Ⓑ Ⓒ Ⓓ Ⓔ

41 Ⓐ Ⓑ Ⓒ Ⓓ Ⓔ
42 Ⓐ Ⓑ Ⓒ Ⓓ Ⓔ
43 Ⓐ Ⓑ Ⓒ Ⓓ Ⓔ
44 Ⓐ Ⓑ Ⓒ Ⓓ Ⓔ
45 Ⓐ Ⓑ Ⓒ Ⓓ Ⓔ
46 Ⓐ Ⓑ Ⓒ Ⓓ Ⓔ
47 Ⓐ Ⓑ Ⓒ Ⓓ Ⓔ
48 Ⓐ Ⓑ Ⓒ Ⓓ Ⓔ

D

6500-6799 Camp
Orchid
4400-4699 Sarah
Ocean
4700-5599 Lang

E

4400-4699 Camp
Forest
4700-5599 Sarah
Pittman
6800-6999 Lang

49. Ocean
50. 6500-6799 Lang
51. 4400-4699 Sarah
52. 6800-6999 Camp
53. 4400-4699 Camp
54. Broad
55. Orchid
56. 5600-6499 Lang

57. 4700-5599 Sarah
58. Pittman
59. 5600-6499 Sarah
60. 6800-6999 Sarah
61. Forest
62. Cox
63. 6500-6799 Camp
64. 5600-6499 Camp

65. 4400-4699 Sarah
66. Pittman
67. Cox
68. 6800-6999 Camp
69. 4700-5599 Camp
70. Forest
71. 4400-4699 Sarah
72. State

73. 6500-6799 Sarah
74. 5600-6499 Lang
75. 5600-6499 Camp
76. Broad
77. Magnolia
78. Oak
79. Pittman
80. 5600-6499 Sarah

81. 4400-4699 Camp
82. 4700-5599 Sarah
83. Ocean
84. State
85. 4400-4699 Lang
86. 6500-6799 Lang
87. Dearman
88. Orchid

49 (A) (B) (C) (D) (E)
50 (A) (B) (C) (D) (E)
51 (A) (B) (C) (D) (E)
52 (A) (B) (C) (D) (E)
53 (A) (B) (C) (D) (E)
54 (A) (B) (C) (D) (E)
55 (A) (B) (C) (D) (E)
56 (A) (B) (C) (D) (E)

57 (A) (B) (C) (D) (E)
58 (A) (B) (C) (D) (E)
59 (A) (B) (C) (D) (E)
60 (A) (B) (C) (D) (E)
61 (A) (B) (C) (D) (E)
62 (A) (B) (C) (D) (E)
63 (A) (B) (C) (D) (E)
64 (A) (B) (C) (D) (E)

65 (A) (B) (C) (D) (E)
66 (A) (B) (C) (D) (E)
67 (A) (B) (C) (D) (E)
68 (A) (B) (C) (D) (E)
69 (A) (B) (C) (D) (E)
70 (A) (B) (C) (D) (E)
71 (A) (B) (C) (D) (E)
72 (A) (B) (C) (D) (E)

73 (A) (B) (C) (D) (E)
74 (A) (B) (C) (D) (E)
75 (A) (B) (C) (D) (E)
76 (A) (B) (C) (D) (E)
77 (A) (B) (C) (D) (E)
78 (A) (B) (C) (D) (E)
79 (A) (B) (C) (D) (E)
80 (A) (B) (C) (D) (E)

81 (A) (B) (C) (D) (E)
82 (A) (B) (C) (D) (E)
83 (A) (B) (C) (D) (E)
84 (A) (B) (C) (D) (E)
85 (A) (B) (C) (D) (E)
86 (A) (B) (C) (D) (E)
87 (A) (B) (C) (D) (E)
88 (A) (B) (C) (D) (E)

COMPLETE PRACTICE EXAM #1
Part B – Address Memory – Segment #4

You have three minutes to answer 88 questions. You must answer from memory. The boxes are not shown. Mark your answers on the sample answer sheet at the bottom of the page. After completing this segment, turn to Segment #5 for further instructions. Begin when you are prepared to time yourself for precisely three minutes.

1. 4400-4699 Sarah
2. Orchid
3. Oak
4. 6500-6799 Camp
5. 5600-6499 Camp
6. Ocean
7. 6800-6999 Lang
8. Dearman

9. 6500-6799 Lang
10. 4400-4699 Lang
11. State
12. Ocean
13. 4400-4699 Sarah
14. 4400-4699 Camp
15. 5600-6499 Sarah
16. Pittman

17. Oak
18. Magnolia
19. Broad
20. 5600-6499 Camp
21. 5600-6499 Lang
22. 6500-6799 Sarah
23. Forest
24. 4700-5599 Camp

25. 6800-6999 Camp
26. Cox
27. Pittman
28. 4400-4699 Sarah
29. 5600-6499 Camp
30. 6500-6799 Camp
31. Cox
32. Forest

33. 6800-6999 Sarah
34. 5600-6499 Sarah
35. Pittman
36. 4700-5599 Sarah
37. 6500-6799 Lang
38. Orchid
39. Broad
40. 4400-4699 Camp

41. 6800-6999 Camp
42. 4400-4699 Sarah
43. 4700-5599 Camp
44. Ocean
45. Magnolia
46. 4400-4699 Lang
47. State
48. 5600-6499 Camp

1 Ⓐ Ⓑ Ⓒ Ⓓ Ⓔ
2 Ⓐ Ⓑ Ⓒ Ⓓ Ⓔ
3 Ⓐ Ⓑ Ⓒ Ⓓ Ⓔ
4 Ⓐ Ⓑ Ⓒ Ⓓ Ⓔ
5 Ⓐ Ⓑ Ⓒ Ⓓ Ⓔ
6 Ⓐ Ⓑ Ⓒ Ⓓ Ⓔ
7 Ⓐ Ⓑ Ⓒ Ⓓ Ⓔ
8 Ⓐ Ⓑ Ⓒ Ⓓ Ⓔ
9 Ⓐ Ⓑ Ⓒ Ⓓ Ⓔ
10 Ⓐ Ⓑ Ⓒ Ⓓ Ⓔ
11 Ⓐ Ⓑ Ⓒ Ⓓ Ⓔ
12 Ⓐ Ⓑ Ⓒ Ⓓ Ⓔ
13 Ⓐ Ⓑ Ⓒ Ⓓ Ⓔ
14 Ⓐ Ⓑ Ⓒ Ⓓ Ⓔ
15 Ⓐ Ⓑ Ⓒ Ⓓ Ⓔ
16 Ⓐ Ⓑ Ⓒ Ⓓ Ⓔ

17 Ⓐ Ⓑ Ⓒ Ⓓ Ⓔ
18 Ⓐ Ⓑ Ⓒ Ⓓ Ⓔ
19 Ⓐ Ⓑ Ⓒ Ⓓ Ⓔ
20 Ⓐ Ⓑ Ⓒ Ⓓ Ⓔ
21 Ⓐ Ⓑ Ⓒ Ⓓ Ⓔ
22 Ⓐ Ⓑ Ⓒ Ⓓ Ⓔ
23 Ⓐ Ⓑ Ⓒ Ⓓ Ⓔ
24 Ⓐ Ⓑ Ⓒ Ⓓ Ⓔ
25 Ⓐ Ⓑ Ⓒ Ⓓ Ⓔ
26 Ⓐ Ⓑ Ⓒ Ⓓ Ⓔ
27 Ⓐ Ⓑ Ⓒ Ⓓ Ⓔ
28 Ⓐ Ⓑ Ⓒ Ⓓ Ⓔ
29 Ⓐ Ⓑ Ⓒ Ⓓ Ⓔ
30 Ⓐ Ⓑ Ⓒ Ⓓ Ⓔ
31 Ⓐ Ⓑ Ⓒ Ⓓ Ⓔ
32 Ⓐ Ⓑ Ⓒ Ⓓ Ⓔ

33 Ⓐ Ⓑ Ⓒ Ⓓ Ⓔ
34 Ⓐ Ⓑ Ⓒ Ⓓ Ⓔ
35 Ⓐ Ⓑ Ⓒ Ⓓ Ⓔ
36 Ⓐ Ⓑ Ⓒ Ⓓ Ⓔ
37 Ⓐ Ⓑ Ⓒ Ⓓ Ⓔ
38 Ⓐ Ⓑ Ⓒ Ⓓ Ⓔ
39 Ⓐ Ⓑ Ⓒ Ⓓ Ⓔ
40 Ⓐ Ⓑ Ⓒ Ⓓ Ⓔ
41 Ⓐ Ⓑ Ⓒ Ⓓ Ⓔ
42 Ⓐ Ⓑ Ⓒ Ⓓ Ⓔ
43 Ⓐ Ⓑ Ⓒ Ⓓ Ⓔ
44 Ⓐ Ⓑ Ⓒ Ⓓ Ⓔ
45 Ⓐ Ⓑ Ⓒ Ⓓ Ⓔ
46 Ⓐ Ⓑ Ⓒ Ⓓ Ⓔ
47 Ⓐ Ⓑ Ⓒ Ⓓ Ⓔ
48 Ⓐ Ⓑ Ⓒ Ⓓ Ⓔ

49. Dearman
50. Cox
51. Forest
52. 4700-5599 Camp
53. 6800-6999 Sarah
54. 4400-4699 Camp
55. 6500-6799 Camp
56. 6800-6999 Lang

57. Cox
58. Magnolia
59. 5600-6499 Lang
60. 4700-5599 Sarah
61. Pittman
62. 6500-6799 Lang
63. Dearman
64. 5600-6499 Sarah

65. Broad
66. 5600-6499 Camp
67. Forest
68. Oak
69. 5600-6499 Lang
70. 6500-6799 Sarah
71. 4400-4699 Sarah
72. 6800-6999 Camp

73. Orchid
74. 5600-6499 Sarah
75. Forest
76. State
77. 4400-4699 Sarah
78. 4700-5599 Lang
79. Magnolia
80. Broad

81. 4400-4699 Lang
82. 4400-4699 Camp
83. 4700-5599 Camp
84. Pittman
85. 6800-6999 Lang
86. 6500-6799 Camp
87. Ocean
88. Cox

49 Ⓐ Ⓑ Ⓒ Ⓓ Ⓔ
50 Ⓐ Ⓑ Ⓒ Ⓓ Ⓔ
51 Ⓐ Ⓑ Ⓒ Ⓓ Ⓔ
52 Ⓐ Ⓑ Ⓒ Ⓓ Ⓔ
53 Ⓐ Ⓑ Ⓒ Ⓓ Ⓔ
54 Ⓐ Ⓑ Ⓒ Ⓓ Ⓔ
55 Ⓐ Ⓑ Ⓒ Ⓓ Ⓔ
56 Ⓐ Ⓑ Ⓒ Ⓓ Ⓔ

57 Ⓐ Ⓑ Ⓒ Ⓓ Ⓔ
58 Ⓐ Ⓑ Ⓒ Ⓓ Ⓔ
59 Ⓐ Ⓑ Ⓒ Ⓓ Ⓔ
60 Ⓐ Ⓑ Ⓒ Ⓓ Ⓔ
61 Ⓐ Ⓑ Ⓒ Ⓓ Ⓔ
62 Ⓐ Ⓑ Ⓒ Ⓓ Ⓔ
63 Ⓐ Ⓑ Ⓒ Ⓓ Ⓔ
64 Ⓐ Ⓑ Ⓒ Ⓓ Ⓔ

65 Ⓐ Ⓑ Ⓒ Ⓓ Ⓔ
66 Ⓐ Ⓑ Ⓒ Ⓓ Ⓔ
67 Ⓐ Ⓑ Ⓒ Ⓓ Ⓔ
68 Ⓐ Ⓑ Ⓒ Ⓓ Ⓔ
69 Ⓐ Ⓑ Ⓒ Ⓓ Ⓔ
70 Ⓐ Ⓑ Ⓒ Ⓓ Ⓔ
71 Ⓐ Ⓑ Ⓒ Ⓓ Ⓔ
72 Ⓐ Ⓑ Ⓒ Ⓓ Ⓔ

73 Ⓐ Ⓑ Ⓒ Ⓓ Ⓔ
74 Ⓐ Ⓑ Ⓒ Ⓓ Ⓔ
75 Ⓐ Ⓑ Ⓒ Ⓓ Ⓔ
76 Ⓐ Ⓑ Ⓒ Ⓓ Ⓔ
77 Ⓐ Ⓑ Ⓒ Ⓓ Ⓔ
78 Ⓐ Ⓑ Ⓒ Ⓓ Ⓔ
79 Ⓐ Ⓑ Ⓒ Ⓓ Ⓔ
80 Ⓐ Ⓑ Ⓒ Ⓓ Ⓔ

81 Ⓐ Ⓑ Ⓒ Ⓓ Ⓔ
82 Ⓐ Ⓑ Ⓒ Ⓓ Ⓔ
83 Ⓐ Ⓑ Ⓒ Ⓓ Ⓔ
84 Ⓐ Ⓑ Ⓒ Ⓓ Ⓔ
85 Ⓐ Ⓑ Ⓒ Ⓓ Ⓔ
86 Ⓐ Ⓑ Ⓒ Ⓓ Ⓔ
87 Ⓐ Ⓑ Ⓒ Ⓓ Ⓔ
88 Ⓐ Ⓑ Ⓒ Ⓓ Ⓔ

74

COMPLETE PRACTICE EXAM #1
Part B – Address Memory – Segment #5

In this segment, you are given five minutes to study the addresses. There are no questions to answer in this segment – it is a study period only. As before, the boxes are not reprinted here for your use. Instead, you are instructed to turn back to Address Memory Segment #1 and to spend five minutes studying the boxes displayed there. After studying for five minutes, turn to Segment #6 for directions on how to continue. Turn back to Segment #1 and begin studying when you are prepared to time yourself for precisely five minutes.

You have five minutes to answer 88 questions. Try to answer from memory, but the boxes are shown if you need to refer to them. Mark your answers on the sample answer sheet at the bottom of the page. After completing this segment, turn to Segment #7 for further instructions. Begin when you are prepared to time yourself for precisely five minutes.

A

4700-5599 Camp Oak
5600-6499 Sarah Magnolia
4400-4699 Lang

B

6800-6999 Camp Broad
6500-6799 Sarah Dearman
5600-6499 Lang

C

5600-6499 Camp State
6800-6999 Sarah Cox
6500-6799 Lang

1. 5600-6499 Lang
2. Forest
3. State
4. 4400-4699 Sarah
5. 4700-5599 Lang
6. Magnolia
7. Broad
8. 4400-4699 Lang

9. 4400-4699 Camp
10. 4700-5599 Camp
11. Pittman
12. 6800-6999 Lang
13. 6500-6799 Camp
14. Ocean
15. Cox
16. 4700-5599 Sarah

17. Oak
18. 5600-6499 Camp
19. 5600-6499 Sarah
20. Orchid
21. 6800-6999 Camp
22. 4400-4699 Sarah
23. 6500-6799 Sarah
24. 5600-6499 Lang

25. Oak
26. Forest
27. 5600-6499 Camp
28. Broad
29. 5600-6499 Sarah
30. Dearman
31. 6500-6799 Lang
32. Pittman

33. 4700-5599 Sarah
34. 5600-6499 Lang
35. Magnolia
36. Cox
37. 6800-6999 Lang
38. 6500-6799 Camp
39. 4400-4699 Camp
40. 6800-6999 Sarah

41. 4700-5599 Camp
42. Forest
43. Cox
44. Dearman
45. 5600-6499 Camp
46. State
47. 4400-4699 Lang
48. Magnolia

1 Ⓐ Ⓑ Ⓒ Ⓓ Ⓔ
2 Ⓐ Ⓑ Ⓒ Ⓓ Ⓔ
3 Ⓐ Ⓑ Ⓒ Ⓓ Ⓔ
4 Ⓐ Ⓑ Ⓒ Ⓓ Ⓔ
5 Ⓐ Ⓑ Ⓒ Ⓓ Ⓔ
6 Ⓐ Ⓑ Ⓒ Ⓓ Ⓔ
7 Ⓐ Ⓑ Ⓒ Ⓓ Ⓔ
8 Ⓐ Ⓑ Ⓒ Ⓓ Ⓔ

9 Ⓐ Ⓑ Ⓒ Ⓓ Ⓔ
10 Ⓐ Ⓑ Ⓒ Ⓓ Ⓔ
11 Ⓐ Ⓑ Ⓒ Ⓓ Ⓔ
12 Ⓐ Ⓑ Ⓒ Ⓓ Ⓔ
13 Ⓐ Ⓑ Ⓒ Ⓓ Ⓔ
14 Ⓐ Ⓑ Ⓒ Ⓓ Ⓔ
15 Ⓐ Ⓑ Ⓒ Ⓓ Ⓔ
16 Ⓐ Ⓑ Ⓒ Ⓓ Ⓔ

17 Ⓐ Ⓑ Ⓒ Ⓓ Ⓔ
18 Ⓐ Ⓑ Ⓒ Ⓓ Ⓔ
19 Ⓐ Ⓑ Ⓒ Ⓓ Ⓔ
20 Ⓐ Ⓑ Ⓒ Ⓓ Ⓔ
21 Ⓐ Ⓑ Ⓒ Ⓓ Ⓔ
22 Ⓐ Ⓑ Ⓒ Ⓓ Ⓔ
23 Ⓐ Ⓑ Ⓒ Ⓓ Ⓔ
24 Ⓐ Ⓑ Ⓒ Ⓓ Ⓔ

25 Ⓐ Ⓑ Ⓒ Ⓓ Ⓔ
26 Ⓐ Ⓑ Ⓒ Ⓓ Ⓔ
27 Ⓐ Ⓑ Ⓒ Ⓓ Ⓔ
28 Ⓐ Ⓑ Ⓒ Ⓓ Ⓔ
29 Ⓐ Ⓑ Ⓒ Ⓓ Ⓔ
30 Ⓐ Ⓑ Ⓒ Ⓓ Ⓔ
31 Ⓐ Ⓑ Ⓒ Ⓓ Ⓔ
32 Ⓐ Ⓑ Ⓒ Ⓓ Ⓔ

33 Ⓐ Ⓑ Ⓒ Ⓓ Ⓔ
34 Ⓐ Ⓑ Ⓒ Ⓓ Ⓔ
35 Ⓐ Ⓑ Ⓒ Ⓓ Ⓔ
36 Ⓐ Ⓑ Ⓒ Ⓓ Ⓔ
37 Ⓐ Ⓑ Ⓒ Ⓓ Ⓔ
38 Ⓐ Ⓑ Ⓒ Ⓓ Ⓔ
39 Ⓐ Ⓑ Ⓒ Ⓓ Ⓔ
40 Ⓐ Ⓑ Ⓒ Ⓓ Ⓔ

41 Ⓐ Ⓑ Ⓒ Ⓓ Ⓔ
42 Ⓐ Ⓑ Ⓒ Ⓓ Ⓔ
43 Ⓐ Ⓑ Ⓒ Ⓓ Ⓔ
44 Ⓐ Ⓑ Ⓒ Ⓓ Ⓔ
45 Ⓐ Ⓑ Ⓒ Ⓓ Ⓔ
46 Ⓐ Ⓑ Ⓒ Ⓓ Ⓔ
47 Ⓐ Ⓑ Ⓒ Ⓓ Ⓔ
48 Ⓐ Ⓑ Ⓒ Ⓓ Ⓔ

D

6500-6799 Camp Orchid
4400-4699 Sarah Ocean
4700-5599 Lang

E

4400-4699 Camp Forest
4700-5599 Sarah Pittman
6800-6999 Lang

49. Ocean
50. 6500-6799 Lang
51. 4400-4699 Sarah
52. 6800-6999 Camp
53. 4400-4699 Camp
54. Broad
55. Orchid
56. 5600-6499 Lang

57. 4700-5599 Sarah
58. Pittman
59. 5600-6499 Sarah
60. 6800-6999 Sarah
61. Forest
62. Cox
63. 6500-6799 Camp
64. 5600-6499 Camp

65. 4400-4699 Sarah
66. Pittman
67. Cox
68. 6800-6999 Camp
69. 4700-5599 Camp
70. Forest
71. 4400-4699 Sarah
72. State

73. 6500-6799 Sarah
74. 5600-6499 Lang
75. 5600-6499 Camp
76. Broad
77. Magnolia
78. Oak
79. Pittman
80. 5600-6499 Sarah

81. 4400-4699 Camp
82. 4700-5599 Sarah
83. Ocean
84. State
85. 4400-4699 Lang
86. 6500-6799 Lang
87. Dearman
88. Orchid

49. Ⓐ Ⓑ Ⓒ Ⓓ Ⓔ
50. Ⓐ Ⓑ Ⓒ Ⓓ Ⓔ
51. Ⓐ Ⓑ Ⓒ Ⓓ Ⓔ
52. Ⓐ Ⓑ Ⓒ Ⓓ Ⓔ
53. Ⓐ Ⓑ Ⓒ Ⓓ Ⓔ
54. Ⓐ Ⓑ Ⓒ Ⓓ Ⓔ
55. Ⓐ Ⓑ Ⓒ Ⓓ Ⓔ
56. Ⓐ Ⓑ Ⓒ Ⓓ Ⓔ

57. Ⓐ Ⓑ Ⓒ Ⓓ Ⓔ
58. Ⓐ Ⓑ Ⓒ Ⓓ Ⓔ
59. Ⓐ Ⓑ Ⓒ Ⓓ Ⓔ
60. Ⓐ Ⓑ Ⓒ Ⓓ Ⓔ
61. Ⓐ Ⓑ Ⓒ Ⓓ Ⓔ
62. Ⓐ Ⓑ Ⓒ Ⓓ Ⓔ
63. Ⓐ Ⓑ Ⓒ Ⓓ Ⓔ
64. Ⓐ Ⓑ Ⓒ Ⓓ Ⓔ

65. Ⓐ Ⓑ Ⓒ Ⓓ Ⓔ
66. Ⓐ Ⓑ Ⓒ Ⓓ Ⓔ
67. Ⓐ Ⓑ Ⓒ Ⓓ Ⓔ
68. Ⓐ Ⓑ Ⓒ Ⓓ Ⓔ
69. Ⓐ Ⓑ Ⓒ Ⓓ Ⓔ
70. Ⓐ Ⓑ Ⓒ Ⓓ Ⓔ
71. Ⓐ Ⓑ Ⓒ Ⓓ Ⓔ
72. Ⓐ Ⓑ Ⓒ Ⓓ Ⓔ

73. Ⓐ Ⓑ Ⓒ Ⓓ Ⓔ
74. Ⓐ Ⓑ Ⓒ Ⓓ Ⓔ
75. Ⓐ Ⓑ Ⓒ Ⓓ Ⓔ
76. Ⓐ Ⓑ Ⓒ Ⓓ Ⓔ
77. Ⓐ Ⓑ Ⓒ Ⓓ Ⓔ
78. Ⓐ Ⓑ Ⓒ Ⓓ Ⓔ
79. Ⓐ Ⓑ Ⓒ Ⓓ Ⓔ
80. Ⓐ Ⓑ Ⓒ Ⓓ Ⓔ

81. Ⓐ Ⓑ Ⓒ Ⓓ Ⓔ
82. Ⓐ Ⓑ Ⓒ Ⓓ Ⓔ
83. Ⓐ Ⓑ Ⓒ Ⓓ Ⓔ
84. Ⓐ Ⓑ Ⓒ Ⓓ Ⓔ
85. Ⓐ Ⓑ Ⓒ Ⓓ Ⓔ
86. Ⓐ Ⓑ Ⓒ Ⓓ Ⓔ
87. Ⓐ Ⓑ Ⓒ Ⓓ Ⓔ
88. Ⓐ Ⓑ Ⓒ Ⓓ Ⓔ

COMPLETE PRACTICE EXAM #1
Part B – Address Memory – Segment #7

You have five minutes to answer 88 questions. You must answer from memory. The boxes are not shown. Mark your answers on the Complete Practice Exam Answer Sheet. After completing this segment, turn to the Number Series section for instructions on how to continue. Begin when you are prepared to time yourself for precisely five minutes.

1. 4400-4699 Sarah
2. Orchid
3. Oak
4. 6500-6799 Camp
5. 5600-6499 Camp
6. Ocean
7. 6800-6999 Lang
8. Dearman

9. 6500-6799 Lang
10. 4400-4699 Lang
11. State
12. Ocean
13. 4400-4699 Sarah
14. 4400-4699 Camp
15. 5600-6499 Sarah
16. Pittman

17. Oak
18. Magnolia
19. Broad
20. 5600-6499 Camp
21. 5600-6499 Lang
22. 6500-6799 Sarah
23. Forest
24. 4700-5599 Camp

25. 6800-6999 Camp
26. Cox
27. Pittman
28. 4400-4699 Sarah
29. 5600-6499 Camp
30. 6500-6799 Camp
31. Cox
32. Forest

33. 6800-6999 Sarah
34. 5600-6499 Sarah
35. Pittman
36. 4700-5599 Sarah
37. 6500-6799 Lang
38. Orchid
39. Broad
40. 4400-4699 Camp

41. 6800-6999 Camp
42. 4400-4699 Sarah
43. 4700-5599 Camp
44. Ocean
45. Magnolia
46. 4400-4699 Lang
47. State
48. 5600-6499 Camp

49. Dearman
50. Cox
51. Forest
52. 4700-5599 Camp
53. 6800-6999 Sarah
54. 4400-4699 Camp
55. 6500-6799 Camp
56. 6800-6999 Lang

57. Cox
58. Magnolia
59. 5600-6499 Lang
60. 4700-5599 Sarah
61. Pittman
62. 6500-6799 Lang
63. Dearman
64. 5600-6499 Sarah

65. Broad
66. 5600-6499 Camp
67. Forest
68. Oak
69. 5600-6499 Lang
70. 6500-6799 Sarah
71. 4400-4699 Sarah
72. 6800-6999 Camp

73. Orchid
74. 5600-6499 Sarah
75. Forest
76. State
77. 4400-4699 Sarah
78. 4700-5599 Lang
79. Magnolia
80. Broad

81. 4400-4699 Lang
82. 4400-4699 Camp
83. 4700-5599 Camp
84. Pittman
85. 6800-6999 Lang
86. 6500-6799 Camp
87. Ocean
88. Cox

COMPLETE PRACTICE EXAM #1
Part C – Number Series

You have 20 minutes to answer 24 questions. Each question is a series of numbers followed by two blanks. You are to find which two numbers would logically follow in the series. Mark your answers on the Complete Practice Exam Answer Sheet. After completing this section, turn to the Following Oral Instructions section. Begin when you are prepared to time yourself for precisely 20 minutes.

1. 31 32 33 34 35 36 ___ ___   (A) 38,37 (B) 37,38 (C) 38,40 (D) 35,34 (E) 39,41

2. 5 5 5 10 5 5 5 10 5 5 ___ ___   (A) 5,10 (B) 10,5 (C) 5,5 (D) 5,0 (E) 0,5

3. 22 10 22 9 22 8 22 7 ___ ___   (A) 6,22 (B) 20,22 (C) 6,8 (D) 8,6 (E) 22,6

4. 1 2 4 5 7 8 10 ___ ___   (A) 11,13 (B) 10,9 (C) 8,7 (D) 12,14 (E) 13,29

5. 1 2 0 3 4 0 5 6 0 7 ___ ___   (A) 8,0 (B) 0,8 (C) 9,0 (D) 12,13 (E) 7,0

6. 2 5 9 12 16 19 23 ___ ___   (A) 25,29 (B) 27,31 (C) 26,30 (D) 30,34 (E) 32,36

7. 2 4 6 10 16 26 ___ ___   (A) 42,68 (B) 28,64 (C) 68,84 (D) 42,86 (E) 44,48

8. 89 88 87 86 85 ___ ___   (A) 82,81 (B) 85,86 (C) 84,83 (D) 84,81 (E) 85,83

9. 2 4 8 16 ___ ___   (A) 32,64 (B) 34,64 (C) 30,64 (D) 42,74 (E) 52,84

10. 2 17 32 47 ___ ___   (A) 60,75 (B) 32,47 (C) 85,97 (D) 62,77 (E) 68,79

11. 16 16 33 33 16 16 33 ___ ___   (A) 31,17 (B) 30,20 (C) 33,16 (D) 29,21 (E) 28,27

12. 65 20 55 30 45 40 35 ___ ___   (A) 60,35 (B) 40,15 (C) 30,45 (D) 40,25 (E) 50,25

13. 18 18 15 15 12 12 9 ___ ___   (A) 9,9 (B) 6,6 (C) 9,7 (D) 12,9 (E) 9,6

14. 1 14 27 40 ___ ___   (A) 51,64 (B) 53,66 (C) 50,63 (D) 63,76 (E) 50,65

15. 8 29 11 26 14 23 17 20 20 ___ ___   (A) 21,21 (B) 17,23 (C) 23,15 (D) 18,21 (E) 18,24

16. 2 4 8 10 14 16 20 ___ ___   (A) 22,24 (B) 20,26 (C) 22,26 (D) 26,28 (E) 21,23

17. 3 6 9 15 18 21 27 30 ___ ___   (A) 33,36 (B) 33,39 (C) 36,39 (D) 40,43 (E) 41,44

18. 80 50 70 60 60 70 50 ___ ___   (A) 70,30 (B) 50,60 (C) 80,40 (D) 20,40 (E) 90,50

19. 13 83 23 63 33 43 ___ ___   (A) 13,44 (B) 32,67 (C) 45,46 (D) 43,23 (E) 28,59

20. 31 3 31 4 31 5 31 ___ ___   (A) 4,28 (B) 3,21 (C) 6,31 (D) 8,32 (E) 10,37

21. 8 16 24 32 40 ___ ___   (A) 45,50 (B) 46,52 (C) 47,54 (D) 48,56 (E) 49,58

22. 1 5 25 15 49 25 ___ ___   (A) 45,93 (B) 43,35 (C) 73,35 (D) 76,65 (E) 53,65

23. 21 18 10 8 15 12 6 ___ ___   (A) 8,10 (B) 4,9 (C) 5,8 (D) 3,7 (E) 2,6

24. 10 6 12 5 14 4 16 ___ ___   (A) 2,15 (B) 3,18 (C) 4,20 (D) 5,17 (E) 5,21

82

COMPLETE PRACTICE EXAM #1
Part D – Following Oral Instructions

On this section, questions/instructions are presented verbally that lead you to the correct answers. Mark your answers on the Complete Practice Exam Answer Sheet. When you complete the Following Oral Instructions section, you have finished the complete practice exam. Begin when you are prepared to listen to the questions from the author's recording or from someone who will read them to you.

1.   3_____

2.   7   3   9   5

3.   1   C   5   E

4.   3   6   8   9   1

5.   C   D   E   G

6.   [A_____]   [C_____]   [D_____]   [E_____]

7.   33_____   39_____   45_____   58_____   69_____

8.   [10__]   (6__)   [15__]   (2__)

9.   C____   A____   E____   D____

10.   [12__]   [8__]   [19__]   [72__]

11.   [77__]   (11__)   [13__]   (16__)

12.   C____   D____   C____   B____   A____

13.   (B 1:30)   (C 12:30)   (D 1:10)   (E 6:30)   (F 8:45)

14.   [A]   (B)   [C]   (D)

15.   [1:15]   [1:45]   [2:45]   [3:25]

16.   [32__]   [28__]   [39__]   [62__]

83

17. (72)   (11)   (54)   (13)

18. _____

19. [1:30]   [3:30]   [1:45]   [4:45]

20.   47   32   28   33

21. [DENVER]   [CLEVELAND]   [CHICAGO]   [DALLAS]

22.   16F

23.   13   22   31   15

24. [81___]   [17___]   [6___]

25. ___E   ___D   ___C   ___A   ___B

26. (41___)   (82___)   (27___)

27. [Town 27 ___   Pop. 837]   [Town 82 ___   Pop. 3,781]   [Town 16 ___   Pop. 631]

COMPLETE PRACTICE EXAM #2

This complete practice exam contains all four sections of the actual exam. The instructions given are similar to those on the actual exam. The format of this practice exam is identical to the actual exam.

It is imperative that you take the practice exam in as realistic a fashion as possible. **Your practice will have no value unless it is done realistically.** Therefore, you must precisely time yourself on the Address Checking, Address Memory, and Number Series sections. Our Timed Practice Test CD is a convenient way to practice realistically and time yourself precisely. Also, you must listen to the Following Oral Instructions questions on our Oral Instructions Practice Tests CD or have someone read them to you - *do not read the questions yourself!* The Following Oral Instructions questions can be found in the back of your book if someone will be reading them to you.

When taking a practice exam, first turn to the back of your book and tear out one of the **Complete Practice Exam Answer Sheets.** Mark the answers to the scored segments of the exam on this answer sheet. Remember, of the seven segments on the Address Memory Section, only the final one is scored. Accordingly, you should mark answers for only the final Address Memory segment on your Complete Practice Exam Answer Sheet. The other segments of the Address Memory Section that call for answers have their own sample answer sheets where you should mark answers.

Answer keys are provided in the back of your book. Immediately upon completing each section of a practice exam, **it is imperative that you score yourself** using the formulas given in the Scoring Formulas section of the book. Scoring is necessary in order to gauge your progress and to identify your individual areas of weakness that may need extra attention.

After completing and scoring each practice exam, move on to the next. **After finishing all six exams, you should be prepared for the actual exam.** If you feel the need for more practice after completing six practice exams, see page 60 for details on our free extra practice tests.

Do not look over the practice exam questions until you are ready to start - usually meaning either until (1) you have started the Timed Practice Test CD or the Oral Instructions Practice Tests CD or (2) you have set a timer for the allotted period of time. Similarly, after completing one section of the practice test, do not look over the next one until your are ready to start it. Likewise, stop working and put down your pencil immediately when the allotted period of time has expired. As has been emphasized before but cannot be emphasized enough, your practice is of absolutely no value unless it is done realistically. Also, you must train yourself (1) to not open your test booklet or pick up your pencil until instructed to do so and (2) to close your booklet and put down your pencil immediately upon being so instructed. The Postal Service has zero tolerance on these matters. Any variance may be viewed as cheating and may result in your disqualification.

COMPLETE PRACTICE EXAM #2
Part A – Address Checking

Directions

In the Address Checking section, you are to decide whether two addresses are alike or different. You have 6 minutes to answer 95 questions. Each question consists of a pair of addresses. If the two addresses in the pair are exactly alike in every way, darken the oval with the letter "A" for *Alike*. If the two addresses are different in any way, darken the oval with the letter "D" for *Different*. Mark your answers on the Complete Practice Exam Answer Sheet in the section entitled Address Checking. Begin when you are prepared to time yourself for precisely 6 minutes.

Notes:
- *You will notice that the questions on this section of your practice exam are spread across two pages. This is the exact format of the Address Checking section on the real exam. To save printing costs, some study guides condense the two pages of this section down to only one. Other study guides, for reasons we cannot even begin to guess, stretch the Address Checking section out over several pages.*
- *You will also notice that the Address Checking questions are presented in a font, or type of print, that is different from the rest of the book. This font closely matches the type of print used on the real exam, and - as you will see - it makes this section even more challenging.*
- *It is imperative that you practice realistically and that you become acquainted with the actual format of the test. We have therefore formatted the page layout and the font of the Address Checking section on this practice exam realistically for your benefit.*

1.	8757 Lee Blvd.	8757 Lee Blvd.
2.	Roundfield, Mass. 78645-5645	Roundfield, Mass. 78654-5645
3.	109 Boggs Circle SW	109 Boggs Circle SW
4.	315 E. Fourth St.	315 E. Fourth St.
5.	Lurch, Az. 22344-3347	Lurch, Az. 23344-3347
6.	555 Van Buren Ave.	55 Van Buren Ave.
7.	2343 Camron Mills	2343 Canron Mills
8.	Rolling Fork, Ms. 39255-2516	Rolling Fork, Ms. 39255-2516
9.	Hinds, N.H.	Hinds, N.H.
10.	456 Cuevas Dr., Ronkonkoma, NY	456 Cuevas Dr., Ronkonkoma, NY
11.	9834 Wellings NW	9834 Willings NW
12.	982 Brymnawr Ave.	982 Brynmawr Ave.
13.	Kinston, S.C. 77896-4576	Kingston, S.C. 77896-4576
14.	212 Columbia Rd.	212 Columbia R.
15.	2000 Sylva Mannor Dr.	2000 Sylva Mannor Dr.
16.	305 Park Row, Sagaponack, OR	305 Park Row, Sagaponack, OR
17.	1335 Main Road East	1334 Main Road East
18.	999 Jefferson Davis Cir.	999 Jefferson Davis Cir.
19.	Mt. Olive, N.S. 35074-5653	Mt. Olive, N.S. 35047-5653
20.	878 St. George Sq.	878 St. George Sq.
21.	215 Beaumont Dr. West	215 Beaumont Dr. East
22.	Summit, Wash. 94590-9981	Summit, Wash. 94590-9981
23.	220 West Beach	220 West Beach
24.	6242 Lynnwood Cir. East	6244 Lynnwood Cir. East
25.	Portland, Org. 95580-1940	Portland, Org. 95580-1940
26.	905 Morse Code Rd.	905 Morse Code Rd.
27.	1221 North Street East	1221 East Street North
28.	5544 Mockingbird Lane, Amagansett, RI	4455 Mockingbird Land, Amagansett, RI
29.	104-A N. Island View	104-A N. Island View
30.	106 Carroll Ave. South	106 Carrol Ave. South
31.	1001 Mitchell Blvd. NW Suite 1422	1001 Mitchell Blvd. NE Suite 1422
32.	Eaton Village, Okla.	Eaton Village, Okla.
33.	255 Ann St. South	255 Ane St. South
34.	605 Camp Ave., Massapequa, Mass	605 Camp Ave., Massapequa, Mass
35.	3007 Memory Lane	3007 Mimory Lane
36.	Miller, W. Va. 55665-4356	Miller, W.Va. 56655-4356
37.	905 Coutel blvd. North	905 Coutel blvd. North
38.	101 Westwood Pl.	101 Westwood Pl.
39.	102 Trautman Ave.	102 Trautman Dr.
40.	209 Jeff Davis SE	209 Jeff Davis SE
41.	956 Powers Pl., Wyandanch, OK	956 Powers Pl., Wyandanch, OK
42.	St. Bay Louis, Mich. 78655-1776	St. Bay Louis, Mich. 78556-1776
43.	1952 Bilmar Dr.	1952 Bilmar Dr.
44.	504 Gulf View N	405 Gulf View N
45.	303 Mesa Villa Rd., Guanajuato, NM	303 Mesa Vila Rd., Guanajuato, NM
46.	4004 Oak Place	4004 Oak Place
47.	217 Leigh St. NW	217 Lee St. NW
48.	5064 E Mission Lane, Nayarit, Calif.	5064 E Mission Lane, Nayarit, Calif.

49.	Great Andes, Calif. 99033-5464	Great Ander, Calif. 99033-5464
50.	Beach Oak Apts. NW	Beach Oak Apts. NE
51.	4234 Newton Park	4324 Newton Park
52.	205-B Ranch Road East	205-B Ranch Road East
53.	Houston, Texas 77055-2662	Houston, Texas 77050-2662
54.	0489 East Old Pass Road	0489 East Old Pass Rd.
55.	515 W. Nicholson Ave.	515 W. Nicholson Ave.
56.	Orange Grove, Fla. 40097-8941	Orange Grove, Fla. 40097-8941
57.	909 Sinwell Market St.	909 Sinwell Market Ave.
58.	4763 Oak Pl. Apt 6-B	4763 Oak Ct. Apt, 6-B
59.	6749 Beach Ct., Andalouisa, LA	6794 Beach Ct., Andalouisa, LA
60.	00601 Area Blvd.	06001 Area Blvd.
61.	321-B Menarney St.	321-B Menarney St.
62.	1724 Maple Ct.	1742 Maple Ct.
63.	303-D Sweeney Dr.	303-B Sweeney Dr.
64.	Vandenburg, VA 67495-3214	Vandenburg, VA 67945-3214
65.	09572 Waycross Dr.	09572 Waycross Dr.
66.	07523 Bienville Dr.	07253 Bienville Dr.
67.	Holly Hills, KY 38572-5613	Holly Hills, KY 38572-5613
68.	399 Santa Maria Cr.	339 Santa Maria Cr.
69.	3097 Rodenburg Ave.	3097 Rodenburg Ave.
70.	0132 Regency Blvd.	0123 Regency Blvd.
71.	Merigold, Mass. 68975-0021	Meriglod, Miss. 68975-0021
72.	212 South Shore St.	212 South Shore Ct.
73.	Kensington, LA 57391	Kensington, LA 57931
74.	696 Camp Wilkes	696 Camp Willie
75.	1658 Cherry Circle	1658 Cherry Circle
76.	Sycamore, NY 76983-9999	Sycamore, NY 76983-9999
77.	0060 DeMountluzin Ave.	00600 De Montluzin Ave.
78.	44-B Daisy Vestry Rd.	44-B Daisy View Rd.
79.	717 Acacia Apt. A	717 Acacia Apt. A
80.	397 N Paradise Pt.	379 N Paradise Pt.
81.	112 Felicity View W, Suite 154C	122 Felicity View W, Suite 154C
82.	0435 Ballentine N	0453 Ballentine W
83.	17 S Crawford Court	17 S Crawford Circle
84.	Lameuse, Texas 48275-1255	Lameuse, Texas 48725-1255
85.	47-C Rolling Hills Ave.	47-C Rolling Hills Ave.
86.	Everbreeze, S.D. 29402	Evergreen, S.D. 29042
87.	Grand Island, Nebraska 00	Grand Isle, Nebraska 07001
88.	Rock Chester, NJ 79538-7001	Rock Chester, NM 97358-7001
89.	07864 Knollwood Dr.	07684 Knollwood Dr.
90.	001 E. Rustwood St.	001 E. Rustwood St.
91.	W. Vandenburg Heights #68	W. Vandenburg Heights #86
92.	Muskego, Ohio 35426-9933	Muskego, Ohio 35246-9933
93.	Yorkshire N Apt. 66	Yorkshire N Apt. 66
94.	6226 Heibenhein Ct.	6262 Heibenhein Ct.
95.	Shasta Place #242 W	Shasta Place #424 W

COMPLETE PRACTICE EXAM #2
Part B – Address Memory

Directions

In the Address Memory section, you are to memorize the locations of 25 addresses in five boxes. During this section, you will have several study periods and practice exercises to help you memorize the location of the addresses shown in the five boxes. Answer the questions by darkening the oval containing the letter (A, B, C, D, E) of the box the address came from - Box A, Box B, Box C, Box D, or Box E. At the end of each segment, you will be given instructions on how and where to continue. After completing six preliminary segments, the actual test will be given as segment #7.

Turn the page to begin Segment #1 of the Address Memory section.

Note: You will notice in this practice exam that segments 3, 4, and 6 of the Address Memory section are spread across two pages. The five boxes, the 88 questions, and the sample answer sheet in these segments are spread across two facing pages. This is the exact same format that you will experience on Address Memory segments 3, 4, and 6 of the actual exam. To save printing costs, other study guides frequently condense these segments down from two pages to only one. However, it is imperative that you practice realistically and that you become acquainted with the actual format of the test. We have therefore formatted the Address Memory section on this practice exam realistically for your benefit.

COMPLETE PRACTICE EXAM #2
Part B – Address Memory – Segment #1

The purpose of this small exercise is to acquaint you with the format of the Address Memory section. The first two questions are answered for you. You are to spend three minutes studying this page and answering sample questions 3, 4, and 5. After completing Segment #1, turn to Segment #2 for further instructions. Begin when you are prepared to time yourself for precisely three minutes.

A	B	C	D	E
6800-7599 Beach Island View 7700-8499 West Carroll 6500-6699 Samuel	8900-8999 Beach Galloway 8600-8799 West Runnels 7700-8499 Samuel	7700-8499 Beach Alexander 8900-8999 West Driftwood 8600-8799 Samuel	8600-8799 Beach Mathison 6500-6699 West Pirate 6800-7599 Samuel	6500-6699 Beach Clifford 6800-7599 West Lynwood 8900-8999 Samuel

1. Clifford   Ⓐ Ⓑ Ⓒ Ⓓ **Ⓔ**
   This address came from Box E, so we sill darken the oval with the letter E.

2. 6500-6699 Samuel   **Ⓐ** Ⓑ Ⓒ Ⓓ Ⓔ
   This address came from Box A, so we will darken the oval with the letter A.

3. 8900-8999 West   Ⓐ Ⓑ Ⓒ Ⓓ Ⓔ
   Now that you know how to answer, you do questions 3, 4, and 5.

4. 7700-8499 Samuel   Ⓐ Ⓑ Ⓒ Ⓓ Ⓔ

5. Alexander   Ⓐ Ⓑ Ⓒ Ⓓ Ⓔ

The correct answers are E, A, C, B, and C.

COMPLETE PRACTICE EXAM #2
Part B – Address Memory – Segment #2

In this segment, you are given three minutes to study and memorize the addresses. There are no questions to answer in this segment - it is a study period only. However, on the actual exam, the boxes are not reprinted for your use. Instead, you are instructed to turn back to Address Memory Segment #1 and to spend three minutes studying the boxes displayed there. So, we will do the very same on this practice exam. After studying for three minutes, turn to Segment #3 for directions on how to continue the Address Memory Section of the exam. Begin studying when you are prepared to time yourself for precisely three minutes.

COMPLETE PRACTICE EXAM #2
Part B – Address Memory – Segment #3

You have three minutes to answer 88 questions. Try to answer from memory, but the boxes are shown if you need to refer to them. Mark your answers on the sample answer sheet at the bottom of the pages. After completing this segment, turn to Segment #4 for further instructions. Begin when you are prepared to time yourself for precisely three minutes.

A	B	C
6800-7599 Beach Island View 7700-8499 West Carroll 6500-6699 Samuel	8900-8999 Beach Galloway 8600-8799 West Runnels 7700-8499 Samuel	7700-8499 Beach Alexander 8900-8999 West Driftwood 8600-8799 Samuel

1. 8600-8799 West
2. Alexander
3. 6500-6699 West
4. Mathison
5. 6800-7599 Beach
6. 8900-8999 Samuel
7. Carroll
8. 7700-8499 Beach

9. Lynwood
10. Island View
11. 6500-6699 Samuel
12. 8900-8999 Beach
13. Pirate
14. 7700-8499 West
15. Clifford
16. 6500-6699 Beach

17. 8900-8999 West
18. 7700-8499 Samuel
19. Driftwood
20. 6800-7599 Samuel
21. Galloway
22. Mathison
23. 8600-8799 Samuel
24. 6800-7599 Beach

25. 6500-6699 Beach
26. Runnels
27. 7700-8499 West
28. 6800-7599 West
29. 7700-8499 Beach
30. Pirate
31. 6500-6699 West
32. Lynwood

33. Alexander
34. 8900-8999 West
35. 7700-8499 Samuel
36. 6500-6699 Beach
37. 6500-6699 Samuel
38. 8900-8999 Beach
39. 8600-8799 West
40. 6800-7599 Samuel

41. Island View
42. Carroll
43. 7700-8499 West
44. Driftwood
45. Galloway
46. 6800-7599 Beach
47. 8900-8999 Samuel
48. Mathison

1 Ⓐ Ⓑ Ⓒ Ⓓ Ⓔ
2 Ⓐ Ⓑ Ⓒ Ⓓ Ⓔ
3 Ⓐ Ⓑ Ⓒ Ⓓ Ⓔ
4 Ⓐ Ⓑ Ⓒ Ⓓ Ⓔ
5 Ⓐ Ⓑ Ⓒ Ⓓ Ⓔ
6 Ⓐ Ⓑ Ⓒ Ⓓ Ⓔ
7 Ⓐ Ⓑ Ⓒ Ⓓ Ⓔ
8 Ⓐ Ⓑ Ⓒ Ⓓ Ⓔ

9 Ⓐ Ⓑ Ⓒ Ⓓ Ⓔ
10 Ⓐ Ⓑ Ⓒ Ⓓ Ⓔ
11 Ⓐ Ⓑ Ⓒ Ⓓ Ⓔ
12 Ⓐ Ⓑ Ⓒ Ⓓ Ⓔ
13 Ⓐ Ⓑ Ⓒ Ⓓ Ⓔ
14 Ⓐ Ⓑ Ⓒ Ⓓ Ⓔ
15 Ⓐ Ⓑ Ⓒ Ⓓ Ⓔ
16 Ⓐ Ⓑ Ⓒ Ⓓ Ⓔ

17 Ⓐ Ⓑ Ⓒ Ⓓ Ⓔ
18 Ⓐ Ⓑ Ⓒ Ⓓ Ⓔ
19 Ⓐ Ⓑ Ⓒ Ⓓ Ⓔ
20 Ⓐ Ⓑ Ⓒ Ⓓ Ⓔ
21 Ⓐ Ⓑ Ⓒ Ⓓ Ⓔ
22 Ⓐ Ⓑ Ⓒ Ⓓ Ⓔ
23 Ⓐ Ⓑ Ⓒ Ⓓ Ⓔ
24 Ⓐ Ⓑ Ⓒ Ⓓ Ⓔ

25 Ⓐ Ⓑ Ⓒ Ⓓ Ⓔ
26 Ⓐ Ⓑ Ⓒ Ⓓ Ⓔ
27 Ⓐ Ⓑ Ⓒ Ⓓ Ⓔ
28 Ⓐ Ⓑ Ⓒ Ⓓ Ⓔ
29 Ⓐ Ⓑ Ⓒ Ⓓ Ⓔ
30 Ⓐ Ⓑ Ⓒ Ⓓ Ⓔ
31 Ⓐ Ⓑ Ⓒ Ⓓ Ⓔ
32 Ⓐ Ⓑ Ⓒ Ⓓ Ⓔ

33 Ⓐ Ⓑ Ⓒ Ⓓ Ⓔ
34 Ⓐ Ⓑ Ⓒ Ⓓ Ⓔ
35 Ⓐ Ⓑ Ⓒ Ⓓ Ⓔ
36 Ⓐ Ⓑ Ⓒ Ⓓ Ⓔ
37 Ⓐ Ⓑ Ⓒ Ⓓ Ⓔ
38 Ⓐ Ⓑ Ⓒ Ⓓ Ⓔ
39 Ⓐ Ⓑ Ⓒ Ⓓ Ⓔ
40 Ⓐ Ⓑ Ⓒ Ⓓ Ⓔ

41 Ⓐ Ⓑ Ⓒ Ⓓ Ⓔ
42 Ⓐ Ⓑ Ⓒ Ⓓ Ⓔ
43 Ⓐ Ⓑ Ⓒ Ⓓ Ⓔ
44 Ⓐ Ⓑ Ⓒ Ⓓ Ⓔ
45 Ⓐ Ⓑ Ⓒ Ⓓ Ⓔ
46 Ⓐ Ⓑ Ⓒ Ⓓ Ⓔ
47 Ⓐ Ⓑ Ⓒ Ⓓ Ⓔ
48 Ⓐ Ⓑ Ⓒ Ⓓ Ⓔ

D	E
8600-8799 Beach Mathison 6500-6699 West Pirate 6800-7599 Samuel	6500-6699 Beach Clifford 6800-7599 West Lynwood 8900-8999 Samuel

49. Clifford
50. 6800-7599 West
51. 6500-6699 Samuel
52. 8600-8799 Samuel
53. Island View
54. 7700-8499 Beach
55. Runnels
56. Lynwood

57. 8600-8799 West
58. 6500-6699 West
59. Pirate
60. 6500-6699 Beach
61. Galloway
62. 8900-8999 Beach
63. 7700-8499 West
64. Clifford

65. 8600-8799 Beach
66. 6800-7599 Samuel
67. Alexander
68. 8900-8999 West
69. Driftwood
70. Carroll
71. 6800-7599 Beach
72. 8900-8999 Samuel

73. 7700-8499 Beach
74. Galloway
75. Clifford
76. 8600-8799 Samuel
77. 8900-8999 Beach
78. 6800-7599 Beach
79. Lynwood
80. 8600-8799 West

81. Mathison
82. 7700-8499 Beach
83. 6500-6699 Samuel
84. 7700-8499 Samuel
85. 6500-6699 West
86. Driftwood
87. Island View
88. 6800-7599 West

49 Ⓐ Ⓑ Ⓒ Ⓓ Ⓔ
50 Ⓐ Ⓑ Ⓒ Ⓓ Ⓔ
51 Ⓐ Ⓑ Ⓒ Ⓓ Ⓔ
52 Ⓐ Ⓑ Ⓒ Ⓓ Ⓔ
53 Ⓐ Ⓑ Ⓒ Ⓓ Ⓔ
54 Ⓐ Ⓑ Ⓒ Ⓓ Ⓔ
55 Ⓐ Ⓑ Ⓒ Ⓓ Ⓔ
56 Ⓐ Ⓑ Ⓒ Ⓓ Ⓔ

57 Ⓐ Ⓑ Ⓒ Ⓓ Ⓔ
58 Ⓐ Ⓑ Ⓒ Ⓓ Ⓔ
59 Ⓐ Ⓑ Ⓒ Ⓓ Ⓔ
60 Ⓐ Ⓑ Ⓒ Ⓓ Ⓔ
61 Ⓐ Ⓑ Ⓒ Ⓓ Ⓔ
62 Ⓐ Ⓑ Ⓒ Ⓓ Ⓔ
63 Ⓐ Ⓑ Ⓒ Ⓓ Ⓔ
64 Ⓐ Ⓑ Ⓒ Ⓓ Ⓔ

65 Ⓐ Ⓑ Ⓒ Ⓓ Ⓔ
66 Ⓐ Ⓑ Ⓒ Ⓓ Ⓔ
67 Ⓐ Ⓑ Ⓒ Ⓓ Ⓔ
68 Ⓐ Ⓑ Ⓒ Ⓓ Ⓔ
69 Ⓐ Ⓑ Ⓒ Ⓓ Ⓔ
70 Ⓐ Ⓑ Ⓒ Ⓓ Ⓔ
71 Ⓐ Ⓑ Ⓒ Ⓓ Ⓔ
72 Ⓐ Ⓑ Ⓒ Ⓓ Ⓔ

73 Ⓐ Ⓑ Ⓒ Ⓓ Ⓔ
74 Ⓐ Ⓑ Ⓒ Ⓓ Ⓔ
75 Ⓐ Ⓑ Ⓒ Ⓓ Ⓔ
76 Ⓐ Ⓑ Ⓒ Ⓓ Ⓔ
77 Ⓐ Ⓑ Ⓒ Ⓓ Ⓔ
78 Ⓐ Ⓑ Ⓒ Ⓓ Ⓔ
79 Ⓐ Ⓑ Ⓒ Ⓓ Ⓔ
80 Ⓐ Ⓑ Ⓒ Ⓓ Ⓔ

81 Ⓐ Ⓑ Ⓒ Ⓓ Ⓔ
82 Ⓐ Ⓑ Ⓒ Ⓓ Ⓔ
83 Ⓐ Ⓑ Ⓒ Ⓓ Ⓔ
84 Ⓐ Ⓑ Ⓒ Ⓓ Ⓔ
85 Ⓐ Ⓑ Ⓒ Ⓓ Ⓔ
86 Ⓐ Ⓑ Ⓒ Ⓓ Ⓔ
87 Ⓐ Ⓑ Ⓒ Ⓓ Ⓔ
88 Ⓐ Ⓑ Ⓒ Ⓓ Ⓔ

COMPLETE PRACTICE EXAM #2
Part B – Address Memory – Segment #4

You have three minutes to answer 88 questions. You must answer from memory. The boxes are not shown. Mark your answers on the sample answer sheet at the bottom of the page. After completing this segment, turn to Segment #5 for further instructions. Begin when you are prepared to time yourself for precisely three minutes.

1. Clifford
2. 8900-8999 Samuel
3. 8900-8999 West
4. 7700-8499 Samuel
5. Alexander
6. 6500-6699 Beach
7. 6800-7599 West
8. 8600-8799 Samuel

9. Driftwood
10. Island View
11. 8600-8799 West
12. 7700-8499 West
13. 8900-8999 Samuel
14. Runnels
15. 8900-8999 Beach
16. 6500-6699 West

17. 7700-8499 Beach
18. Pirate
19. Carroll
20. Clifford
21. 6800-7599 Samuel
22. 8900-8999 West
23. 8600-8799 Beach
24. 6800-7599 Beach

25. Galloway
26. 6800-7599 West
27. 8600-8799 West
28. 8900-8999 Samuel
29. Driftwood
30. 7700-8499 West
31. 6800-7599 Beach
32. Lynwood

33. Mathison
34. Clifford
35. 8900-8999 Beach
36. 6800-7599 Samuel
37. 7700-8499 Beach
38. Island View
39. 6500-6699 West
40. 6500-6699 Beach

41. Carroll
42. 6500-6699 Samuel
43. 8600-8799 Beach
44. Alexander
45. 8900-8999 Beach
46. 8600-8799 Samuel
47. Runnels
48. Pirate

1 Ⓐ Ⓑ Ⓒ Ⓓ Ⓔ	17 Ⓐ Ⓑ Ⓒ Ⓓ Ⓔ	33 Ⓐ Ⓑ Ⓒ Ⓓ Ⓔ
2 Ⓐ Ⓑ Ⓒ Ⓓ Ⓔ	18 Ⓐ Ⓑ Ⓒ Ⓓ Ⓔ	34 Ⓐ Ⓑ Ⓒ Ⓓ Ⓔ
3 Ⓐ Ⓑ Ⓒ Ⓓ Ⓔ	19 Ⓐ Ⓑ Ⓒ Ⓓ Ⓔ	35 Ⓐ Ⓑ Ⓒ Ⓓ Ⓔ
4 Ⓐ Ⓑ Ⓒ Ⓓ Ⓔ	20 Ⓐ Ⓑ Ⓒ Ⓓ Ⓔ	36 Ⓐ Ⓑ Ⓒ Ⓓ Ⓔ
5 Ⓐ Ⓑ Ⓒ Ⓓ Ⓔ	21 Ⓐ Ⓑ Ⓒ Ⓓ Ⓔ	37 Ⓐ Ⓑ Ⓒ Ⓓ Ⓔ
6 Ⓐ Ⓑ Ⓒ Ⓓ Ⓔ	22 Ⓐ Ⓑ Ⓒ Ⓓ Ⓔ	38 Ⓐ Ⓑ Ⓒ Ⓓ Ⓔ
7 Ⓐ Ⓑ Ⓒ Ⓓ Ⓔ	23 Ⓐ Ⓑ Ⓒ Ⓓ Ⓔ	39 Ⓐ Ⓑ Ⓒ Ⓓ Ⓔ
8 Ⓐ Ⓑ Ⓒ Ⓓ Ⓔ	24 Ⓐ Ⓑ Ⓒ Ⓓ Ⓔ	40 Ⓐ Ⓑ Ⓒ Ⓓ Ⓔ
9 Ⓐ Ⓑ Ⓒ Ⓓ Ⓔ	25 Ⓐ Ⓑ Ⓒ Ⓓ Ⓔ	41 Ⓐ Ⓑ Ⓒ Ⓓ Ⓔ
10 Ⓐ Ⓑ Ⓒ Ⓓ Ⓔ	26 Ⓐ Ⓑ Ⓒ Ⓓ Ⓔ	42 Ⓐ Ⓑ Ⓒ Ⓓ Ⓔ
11 Ⓐ Ⓑ Ⓒ Ⓓ Ⓔ	27 Ⓐ Ⓑ Ⓒ Ⓓ Ⓔ	43 Ⓐ Ⓑ Ⓒ Ⓓ Ⓔ
12 Ⓐ Ⓑ Ⓒ Ⓓ Ⓔ	28 Ⓐ Ⓑ Ⓒ Ⓓ Ⓔ	44 Ⓐ Ⓑ Ⓒ Ⓓ Ⓔ
13 Ⓐ Ⓑ Ⓒ Ⓓ Ⓔ	29 Ⓐ Ⓑ Ⓒ Ⓓ Ⓔ	45 Ⓐ Ⓑ Ⓒ Ⓓ Ⓔ
14 Ⓐ Ⓑ Ⓒ Ⓓ Ⓔ	30 Ⓐ Ⓑ Ⓒ Ⓓ Ⓔ	46 Ⓐ Ⓑ Ⓒ Ⓓ Ⓔ
15 Ⓐ Ⓑ Ⓒ Ⓓ Ⓔ	31 Ⓐ Ⓑ Ⓒ Ⓓ Ⓔ	47 Ⓐ Ⓑ Ⓒ Ⓓ Ⓔ
16 Ⓐ Ⓑ Ⓒ Ⓓ Ⓔ	32 Ⓐ Ⓑ Ⓒ Ⓓ Ⓔ	48 Ⓐ Ⓑ Ⓒ Ⓓ Ⓔ

49. 8600-8799 Beach
50. Clifford
51. 7700-8499 West
52. 6800-7599 Samuel
53. Galloway
54. 6500-6699 Samuel
55. 6500-6699 Beach
56. 8600-8799 West

57. 8900-8999 West
58. 6800-7599 Samuel
59. Clifford
60. Lynwood
61. 6500-6699 Beach
62. 8600-8799 West
63. Carroll
64. 8600-8799 Samuel

65. 6800-7599 West
66. 8900-8999 West
67. Island View
68. 8900-8999 Samuel
69. 7700-8499 Samuel
70. Mathison
71. Pirate
72. 6500-6699 West

73. 8900-8999 Beach
74. 6500-6699 West
75. Alexander
76. Driftwood
77. Galloway
78. 7700-8499 Samuel
79. 6800-7599 Beach
80. 8900-8999 Samuel

81. Lynwood
82. 8600-8799 Beach
83. Runnels
84. 6800-7599 Beach
85. 6500-6699 Samuel
86. 6800-7599 West
87. 6500-6699 Samuel
88. 8900-8999 Beach

49. Ⓐ Ⓑ Ⓒ Ⓓ Ⓔ
50. Ⓐ Ⓑ Ⓒ Ⓓ Ⓔ
51. Ⓐ Ⓑ Ⓒ Ⓓ Ⓔ
52. Ⓐ Ⓑ Ⓒ Ⓓ Ⓔ
53. Ⓐ Ⓑ Ⓒ Ⓓ Ⓔ
54. Ⓐ Ⓑ Ⓒ Ⓓ Ⓔ
55. Ⓐ Ⓑ Ⓒ Ⓓ Ⓔ
56. Ⓐ Ⓑ Ⓒ Ⓓ Ⓔ

57. Ⓐ Ⓑ Ⓒ Ⓓ Ⓔ
58. Ⓐ Ⓑ Ⓒ Ⓓ Ⓔ
59. Ⓐ Ⓑ Ⓒ Ⓓ Ⓔ
60. Ⓐ Ⓑ Ⓒ Ⓓ Ⓔ
61. Ⓐ Ⓑ Ⓒ Ⓓ Ⓔ
62. Ⓐ Ⓑ Ⓒ Ⓓ Ⓔ
63. Ⓐ Ⓑ Ⓒ Ⓓ Ⓔ
64. Ⓐ Ⓑ Ⓒ Ⓓ Ⓔ

65. Ⓐ Ⓑ Ⓒ Ⓓ Ⓔ
66. Ⓐ Ⓑ Ⓒ Ⓓ Ⓔ
67. Ⓐ Ⓑ Ⓒ Ⓓ Ⓔ
68. Ⓐ Ⓑ Ⓒ Ⓓ Ⓔ
69. Ⓐ Ⓑ Ⓒ Ⓓ Ⓔ
70. Ⓐ Ⓑ Ⓒ Ⓓ Ⓔ
71. Ⓐ Ⓑ Ⓒ Ⓓ Ⓔ
72. Ⓐ Ⓑ Ⓒ Ⓓ Ⓔ

73. Ⓐ Ⓑ Ⓒ Ⓓ Ⓔ
74. Ⓐ Ⓑ Ⓒ Ⓓ Ⓔ
75. Ⓐ Ⓑ Ⓒ Ⓓ Ⓔ
76. Ⓐ Ⓑ Ⓒ Ⓓ Ⓔ
77. Ⓐ Ⓑ Ⓒ Ⓓ Ⓔ
78. Ⓐ Ⓑ Ⓒ Ⓓ Ⓔ
79. Ⓐ Ⓑ Ⓒ Ⓓ Ⓔ
80. Ⓐ Ⓑ Ⓒ Ⓓ Ⓔ

81. Ⓐ Ⓑ Ⓒ Ⓓ Ⓔ
82. Ⓐ Ⓑ Ⓒ Ⓓ Ⓔ
83. Ⓐ Ⓑ Ⓒ Ⓓ Ⓔ
84. Ⓐ Ⓑ Ⓒ Ⓓ Ⓔ
85. Ⓐ Ⓑ Ⓒ Ⓓ Ⓔ
86. Ⓐ Ⓑ Ⓒ Ⓓ Ⓔ
87. Ⓐ Ⓑ Ⓒ Ⓓ Ⓔ
88. Ⓐ Ⓑ Ⓒ Ⓓ Ⓔ

COMPLETE PRACTICE EXAM #2
Part B – Address Memory – Segment #5

In this segment, you are given five minutes to study the addresses. There are no questions to answer in this segment – it is a study period only. As before, the boxes are not reprinted here for your use. Instead, you are instructed to turn back to Address Memory Segment #1 and to spend five minutes studying the boxes displayed there. After studying for five minutes, turn to Segment #6 for directions on how to continue. Turn back to Segment #1 and begin studying when you are prepared to time yourself for precisely five minutes.

COMPLETE PRACTICE EXAM #2
Part B – Address Memory – Segment #6

You have five minutes to answer 88 questions. Try to answer from memory, but the boxes are shown if you need to refer to them. Mark your answers on the sample answer sheet at the bottom of the page. After completing this segment, turn to Segment #7 for further instructions. Begin when you are prepared to time yourself for precisely five minutes.

A	B	C
6800-7599 Beach Island View 7700-8499 West Carroll 6500-6699 Samuel	8900-8999 Beach Galloway 8600-8799 West Runnels 7700-8499 Samuel	7700-8499 Beach Alexander 8900-8999 West Driftwood 8600-8799 Samuel

1. 8600-8799 West
2. Alexander
3. 6500-6699 West
4. Mathison
5. 6800-7599 Beach
6. 8900-8999 Samuel
7. Carroll
8. 7700-8499 Beach

9. Lynwood
10. Island View
11. 6500-6699 Samuel
12. 8900-8999 Beach
13. Pirate
14. 7700-8499 West
15. Clifford
16. 6500-6699 Beach

17. 8900-8999 West
18. 7700-8499 Samuel
19. Driftwood
20. 6800-7599 Samuel
21. Galloway
22. Mathison
23. 8600-8799 Samuel
24. 6800-7599 Beach

25. 6500-6699 Beach
26. Runnels
27. 7700-8499 West
28. 6800-7599 West
29. 7700-8499 Beach
30. Pirate
31. 6500-6699 West
32. Lynwood

33. Alexander
34. 8900-8999 West
35. 7700-8499 Samuel
36. 6500-6699 Beach
37. 6500-6699 Samuel
38. 8900-8999 Beach
39. 8600-8799 West
40. 6800-7599 Samuel

41. Island View
42. Carroll
43. 7700-8499 West
44. Driftwood
45. Galloway
46. 6800-7599 Beach
47. 8900-8999 Samuel
48. Mathison

1 Ⓐ Ⓑ Ⓒ Ⓓ Ⓔ
2 Ⓐ Ⓑ Ⓒ Ⓓ Ⓔ
3 Ⓐ Ⓑ Ⓒ Ⓓ Ⓔ
4 Ⓐ Ⓑ Ⓒ Ⓓ Ⓔ
5 Ⓐ Ⓑ Ⓒ Ⓓ Ⓔ
6 Ⓐ Ⓑ Ⓒ Ⓓ Ⓔ
7 Ⓐ Ⓑ Ⓒ Ⓓ Ⓔ
8 Ⓐ Ⓑ Ⓒ Ⓓ Ⓔ
9 Ⓐ Ⓑ Ⓒ Ⓓ Ⓔ
10 Ⓐ Ⓑ Ⓒ Ⓓ Ⓔ
11 Ⓐ Ⓑ Ⓒ Ⓓ Ⓔ
12 Ⓐ Ⓑ Ⓒ Ⓓ Ⓔ
13 Ⓐ Ⓑ Ⓒ Ⓓ Ⓔ
14 Ⓐ Ⓑ Ⓒ Ⓓ Ⓔ
15 Ⓐ Ⓑ Ⓒ Ⓓ Ⓔ
16 Ⓐ Ⓑ Ⓒ Ⓓ Ⓔ

17 Ⓐ Ⓑ Ⓒ Ⓓ Ⓔ
18 Ⓐ Ⓑ Ⓒ Ⓓ Ⓔ
19 Ⓐ Ⓑ Ⓒ Ⓓ Ⓔ
20 Ⓐ Ⓑ Ⓒ Ⓓ Ⓔ
21 Ⓐ Ⓑ Ⓒ Ⓓ Ⓔ
22 Ⓐ Ⓑ Ⓒ Ⓓ Ⓔ
23 Ⓐ Ⓑ Ⓒ Ⓓ Ⓔ
24 Ⓐ Ⓑ Ⓒ Ⓓ Ⓔ
25 Ⓐ Ⓑ Ⓒ Ⓓ Ⓔ
26 Ⓐ Ⓑ Ⓒ Ⓓ Ⓔ
27 Ⓐ Ⓑ Ⓒ Ⓓ Ⓔ
28 Ⓐ Ⓑ Ⓒ Ⓓ Ⓔ
29 Ⓐ Ⓑ Ⓒ Ⓓ Ⓔ
30 Ⓐ Ⓑ Ⓒ Ⓓ Ⓔ
31 Ⓐ Ⓑ Ⓒ Ⓓ Ⓔ
32 Ⓐ Ⓑ Ⓒ Ⓓ Ⓔ

33 Ⓐ Ⓑ Ⓒ Ⓓ Ⓔ
34 Ⓐ Ⓑ Ⓒ Ⓓ Ⓔ
35 Ⓐ Ⓑ Ⓒ Ⓓ Ⓔ
36 Ⓐ Ⓑ Ⓒ Ⓓ Ⓔ
37 Ⓐ Ⓑ Ⓒ Ⓓ Ⓔ
38 Ⓐ Ⓑ Ⓒ Ⓓ Ⓔ
39 Ⓐ Ⓑ Ⓒ Ⓓ Ⓔ
40 Ⓐ Ⓑ Ⓒ Ⓓ Ⓔ
41 Ⓐ Ⓑ Ⓒ Ⓓ Ⓔ
42 Ⓐ Ⓑ Ⓒ Ⓓ Ⓔ
43 Ⓐ Ⓑ Ⓒ Ⓓ Ⓔ
44 Ⓐ Ⓑ Ⓒ Ⓓ Ⓔ
45 Ⓐ Ⓑ Ⓒ Ⓓ Ⓔ
46 Ⓐ Ⓑ Ⓒ Ⓓ Ⓔ
47 Ⓐ Ⓑ Ⓒ Ⓓ Ⓔ
48 Ⓐ Ⓑ Ⓒ Ⓓ Ⓔ

D

8600-8799 Beach
Mathison
6500-6699 West
Pirate
6800-7599 Samuel

E

6500-6699 Beach
Clifford
6800-7599 West
Lynwood
8900-8999 Samuel

49. Clifford
50. 6800-7599 West
51. 6500-6699 Samuel
52. 8600-8799 Samuel
53. Island View
54. 7700-8499 Beach
55. Runnels
56. Lynwood

57. 8600-8799 West
58. 6500-6699 West
59. Pirate
60. 6500-6699 Beach
61. Galloway
62. 8900-8999 Beach
63. 7700-8499 West
64. Clifford

65. 8600-8799 Beach
66. 6800-7599 Samuel
67. Alexander
68. 8900-8999 West
69. Driftwood
70. Carroll
71. 6800-7599 Beach
72. 8900-8999 Samuel

73. 7700-8499 Beach
74. Galloway
75. Clifford
76. 8600-8799 Samuel
77. 8900-8999 Beach
78. 6800-7599 Beach
79. Lynwood
80. 8600-8799 West

81. Mathison
82. 7700-8499 Beach
83. 6500-6699 Samuel
84. 7700-8499 Samuel
85. 6500-6699 West
86. Driftwood
87. Island View
88. 6800-7599 West

49. Ⓐ Ⓑ Ⓒ Ⓓ Ⓔ
50. Ⓐ Ⓑ Ⓒ Ⓓ Ⓔ
51. Ⓐ Ⓑ Ⓒ Ⓓ Ⓔ
52. Ⓐ Ⓑ Ⓒ Ⓓ Ⓔ
53. Ⓐ Ⓑ Ⓒ Ⓓ Ⓔ
54. Ⓐ Ⓑ Ⓒ Ⓓ Ⓔ
55. Ⓐ Ⓑ Ⓒ Ⓓ Ⓔ
56. Ⓐ Ⓑ Ⓒ Ⓓ Ⓔ

57. Ⓐ Ⓑ Ⓒ Ⓓ Ⓔ
58. Ⓐ Ⓑ Ⓒ Ⓓ Ⓔ
59. Ⓐ Ⓑ Ⓒ Ⓓ Ⓔ
60. Ⓐ Ⓑ Ⓒ Ⓓ Ⓔ
61. Ⓐ Ⓑ Ⓒ Ⓓ Ⓔ
62. Ⓐ Ⓑ Ⓒ Ⓓ Ⓔ
63. Ⓐ Ⓑ Ⓒ Ⓓ Ⓔ
64. Ⓐ Ⓑ Ⓒ Ⓓ Ⓔ

65. Ⓐ Ⓑ Ⓒ Ⓓ Ⓔ
66. Ⓐ Ⓑ Ⓒ Ⓓ Ⓔ
67. Ⓐ Ⓑ Ⓒ Ⓓ Ⓔ
68. Ⓐ Ⓑ Ⓒ Ⓓ Ⓔ
69. Ⓐ Ⓑ Ⓒ Ⓓ Ⓔ
70. Ⓐ Ⓑ Ⓒ Ⓓ Ⓔ
71. Ⓐ Ⓑ Ⓒ Ⓓ Ⓔ
72. Ⓐ Ⓑ Ⓒ Ⓓ Ⓔ

73. Ⓐ Ⓑ Ⓒ Ⓓ Ⓔ
74. Ⓐ Ⓑ Ⓒ Ⓓ Ⓔ
75. Ⓐ Ⓑ Ⓒ Ⓓ Ⓔ
76. Ⓐ Ⓑ Ⓒ Ⓓ Ⓔ
77. Ⓐ Ⓑ Ⓒ Ⓓ Ⓔ
78. Ⓐ Ⓑ Ⓒ Ⓓ Ⓔ
79. Ⓐ Ⓑ Ⓒ Ⓓ Ⓔ
80. Ⓐ Ⓑ Ⓒ Ⓓ Ⓔ

81. Ⓐ Ⓑ Ⓒ Ⓓ Ⓔ
82. Ⓐ Ⓑ Ⓒ Ⓓ Ⓔ
83. Ⓐ Ⓑ Ⓒ Ⓓ Ⓔ
84. Ⓐ Ⓑ Ⓒ Ⓓ Ⓔ
85. Ⓐ Ⓑ Ⓒ Ⓓ Ⓔ
86. Ⓐ Ⓑ Ⓒ Ⓓ Ⓔ
87. Ⓐ Ⓑ Ⓒ Ⓓ Ⓔ
88. Ⓐ Ⓑ Ⓒ Ⓓ Ⓔ

COMPLETE PRACTICE EXAM #2
Part B – Address Memory – Segment #7

You have five minutes to answer 88 questions. You must answer from memory. The boxes are not shown. Mark your answers on the Complete Practice Exam Answer Sheet. After completing this segment, turn to the Number Series section for instructions on how to continue. Begin when you are prepared to time yourself for precisely five minutes.

1. Clifford
2. 8900-8999 Samuel
3. 8900-8999 West
4. 7700-8499 Samuel
5. Alexander
6. 6500-6699 Beach
7. 6800-7599 West
8. 8600-8799 Samuel

9. Driftwood
10. Island View
11. 8600-8799 West
12. 7700-8499 West
13. 8900-8999 Samuel
14. Runnels
15. 8900-8999 Beach
16. 6500-6699 West

17. 7700-8499 Beach
18. Pirate
19. Carroll
20. Clifford
21. 6800-7599 Samuel
22. 8900-8999 West
23. 8600-8799 Beach
24. 6800-7599 Beach

25. Galloway
26. 6800-7599 West
27. 8600-8799 West
28. 8900-8999 Samuel
29. Driftwood
30. 7700-8499 West
31. 6800-7599 Beach
32. Lynwood

33. Mathison
34. Clifford
35. 8900-8999 Beach
36. 6800-7599 Samuel
37. 7700-8499 Beach
38. Island View
39. 6500-6699 West
40. 6500-6699 Beach

41. Carroll
42. 6500-6699 Samuel
43. 8600-8799 Beach
44. Alexander
45. 8900-8999 Beach
46. 8600-8799 Samuel
47. Runnels
48. Pirate

49. 8600-8799 Beach
50. Clifford
51. 7700-8499 West
52. 6800-7599 Samuel
53. Galloway
54. 6500-6699 Samuel
55. 6500-6699 Beach
56. 8600-8799 West

57. 8900-8999 West
58. 6800-7599 Samuel
59. Clifford
60. Lynwood
61. 6500-6699 Beach
62. 8600-8799 West
63. Carroll
64. 8600-8799 Samuel

65. 6800-7599 West
66. 8900-8999 West
67. Island View
68. 8900-8999 Samuel
69. 7700-8499 Samuel
70. Mathison
71. Pirate
72. 6500-6699 West

73. 8900-8999 Beach
74. 6500-6699 West
75. Alexander
76. Driftwood
77. Galloway
78. 7700-8499 Samuel
79. 6800-7599 Beach
80. 8900-8999 Samuel

81. Lynwood
82. 8600-8799 Beach
83. Runnels
84. 6800-7599 Beach
85. 6500-6699 Samuel
86. 6800-7599 West
87. 6500-6699 Samuel
88. 8900-8999 Beach

COMPLETE PRACTICE EXAM #2
Part C – Number Series

You have 20 minutes to answer 24 questions. Each question is a series of numbers followed by two blanks. You are to find which two numbers would logically follow in the series. Mark your answers on the Complete Practice Exam Answer Sheet. After completing this section, turn to the Following Oral Instructions section. Begin when you are prepared to time yourself for precisely 20 minutes.

1. 12 11 10 9 8 7 6 ___ ___   (A) 4,5   (B) 5,4   (C) 2,7   (D) 5,5   (E) 10,10

2. 14 16 18 20 22 24 ___ ___   (A) 26,28 (B) 29,30 (C) 28,26 (D) 26,24 (E) 14,16

3. 4 9 14 19 24 ___ ___   (A) 4,9   (B) 25,29 (C) 29,35 (D) 29,34 (E) 8,34

4. 2 5 3 11 4 17 ___ ___   (A) 7,11 (B) 5,23   (C) 23,5 (D) 5,9   (E) 23,25

5. 3 8 11 13 19 18 ___ ___   (A) 27,23 (B) 23,28 (C) 28,41 (D) 33,48 (E) 48,51

6. 28 25 10 12 22 19 14 ___ ___   (A) 14,15 (B) 12,16 (C) 16,16 (D) 25,30 (E) 33,16

7. 33 66 44 55 55 44 ___ ___   (A) 65,32 (B) 68,90 (C) 66,77 (D) 66,33 (E) 33,22

8. 21 87 24 85 27 83 ___ ___   (A) 30,90 (B) 28,40 (C) 81,96 (D) 30,81 (E) 40,40

9. 10 30 15 20 35 25 30 ___ ___   (A) 40,35 (B) 35,20 (C) 20,35 (D) 40,25 (E) 36,15

10. 75 8 75 15 75 22 ___ ___   (A) 29,15 (B) 75,8 (C) 15,22 (D) 29,8 (E) 75,29

11. 1 9 8 1 9 8 ___ ___   (A) 1,9   (B) 8,1   (C) 9,8   (D) 9,9   (E) 1,5

12. 13 15 90 35 37 87 ___ ___   (A) 57,37 (B) 89,59 (C) 90,37 (D) 57,59 (E) 59,90

13. 1 2 4 5 7 8 10 ___ ___   (A) 13,8 (B) 11,4   (C) 13,7 (D) 11,7 (E) 11,13

14. 41 36 63 68 31 26 73 ___ ___   (A) 78,68 (B) 78,21 (C) 21,41 (D) 78,31 (E) 21,73

15. 7 12 37 17 22 40 27 ___ ___   (A) 32,43 (B) 43,37 (C) 22,43 (D) 32,17 (E) 27,27

16. 14 14 14 26 17 17 17 40 20 ___ ___   (A) 20,40 (B) 17,17 (C) 20,20 (D) 14,26 (E) 20,17

17. 24 22 21 34 20 19 44 ___ ___   (A) 43,42 (B) 17,18 (C) 18,17 (D) 23,43 (E) 43, 23

18. 1 3 4 7 11 18 ___ ___   (A) 11,47 (B) 18,4 (C) 29,47 (D) 29,32 (E) 7,4

19. 2 7 12 17 ___ ___   (A) 27,27 (B) 22,12 (C) 20,11 (D) 17,7 (E) 22,27

20. 13 14 44 42 40 15 16 38 ___ ___   (A) 36,34 (B) 44,40 (C) 34,14 (D) 15,36 (E) 15,38

21. 9 10 30 28 11 12 ___ ___   (A) 30,26 (B) 26,24 (C) 28,12 (D) 11,20 (E) 24,30

22. 33 32 31 31 29 30 27 ___ ___   (A) 28,26 (B) 29,29 (C) 29,25 (D) 25,23 (E) 31,29

23. 10 30 29 28 9 27 26 25 8 ___ ___   (A) 23,22 (B) 25,30 (C) 29,24 (D) 24,23 (E) 32,21

24. 8 45 40 28 35 30 48 ___ ___   (A) 24,19 (B) 21,26 (C) 32,40 (D) 22,34 (E) 25,20

COMPLETE PRACTICE EXAM #2
Part D – Following Oral Instructions

On this section, questions/instructions are presented verbally that lead you to the correct answers. Mark your answers on the Complete Practice Exam Answer Sheet. When you complete the Following Oral Instructions section, you have finished the complete practice exam. Begin when you are prepared to listen to the questions from the author's recording or from someone who will read them to you.

1.   7   11   14   22

2.   A   D   E   S   B

3.   A   12   14   C   3   D

4.   78   82   52   12

5.   R_____   D_____   A_____   C_____

6. | 6_____ | | 8_____ | | 5_____ | | 10_____ |

7.   27   36   52   87

8. | 7__ | (4__)   (9__) | 6__ |

9. | 22_____ | | 12_____ | | 71_____ | | 9_____ |

10.   ____E   ____C   ____D   ____B   ____A

11.   (1)   (3) | 7 | | 2 |

12.   62_____   47_____   94_____   13_____   51_____

13.   D A Y S

    __   __   __   __

14.

2:20 PM	12:05 AM	6:10 PM	9:45 AM	1:15 PM
___	___	___	___	___

15. _____

16.

9___	32___	57___	64___

17.

Chicago 91	Dallas 52	Denver 12	Akron 72

18.

12:00 AM	3:00 PM	6:00 AM

19.   R   S   H   W   E

20.   32___   14___   79___   51___

21.   11___   49___   1___   17___   29___

22. _____

23.   A____   B____   C____   D____   E____

24.

Gulfport 81_____	Gainsville 71_____

25.   87   21   58   88   68

26.   MATH PROBLEM

COMPLETE PRACTICE EXAM #3

This complete practice exam contains all four sections of the actual exam. The instructions given are similar to those on the actual exam. The format of this practice exam is identical to the actual exam.

It is imperative that you take the practice exam in as realistic a fashion as possible. **Your practice will have no value unless it is done realistically.** Therefore, you must precisely time yourself on the Address Checking, Address Memory, and Number Series sections. Our Timed Practice Test CD is a convenient way to practice realistically and time yourself precisely. Also, you must listen to the Following Oral Instructions questions on our Oral Instructions Practice Tests CD or have someone read them to you - *do not read the questions yourself!* The Following Oral Instructions questions can be found in the back of your book if someone will be reading them to you.

When taking a practice exam, first turn to the back of your book and tear out one of the **Complete Practice Exam Answer Sheets.** Mark the answers to the scored segments of the exam on this answer sheet. Remember, of the seven segments on the Address Memory Section, only the final one is scored. Accordingly, you should mark answers for only the final Address Memory segment on your Complete Practice Exam Answer Sheet. The other segments of the Address Memory Section that call for answers have their own sample answer sheets where you should mark answers.

Answer keys are provided in the back of your book. Immediately upon completing each section of a practice exam, **it is imperative that you score yourself** using the formulas given in the Scoring Formulas section of the book. Scoring is necessary in order to gauge your progress and to identify your individual areas of weakness that may need extra attention.

After completing and scoring each practice exam, move on to the next. **After finishing all six exams, you should be prepared for the actual exam.** If you feel the need for more practice after completing six practice exams, see page 60 for details on our free extra practice tests.

Do not look over the practice exam questions until you are ready to start - usually meaning either until (1) you have started the Timed Practice Test CD or the Oral Instructions Practice Tests CD or (2) you have set a timer for the allotted period of time. Similarly, after completing one section of the practice test, do not look over the next one until your are ready to start it. Likewise, stop working and put down your pencil immediately when the allotted period of time has expired. As has been emphasized before but cannot be emphasized enough, your practice is of absolutely no value unless it is done realistically. Also, you must train yourself (1) to not open your test booklet or pick up your pencil until instructed to do so and (2) to close your booklet and put down your pencil immediately upon being so instructed. The Postal Service has zero tolerance on these matters. Any variance may be viewed as cheating and may result in your disqualification.

COMPLETE PRACTICE EXAM #3
Part A – Address Checking

Directions

In the Address Checking section, you are to decide whether two addresses are alike or different. You have 6 minutes to answer 95 questions. Each question consists of a pair of addresses. If the two addresses in the pair are exactly alike in every way, darken the oval with the letter "A" for _Alike_. If the two addresses are different in any way, darken the oval with the letter "D" for _Different_. Mark your answers on the Complete Practice Exam Answer Sheet in the section entitled Address Checking. Begin when you are prepared to time yourself for precisely 6 minutes.

Notes:
- _You will notice that the questions on this section of your practice exam are spread across two pages. This is the exact format of the Address Checking section on the real exam. To save printing costs, some study guides condense the two pages of this section down to only one. Other study guides, for reasons we cannot even begin to guess, stretch the Address Checking section out over several pages._
- _You will also notice that the Address Checking questions are presented in a font, or type of print, that is different from the rest of the book. This font closely matches the type of print used on the real exam, and - as you will see - it makes this section even more challenging._
- _It is imperative that you practice realistically and that you become acquainted with the actual format of the test. We have therefore formatted the page layout and the font of the Address Checking section on this practice exam realistically for your benefit._

1.	3539 North Causeway, Plaissance, LA	3593 North Causeway, Plaissance, LA
2.	Plainsville, Ill. 36962-5633	Plainvill, Ill. 36962-5633
3.	352 N. 5th Ave.	352 N. 5th Ave.
4.	Saunemin, Md. 20584-8453	Saumenin, Md. 20584-8453
5.	#255 Apt. D-45	#255 Apt. B-45
6.	Zalma, Mo. 68975-1492	Zalma, Mo. 68975-1492
7.	1558 Cuevas Estates	1558 Cuevas Estates
8.	312 Jackson Square Notting	313 Jackson Square Notting
9.	Morris Landing, Wyo. 80399	Morris Landing, Wyo. 80399
10.	82499 West Plum Rd.	82499 East Plum Rd.
11.	104 Runnels Ave. South	104 Runnels Ave. South
12.	Collinsville, N.D. 34569-8799	Collinsville, N.H. 93658-8799
13.	#790 Royal Oak Roadway	#790 Royal Oak Roadway
14.	7778 Tower Hill	7778 Tower Hill
15.	Tiffany Gardens Apt. #101	Tiffany Gardens Apt. #101
16.	Metamorassa, Fla. 78232-6546	Metmorassa, Fla. 78232-6546
17.	975 Misson Sothe N.W.	975 Misson Sothe N.W.
18.	del Amos Hwy. 57 South	del Amos Hwy. 57 South
19.	5275 West Water Way	5725 West Water Way
20.	North Ridge, Ga. 43189-4213	North Ridge, Ga. 43189-4213
21.	545 Hewes Ave. S.W.	454 Hewes Ave. S.W.
22.	1106 East Old Pass Rd.	1106 East Old Pass Rd.
23.	3992 Leigh High Blvd.	3992 Leigh High Blvd.
24.	45 Townhall Express Way	45 Townhall Express Way
25.	Lake Byron, Minn. 40025-8888	Lake Pyron, Maine 00425-8888
26.	1212 Rual del Haban	1212 Rual del Haban
27.	Reno, Nev. 70900-0024	Reno, Nev. 70909-0024
28.	10004 St. Charles	1004 St. Charles
29.	67439 Ethel Avenue	67349 Ethel Avenue
30.	St. John, Maine 67948	St. John, Maine 67948
31.	2745 Cookie Ct.	2745 Cookie Ct.
32.	Juneville, N.C. 57684	Juneville, N.D. 57864
33.	147 Flower St. Michoacan AZ	1470 Flower St. Michoacan AZ
34.	Coronet, N.Y. 95847	Coronet, N.H. 95487
35.	1647 Clearview St. Apt. 6	1647 Clearview St. Apt. 6
36.	Wheatsdale, Ohio 45264-2646	Wheatsville, Ohio 45624-2646
37.	1684 Mushroom Blvd. N.W.	1684 Mushroom Blvd. N.
38.	88B Cinnamon Cirlce	888 Cinnamon Circle
39.	Flagg, Minn. 74925	Flagg, Minn. 74925
40.	Rustway Blvd. 69 N.E.	Rustway Blvd. 96 N.E.
41.	168500 Independence Blvd.	165860 Independence Blvd.
42.	Congress, Wash. D.C. 26734	Congress, Wash. D.C. 26374
43.	Rockchester, N.Y. 73593-1952	Rockchester, N.Y. 73593-1952
44.	1786 Empire St. N.E.	1789 Empire St. N.E.
45.	1475 North Shore Parkway	1475 North Shore Roadway
46.	1976 Colonial Road	1796 Colonial Road
47.	Alden Manor, West Virginia	Alden Manor, West Virginia
48.	14 Fair Lawn & Paramus N.	14 Fair Lawn & Pampas N.

49.	Staten Island, N.Y. 95874-5512	Staten Island, N.Y. 95784-5512
50.	369 New Haven Avenue E.	396 New Haven Avenue E.
51.	46-D Bridgeport St.	46-D Bridgeport St.
52.	7345 East Overhead Drive	7354 East Overhead Drive
53.	Billings, Mont. 88535-9999	Billings, Mont. 88535-9999
54.	303 Marice Drive NW	303 Marice Drive NW
55.	3906 Castille Dr.	3906 Castille Dr.
56.	4503 46th Ave. South	4503 46th Ave. North
57.	Parkwood, Del. 20643	Parkwood, Del. 20643
58.	3712 Reynosa Road, Chihuahua, NV	3712 Reynosa Road, Chihuahua, NV
59.	Bel-Aire Moble Home Pk.	Bel-Aire Mobil Home Pk.
60.	1700 John Quincy Adams W	1700 John Quincy Adams E
61.	#44 Racquet Club Riviere-du-Portage MT	#44 Racquet Club Riviere-du-Portage MT
62.	Crest View, Wash. 80025	Crest View, Wash. 80225
63.	1415 Avolone-Topango Rd.	1415 Avolone-Topango Rd.
64.	01800 E. Beach Blvd.	01800 E. Beach Blvd.
65.	Daemions, N.C. 75498-4521	Deamions, N.C. 75498-4521
66.	813 Allendale St.	813 Allendale St.
67.	1412 Genevieve Race	1413 Genevieve Race
68.	#3 Carondelet Apt.	#3 Carondlet Apt.
69.	Sherwood Village, Id. 69008	Sherwood Village, Wah. 99670
70.	Maison D'Orleans Apt. 72	Maison D'Orleans Apt. 72
71.	537 Delauney Cir. North	537 Delauney Cir. North
72.	6809 Mescalero, Ixtapaluca, TX	6809 Mesclaro, Ixtapaluca, TX
73.	Santa Maria Del Mar SW	Del Maria Mar SW
74.	875 Gorenflo Ave.	875 Gorenflo Ave.
75.	14220 Lemoyne Blvd.	14220 Lemoyne Blvd.
76.	Redding, W.V. 73996-8948	Redding, Va. 79936-8948
77.	8714-B 29th St. South	8714-A 29th St. South
78.	16485 Lorraine Cir.	16485 Lorraine Cir.
79.	101 Beauvoir Manor Apts.	101 Beauvoir Manor Apts.
80.	Howard, Fla. 74469	Howard, Fla. 74469
81.	517 Jefferson Davis Ave.	715 Jefferson Davis Ave.
82.	4686 Virginia Blvd. NE	4684 Virginia Blvd. NE
83.	602 West Pass, Nunapitchuk, WA	602 West Pass, Nunapitchuk, WA
84.	3432 Washington Square	3234 Washington Square
85.	1910 Switzer Dr.	1910 Switzer Dr.
86.	97 West 58th Ave. NW	97 West 58th St. NW
87.	Bullis, La. 22856-6486	Bullis, La. 22856-6486
88.	2423 Middlecoffe Dr.	2423 Middlecoffe Dr.
89.	1011-B Ladd Cir.	1101-B Ladd Cir.
90.	Opal, Ohio 55334	Opal, Ohio 55334
91.	14334 Jo Ellen End	1434 Jo Ellen End
92.	#56 Alexander Rd.	#56 Alexander Rd.
93.	503 Cypress Cove	503 Cypress Cove
94.	130 Richards Ave.	130 Richard Ave.
95.	137 Beach Park Place	137 Beach Park Place

COMPLETE PRACTICE EXAM #3
Part B – Address Memory

Directions

In the Address Memory section, you are to memorize the locations of 25 addresses in five boxes. During this section, you will have several study periods and practice exercises to help you memorize the location of the addresses shown in the five boxes. Answer the questions by darkening the oval containing the letter (A, B, C, D, E) of the box the address came from - Box A, Box B, Box C, Box D, or Box E. At the end of each segment, you will be given instructions on how and where to continue. After completing six preliminary segments, the actual test will be given as segment #7.

Turn the page to begin Segment #1 of the Address Memory section.

Note: You will notice in this practice exam that segments 3, 4, and 6 of the Address Memory section are spread across two pages. The five boxes, the 88 questions, and the sample answer sheet in these segments are spread across two facing pages. This is the exact same format that you will experience on Address Memory segments 3, 4, and 6 of the actual exam. To save printing costs, other study guides frequently condense these segments down from two pages to only one. However, it is imperative that you practice realistically and that you become acquainted with the actual format of the test. We have therefore formatted the Address Memory section on this practice exam realistically for your benefit.

COMPLETE PRACTICE EXAM #3
Part B – Address Memory – Segment #1

The purpose of this small exercise is to acquaint you with the format of the Address Memory section. The first two questions are answered for you. You are to spend three minutes studying this page and answering sample questions 3, 4, and 5. After completing Segment #1, turn to Segment #2 for further instructions. Begin when you are prepared to time yourself for precisely three minutes.

A	B	C	D	E
1500-2399 Savannah Grafton 2400-3299 Candy Cleveland 1200-1499 Latil	3600-3999 Savannah Dambrino 3300-3599 Candy Ridge 2400-3299 Latil	2400-3299 Savannah Casper 3600-3999 Candy Mills 3300-3599 Latil	3300-3599 Savannah Richardson 1200-1499 Candy Lewis 1500-2399 Latil	1200-1499 Savannah Maxey 1500-2399 Candy Boggs 3600-3999 Latil

1. Maxey   Ⓐ Ⓑ Ⓒ Ⓓ ⬤
   This address came from Box E, so we sill darken the oval with the letter E.

2. Mills   Ⓐ Ⓑ ⬤ Ⓓ Ⓔ
   This address came from Box C, so we will darken the oval with the letter C.

3. Ridge   Ⓐ Ⓑ Ⓒ Ⓓ Ⓔ
   Now that you know how to answer, you do questions 3, 4, and 5.

4. 1500-2399 Candy   Ⓐ Ⓑ Ⓒ Ⓓ Ⓔ

5. Lewis   Ⓐ Ⓑ Ⓒ Ⓓ Ⓔ

The correct answers are E, C, B, E, and D.

115

COMPLETE PRACTICE EXAM #3
Part B – Address Memory – Segment #2

In this segment, you are given three minutes to study and memorize the addresses. There are no questions to answer in this segment - it is a study period only. However, on the actual exam, the boxes are not reprinted for your use. Instead, you are instructed to turn back to Address Memory Segment #1 and to spend three minutes studying the boxes displayed there. So, we will do the very same on this practice exam. After studying for three minutes, turn to Segment #3 for directions on how to continue the Address Memory Section of the exam. Begin studying when you are prepared to time yourself for precisely three minutes.

COMPLETE PRACTICE EXAM #3
Part B – Address Memory – Segment #3

You have three minutes to answer 88 questions. Try to answer from memory, but the boxes are shown if you need to refer to them. Mark your answers on the sample answer sheet at the bottom of the pages. After completing this segment, turn to Segment #4 for further instructions. Begin when you are prepared to time yourself for precisely three minutes.

A	B	C
1500-2399 Savannah Grafton 2400-3299 Candy Cleveland 1200-1499 Latil	3600-3999 Savannah Dambrino 3300-3599 Candy Ridge 2400-3299 Latil	2400-3299 Savannah Casper 3600-3999 Candy Mills 3300-3599 Latil

1. Ridge
2. 3600-3999 Savannah
3. 1200-1499 Latil
4. Lewis
5. 2400-3299 Latil
6. 1200-1499 Savannah
7. Dambrino
8. 3600-3999 Latil

9. 3300-3599 Candy
10. 2400-3299 Savannah
11. 1200-1499 Candy
12. Maxey
13. Grafton
14. Casper
15. 1500-2399 Latil
16. Cleveland

17. 2400-3299 Candy
18. 1500-2399 Candy
19. 3300-3599 Savannah
20. 2400-3299 Latil
21. Boggs
22. Mills
23. 1500-2399 Savannah
24. 1200-1499 Latil

25. 3300-3599 Latil
26. Maxey
27. Dambrino
28. 1500-2399 Latil
29. 3600-3999 Savannah
30. Grafton
31. Lewis
32. 2400-3299 Candy

33. 1200-1499 Savannah
34. 1200-1499 Latil
35. Mills
36. 3300-3599 Latil
37. 2400-3299 Savannah
38. 1200-1499 Candy
39. 3600-3999 Latil
40. 2400-3299 Latil

41. 3300-3599 Savannah
42. Dambrino
43. 3300-3599 Candy
44. Cleveland
45. Ridge
46. Richardson
47. 1500-2399 Savannah
48. Casper

1 Ⓐ Ⓑ Ⓒ Ⓓ Ⓔ
2 Ⓐ Ⓑ Ⓒ Ⓓ Ⓔ
3 Ⓐ Ⓑ Ⓒ Ⓓ Ⓔ
4 Ⓐ Ⓑ Ⓒ Ⓓ Ⓔ
5 Ⓐ Ⓑ Ⓒ Ⓓ Ⓔ
6 Ⓐ Ⓑ Ⓒ Ⓓ Ⓔ
7 Ⓐ Ⓑ Ⓒ Ⓓ Ⓔ
8 Ⓐ Ⓑ Ⓒ Ⓓ Ⓔ

9 Ⓐ Ⓑ Ⓒ Ⓓ Ⓔ
10 Ⓐ Ⓑ Ⓒ Ⓓ Ⓔ
11 Ⓐ Ⓑ Ⓒ Ⓓ Ⓔ
12 Ⓐ Ⓑ Ⓒ Ⓓ Ⓔ
13 Ⓐ Ⓑ Ⓒ Ⓓ Ⓔ
14 Ⓐ Ⓑ Ⓒ Ⓓ Ⓔ
15 Ⓐ Ⓑ Ⓒ Ⓓ Ⓔ
16 Ⓐ Ⓑ Ⓒ Ⓓ Ⓔ

17 Ⓐ Ⓑ Ⓒ Ⓓ Ⓔ
18 Ⓐ Ⓑ Ⓒ Ⓓ Ⓔ
19 Ⓐ Ⓑ Ⓒ Ⓓ Ⓔ
20 Ⓐ Ⓑ Ⓒ Ⓓ Ⓔ
21 Ⓐ Ⓑ Ⓒ Ⓓ Ⓔ
22 Ⓐ Ⓑ Ⓒ Ⓓ Ⓔ
23 Ⓐ Ⓑ Ⓒ Ⓓ Ⓔ
24 Ⓐ Ⓑ Ⓒ Ⓓ Ⓔ

25 Ⓐ Ⓑ Ⓒ Ⓓ Ⓔ
26 Ⓐ Ⓑ Ⓒ Ⓓ Ⓔ
27 Ⓐ Ⓑ Ⓒ Ⓓ Ⓔ
28 Ⓐ Ⓑ Ⓒ Ⓓ Ⓔ
29 Ⓐ Ⓑ Ⓒ Ⓓ Ⓔ
30 Ⓐ Ⓑ Ⓒ Ⓓ Ⓔ
31 Ⓐ Ⓑ Ⓒ Ⓓ Ⓔ
32 Ⓐ Ⓑ Ⓒ Ⓓ Ⓔ

33 Ⓐ Ⓑ Ⓒ Ⓓ Ⓔ
34 Ⓐ Ⓑ Ⓒ Ⓓ Ⓔ
35 Ⓐ Ⓑ Ⓒ Ⓓ Ⓔ
36 Ⓐ Ⓑ Ⓒ Ⓓ Ⓔ
37 Ⓐ Ⓑ Ⓒ Ⓓ Ⓔ
38 Ⓐ Ⓑ Ⓒ Ⓓ Ⓔ
39 Ⓐ Ⓑ Ⓒ Ⓓ Ⓔ
40 Ⓐ Ⓑ Ⓒ Ⓓ Ⓔ

41 Ⓐ Ⓑ Ⓒ Ⓓ Ⓔ
42 Ⓐ Ⓑ Ⓒ Ⓓ Ⓔ
43 Ⓐ Ⓑ Ⓒ Ⓓ Ⓔ
44 Ⓐ Ⓑ Ⓒ Ⓓ Ⓔ
45 Ⓐ Ⓑ Ⓒ Ⓓ Ⓔ
46 Ⓐ Ⓑ Ⓒ Ⓓ Ⓔ
47 Ⓐ Ⓑ Ⓒ Ⓓ Ⓔ
48 Ⓐ Ⓑ Ⓒ Ⓓ Ⓔ

D	E
3300-3599 Savannah Richardson 1200-1499 Candy Lewis 1500-2399 Latil	1200-1499 Savannah Maxey 1500-2399 Candy Boggs 3600-3999 Latil

49. 3600-3999 Candy
50. Boggs
51. 1200-1499 Candy
52. 1200-1499 Savannah
53. 2400-3299 Latil
54. Grafton
55. 2400-3299 Candy
56. 3600-3999 Latil

57. Ridge
58. 2400-3299 Savannah
59. Lewis
60. 3300-3599 Latil
61. 1500-2399 Latil
62. 1500-2399 Candy
63. Maxey
64. 3600-3999 Savannah

65. 1200-1499 Latil
66. 1500-2399 Savannah
67. 3300-3599 Savannah
68. 1200-1499 Savannah
69. Mills
70. Richardson
71. 3300-3599 Candy
72. Dambrino

73. 2400-3299 Candy
74. 1500-2399 Latil
75. 1200-1499 Candy
76. Grafton
77. Cleveland
78. Casper
79. 3600-3999 Latil
80. 2400-3299 Latil

81. 3300-3599 Latil
82. 2400-3299 Candy
83. 2400-3299 Savannah
84. Lewis
85. 1500-2399 Candy
86. Ridge
87. Mills
88. Maxey

49 Ⓐ Ⓑ Ⓒ Ⓓ Ⓔ
50 Ⓐ Ⓑ Ⓒ Ⓓ Ⓔ
51 Ⓐ Ⓑ Ⓒ Ⓓ Ⓔ
52 Ⓐ Ⓑ Ⓒ Ⓓ Ⓔ
53 Ⓐ Ⓑ Ⓒ Ⓓ Ⓔ
54 Ⓐ Ⓑ Ⓒ Ⓓ Ⓔ
55 Ⓐ Ⓑ Ⓒ Ⓓ Ⓔ
56 Ⓐ Ⓑ Ⓒ Ⓓ Ⓔ

57 Ⓐ Ⓑ Ⓒ Ⓓ Ⓔ
58 Ⓐ Ⓑ Ⓒ Ⓓ Ⓔ
59 Ⓐ Ⓑ Ⓒ Ⓓ Ⓔ
60 Ⓐ Ⓑ Ⓒ Ⓓ Ⓔ
61 Ⓐ Ⓑ Ⓒ Ⓓ Ⓔ
62 Ⓐ Ⓑ Ⓒ Ⓓ Ⓔ
63 Ⓐ Ⓑ Ⓒ Ⓓ Ⓔ
64 Ⓐ Ⓑ Ⓒ Ⓓ Ⓔ

65 Ⓐ Ⓑ Ⓒ Ⓓ Ⓔ
66 Ⓐ Ⓑ Ⓒ Ⓓ Ⓔ
67 Ⓐ Ⓑ Ⓒ Ⓓ Ⓔ
68 Ⓐ Ⓑ Ⓒ Ⓓ Ⓔ
69 Ⓐ Ⓑ Ⓒ Ⓓ Ⓔ
70 Ⓐ Ⓑ Ⓒ Ⓓ Ⓔ
71 Ⓐ Ⓑ Ⓒ Ⓓ Ⓔ
72 Ⓐ Ⓑ Ⓒ Ⓓ Ⓔ

73 Ⓐ Ⓑ Ⓒ Ⓓ Ⓔ
74 Ⓐ Ⓑ Ⓒ Ⓓ Ⓔ
75 Ⓐ Ⓑ Ⓒ Ⓓ Ⓔ
76 Ⓐ Ⓑ Ⓒ Ⓓ Ⓔ
77 Ⓐ Ⓑ Ⓒ Ⓓ Ⓔ
78 Ⓐ Ⓑ Ⓒ Ⓓ Ⓔ
79 Ⓐ Ⓑ Ⓒ Ⓓ Ⓔ
80 Ⓐ Ⓑ Ⓒ Ⓓ Ⓔ

81 Ⓐ Ⓑ Ⓒ Ⓓ Ⓔ
82 Ⓐ Ⓑ Ⓒ Ⓓ Ⓔ
83 Ⓐ Ⓑ Ⓒ Ⓓ Ⓔ
84 Ⓐ Ⓑ Ⓒ Ⓓ Ⓔ
85 Ⓐ Ⓑ Ⓒ Ⓓ Ⓔ
86 Ⓐ Ⓑ Ⓒ Ⓓ Ⓔ
87 Ⓐ Ⓑ Ⓒ Ⓓ Ⓔ
88 Ⓐ Ⓑ Ⓒ Ⓓ Ⓔ

COMPLETE PRACTICE EXAM #3
Part B – Address Memory – Segment #4

You have three minutes to answer 88 questions. You must answer from memory. The boxes are not shown. Mark your answers on the sample answer sheet at the bottom of the page. After completing this segment, turn to Segment #5 for further instructions. Begin when you are prepared to time yourself for precisely three minutes.

1. Maxey
2. Mills
3. Ridge
4. 1500-2399 Candy
5. Lewis
6. 2400-3299 Savannah
7. 2400-3299 Candy
8. 3300-3599 Latil

9. 2400-3299 Latil
10. 3600-3999 Latil
11. Casper
12. Cleveland
13. Grafton
14. 1200-1499 Candy
15. Dambrino
16. 3300-3599 Candy

17. Richardson
18. Mills
19. 1200-1499 Savannah
20. 3300-3599 Savannah
21. 1500-2399 Savannah
22. 1200-1499 Latil
23. 3600-3999 Savannah
24. Maxey

25. 1500-2399 Candy
26. 1500-2399 Latil
27. 3300-3599 Latil
28. Lewis
29. 2400-3299 Savannah
30. Ridge
31. 3600-3999 Latil
32. 2400-3299 Candy

33. Grafton
34. 2400-3299 Latil
35. 1200-1499 Savannah
36. 1200-1499 Candy
37. Boggs
38. 3600-3999 Candy
39. Casper
40. 1500-2399 Savannah

41. Richardson
42. Ridge
43. Cleveland
44. 3300-3599 Candy
45. Dambrino
46. 3300-3599 Savannah
47. 2400-3299 Latil
48. 3600-3999 Latil

---

1 Ⓐ Ⓑ Ⓒ Ⓓ Ⓔ
2 Ⓐ Ⓑ Ⓒ Ⓓ Ⓔ
3 Ⓐ Ⓑ Ⓒ Ⓓ Ⓔ
4 Ⓐ Ⓑ Ⓒ Ⓓ Ⓔ
5 Ⓐ Ⓑ Ⓒ Ⓓ Ⓔ
6 Ⓐ Ⓑ Ⓒ Ⓓ Ⓔ
7 Ⓐ Ⓑ Ⓒ Ⓓ Ⓔ
8 Ⓐ Ⓑ Ⓒ Ⓓ Ⓔ

9 Ⓐ Ⓑ Ⓒ Ⓓ Ⓔ
10 Ⓐ Ⓑ Ⓒ Ⓓ Ⓔ
11 Ⓐ Ⓑ Ⓒ Ⓓ Ⓔ
12 Ⓐ Ⓑ Ⓒ Ⓓ Ⓔ
13 Ⓐ Ⓑ Ⓒ Ⓓ Ⓔ
14 Ⓐ Ⓑ Ⓒ Ⓓ Ⓔ
15 Ⓐ Ⓑ Ⓒ Ⓓ Ⓔ
16 Ⓐ Ⓑ Ⓒ Ⓓ Ⓔ

17 Ⓐ Ⓑ Ⓒ Ⓓ Ⓔ
18 Ⓐ Ⓑ Ⓒ Ⓓ Ⓔ
19 Ⓐ Ⓑ Ⓒ Ⓓ Ⓔ
20 Ⓐ Ⓑ Ⓒ Ⓓ Ⓔ
21 Ⓐ Ⓑ Ⓒ Ⓓ Ⓔ
22 Ⓐ Ⓑ Ⓒ Ⓓ Ⓔ
23 Ⓐ Ⓑ Ⓒ Ⓓ Ⓔ
24 Ⓐ Ⓑ Ⓒ Ⓓ Ⓔ

25 Ⓐ Ⓑ Ⓒ Ⓓ Ⓔ
26 Ⓐ Ⓑ Ⓒ Ⓓ Ⓔ
27 Ⓐ Ⓑ Ⓒ Ⓓ Ⓔ
28 Ⓐ Ⓑ Ⓒ Ⓓ Ⓔ
29 Ⓐ Ⓑ Ⓒ Ⓓ Ⓔ
30 Ⓐ Ⓑ Ⓒ Ⓓ Ⓔ
31 Ⓐ Ⓑ Ⓒ Ⓓ Ⓔ
32 Ⓐ Ⓑ Ⓒ Ⓓ Ⓔ

33 Ⓐ Ⓑ Ⓒ Ⓓ Ⓔ
34 Ⓐ Ⓑ Ⓒ Ⓓ Ⓔ
35 Ⓐ Ⓑ Ⓒ Ⓓ Ⓔ
36 Ⓐ Ⓑ Ⓒ Ⓓ Ⓔ
37 Ⓐ Ⓑ Ⓒ Ⓓ Ⓔ
38 Ⓐ Ⓑ Ⓒ Ⓓ Ⓔ
39 Ⓐ Ⓑ Ⓒ Ⓓ Ⓔ
40 Ⓐ Ⓑ Ⓒ Ⓓ Ⓔ

41 Ⓐ Ⓑ Ⓒ Ⓓ Ⓔ
42 Ⓐ Ⓑ Ⓒ Ⓓ Ⓔ
43 Ⓐ Ⓑ Ⓒ Ⓓ Ⓔ
44 Ⓐ Ⓑ Ⓒ Ⓓ Ⓔ
45 Ⓐ Ⓑ Ⓒ Ⓓ Ⓔ
46 Ⓐ Ⓑ Ⓒ Ⓓ Ⓔ
47 Ⓐ Ⓑ Ⓒ Ⓓ Ⓔ
48 Ⓐ Ⓑ Ⓒ Ⓓ Ⓔ

49. 1200-1499 Candy
50. 2400-3299 Savannah
51. 3300-3599 Latil
52. Mills
53. 1200-1499 Latil
54. 1200-1499 Savannah
55. 2400-3299 Candy
56. Lewis

57. Grafton
58. 3600-3999 Savannah
59. 1500-2399 Latil
60. Dambrino
61. Maxey
62. 3300-3599 Latil
63. 1200-1499 Latil
64. 1500-2399 Savannah

65. Mills
66. Boggs
67. 2400-3299 Latil
68. 3300-3599 Savannah
69. 1500-2399 Candy
70. 2400-3299 Candy
71. Cleveland
72. 1500-2399 Latil

73. Casper
74. Grafton
75. Maxey
76. 1200-1499 Candy
77. 2400-3299 Savannah
78. 3300-3599 Candy
79. 3600-3999 Latil
80. Dambrino

81. 1200-1499 Savannah
82. 2400-3299 Latil
83. Lewis
84. 1200-1499 Latil
85. 3600-3999 Savannah
86. Ridge
87. Boggs
88. 1500-2399 Candy

49 Ⓐ Ⓑ Ⓒ Ⓓ Ⓔ
50 Ⓐ Ⓑ Ⓒ Ⓓ Ⓔ
51 Ⓐ Ⓑ Ⓒ Ⓓ Ⓔ
52 Ⓐ Ⓑ Ⓒ Ⓓ Ⓔ
53 Ⓐ Ⓑ Ⓒ Ⓓ Ⓔ
54 Ⓐ Ⓑ Ⓒ Ⓓ Ⓔ
55 Ⓐ Ⓑ Ⓒ Ⓓ Ⓔ
56 Ⓐ Ⓑ Ⓒ Ⓓ Ⓔ

57 Ⓐ Ⓑ Ⓒ Ⓓ Ⓔ
58 Ⓐ Ⓑ Ⓒ Ⓓ Ⓔ
59 Ⓐ Ⓑ Ⓒ Ⓓ Ⓔ
60 Ⓐ Ⓑ Ⓒ Ⓓ Ⓔ
61 Ⓐ Ⓑ Ⓒ Ⓓ Ⓔ
62 Ⓐ Ⓑ Ⓒ Ⓓ Ⓔ
63 Ⓐ Ⓑ Ⓒ Ⓓ Ⓔ
64 Ⓐ Ⓑ Ⓒ Ⓓ Ⓔ

65 Ⓐ Ⓑ Ⓒ Ⓓ Ⓔ
66 Ⓐ Ⓑ Ⓒ Ⓓ Ⓔ
67 Ⓐ Ⓑ Ⓒ Ⓓ Ⓔ
68 Ⓐ Ⓑ Ⓒ Ⓓ Ⓔ
69 Ⓐ Ⓑ Ⓒ Ⓓ Ⓔ
70 Ⓐ Ⓑ Ⓒ Ⓓ Ⓔ
71 Ⓐ Ⓑ Ⓒ Ⓓ Ⓔ
72 Ⓐ Ⓑ Ⓒ Ⓓ Ⓔ

73 Ⓐ Ⓑ Ⓒ Ⓓ Ⓔ
74 Ⓐ Ⓑ Ⓒ Ⓓ Ⓔ
75 Ⓐ Ⓑ Ⓒ Ⓓ Ⓔ
76 Ⓐ Ⓑ Ⓒ Ⓓ Ⓔ
77 Ⓐ Ⓑ Ⓒ Ⓓ Ⓔ
78 Ⓐ Ⓑ Ⓒ Ⓓ Ⓔ
79 Ⓐ Ⓑ Ⓒ Ⓓ Ⓔ
80 Ⓐ Ⓑ Ⓒ Ⓓ Ⓔ

81 Ⓐ Ⓑ Ⓒ Ⓓ Ⓔ
82 Ⓐ Ⓑ Ⓒ Ⓓ Ⓔ
83 Ⓐ Ⓑ Ⓒ Ⓓ Ⓔ
84 Ⓐ Ⓑ Ⓒ Ⓓ Ⓔ
85 Ⓐ Ⓑ Ⓒ Ⓓ Ⓔ
86 Ⓐ Ⓑ Ⓒ Ⓓ Ⓔ
87 Ⓐ Ⓑ Ⓒ Ⓓ Ⓔ
88 Ⓐ Ⓑ Ⓒ Ⓓ Ⓔ

In this segment, you are given five minutes to study the addresses. There are no questions to answer in this segment – it is a study period only. As before, the boxes are not reprinted here for your use. Instead, you are instructed to turn back to Address Memory Segment #1 and to spend five minutes studying the boxes displayed there. After studying for five minutes, turn to Segment #6 for directions on how to continue. Turn back to Segment #1 and begin studying when you are prepared to time yourself for precisely five minutes.

COMPLETE PRACTICE EXAM #3
Part B – Address Memory – Segment #6

You have five minutes to answer 88 questions. Try to answer from memory, but the boxes are shown if you need to refer to them. Mark your answers on the sample answer sheet at the bottom of the page. After completing this segment, turn to Segment #7 for further instructions. Begin when you are prepared to time yourself for precisely five minutes.

A	B	C
1500-2399 Savannah Grafton 2400-3299 Candy Cleveland 1200-1499 Latil	3600-3999 Savannah Dambrino 3300-3599 Candy Ridge 2400-3299 Latil	2400-3299 Savannah Casper 3600-3999 Candy Mills 3300-3599 Latil

1. Ridge
2. 3600-3999 Savannah
3. 1200-1499 Latil
4. Lewis
5. 2400-3299 Latil
6. 1200-1499 Savannah
7. Dambrino
8. 3600-3999 Latil

9. 3300-3599 Candy
10. 2400-3299 Savannah
11. 1200-1499 Candy
12. Maxey
13. Grafton
14. Casper
15. 1500-2399 Latil
16. Cleveland

17. 2400-3299 Candy
18. 1500-2399 Candy
19. 3300-3599 Savannah
20. 2400-3299 Latil
21. Boggs
22. Mills
23. 1500-2399 Savannah
24. 1200-1499 Latil

25. 3300-3599 Latil
26. Maxey
27. Dambrino
28. 1500-2399 Latil
29. 3600-3999 Savannah
30. Grafton
31. Lewis
32. 2400-3299 Candy

33. 1200-1499 Savannah
34. 1200-1499 Latil
35. Mills
36. 3300-3599 Latil
37. 2400-3299 Savannah
38. 1200-1499 Candy
39. 3600-3999 Latil
40. 2400-3299 Latil

41. 3300-3599 Savannah
42. Dambrino
43. 3300-3599 Candy
44. Cleveland
45. Ridge
46. Richardson
47. 1500-2399 Savannah
48. Casper

1 Ⓐ Ⓑ Ⓒ Ⓓ Ⓔ
2 Ⓐ Ⓑ Ⓒ Ⓓ Ⓔ
3 Ⓐ Ⓑ Ⓒ Ⓓ Ⓔ
4 Ⓐ Ⓑ Ⓒ Ⓓ Ⓔ
5 Ⓐ Ⓑ Ⓒ Ⓓ Ⓔ
6 Ⓐ Ⓑ Ⓒ Ⓓ Ⓔ
7 Ⓐ Ⓑ Ⓒ Ⓓ Ⓔ
8 Ⓐ Ⓑ Ⓒ Ⓓ Ⓔ

9 Ⓐ Ⓑ Ⓒ Ⓓ Ⓔ
10 Ⓐ Ⓑ Ⓒ Ⓓ Ⓔ
11 Ⓐ Ⓑ Ⓒ Ⓓ Ⓔ
12 Ⓐ Ⓑ Ⓒ Ⓓ Ⓔ
13 Ⓐ Ⓑ Ⓒ Ⓓ Ⓔ
14 Ⓐ Ⓑ Ⓒ Ⓓ Ⓔ
15 Ⓐ Ⓑ Ⓒ Ⓓ Ⓔ
16 Ⓐ Ⓑ Ⓒ Ⓓ Ⓔ

17 Ⓐ Ⓑ Ⓒ Ⓓ Ⓔ
18 Ⓐ Ⓑ Ⓒ Ⓓ Ⓔ
19 Ⓐ Ⓑ Ⓒ Ⓓ Ⓔ
20 Ⓐ Ⓑ Ⓒ Ⓓ Ⓔ
21 Ⓐ Ⓑ Ⓒ Ⓓ Ⓔ
22 Ⓐ Ⓑ Ⓒ Ⓓ Ⓔ
23 Ⓐ Ⓑ Ⓒ Ⓓ Ⓔ
24 Ⓐ Ⓑ Ⓒ Ⓓ Ⓔ

25 Ⓐ Ⓑ Ⓒ Ⓓ Ⓔ
26 Ⓐ Ⓑ Ⓒ Ⓓ Ⓔ
27 Ⓐ Ⓑ Ⓒ Ⓓ Ⓔ
28 Ⓐ Ⓑ Ⓒ Ⓓ Ⓔ
29 Ⓐ Ⓑ Ⓒ Ⓓ Ⓔ
30 Ⓐ Ⓑ Ⓒ Ⓓ Ⓔ
31 Ⓐ Ⓑ Ⓒ Ⓓ Ⓔ
32 Ⓐ Ⓑ Ⓒ Ⓓ Ⓔ

33 Ⓐ Ⓑ Ⓒ Ⓓ Ⓔ
34 Ⓐ Ⓑ Ⓒ Ⓓ Ⓔ
35 Ⓐ Ⓑ Ⓒ Ⓓ Ⓔ
36 Ⓐ Ⓑ Ⓒ Ⓓ Ⓔ
37 Ⓐ Ⓑ Ⓒ Ⓓ Ⓔ
38 Ⓐ Ⓑ Ⓒ Ⓓ Ⓔ
39 Ⓐ Ⓑ Ⓒ Ⓓ Ⓔ
40 Ⓐ Ⓑ Ⓒ Ⓓ Ⓔ

41 Ⓐ Ⓑ Ⓒ Ⓓ Ⓔ
42 Ⓐ Ⓑ Ⓒ Ⓓ Ⓔ
43 Ⓐ Ⓑ Ⓒ Ⓓ Ⓔ
44 Ⓐ Ⓑ Ⓒ Ⓓ Ⓔ
45 Ⓐ Ⓑ Ⓒ Ⓓ Ⓔ
46 Ⓐ Ⓑ Ⓒ Ⓓ Ⓔ
47 Ⓐ Ⓑ Ⓒ Ⓓ Ⓔ
48 Ⓐ Ⓑ Ⓒ Ⓓ Ⓔ

D	**E**
3300-3599 Savannah Richardson 1200-1499 Candy Lewis 1500-2399 Latil	1200-1499 Savannah Maxey 1500-2399 Candy Boggs 3600-3999 Latil

49. 3600-3999 Candy
50. Boggs
51. 1200-1499 Candy
52. 1200-1499 Savannah
53. 2400-3299 Latil
54. Grafton
55. 2400-3299 Candy
56. 3600-3999 Latil

57. Ridge
58. 2400-3299 Savannah
59. Lewis
60. 3300-3599 Latil
61. 1500-2399 Latil
62. 1500-2399 Candy
63. Maxey
64. 3600-3999 Savannah

65. 1200-1499 Latil
66. 1500-2399 Savannah
67. 3300-3599 Savannah
68. 1200-1499 Savannah
69. Mills
70. Richardson
71. 3300-3599 Candy
72. Dambrino

73. 2400-3299 Candy
74. 1500-2399 Latil
75. 1200-1499 Candy
76. Grafton
77. Cleveland
78. Casper
79. 3600-3999 Latil
80. 2400-3299 Latil

81. 3300-3599 Latil
82. 2400-3299 Candy
83. 2400-3299 Savannah
84. Lewis
85. 1500-2399 Candy
86. Ridge
87. Mills
88. Maxey

49 Ⓐ Ⓑ Ⓒ Ⓓ Ⓔ
50 Ⓐ Ⓑ Ⓒ Ⓓ Ⓔ
51 Ⓐ Ⓑ Ⓒ Ⓓ Ⓔ
52 Ⓐ Ⓑ Ⓒ Ⓓ Ⓔ
53 Ⓐ Ⓑ Ⓒ Ⓓ Ⓔ
54 Ⓐ Ⓑ Ⓒ Ⓓ Ⓔ
55 Ⓐ Ⓑ Ⓒ Ⓓ Ⓔ
56 Ⓐ Ⓑ Ⓒ Ⓓ Ⓔ

57 Ⓐ Ⓑ Ⓒ Ⓓ Ⓔ
58 Ⓐ Ⓑ Ⓒ Ⓓ Ⓔ
59 Ⓐ Ⓑ Ⓒ Ⓓ Ⓔ
60 Ⓐ Ⓑ Ⓒ Ⓓ Ⓔ
61 Ⓐ Ⓑ Ⓒ Ⓓ Ⓔ
62 Ⓐ Ⓑ Ⓒ Ⓓ Ⓔ
63 Ⓐ Ⓑ Ⓒ Ⓓ Ⓔ
64 Ⓐ Ⓑ Ⓒ Ⓓ Ⓔ

65 Ⓐ Ⓑ Ⓒ Ⓓ Ⓔ
66 Ⓐ Ⓑ Ⓒ Ⓓ Ⓔ
67 Ⓐ Ⓑ Ⓒ Ⓓ Ⓔ
68 Ⓐ Ⓑ Ⓒ Ⓓ Ⓔ
69 Ⓐ Ⓑ Ⓒ Ⓓ Ⓔ
70 Ⓐ Ⓑ Ⓒ Ⓓ Ⓔ
71 Ⓐ Ⓑ Ⓒ Ⓓ Ⓔ
72 Ⓐ Ⓑ Ⓒ Ⓓ Ⓔ

73 Ⓐ Ⓑ Ⓒ Ⓓ Ⓔ
74 Ⓐ Ⓑ Ⓒ Ⓓ Ⓔ
75 Ⓐ Ⓑ Ⓒ Ⓓ Ⓔ
76 Ⓐ Ⓑ Ⓒ Ⓓ Ⓔ
77 Ⓐ Ⓑ Ⓒ Ⓓ Ⓔ
78 Ⓐ Ⓑ Ⓒ Ⓓ Ⓔ
79 Ⓐ Ⓑ Ⓒ Ⓓ Ⓔ
80 Ⓐ Ⓑ Ⓒ Ⓓ Ⓔ

81 Ⓐ Ⓑ Ⓒ Ⓓ Ⓔ
82 Ⓐ Ⓑ Ⓒ Ⓓ Ⓔ
83 Ⓐ Ⓑ Ⓒ Ⓓ Ⓔ
84 Ⓐ Ⓑ Ⓒ Ⓓ Ⓔ
85 Ⓐ Ⓑ Ⓒ Ⓓ Ⓔ
86 Ⓐ Ⓑ Ⓒ Ⓓ Ⓔ
87 Ⓐ Ⓑ Ⓒ Ⓓ Ⓔ
88 Ⓐ Ⓑ Ⓒ Ⓓ Ⓔ

COMPLETE PRACTICE EXAM #3
Part B – Address Memory – Segment #7

You have five minutes to answer 88 questions. You must answer from memory. The boxes are not shown. Mark your answers on the Complete Practice Exam Answer Sheet. After completing this segment, turn to the Number Series section for instructions on how to continue. Begin when you are prepared to time yourself for precisely five minutes.

1. Maxey
2. Mills
3. Ridge
4. 1500-2399 Candy
5. Lewis
6. 2400-3299 Savannah
7. 2400-3299 Candy
8. 3300-3599 Latil

9. 2400-3299 Latil
10. 3600-3999 Latil
11. Casper
12. Cleveland
13. Grafton
14. 1200-1499 Candy
15. Dambrino
16. 3300-3599 Candy

17. Richardson
18. Mills
19. 1200-1499 Savannah
20. 3300-3599 Savannah
21. 1500-2399 Savannah
22. 1200-1499 Latil
23. 3600-3999 Savannah
24. Maxey

25. 1500-2399 Candy
26. 1500-2399 Latil
27. 3300-3599 Latil
28. Lewis
29. 2400-3299 Savannah
30. Ridge
31. 3600-3999 Latil
32. 2400-3299 Candy

33. Grafton
34. 2400-3299 Latil
35. 1200-1499 Savannah
36. 1200-1499 Candy
37. Boggs
38. 3600-3999 Candy
39. Casper
40. 1500-2399 Savannah

41. Richardson
42. Ridge
43. Cleveland
44. 3300-3599 Candy
45. Dambrino
46. 3300-3599 Savannah
47. 2400-3299 Latil
48. 3600-3999 Latil

49. 1200-1499 Candy
50. 2400-3299 Savannah
51. 3300-3599 Latil
52. Mills
53. 1200-1499 Latil
54. 1200-1499 Savannah
55. 2400-3299 Candy
56. Lewis

57. Grafton
58. 3600-3999 Savannah
59. 1500-2399 Latil
60. Dambrino
61. Maxey
62. 3300-3599 Latil
63. 1200-1499 Latil
64. 1500-2399 Savannah

65. Mills
66. Boggs
67. 2400-3299 Latil
68. 3300-3599 Savannah
69. 1500-2399 Candy
70. 2400-3299 Candy
71. Cleveland
72. 1500-2399 Latil

73. Casper
74. Grafton
75. Maxey
76. 1200-1499 Candy
77. 2400-3299 Savannah
78. 3300-3599 Candy
79. 3600-3999 Latil
80. Dambrino

81. 1200-1499 Savannah
82. 2400-3299 Latil
83. Lewis
84. 1200-1499 Latil
85. 3600-3999 Savannah
86. Ridge
87. Boggs
88. 1500-2399 Candy

128

COMPLETE PRACTICE EXAM #3
Part C – Number Series

You have 20 minutes to answer 24 questions. Each question is a series of numbers followed by two blanks. You are to find which two numbers would logically follow in the series. Mark your answers on the Complete Practice Exam Answer Sheet. After completing this section, turn to the Following Oral Instructions section. Begin when you are prepared to time yourself for precisely 20 minutes.

1. 3 5 7 9 11 13 15 ___ ___   (A) 18,21   (B) 19,23   (C) 17,19   (D) 16,17   (E) 39,41

2. 1 7 13 19 25 31 37 ___ ___   (A) 38,45   (B) 43,50   (C) 38,46   (D) 47,57   (E) 43,49

3. 12 15 18 21 24 27 30 ___ ___   (A) 33,36   (B) 34,37   (C) 33,38   (D) 40,50   (E) 30,36

4. 21 28 35 42 49 56 63 ___ ___   (A) 72,79   (B) 70,77   (C) 70,80   (D) 70,78   (E) 73,83

5. 62 60 58 56 54 52 50 ___ ___   (A) 48,44   (B) 52,54   (C) 46,44   (D) 48,46   (E) 42,40

6. 82 71 60 49 38 27 ___ ___   (A) 16,5   (B) 15,4   (C) 17,6   (D) 18,8   (E) 19,9

7. 16 20 24 28 32 36 40 ___ ___   (A) 42,44   (B) 43,47   (C) 45,49   (D) 50,54   (E) 44,48

8. 58 55 52 49 46 43 40 ___ ___   (A) 36,33   (B) 38,35   (C) 37,34   (D) 40,37   (E) 42,39

9. 4 5 8 6 7 11 8 ___ ___   (A) 8,13   (B) 9,14   (C) 10,15   (D) 16,18   (E) 12,17

10. 19 21 50 23 25 47 27 ___ ___   (A) 30,45   (B) 28,43   (C) 27,42   (D) 29,44   (E) 25,45

11. 3 9 15 21 27 33 39 ___ ___   (A) 45,51   (B) 35,41   (C) 55,61   (D) 56,66   (E) 56,63

12. 12 11 10 37 9 8 7 36 ___ ___   (A) 9,2   (B) 9,3   (C) 8,4   (D) 7,5   (E) 6,5

13. 42 37 64 69 32 27 74 ___ ___   (A) 79,20   (B) 80,21   (C) 82,17   (D) 76,20   (E) 79,22

14. 71 76 31 29 81 86 27 ___ ___   (A) 24,90   (B) 26,92   (C) 25,91   (D) 26,91   (E) 26,93

15. 1 13 7 19 13 25 19 ___ ___   (A) 30,24   (B) 31,25   (C) 32,26   (D) 34,28   (E) 30,20

16. 21 21 14 18 18 52 15 ___ ___   (A) 15,92   (B) 16,40   (C) 14,52   (D) 15,90   (E) 45,90

17. 36 7 5 39 39 3 1 ___ ___   (A) 47,47   (B) 42,42   (C) 42,1   (D) 3,42   (E) 0,48

18. 27 37 61 21 85 109 15 ___ ___   (A) 133,157 (B) 133,158 (C) 132,159 (D) 159,165 (E) 131,150

19. 11 17 7 7 7 23 3 3 ___ ___   (A) 3,28   (B) 3,3   (C) 27,3   (D) 29,28   (E) 3,29

20. 80 14 32 69 65 17 35 54 50 20 ___ ___   (A) 37,38   (B) 18,39   (C) 38,39   (D) 36,38   (E) 32,40

21. 15 22 25 32 35 42 45 ___ ___   (A) 52,55   (B) 53,54   (C) 54,60   (D) 52,59   (E) 55,60

22. 96 96 11 75 75 14 54 ___ ___   (A) 17,54   (B) 54,54   (C) 14,54   (D) 54,17   (E) 75,17

23. 27 42 57 72 87 ___ ___   (A) 92,107   (B) 103,116 (C) 102,117 (D) 103,118 (E) 101,126

24. 6 7 21 10 11 26 15 ___ ___   (A) 16,30   (B) 17,25   (C) 18,33   (D) 31,17   (E) 16,31

COMPLETE PRACTICE EXAM #3
Part D – Following Oral Instructions

On this section, questions/instructions are presented verbally that lead you to the correct answers. Mark your answers on the Complete Practice Exam Answer Sheet. When you complete the Following Oral Instructions section, you have finished the complete practice exam. Begin when you are prepared to listen to the questions from the author's recording or from someone who will read them to you.

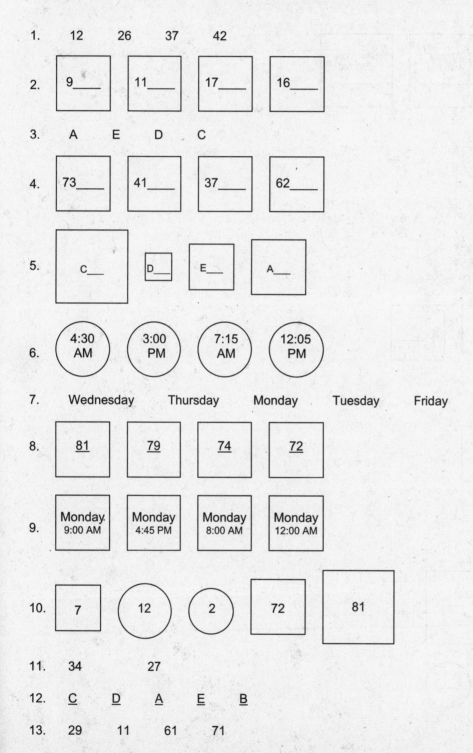

1. 12   26   37   42

2. 9____   11____   17____   16____

3. A   E   D   C

4. 73____   41____   37____   62____

5. C__   D__   E__   A__

6. 4:30 AM   3:00 PM   7:15 AM   12:05 PM

7. Wednesday   Thursday   Monday   Tuesday   Friday

8. <u>81</u>   <u>79</u>   <u>74</u>   <u>72</u>

9. Monday 9:00 AM   Monday 4:45 PM   Monday 8:00 AM   Monday 12:00 AM

10. 7   12   2   72   81

11. 34   27

12. <u>C</u>   <u>D</u>   <u>A</u>   <u>E</u>   <u>B</u>

13. 29   11   61   71

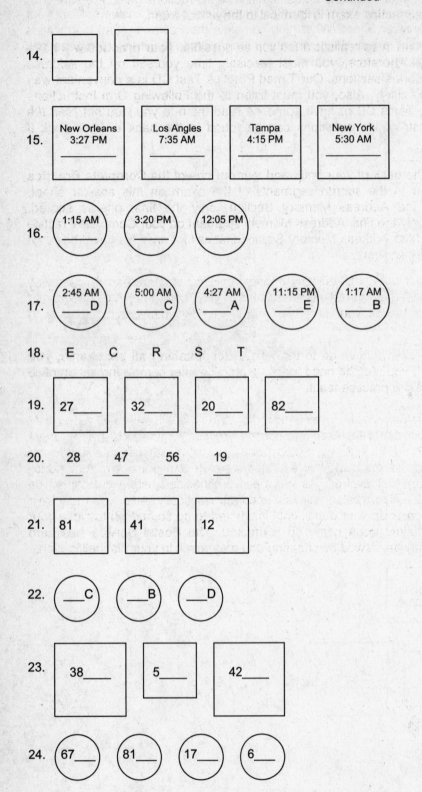

14. ▭ ▭

15. | New Orleans 3:27 PM | Los Angles 7:35 AM | Tampa 4:15 PM | New York 5:30 AM |

16. 1:15 AM   3:20 PM   12:05 PM

17. 2:45 AM ___D   5:00 AM ___C   4:27 AM ___A   11:15 PM ___E   1:17 AM ___B

18. E   C   R   S   T

19. 27___   32___   20___   82___

20. 28   47   56   19

21. 81   41   12

22. ___C   ___B   ___D

23. 38___   5___   42___

24. 67___   81___   17___   6___

COMPLETE PRACTICE EXAM #4

This complete practice exam contains all four sections of the actual exam. The instructions given are similar to those on the actual exam. The format of this practice exam is identical to the actual exam.

It is imperative that you take the practice exam in as realistic a fashion as possible. **Your practice will have no value unless it is done realistically.** Therefore, you must precisely time yourself on the Address Checking, Address Memory, and Number Series sections. Our Timed Practice Test CD is a convenient way to practice realistically and time yourself precisely. Also, you must listen to the Following Oral Instructions questions on our Oral Instructions Practice Tests CD or have someone read them to you - *do not read the questions yourself!* The Following Oral Instructions questions can be found in the back of your book if someone will be reading them to you.

When taking a practice exam, first turn to the back of your book and tear out one of the **Complete Practice Exam Answer Sheets.** Mark the answers to the scored segments of the exam on this answer sheet. Remember, of the seven segments on the Address Memory Section, only the final one is scored. Accordingly, you should mark answers for only the final Address Memory segment on your Complete Practice Exam Answer Sheet. The other segments of the Address Memory Section that call for answers have their own sample answer sheets where you should mark answers.

Answer keys are provided in the back of your book. Immediately upon completing each section of a practice exam, **it is imperative that you score yourself** using the formulas given in the Scoring Formulas section of the book. Scoring is necessary in order to gauge your progress and to identify your individual areas of weakness that may need extra attention.

After completing and scoring each practice exam, move on to the next. **After finishing all six exams, you should be prepared for the actual exam.** If you feel the need for more practice after completing six practice exams, see page 60 for details on our free extra practice tests.

Do not look over the practice exam questions until you are ready to start - usually meaning either until (1) you have started the Timed Practice Test CD or the Oral Instructions Practice Tests CD or (2) you have set a timer for the allotted period of time. Similarly, after completing one section of the practice test, do not look over the next one until your are ready to start it. Likewise, stop working and put down your pencil immediately when the allotted period of time has expired. As has been emphasized before but cannot be emphasized enough, your practice is of absolutely no value unless it is done realistically. Also, you must train yourself (1) to not open your test booklet or pick up your pencil until instructed to do so and (2) to close your booklet and put down your pencil immediately upon being so instructed. The Postal Service has zero tolerance on these matters. Any variance may be viewed as cheating and may result in your disqualification.

COMPLETE PRACTICE EXAM #4
Part A – Address Checking

Directions

In the Address Checking section, you are to decide whether two addresses are alike or different. You have 6 minutes to answer 95 questions. Each question consists of a pair of addresses. If the two addresses in the pair are exactly alike in every way, darken the oval with the letter "A" for _Alike_. If the two addresses are different in any way, darken the oval with the letter "D" for _Different_. Mark your answers on the Complete Practice Exam Answer Sheet in the section entitled Address Checking. Begin when you are prepared to time yourself for precisely 6 minutes.

Notes:
- *You will notice that the questions on this section of your practice exam are spread across two pages. This is the exact format of the Address Checking section on the real exam. To save printing costs, some study guides condense the two pages of this section down to only one. Other study guides, for reasons we cannot even begin to guess, stretch the Address Checking section out over several pages.*
- *You will also notice that the Address Checking questions are presented in a font, or type of print, that is different from the rest of the book. This font closely matches the type of print used on the real exam, and - as you will see - it makes this section even more challenging.*
- *It is imperative that you practice realistically and that you become acquainted with the actual format of the test. We have therefore formatted the page layout and the font of the Address Checking section on this practice exam realistically for your benefit.*

COMPLETE PRACTICE EXAM #4
Part A – Address Checking

1.	Racine WI 10697-2988	Racine WI 10697-2988
2.	4717 W 31st Ave	4717 W 31st Ave
3.	3908 N Robinson Ln	3908 N Robinson Ln
4.	8079 Woodstook Cir	8079 Woodstork Cir
5.	3179 Simonaux Dr, Hesperia, AR	3179 Simonaux Dr, Hesperia, AR
6.	Odgen UT 96781-1661	Ogden UT 96781-1661
7.	426 Heidenheim Ct	426 Heidenheim Ct
8.	9458 Darlene Dr	9584 Darlene Dr.
9.	1681 Irish Hill Dr	1681 Irish Hill Dr
10.	New Orleans LA 40995-3056	New London LA 40995-3056
11.	6450 S Balboa Cir, San Luis Obispo, CA	6450 S Ballbe Cir, San Luis Obispo, CA
12.	8721 Shawna Park	8721 Shawna Park
13.	2000 Liverpool Ave	2000 Liverpoole Ave
14.	Corpus Christi TX 93598-8676	Corpus Christi TX 93598-8676
15.	5154 Cooperslade Pt	5145 Cooperslade Pt
16.	4144 Marshall Ln, Sidewinder, NV	4144 Marshall Ln, Sidewinder, NV
17.	1514 Kensington Pl	1514 Kensington Pl
18.	San Francisco CA 91191	San Francisco CA 91911
19.	9003 Tennyson Cir	9003 Tennyson Cir
20.	8698 Rossmann Ln	8698 Rossmann Rd
21.	6628 W Sandypoint Tr	6628 W Sandypoint Terr
22.	Schenectady NY 67845-6863	Schenectady NY 67845-6863
23.	2315 Saratoga Dr	2315 Saratoga Dr
24.	6671 Barkwood Cir	6671 Bartworth Cir
25.	2583 Robertsdale Pl Okeechobee FL	2583 Robertsdale Pt Okeechobee FL
26.	2303 N Cleveland Ave	2303 N Cleveland Ave
27.	Minneapolis MN 49575	Minneapolaris MN 49575
28.	6967 W 85th St, Okeefenokee, GA	6967 W 85th Star, Okeefenokee, GA
29.	1411 Woolmarket Jct	1411 Woolmarket Jct
30.	Titusville Fl 32217-8228	Titusville Fl 32217-8228
31.	4252 Community Ave	4252 Community Ave
32.	2630 Rushing Waters Way	2630 Rusing Waters Bay
33.	2207 Shadowood Ct	2207 Shadowood Ct
34.	Kalamazoo MI 10240	Kalamazoo MS 10240
35.	8647 Grasslawn Plaza	8647 Grasslawn Plaza
36.	Chattanooga Tn 90108	Chattanooga Tn 90108
37.	7327 Horace Rd	7327 Horrace Rd
38.	3020 General Sherman St	3020 General Sherman St
39.	4100 McNamee Bridge	4100 McNamee Bridge
40.	1137 Quailridge Rd	1173 Quailridge Rd
41.	Melbourne Fl 21907	Melbourne Fl 21907
42.	2686 51st Ave, Kamouraska, MI	2686 51st Ave, Kamouraska, MI
43.	2117 E Princeton Dr	2117 W Princeton Dr
44.	1607 Mary Ellen Dr	1609 Mary Ellen Dr
45.	2882 Flounder Pt	2882 Flounder Pt
46.	Fayetteville NC 71673-4229	Fayettetown NC 71673-4229
47.	4984 W Ruffin Ln	4984 W Ruffin Ln
48.	8777 Partridge Pl	8777 Partridge Pl

49.	3043 Sampson Ct	3043 Sapsonite Ct
50.	1024 Greenbriar Rd	1024 Greenbriar Rd
51.	Bethlehem PA 84297-1982	Bethleham PA 84297-1982
52.	6051 Riverview Ln	6051 Riverview Ln
53.	1769 English Village Dr	1769 English Village Dr
54.	4217 St Augustine Pl	4772 St Augustine Pl
55.	2280 E 2nd St Mattawamkeag NY	2280 E 2nd St Mattawamkeag NY
56.	Atlantic City NJ 63636-2555	Atlantic City NJ 63636-2555
57.	8633 Satchfield Jct	8633 Satchfore Jct
58.	1357 Cloverdale Rd	1357 W Cloverdale Rd
59.	7877 Whorton Blvd	7877 Whorton Bd
60.	2142 Hollyheath Pt	2142 Hollyheath Pt
61.	Colorado Springs CO 16560	Colorado Springs CO 15606
62.	2481 W Stanfield Rd	2481 W Stanfold Rd
63.	6718 Bamboo Cir	6718 Bamboo Cir
64.	745 Schindler Cove	745 Schindler Cape
65.	Hot Springs AR 89651-2656	Hot Springs AR 89651-2656
66.	9827 Schumacker Ln	9827 Schumaker Ln
67.	5621 Annelore Pl	5621 Annelore Pl
68.	4177 Tantaloon Rd	4177 Telephone Rd
69.	6010 Railroad St, Obo, OR	6010 Railroad St, Obo, OR
70.	Saskatoon MN 11257	Sascatoon MN 11257
71.	Biloxi MS 39806	Buloxi Ms 39806
72.	3674 22nd St, East Millinocket, ME	3674 22nd St, East Millinocket, ME
73.	9558 W Jackson Ln	9558 E Jackson Ln
74.	2555 Ransom Way	2555 Ranson Way
75.	Jacksonville Fl 32790-1953	Jacksonville MS 32790-1953
76.	3910 Stephanie Bridge	3910 Stephanie Bridge
77.	8210 Tyrone Blvd	8210 Tyrone Blvd
78.	7411 W 84th St Mastigouche MT	7477 W 84th St Mastigouche MT
79.	Fort Lauderdale Fl 76708	Fort Lauderdale Fl 76708
80.	2004 Barracuda Pt	2004 Barracuda Pt
81.	3271 E Clarence	3271 E Clarence
82.	1186 Jefferson Ave	1186 S Jefferson Ave
83.	Millinocket NH 13270-2002	Millinocket NH 13270-2002
84.	6665 N Nottingham Cir	6665 S Nottingham Cir
85.	3330 Meadowlark Jct	3330 Meadowlark Jct
86.	1579 Rosebud Trail	1659 Rosebud Trail
87.	Winnemucca NV 56707-4704	Winnemucca NV 56701-4704
88.	8814 Hampstead Way	8814 Hampstead Way
89.	4969 87th Ave	4969 87th Ave
90.	6957 Homestead Ln	6957 Homestead Ln
91.	2121 Campbell Blvd Suite 3356B	2121 Campbell Blvd Suite 3356B
92.	Alamogorda NM 66712	Alamogordy NM 66712
93.	5111 Orchard Park	5111 Orchard Bark
94.	8814 W 15th St	8814 W 15th St
95.	Devils Lake ND 77216-9657	Devils Lake ND 77216-9657

COMPLETE PRACTICE EXAM #4
Part B – Address Memory

Directions

In the Address Memory section, you are to memorize the locations of 25 addresses in five boxes. During this section, you will have several study periods and practice exercises to help you memorize the location of the addresses shown in the five boxes. Answer the questions by darkening the oval containing the letter (A, B, C, D, E) of the box the address came from - Box A, Box B, Box C, Box D, or Box E. At the end of each segment, you will be given instructions on how and where to continue. After completing six preliminary segments, the actual test will be given as segment #7.

Turn the page to begin Segment #1 of the Address Memory section.

Note: You will notice in this practice exam that segments 3, 4, and 6 of the Address Memory section are spread across two pages. The five boxes, the 88 questions, and the sample answer sheet in these segments are spread across two facing pages. This is the exact same format that you will experience on Address Memory segments 3, 4, and 6 of the actual exam. To save printing costs, other study guides frequently condense these segments down from two pages to only one. However, it is imperative that you practice realistically and that you become acquainted with the actual format of the test. We have therefore formatted the Address Memory section on this practice exam realistically for your benefit.

COMPLETE PRACTICE EXAM #4
Part B – Address Memory – Segment #1

The purpose of this small exercise is to acquaint you with the format of the Address Memory section. The first two questions are answered for you. You are to spend three minutes studying this page and answering sample questions 3, 4, and 5. After completing Segment #1, turn to Segment #2 for further instructions. Begin when you are prepared to time yourself for precisely three minutes.

A	B	C	D	E
5100-5299 Owen Adolph 3300-3499 Grove Brodie 5800-5999 Tuck	8700-8899 Owen Walda 8200-8399 Grove Eddy 3300-3499 Tuck	3300-3499 Owen Odessa 5800-5999 Grove Halter 8200-8399 Tuck	5800-5999 Owen Sonja 5100-5299 Grove Benoit 8700-8899 Tuck	8200-8399 Owen Bayou 8700-8899 Grove Trehern 5100-5299 Tuck

1. 5100-5299 Owen   Ⓐ Ⓑ Ⓒ Ⓓ Ⓔ
   This address came from Box A, so we sill darken the oval with the letter A.

2. 5800-5999 Grove   Ⓐ Ⓑ Ⓒ Ⓓ Ⓔ
   This address came from Box C, so we will darken the oval with the letter C.

3. 8200-8399 Owen   Ⓐ Ⓑ Ⓒ Ⓓ Ⓔ
   Now that you know how to answer, you do questions 3, 4, and 5.

4. Walda   Ⓐ Ⓑ Ⓒ Ⓓ Ⓔ

5. Bayou   Ⓐ Ⓑ Ⓒ Ⓓ Ⓔ

The correct answers are A, C, E, B, and E.

COMPLETE PRACTICE EXAM #4
Part B – Address Memory – Segment #2

In this segment, you are given three minutes to study and memorize the addresses. There are no questions to answer in this segment - it is a study period only. However, on the actual exam, the boxes are not reprinted for your use. Instead, you are instructed to turn back to Address Memory Segment #1 and to spend three minutes studying the boxes displayed there. So, we will do the very same on this practice exam. After studying for three minutes, turn to Segment #3 for directions on how to continue the Address Memory Section of the exam. Begin studying when you are prepared to time yourself for precisely three minutes.

COMPLETE PRACTICE EXAM #4
Part B – Address Memory – Segment #3

You have three minutes to answer 88 questions. Try to answer from memory, but the boxes are shown if you need to refer to them. Mark your answers on the sample answer sheet at the bottom of the pages. After completing this segment, turn to Segment #4 for further instructions. Begin when you are prepared to time yourself for precisely three minutes.

A	B	C
5100-5299 Owen Adolph 3300-3499 Grove Brodie 5800-5999 Tuck	8700-8899 Owen Walda 8200-8399 Grove Eddy 3300-3499 Tuck	3300-3499 Owen Odessa 5800-5999 Grove Halter 8200-8399 Tuck

1. 8700-8899 Grove
2. Halter
3. Trehern
4. 5100-5299 Grove
5. 5800-5999 Tuck
6. 8200-8399 Tuck
7. 5800-5999 Owen
8. Walda

9. 5100-5299 Owen
10. Benoit
11. 3300-3499 Tuck
12. Bayou
13. 8200-8399 Grove
14. 5100-5299 Grove
15. 8200-8399 Owen
16. Eddy

17. 8700-8899 Grove
18. Odessa
19. 5800-5999 Tuck
20. Adolph
21. Benoit
22. Walda
23. 3300-3499 Tuck
24. Halter

25. Brodie
26. 8200-8399 Tuck
27. 8700-8899 Tuck
28. 8700-8899 Owen
29. 5100-5299 Tuck
30. 3300-3499 Owen
31. 8700-8899 Grove
32. Walda

33. 5100-5299 Owen
34. Bayou
35. 5800-5999 Grove
36. 5100-5299 Tuck
37. 8200-8399 Grove
38. 5800-5999 Owen
39. Trehern
40. 5800-5999 Tuck

41. Odessa
42. 3300-3499 Grove
43. 8200-8399 Grove
44. Halter
45. Eddy
46. Sonja
47. 3300-3499 Owen
48. 5800-5999 Grove

1 ⒶⒷⒸⒹⒺ	17 ⒶⒷⒸⒹⒺ	33 ⒶⒷⒸⒹⒺ
2 ⒶⒷⒸⒹⒺ	18 ⒶⒷⒸⒹⒺ	34 ⒶⒷⒸⒹⒺ
3 ⒶⒷⒸⒹⒺ	19 ⒶⒷⒸⒹⒺ	35 ⒶⒷⒸⒹⒺ
4 ⒶⒷⒸⒹⒺ	20 ⒶⒷⒸⒹⒺ	36 ⒶⒷⒸⒹⒺ
5 ⒶⒷⒸⒹⒺ	21 ⒶⒷⒸⒹⒺ	37 ⒶⒷⒸⒹⒺ
6 ⒶⒷⒸⒹⒺ	22 ⒶⒷⒸⒹⒺ	38 ⒶⒷⒸⒹⒺ
7 ⒶⒷⒸⒹⒺ	23 ⒶⒷⒸⒹⒺ	39 ⒶⒷⒸⒹⒺ
8 ⒶⒷⒸⒹⒺ	24 ⒶⒷⒸⒹⒺ	40 ⒶⒷⒸⒹⒺ
9 ⒶⒷⒸⒹⒺ	25 ⒶⒷⒸⒹⒺ	41 ⒶⒷⒸⒹⒺ
10 ⒶⒷⒸⒹⒺ	26 ⒶⒷⒸⒹⒺ	42 ⒶⒷⒸⒹⒺ
11 ⒶⒷⒸⒹⒺ	27 ⒶⒷⒸⒹⒺ	43 ⒶⒷⒸⒹⒺ
12 ⒶⒷⒸⒹⒺ	28 ⒶⒷⒸⒹⒺ	44 ⒶⒷⒸⒹⒺ
13 ⒶⒷⒸⒹⒺ	29 ⒶⒷⒸⒹⒺ	45 ⒶⒷⒸⒹⒺ
14 ⒶⒷⒸⒹⒺ	30 ⒶⒷⒸⒹⒺ	46 ⒶⒷⒸⒹⒺ
15 ⒶⒷⒸⒹⒺ	31 ⒶⒷⒸⒹⒺ	47 ⒶⒷⒸⒹⒺ
16 ⒶⒷⒸⒹⒺ	32 ⒶⒷⒸⒹⒺ	48 ⒶⒷⒸⒹⒺ

D	E
5800-5999 Owen Sonja 5100-5299 Grove Benoit 8700-8899 Tuck	8200-8399 Owen Bayou 8700-8899 Grove Trehern 5100-5299 Tuck

49. 8700-8899 Tuck
50. Adolph
51. 8200-8399 Owen
52. Odessa
53. 5800-5999 Owen
54. Bayou
55. 8700-8899 Owen
56. 5100-5299 Grove

57. 5800-5999 Grove
58. Brodie
59. 8200-8399 Grove
60. Sonja
61. Benoit
62. 3300-3499 Grove
63. 8700-8899 Grove
64. Halter

65. 5800-5999 Tuck
66. Brodie
67. 5800-5999 Grove
68. 8200-8399 Grove
69. 5100-5299 Tuck
70. 5100-5299 Owen
71. Bayou
72. Eddy

73. 3300-3499 Owen
74. Trehern
75. Brodie
76. 8200-8399 Owen
77. 8700-8899 Owen
78. 8700-8899 Tuck
79. 8200-8399 Tuck
80. Adolph

81. 3300-3499 Tuck
82. 8700-8899 Tuck
83. Benoit
84. 3300-3499 Grove
85. Halter
86. Walda
87. Sonja
88. 8200-8399 Tuck

(Answer bubbles 49–88, options A B C D E)

COMPLETE PRACTICE EXAM #4
Part B – Address Memory – Segment #4

You have three minutes to answer 88 questions. You must answer from memory. The boxes are not shown. Mark your answers on the sample answer sheet at the bottom of the page. After completing this segment, turn to Segment #5 for further instructions. Begin when you are prepared to time yourself for precisely three minutes.

1. 5100-5299 Owen
2. 5800-5999 Grove
3. 8200-8399 Owen
4. Walda
5. Bayou
6. 5800-5999 Owen
7. 5100-5299 Owen
8. 8700-8899 Grove

9. 5100-5299 Tuck
10. Eddy
11. 5100-5299 Grove
12. 5800-5999 Tuck
13. 8700-8899 Tuck
14. 3300-3499 Owen
15. 8200-8399 Grove
16. Adolph

17. Sonja
18. Trehern
19. 8700-8899 Owen
20. Halter
21. 5800-5999 Grove
22. Brodie
23. 8200-8399 Tuck
24. 8700-8899 Tuck

25. 3300-3499 Tuck
26. Benoit
27. 3300-3499 Grove
28. Bayou
29. Odessa
30. 5100-5299 Tuck
31. 8200-8399 Grove
32. 3300-3499 Grove

33. Walda
34. Adolph
35. 8200-8399 Tuck
36. 3300-3499 Owen
37. 5800-5999 Owen
38. Halter
39. 8700-8899 Grove
40. 3300-3499 Grove

41. 5100-5299 Grove
42. 5800-5999 Tuck
43. 8700-8999 Owen
44. Sonja
45. Walda
46. Bayou
47. 5100-5299 Owen
48. Trehern

---

1 Ⓐ Ⓑ Ⓒ Ⓓ Ⓔ
2 Ⓐ Ⓑ Ⓒ Ⓓ Ⓔ
3 Ⓐ Ⓑ Ⓒ Ⓓ Ⓔ
4 Ⓐ Ⓑ Ⓒ Ⓓ Ⓔ
5 Ⓐ Ⓑ Ⓒ Ⓓ Ⓔ
6 Ⓐ Ⓑ Ⓒ Ⓓ Ⓔ
7 Ⓐ Ⓑ Ⓒ Ⓓ Ⓔ
8 Ⓐ Ⓑ Ⓒ Ⓓ Ⓔ

9 Ⓐ Ⓑ Ⓒ Ⓓ Ⓔ
10 Ⓐ Ⓑ Ⓒ Ⓓ Ⓔ
11 Ⓐ Ⓑ Ⓒ Ⓓ Ⓔ
12 Ⓐ Ⓑ Ⓒ Ⓓ Ⓔ
13 Ⓐ Ⓑ Ⓒ Ⓓ Ⓔ
14 Ⓐ Ⓑ Ⓒ Ⓓ Ⓔ
15 Ⓐ Ⓑ Ⓒ Ⓓ Ⓔ
16 Ⓐ Ⓑ Ⓒ Ⓓ Ⓔ

17 Ⓐ Ⓑ Ⓒ Ⓓ Ⓔ
18 Ⓐ Ⓑ Ⓒ Ⓓ Ⓔ
19 Ⓐ Ⓑ Ⓒ Ⓓ Ⓔ
20 Ⓐ Ⓑ Ⓒ Ⓓ Ⓔ
21 Ⓐ Ⓑ Ⓒ Ⓓ Ⓔ
22 Ⓐ Ⓑ Ⓒ Ⓓ Ⓔ
23 Ⓐ Ⓑ Ⓒ Ⓓ Ⓔ
24 Ⓐ Ⓑ Ⓒ Ⓓ Ⓔ

25 Ⓐ Ⓑ Ⓒ Ⓓ Ⓔ
26 Ⓐ Ⓑ Ⓒ Ⓓ Ⓔ
27 Ⓐ Ⓑ Ⓒ Ⓓ Ⓔ
28 Ⓐ Ⓑ Ⓒ Ⓓ Ⓔ
29 Ⓐ Ⓑ Ⓒ Ⓓ Ⓔ
30 Ⓐ Ⓑ Ⓒ Ⓓ Ⓔ
31 Ⓐ Ⓑ Ⓒ Ⓓ Ⓔ
32 Ⓐ Ⓑ Ⓒ Ⓓ Ⓔ

33 Ⓐ Ⓑ Ⓒ Ⓓ Ⓔ
34 Ⓐ Ⓑ Ⓒ Ⓓ Ⓔ
35 Ⓐ Ⓑ Ⓒ Ⓓ Ⓔ
36 Ⓐ Ⓑ Ⓒ Ⓓ Ⓔ
37 Ⓐ Ⓑ Ⓒ Ⓓ Ⓔ
38 Ⓐ Ⓑ Ⓒ Ⓓ Ⓔ
39 Ⓐ Ⓑ Ⓒ Ⓓ Ⓔ
40 Ⓐ Ⓑ Ⓒ Ⓓ Ⓔ

41 Ⓐ Ⓑ Ⓒ Ⓓ Ⓔ
42 Ⓐ Ⓑ Ⓒ Ⓓ Ⓔ
43 Ⓐ Ⓑ Ⓒ Ⓓ Ⓔ
44 Ⓐ Ⓑ Ⓒ Ⓓ Ⓔ
45 Ⓐ Ⓑ Ⓒ Ⓓ Ⓔ
46 Ⓐ Ⓑ Ⓒ Ⓓ Ⓔ
47 Ⓐ Ⓑ Ⓒ Ⓓ Ⓔ
48 Ⓐ Ⓑ Ⓒ Ⓓ Ⓔ

49. 8200-8399 Grove
50. 5800-5999 Owen
51. Brodie
52. 8200-8399 Owen
53. Eddy
54. Odessa
55. 8700-8899 Grove
56. 5800-5999 Tuck

57. Benoit
58. 8200-8399 Tuck
59. Adolph
60. 5100-5299 Tuck
61. 5800-5999 Grove
62. 8700-8899 Owen
63. Walda
64. 8200-8399 Owen

65. Halter
66. 8700-8899 Tuck
67. 5100-5299 Owen
68. 8200-8399 Tuck
69. 5100-5299 Tuck
70. 8200-8399 Grove
71. 8700-8899 Tuck
72. Eddy

73. 8700-8899 Grove
74. Brodie
75. Odessa
76. 5800-5999 Owen
77. 8700-8899 Owen
78. 5100-5299 Grove
79. 3300-3499 Tuck
80. Sonja

81. 3300-3499 Grove
82. 8700-8899 Tuck
83. 3300-3499 Owen
84. Benoit
85. 5800-5999 Tuck
86. Bayou
87. 5800-5999 Grove
88. Trehern

49 Ⓐ Ⓑ Ⓒ Ⓓ Ⓔ
50 Ⓐ Ⓑ Ⓒ Ⓓ Ⓔ
51 Ⓐ Ⓑ Ⓒ Ⓓ Ⓔ
52 Ⓐ Ⓑ Ⓒ Ⓓ Ⓔ
53 Ⓐ Ⓑ Ⓒ Ⓓ Ⓔ
54 Ⓐ Ⓑ Ⓒ Ⓓ Ⓔ
55 Ⓐ Ⓑ Ⓒ Ⓓ Ⓔ
56 Ⓐ Ⓑ Ⓒ Ⓓ Ⓔ

57 Ⓐ Ⓑ Ⓒ Ⓓ Ⓔ
58 Ⓐ Ⓑ Ⓒ Ⓓ Ⓔ
59 Ⓐ Ⓑ Ⓒ Ⓓ Ⓔ
60 Ⓐ Ⓑ Ⓒ Ⓓ Ⓔ
61 Ⓐ Ⓑ Ⓒ Ⓓ Ⓔ
62 Ⓐ Ⓑ Ⓒ Ⓓ Ⓔ
63 Ⓐ Ⓑ Ⓒ Ⓓ Ⓔ
64 Ⓐ Ⓑ Ⓒ Ⓓ Ⓔ

65 Ⓐ Ⓑ Ⓒ Ⓓ Ⓔ
66 Ⓐ Ⓑ Ⓒ Ⓓ Ⓔ
67 Ⓐ Ⓑ Ⓒ Ⓓ Ⓔ
68 Ⓐ Ⓑ Ⓒ Ⓓ Ⓔ
69 Ⓐ Ⓑ Ⓒ Ⓓ Ⓔ
70 Ⓐ Ⓑ Ⓒ Ⓓ Ⓔ
71 Ⓐ Ⓑ Ⓒ Ⓓ Ⓔ
72 Ⓐ Ⓑ Ⓒ Ⓓ Ⓔ

73 Ⓐ Ⓑ Ⓒ Ⓓ Ⓔ
74 Ⓐ Ⓑ Ⓒ Ⓓ Ⓔ
75 Ⓐ Ⓑ Ⓒ Ⓓ Ⓔ
76 Ⓐ Ⓑ Ⓒ Ⓓ Ⓔ
77 Ⓐ Ⓑ Ⓒ Ⓓ Ⓔ
78 Ⓐ Ⓑ Ⓒ Ⓓ Ⓔ
79 Ⓐ Ⓑ Ⓒ Ⓓ Ⓔ
80 Ⓐ Ⓑ Ⓒ Ⓓ Ⓔ

81 Ⓐ Ⓑ Ⓒ Ⓓ Ⓔ
82 Ⓐ Ⓑ Ⓒ Ⓓ Ⓔ
83 Ⓐ Ⓑ Ⓒ Ⓓ Ⓔ
84 Ⓐ Ⓑ Ⓒ Ⓓ Ⓔ
85 Ⓐ Ⓑ Ⓒ Ⓓ Ⓔ
86 Ⓐ Ⓑ Ⓒ Ⓓ Ⓔ
87 Ⓐ Ⓑ Ⓒ Ⓓ Ⓔ
88 Ⓐ Ⓑ Ⓒ Ⓓ Ⓔ

COMPLETE PRACTICE EXAM #4
Part B – Address Memory – Segment #5

Directions

In this segment, you are given five minutes to study the addresses. There are no questions to answer in this segment – it is a study period only. As before, the boxes are not reprinted here for your use. Instead, you are instructed to turn back to Address Memory Segment #1 and to spend five minutes studying the boxes displayed there. After studying for five minutes, turn to Segment #6 for directions on how to continue. Turn back to Segment #1 and begin studying when you are prepared to time yourself for precisely five minutes.

COMPLETE PRACTICE EXAM #4
Part B – Address Memory – Segment #6

You have five minutes to answer 88 questions. Try to answer from memory, but the boxes are shown if you need to refer to them. Mark your answers on the sample answer sheet at the bottom of the page. After completing this segment, turn to Segment #7 for further instructions. Begin when you are prepared to time yourself for precisely five minutes.

A	B	C
5100-5299 Owen Adolph 3300-3499 Grove Brodie 5800-5999 Tuck	8700-8899 Owen Walda 8200-8399 Grove Eddy 3300-3499 Tuck	3300-3499 Owen Odessa 5800-5999 Grove Halter 8200-8399 Tuck

1. 8700-8899 Grove
2. Halter
3. Trehern
4. 5100-5299 Grove
5. 5800-5999 Tuck
6. 8200-8399 Tuck
7. 5800-5999 Owen
8. Walda

9. 5100-5299 Owen
10. Benoit
11. 3300-3499 Tuck
12. Bayou
13. 8200-8399 Grove
14. 5100-5299 Grove
15. 8200-8399 Owen
16. Eddy

17. 8700-8899 Grove
18. Odessa
19. 5800-5999 Tuck
20. Adolph
21. Benoit
22. Walda
23. 3300-3499 Tuck
24. Halter

25. Brodie
26. 8200-8399 Tuck
27. 8700-8899 Tuck
28. 8700-8899 Owen
29. 5100-5299 Tuck
30. 3300-3499 Owen
31. 8700-8899 Grove
32. Walda

33. 5100-5299 Owen
34. Bayou
35. 5800-5999 Grove
36. 5100-5299 Tuck
37. 8200-8399 Grove
38. 5800-5999 Owen
39. Trehern
40. 5800-5999 Tuck

41. Odessa
42. 3300-3499 Grove
43. 8200-8399 Grove
44. Halter
45. Eddy
46. Sonja
47. 3300-3499 Owen
48. 5800-5999 Grove

1 Ⓐ Ⓑ Ⓒ Ⓓ Ⓔ
2 Ⓐ Ⓑ Ⓒ Ⓓ Ⓔ
3 Ⓐ Ⓑ Ⓒ Ⓓ Ⓔ
4 Ⓐ Ⓑ Ⓒ Ⓓ Ⓔ
5 Ⓐ Ⓑ Ⓒ Ⓓ Ⓔ
6 Ⓐ Ⓑ Ⓒ Ⓓ Ⓔ
7 Ⓐ Ⓑ Ⓒ Ⓓ Ⓔ
8 Ⓐ Ⓑ Ⓒ Ⓓ Ⓔ
9 Ⓐ Ⓑ Ⓒ Ⓓ Ⓔ
10 Ⓐ Ⓑ Ⓒ Ⓓ Ⓔ
11 Ⓐ Ⓑ Ⓒ Ⓓ Ⓔ
12 Ⓐ Ⓑ Ⓒ Ⓓ Ⓔ
13 Ⓐ Ⓑ Ⓒ Ⓓ Ⓔ
14 Ⓐ Ⓑ Ⓒ Ⓓ Ⓔ
15 Ⓐ Ⓑ Ⓒ Ⓓ Ⓔ
16 Ⓐ Ⓑ Ⓒ Ⓓ Ⓔ

17 Ⓐ Ⓑ Ⓒ Ⓓ Ⓔ
18 Ⓐ Ⓑ Ⓒ Ⓓ Ⓔ
19 Ⓐ Ⓑ Ⓒ Ⓓ Ⓔ
20 Ⓐ Ⓑ Ⓒ Ⓓ Ⓔ
21 Ⓐ Ⓑ Ⓒ Ⓓ Ⓔ
22 Ⓐ Ⓑ Ⓒ Ⓓ Ⓔ
23 Ⓐ Ⓑ Ⓒ Ⓓ Ⓔ
24 Ⓐ Ⓑ Ⓒ Ⓓ Ⓔ
25 Ⓐ Ⓑ Ⓒ Ⓓ Ⓔ
26 Ⓐ Ⓑ Ⓒ Ⓓ Ⓔ
27 Ⓐ Ⓑ Ⓒ Ⓓ Ⓔ
28 Ⓐ Ⓑ Ⓒ Ⓓ Ⓔ
29 Ⓐ Ⓑ Ⓒ Ⓓ Ⓔ
30 Ⓐ Ⓑ Ⓒ Ⓓ Ⓔ
31 Ⓐ Ⓑ Ⓒ Ⓓ Ⓔ
32 Ⓐ Ⓑ Ⓒ Ⓓ Ⓔ

33 Ⓐ Ⓑ Ⓒ Ⓓ Ⓔ
34 Ⓐ Ⓑ Ⓒ Ⓓ Ⓔ
35 Ⓐ Ⓑ Ⓒ Ⓓ Ⓔ
36 Ⓐ Ⓑ Ⓒ Ⓓ Ⓔ
37 Ⓐ Ⓑ Ⓒ Ⓓ Ⓔ
38 Ⓐ Ⓑ Ⓒ Ⓓ Ⓔ
39 Ⓐ Ⓑ Ⓒ Ⓓ Ⓔ
40 Ⓐ Ⓑ Ⓒ Ⓓ Ⓔ
41 Ⓐ Ⓑ Ⓒ Ⓓ Ⓔ
42 Ⓐ Ⓑ Ⓒ Ⓓ Ⓔ
43 Ⓐ Ⓑ Ⓒ Ⓓ Ⓔ
44 Ⓐ Ⓑ Ⓒ Ⓓ Ⓔ
45 Ⓐ Ⓑ Ⓒ Ⓓ Ⓔ
46 Ⓐ Ⓑ Ⓒ Ⓓ Ⓔ
47 Ⓐ Ⓑ Ⓒ Ⓓ Ⓔ
48 Ⓐ Ⓑ Ⓒ Ⓓ Ⓔ

D	E
5800-5999 Owen	8200-8399 Owen
Sonja	Bayou
5100-5299 Grove	8700-8899 Grove
Benoit	Trehern
8700-8899 Tuck	5100-5299 Tuck

49. 8700-8899 Tuck
50. Adolph
51. 8200-8399 Owen
52. Odessa
53. 5800-5999 Owen
54. Bayou
55. 8700-8899 Owen
56. 5100-5299 Grove

57. 5800-5999 Grove
58. Brodie
59. 8200-8399 Grove
60. Sonja
61. Benoit
62. 3300-3499 Grove
63. 8700-8899 Grove
64. Halter

65. 5800-5999 Tuck
66. Brodie
67. 5800-5999 Grove
68. 8200-8399 Grove
69. 5100-5299 Tuck
70. 5100-5299 Owen
71. Bayou
72. Eddy

73. 3300-3499 Owen
74. Trehern
75. Brodie
76. 8200-8399 Owen
77. 8700-8899 Owen
78. 8700-8899 Tuck
79. 8200-8399 Tuck
80. Adolph

81. 3300-3499 Tuck
82. 8700-8899 Tuck
83. Benoit
84. 3300-3499 Grove
85. Halter
86. Walda
87. Sonja
88. 8200-8399 Tuck

49 (A) (B) (C) (D) (E)
50 (A) (B) (C) (D) (E)
51 (A) (B) (C) (D) (E)
52 (A) (B) (C) (D) (E)
53 (A) (B) (C) (D) (E)
54 (A) (B) (C) (D) (E)
55 (A) (B) (C) (D) (E)
56 (A) (B) (C) (D) (E)

57 (A) (B) (C) (D) (E)
58 (A) (B) (C) (D) (E)
59 (A) (B) (C) (D) (E)
60 (A) (B) (C) (D) (E)
61 (A) (B) (C) (D) (E)
62 (A) (B) (C) (D) (E)
63 (A) (B) (C) (D) (E)
64 (A) (B) (C) (D) (E)

65 (A) (B) (C) (D) (E)
66 (A) (B) (C) (D) (E)
67 (A) (B) (C) (D) (E)
68 (A) (B) (C) (D) (E)
69 (A) (B) (C) (D) (E)
70 (A) (B) (C) (D) (E)
71 (A) (B) (C) (D) (E)
72 (A) (B) (C) (D) (E)

73 (A) (B) (C) (D) (E)
74 (A) (B) (C) (D) (E)
75 (A) (B) (C) (D) (E)
76 (A) (B) (C) (D) (E)
77 (A) (B) (C) (D) (E)
78 (A) (B) (C) (D) (E)
79 (A) (B) (C) (D) (E)
80 (A) (B) (C) (D) (E)

81 (A) (B) (C) (D) (E)
82 (A) (B) (C) (D) (E)
83 (A) (B) (C) (D) (E)
84 (A) (B) (C) (D) (E)
85 (A) (B) (C) (D) (E)
86 (A) (B) (C) (D) (E)
87 (A) (B) (C) (D) (E)
88 (A) (B) (C) (D) (E)

COMPLETE PRACTICE EXAM #4
Part B – Address Memory – Segment #7

You have five minutes to answer 88 questions. You must answer from memory. The boxes are not shown. Mark your answers on the Complete Practice Exam Answer Sheet. After completing this segment, turn to the Number Series section for instructions on how to continue. Begin when you are prepared to time yourself for precisely five minutes.

1. 5100-5299 Owen
2. 5800-5999 Grove
3. 8200-8399 Owen
4. Walda
5. Bayou
6. 5800-5999 Owen
7. 5100-5299 Owen
8. 8700-8899 Grove

9. 5100-5299 Tuck
10. Eddy
11. 5100-5299 Grove
12. 5800-5999 Tuck
13. 8700-8899 Tuck
14. 3300-3499 Owen
15. 8200-8399 Grove
16. Adolph

17. Sonja
18. Trehern
19. 8700-8899 Owen
20. Halter
21. 5800-5999 Grove
22. Brodie
23. 8200-8399 Tuck
24. 8700-8899 Tuck

25. 3300-3499 Tuck
26. Benoit
27. 3300-3499 Grove
28. Bayou
29. Odessa
30. 5100-5299 Tuck
31. 8200-8399 Grove
32. 3300-3499 Grove

33. Walda
34. Adolph
35. 8200-8399 Tuck
36. 3300-3499 Owen
37. 5800-5999 Owen
38. Halter
39. 8700-8899 Grove
40. 3300-3499 Grove

41. 5100-5299 Grove
42. 5800-5999 Tuck
43. 8700-8899 Owen
44. Sonja
45. Walda
46. Bayou
47. 5100-5299 Owen
48. Trehern

49. 8200-8399 Grove
50. 5800-5999 Owen
51. Brodie
52. 8200-8399 Owen
53. Eddy
54. Odessa
55. 8700-8899 Grove
56. 5800-5999 Tuck

57. Benoit
58. 8200-8399 Tuck
59. Adolph
60. 5100-5299 Tuck
61. 5800-5999 Grove
62. 8700-8899 Owen
63. Walda
64. 8200-8399 Owen

65. Halter
66. 8700-8899 Tuck
67. 5100-5299 Owen
68. 8200-8399 Tuck
69. 5100-5299 Tuck
70. 8200-8399 Grove
71. 8700-8899 Tuck
72. Eddy

73. 8700-8899 Grove
74. Brodie
75. Odessa
76. 5800-5999 Owen
77. 8700-8899 Owen
78. 5100-5299 Grove
79. 3300-3499 Tuck
80. Sonja

81. 3300-3499 Grove
82. 8700-8899 Tuck
83. 3300-3499 Owen
84. Benoit
85. 5800-5999 Tuck
86. Bayou
87. 5800-5999 Grove
88. Trehern

COMPLETE PRACTICE EXAM #4
Part C – Number Series

You have 20 minutes to answer 24 questions. Each question is a series of numbers followed by two blanks. You are to find which two numbers would logically follow in the series. Mark your answers on the Complete Practice Exam Answer Sheet. After completing this section, turn to the Following Oral Instructions section. Begin when you are prepared to time yourself for precisely 20 minutes.

1. 5 6 8 10 10 12 15 ___ ___   (A) 12, 15 (B) 14, 16 (C) 12, 14 (D) 16, 18 (E) 15, 17

2. 21 24 27 30 33 ___ ___   (A) 35, 38 (B) 34, 37 (C) 36, 39 (D) 31, 35 (E) 39, 36

3. 1 3 5 5 7 9 9 ___ ___   (A) 12, 10 (B) 11, 12 (C) 13, 10 (D) 11, 13 (E) 14, 12

4. 11 11 10 10 9 9 8 ___ ___   (A) 8, 9 (B) 8, 7 (C) 7, 6 (D) 8, 6 (E) 9, 1

5. 1 31 1 32 1 33 1 ___ ___   (A) 34, 1 (B) 35, 1 (C) 1, 34 (D) 2, 35 (E) 1, 1

6. 14 12 14 13 14 14 ___ ___   (A) 14, 18 (B) 13, 15 (C) 15, 17 (D) 14, 15 (E) 18, 20

7. 11 1 3 15 5 7 19 ___ ___   (A) 8, 10 (B) 10, 12 (C) 9, 21 (D) 18, 22 (E) 9, 11

8. 11 12 14 17 21 26 32 ___ ___   (A) 40, 47 (B) 38, 45 (C) 39, 47 (D) 40, 47 (E) 42, 48

9. 8 8 10 10 12 12 14 ___ ___   (A) 15, 16 (B) 17, 18 (C) 15, 15 (D) 16, 12 (E) 14, 16

10. 3 4 13 8 9 13 13 ___ ___   (A) 14, 13 (B) 12, 11 (C) 15, 14 (D) 13, 15 (E) 17, 19

11. 2 31 2 32 2 33 2 ___ ___   (A) 36, 2 (B) 34, 2 (C) 2, 2 (D) 46, 2 (E) 35, 2

12. 3 2 7 5 11 8 15 ___ ___   (A) 12, 20 (B) 11, 19 (C) 13, 19 (D) 11, 21 (E) 10, 19

13. 16 15 16 16 16 17 16 ___ ___   (A) 17, 16 (B) 16, 17 (C) 15, 17 (D) 18, 16 (E) 17, 18

14. 2 4 4 4 6 4 8 ___ ___   (A) 10, 4 (B) 4, 10 (C) 4, 4 (D) 5, 11 (E) 6, 12

15. 18 6 6 18 12 12 18 ___ ___   (A) 24, 24 (B) 0, 18 (C) 18, 18 (D) 18, 0 (E) 20, 22

16. 1 15 2 16 3 17 ___ ___   (A) 4, 19 (B) 5, 20 (C) 6, 18 (D) 3, 21 (E) 4, 18

17. 2 1 4 3 6 5 8 ___ ___   (A) 7, 10 (B) 9, 10 (C) 12, 10 (D) 9, 7 (E) 12, 11

18. 1 12 2 12 3 12 4 ___ ___   (A) 12, 6 (B) 12, 4 (C) 5, 12 (D) 12, 12 (E) 12, 5

19. 26 2 24 4 22 6 ___ ___   (A) 18, 6 (B) 20, 8 (C) 22, 10 (D) 24, 12 (E) 21, 13

20. 6 13 15 7 17 19 8 ___ ___   (A) 20, 24 (B) 19, 21 (C) 20, 22 (D) 21, 23 (E) 22, 24

21. 9 10 15 11 12 15 13 ___ ___   (A) 13, 16 (B) 14, 16 (C) 16, 19 (D) 12, 14 (E) 14, 15

22. 23 16 18 18 20 22 13 ___ ___   (A) 20, 24 (B) 24, 26 (C) 22, 26 (D) 25, 27 (E) 24, 28

23. 10 11 13 16 20 25 ___ ___   (A) 30, 36 (B) 31, 36 (C) 31, 38 (D) 32, 37 (E) 32, 38

24. 9 10 12 13 15 16 18 ___ ___   (A) 19, 21 (B) 18, 20 (C) 20, 22 (D) 19, 20 (E) 21, 22

COMPLETE PRACTICE EXAM #4
Part D – Following Oral Instructions

On this section, questions/instructions are presented verbally that lead you to the correct answers. Mark your answers on the Complete Practice Exam Answer Sheet. When you complete the Following Oral Instructions section, you have finished the complete practice exam. Begin when you are prepared to listen to the questions from the author's recording or from someone who will read them to you.

1.   B   C   A   E   D

2.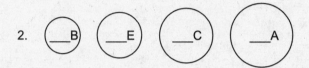
     (__B) (__E) (__C)   (__A)

3.   81   28   57   66   30   43   27   15   41

4.   A   D   E   B   C

5.   (19__) (21__) [37__] [15__]

6.   (7:00) (7:10) (6:51) (6:47) (5:10)
     ‾‾‾‾   ‾‾‾‾   ‾‾‾‾   ‾‾‾‾   ‾‾‾‾

7.   (14__) (37__) (21__)   ABE   DIE   CAB

8.   [85__]   [78__]

9.   OOX   XOO   XXO   XOX   XXO

10. 12___   18___   47___   52___   32___   31__   26___

11. 42   51   73   86   19   23   16

12. [67__]   [43__]   [64__]

13. 57___   82___

155

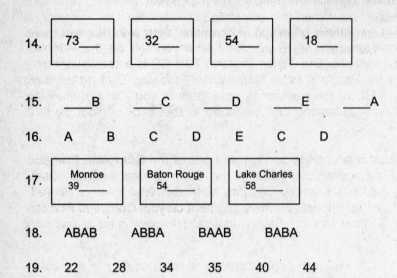

14. 73____   32____   54____   18____

15. ____B   ____C   ____D   ____E   ____A

16. A   B   C   D   E   C   D

17. Monroe   Baton Rouge   Lake Charles
     39____   54____   58____

18. ABAB   ABBA   BAAB   BABA

19. 22   28   34   35   40   44

COMPLETE PRACTICE EXAM #5

This complete practice exam contains all four sections of the actual exam. The instructions given are similar to those on the actual exam. The format of this practice exam is identical to the actual exam.

It is imperative that you take the practice exam in as realistic a fashion as possible. **Your practice will have no value unless it is done realistically.** Therefore, you must precisely time yourself on the Address Checking, Address Memory, and Number Series sections. Our Timed Practice Test CD is a convenient way to practice realistically and time yourself precisely. Also, you must listen to the Following Oral Instructions questions on our Oral Instructions Practice Tests CD or have someone read them to you - *do not read the questions yourself!* The Following Oral Instructions questions can be found in the back of your book if someone will be reading them to you.

When taking a practice exam, first turn to the back of your book and tear out one of the **Complete Practice Exam Answer Sheets.** Mark the answers to the scored segments of the exam on this answer sheet. Remember, of the seven segments on the Address Memory Section, only the final one is scored. Accordingly, you should mark answers for only the final Address Memory segment on your Complete Practice Exam Answer Sheet. The other segments of the Address Memory Section that call for answers have their own sample answer sheets where you should mark answers.

Answer keys are provided in the back of your book. Immediately upon completing each section of a practice exam, **it is imperative that you score yourself** using the formulas given in the Scoring Formulas section of the book. Scoring is necessary in order to gauge your progress and to identify your individual areas of weakness that may need extra attention.

After completing and scoring each practice exam, move on to the next. **After finishing all six exams, you should be prepared for the actual exam.** If you feel the need for more practice after completing six practice exams, see page 60 for details on our free extra practice tests.

Do not look over the practice exam questions until you are ready to start - usually meaning either until (1) you have started the Timed Practice Test CD or the Oral Instructions Practice Tests CD or (2) you have set a timer for the allotted period of time. Similarly, after completing one section of the practice test, do not look over the next one until your are ready to start it. Likewise, stop working and put down your pencil immediately when the allotted period of time has expired. As has been emphasized before but cannot be emphasized enough, your practice is of absolutely no value unless it is done realistically. Also, you must train yourself (1) to not open your test booklet or pick up your pencil until instructed to do so and (2) to close your booklet and put down your pencil immediately upon being so instructed. The Postal Service has zero tolerance on these matters. Any variance may be viewed as cheating and may result in your disqualification.

COMPLETE PRACTICE EXAM #5
Part A – Address Checking

Directions

In the Address Checking section, you are to decide whether two addresses are alike or different. You have 6 minutes to answer 95 questions. Each question consists of a pair of addresses. If the two addresses in the pair are exactly alike in every way, darken the oval with the letter "A" for *Alike*. If the two addresses are different in any way, darken the oval with the letter "D" for *Different*. Mark your answers on the Complete Practice Exam Answer Sheet in the section entitled Address Checking. Begin when you are prepared to time yourself for precisely 6 minutes.

Notes:
- *You will notice that the questions on this section of your practice exam are spread across two pages. This is the exact format of the Address Checking section on the real exam. To save printing costs, some study guides condense the two pages of this section down to only one. Other study guides, for reasons we cannot even begin to guess, stretch the Address Checking section out over several pages.*
- *You will also notice that the Address Checking questions are presented in a font, or type of print, that is different from the rest of the book. This font closely matches the type of print used on the real exam, and - as you will see - it makes this section even more challenging.*
- *It is imperative that you practice realistically and that you become acquainted with the actual format of the test. We have therefore formatted the page layout and the font of the Address Checking section on this practice exam realistically for your benefit.*

COMPLETE PRACTICE EXAM #5
Part A – Address Checking

1.	7172 S 82nd St, Issaquena, OK	7172 S 82nd St, Issaquena, OK
2.	Yakima WA 10345-1922	Yakima WA 10345-1922
3.	3818 Morningview Cape	3818 Morningview Cove
4.	6579 15th St Minnetonka MN	6795 S 15th St Minnetonka MN
5.	3817 Northingham Rd	3817 Northingham Rd
6.	8777 Courthouse Pl	8777 Courthouse Pl
7.	4608 E Ladnier Rd	4608 E Ladner Rd
8.	Melbourne Fl 21907-8582	Melborne Fl 21907-8582
9.	5378 Bayou Oaks Ct	5378 Bayou Oates Ct
10.	4161 Patricia Ln	4161 E Patricia Ln
11.	1579 W Guardian Way	1579 W Guardian Way
12.	9060 Oceanspray Jct	9060 Oceanspray Jct
13.	Montpelier VT 98326	Montpelier VT 98326
14.	1540 Needle St, Needles National Park, NM	1540 Needle St, Needles National Park, NM
15.	1021 Gorenflo Pt	1012 Gorenflo Pt
16.	4969 Heatherwood Ln	4969 Heatherwood Ln
17.	6547 W Hanover St	6547 E Hanover St
18.	Louisville KY 38920-2526	Louisville Ky 38029-2526
19.	9567 Foxworthy Ct	9567 Foxworthy Ct
20.	1474 Tally Ho Cir, Long Beach, CA	1474 Tally Howard Cir, Long Beach, CA
21.	6357 W 28th Ave, Pottawatomie, OK	6357 W 28th Ave, Pottawatomie, OK
22.	9811 N Musella Ave	9811 N Moosella Ave
23.	Laredo TX 48930-6286	Lansing MI 64601-6286
24.	7737 Cambridge Pl	7737 Cambridge Pl
25.	2049 Everbreeze Jct	2049 Everbreeze Jct
26.	1903 W El Bonito St	1903 W El Burito St
27.	5599 Porter Pl, Wahiakum, WA	5599 Porter Pl, Wahiakum, WA
28.	Los Angeles CA 14157-9832	Las Angles CA 14157-9832
29.	408 E Magnolia Dr	409 E Magnolia Dr
30.	5038 Heatherstone Pt	5038 Heatherstone Pt
31.	7519 Arbor Vista Dr	7519 Arbor Vista Dr
32.	Grand Island NE 59487-7878	Grand Island NE 59487-7878
33.	1516 Thornton Ave	1516 Thornton Bay
34.	6473 Northgate Pl	6473 Northgate Pl
35.	6876 E 54th St Puyallop WA	6876 E 54th St Puyallop WA
36.	Flagstaff AZ 64821	Flagstaff AZ 64821
37.	2655 Englewood Rd	2655 Englewood Rd
38.	3709 W Pineview Pl	3709 E Pineview Pl
39.	9860 Plantation Rd	9860 Planter Rd
40.	Butte MT 87562-2003	Butte MT 87562-2003
41.	4050 Llwellyn Grv	4050 Llwellyn Garden
42.	8950 N Badwin Ave	8950 N Baldwin Ave
43.	5673 Bonner Blvd	5673 Bonner Blvd
44.	4441 W Applegate Rd	4444 W Applegate Rd
45.	Kenosha WI 10590-8229	Kenosha WY 10590-8229
46.	4135 E O'Neal Rd	4135 E O'Neal Rd
47.	3100 Abbey Ct, Waushara, Wis	3001 Abbey Ct, Waushara, Wis
48.	3054 Callaghan Cove	3054 Callaghan Cove

49.	3945 Fredinand Ln	3954 Ferdinand Ln
50.	Las Cruces NM 64603-8978	Las Cruces NM 64603-8978
51.	8950 Freeman Bld	8950 Freeman Bld
52.	4957 Humperdinck Pl	4957 Humperdickle Pl
53.	3340 Marco Polo Pt	3340 Marco Polo Pt
54.	9747 McCracken Ln	9747 McCracken Ln
55.	Dallas TX 96261-2566	Dallas TX 96261-2566
56.	1184 Mohammed Bay	1184 Mohammed Bay
57.	6172 Powhatan Ct Cuernavaca AZ	6172 Powhattan Ct Cuernavaca AZ
58.	8211 N 52nd Ave	8211 S 52nd Ave
59.	9172 Ponce DeLeon Way	9172 Ponce DeLeon Way
60.	Scaramento CA 94654-2861	Sacramento CA 94654-2861
61.	2828 Parkman Ave	2828 Parkman Ave
62.	4527 Aleutian Isle	4527 Aleutian Isle
63.	6800 S Welford Blvd	6800 N Welford Blvd
64.	5807 Berkeley Pt	5807 Berkeley Pt
65.	Wilkes-Barre PA 84217-8677	Wilkes-Barre PA 84712-8677
66.	831 Belgrade Cove	831 Belgrade Cove
67.	4504 E Jamestown Blvd	4504 E Jamestown Blvd
68.	5000 Bermuda Bav	5000 Bermuda Beach
69.	1825 W Tulane Ave	1825 W Tulane Ave
70.	Superior WI 50667-6969	Superior WI 50667-6969
71.	2309 Pinehaven Cove	2309 Pinehaven Cove
72.	El Paso TX 92835-1945	El Pasco TX 92835-1945
73.	9417 Meadowlark Pl	9417 Meadowlark Pl
74.	7172 Rebecca Maxey Cove	7712 Rebecca Maxey Cove
75.	5699 N 83rd Blvd	5699 N 83rd Bay
76.	Detroit MI 48207-4452	Detroit MI 48207-4452
77.	3303 Demonica Rd	3303 Demonica Rd
78.	4547 Popps Ferry Rd	4547 Bopps Ferry Rd
79.	8766 Columbus Cir	8766 Columbus Cir
80.	Augusta ME 41939-0012	Augusta ME 41393-0012
81.	20074 Commission Rd	2004 Commission Rd
82.	1711 Sheffield Place	1711 Sheffield Place
83.	1103 N Belair St	1103 W Belair St
84.	1202 W Market St	1202 W Market St
85.	Bettendorf IA 29571	Betteroff IA 29571
86.	1040 Navaho Tr, Suwanee, AL	1040 Navaho Pl, Suwanee, AL
87.	6088 W Primus Pl	6880 W Primus Pl
88.	1975 Northridge Dr	1975 Northridge Dr
89.	Fredrick MD 42995-5441	Fredrick MD 42995-5441
90.	1057 Twin Cedar Ave	1057 Triple Cedar Ave
91.	3176 W Travel Tr	3176 W Travel Tr
92.	2009 Lovers Ln, Peewee Valley, KY	2009 Lovers Ln, Peewee Valley, KY
93.	6357 W Marina Ave	6357 W Martina Ave
94.	Little Rock AR 81415-7457	Little Rock AK 81415-7457
95.	212 W Beach Blvd	212 W Beach Blvd

COMPLETE PRACTICE EXAM #5
Part B – Address Memory

Directions

In the Address Memory section, you are to memorize the locations of 25 addresses in five boxes. During this section, you will have several study periods and practice exercises to help you memorize the location of the addresses shown in the five boxes. Answer the questions by darkening the oval containing the letter (A, B, C, D, E) of the box the address came from - Box A, Box B, Box C, Box D, or Box E. At the end of each segment, you will be given instructions on how and where to continue. After completing six preliminary segments, the actual test will be given as segment #7.

Turn the page to begin Segment #1 of the Address Memory section.

Note: You will notice in this practice exam that segments 3, 4, and 6 of the Address Memory section are spread across two pages. The five boxes, the 88 questions, and the sample answer sheet in these segments are spread across two facing pages. This is the exact same format that you will experience on Address Memory segments 3, 4, and 6 of the actual exam. To save printing costs, other study guides frequently condense these segments down from two pages to only one. However, it is imperative that you practice realistically and that you become acquainted with the actual format of the test. We have therefore formatted the Address Memory section on this practice exam realistically for your benefit.

COMPLETE PRACTICE EXAM #5
Part B – Address Memory – Segment #1

The purpose of this small exercise is to acquaint you with the format of the Address Memory section. The first two questions are answered for you. You are to spend three minutes studying this page and answering sample questions 3, 4, and 5. After completing Segment #1, turn to Segment #2 for further instructions. Begin when you are prepared to time yourself for precisely three minutes.

A	B	C	D	E
9200-9399 Vada Bethel 6700-6899 Bell Ford 9600-9799 Lark	8500-8699 Vada Parker 6300-6499 Bell Finley 9200-9399 Lark	6700-6899 Vada Olivia 9200-9399 Bell Scott 6300-6499 Lark	9600-9799 Vada Lamey 8500-8699 Bell Saratoga 6700-6899 Lark	6300-6499 Vada Verde 9600-9799 Bell Brady 8500-8699 Lark

1. Brady   Ⓐ Ⓑ Ⓒ Ⓓ ⬤
   This address came from Box E, so we sill darken the oval with the letter E.

2. 6300-6499 Lark   Ⓐ Ⓑ ⬤ Ⓓ Ⓔ
   This address came from Box C, so we will darken the oval with the letter C.

3. 9200-9399 Vada   Ⓐ Ⓑ Ⓒ Ⓓ Ⓔ
   Now that you know how to answer, you do questions 3, 4, and 5.

4. Finley   Ⓐ Ⓑ Ⓒ Ⓓ Ⓔ

5. 6300-6499 Vada   Ⓐ Ⓑ Ⓒ Ⓓ Ⓔ

The correct answers are E, C, A, B, and E.

COMPLETE PRACTICE EXAM #5
Part B – Address Memory – Segment #2

Directions

In this segment, you are given three minutes to study and memorize the addresses. There are no questions to answer in this segment - it is a study period only. However, on the actual exam, the boxes are not reprinted for your use. Instead, you are instructed to turn back to Address Memory Segment #1 and to spend three minutes studying the boxes displayed there. So, we will do the very same on this practice exam. After studying for three minutes, turn to Segment #3 for directions on how to continue the Address Memory Section of the exam. Begin studying when you are prepared to time yourself for precisely three minutes.

COMPLETE PRACTICE EXAM #5
Part B – Address Memory – Segment #3

You have three minutes to answer 88 questions. Try to answer from memory, but the boxes are shown if you need to refer to them. Mark your answers on the sample answer sheet at the bottom of the pages. After completing this segment, turn to Segment #4 for further instructions. Begin when you are prepared to time yourself for precisely three minutes.

A	B	C
9200-9399 Vada Bethel 6700-6899 Bell Ford 9600-9799 Lark	8500-8699 Vada Parker 6300-6499 Bell Finley 9200-9399 Lark	6700-6899 Vada Olivia 9200-9399 Bell Scott 6300-6499 Lark

1. 6700-6899 Lark
2. Verde
3. 9200-9399 Lark
4. Lamey
5. Ford
6. 6700-6899 Bell
7. Saratoga
8. 6300-6499 Lark

9. 9600-9799 Vada
10. 9200-9399 Vada
11. 8500-8699 Bell
12. 6300-6499 Bell
13. Finley
14. 8500-8699 Vada
15. 9600-9799 Bell
16. 6700-6899 Vada

17. Bethel
18. 9200-9399 Bell
19. 6300-6499 Vada
20. Parker
21. 8500-8699 Bell
22. 9600-9799 Bell
23. Ford
24. Brady

25. 6700-6899 Vada
26. 6300-6499 Bell
27. Scott
28. 9200-9399 Vada
29. 9600-9799 Lark
30. Verde
31. 6300-6499 Vada
32. 8500-8699 Lark

33. Finley
34. 6300-6499 Lark
35. 9200-9399 Vada
36. Saratoga
37. 6300-6499 Bell
38. 6700-6899 Lark
39. 8500-8699 Vada
40. Olivia

41. 9200-9399 Lark
42. 6700-6899 Bell
43. 9600-9799 Vada
44. Parker
45. Bethel
46. 6300-6499 Vada
47. 9600-9799 Bell
48. Scott

1 Ⓐ Ⓑ Ⓒ Ⓓ Ⓔ
2 Ⓐ Ⓑ Ⓒ Ⓓ Ⓔ
3 Ⓐ Ⓑ Ⓒ Ⓓ Ⓔ
4 Ⓐ Ⓑ Ⓒ Ⓓ Ⓔ
5 Ⓐ Ⓑ Ⓒ Ⓓ Ⓔ
6 Ⓐ Ⓑ Ⓒ Ⓓ Ⓔ
7 Ⓐ Ⓑ Ⓒ Ⓓ Ⓔ
8 Ⓐ Ⓑ Ⓒ Ⓓ Ⓔ

9 Ⓐ Ⓑ Ⓒ Ⓓ Ⓔ
10 Ⓐ Ⓑ Ⓒ Ⓓ Ⓔ
11 Ⓐ Ⓑ Ⓒ Ⓓ Ⓔ
12 Ⓐ Ⓑ Ⓒ Ⓓ Ⓔ
13 Ⓐ Ⓑ Ⓒ Ⓓ Ⓔ
14 Ⓐ Ⓑ Ⓒ Ⓓ Ⓔ
15 Ⓐ Ⓑ Ⓒ Ⓓ Ⓔ
16 Ⓐ Ⓑ Ⓒ Ⓓ Ⓔ

17 Ⓐ Ⓑ Ⓒ Ⓓ Ⓔ
18 Ⓐ Ⓑ Ⓒ Ⓓ Ⓔ
19 Ⓐ Ⓑ Ⓒ Ⓓ Ⓔ
20 Ⓐ Ⓑ Ⓒ Ⓓ Ⓔ
21 Ⓐ Ⓑ Ⓒ Ⓓ Ⓔ
22 Ⓐ Ⓑ Ⓒ Ⓓ Ⓔ
23 Ⓐ Ⓑ Ⓒ Ⓓ Ⓔ
24 Ⓐ Ⓑ Ⓒ Ⓓ Ⓔ

25 Ⓐ Ⓑ Ⓒ Ⓓ Ⓔ
26 Ⓐ Ⓑ Ⓒ Ⓓ Ⓔ
27 Ⓐ Ⓑ Ⓒ Ⓓ Ⓔ
28 Ⓐ Ⓑ Ⓒ Ⓓ Ⓔ
29 Ⓐ Ⓑ Ⓒ Ⓓ Ⓔ
30 Ⓐ Ⓑ Ⓒ Ⓓ Ⓔ
31 Ⓐ Ⓑ Ⓒ Ⓓ Ⓔ
32 Ⓐ Ⓑ Ⓒ Ⓓ Ⓔ

33 Ⓐ Ⓑ Ⓒ Ⓓ Ⓔ
34 Ⓐ Ⓑ Ⓒ Ⓓ Ⓔ
35 Ⓐ Ⓑ Ⓒ Ⓓ Ⓔ
36 Ⓐ Ⓑ Ⓒ Ⓓ Ⓔ
37 Ⓐ Ⓑ Ⓒ Ⓓ Ⓔ
38 Ⓐ Ⓑ Ⓒ Ⓓ Ⓔ
39 Ⓐ Ⓑ Ⓒ Ⓓ Ⓔ
40 Ⓐ Ⓑ Ⓒ Ⓓ Ⓔ

41 Ⓐ Ⓑ Ⓒ Ⓓ Ⓔ
42 Ⓐ Ⓑ Ⓒ Ⓓ Ⓔ
43 Ⓐ Ⓑ Ⓒ Ⓓ Ⓔ
44 Ⓐ Ⓑ Ⓒ Ⓓ Ⓔ
45 Ⓐ Ⓑ Ⓒ Ⓓ Ⓔ
46 Ⓐ Ⓑ Ⓒ Ⓓ Ⓔ
47 Ⓐ Ⓑ Ⓒ Ⓓ Ⓔ
48 Ⓐ Ⓑ Ⓒ Ⓓ Ⓔ

D	**E**
9600-9799 Vada Lamey 8500-8699 Bell Saratoga 6700-6899 Lark	6300-6499 Vada Verde 9600-9799 Bell Brady 8500-8699 Lark

49. Olivia
50. 6300-6499 Vada
51. 9600-9799 Lark
52. 8500-8699 Bell
53. 9200-9399 Vada
54. Bethel
55. 6300-6499 Bell
56. 6700-6899 Vada

57. Parker
58. 9600-9799 Vada
59. Lamey
60. 9200-9399 Bell
61. Ford
62. Saratoga
63. Brady
64. Olivia

65. Scott
66. Ford
67. Verde
68. 6300-6499 Lark
69. 6700-6899 Bell
70. 9600-9799 Bell
71. 6300-6499 Vada
72. 8500-8699 Vada

73. 9200-9399 Lark
74. Saratoga
75. 9200-9399 Vada
76. 8500-8699 Bell
77. Finley
78. 6700-6899 Vada
79. 9600-9799 Lark
80. Brady

81. 9200-9399 Bell
82. 6300-6499 Lark
83. Lamey
84. Scott
85. Ford
86. 6700-6899 Lark
87. 6300-6499 Bell
88. 8500-8699 Lark

49. Ⓐ Ⓑ Ⓒ Ⓓ Ⓔ
50. Ⓐ Ⓑ Ⓒ Ⓓ Ⓔ
51. Ⓐ Ⓑ Ⓒ Ⓓ Ⓔ
52. Ⓐ Ⓑ Ⓒ Ⓓ Ⓔ
53. Ⓐ Ⓑ Ⓒ Ⓓ Ⓔ
54. Ⓐ Ⓑ Ⓒ Ⓓ Ⓔ
55. Ⓐ Ⓑ Ⓒ Ⓓ Ⓔ
56. Ⓐ Ⓑ Ⓒ Ⓓ Ⓔ

57. Ⓐ Ⓑ Ⓒ Ⓓ Ⓔ
58. Ⓐ Ⓑ Ⓒ Ⓓ Ⓔ
59. Ⓐ Ⓑ Ⓒ Ⓓ Ⓔ
60. Ⓐ Ⓑ Ⓒ Ⓓ Ⓔ
61. Ⓐ Ⓑ Ⓒ Ⓓ Ⓔ
62. Ⓐ Ⓑ Ⓒ Ⓓ Ⓔ
63. Ⓐ Ⓑ Ⓒ Ⓓ Ⓔ
64. Ⓐ Ⓑ Ⓒ Ⓓ Ⓔ

65. Ⓐ Ⓑ Ⓒ Ⓓ Ⓔ
66. Ⓐ Ⓑ Ⓒ Ⓓ Ⓔ
67. Ⓐ Ⓑ Ⓒ Ⓓ Ⓔ
68. Ⓐ Ⓑ Ⓒ Ⓓ Ⓔ
69. Ⓐ Ⓑ Ⓒ Ⓓ Ⓔ
70. Ⓐ Ⓑ Ⓒ Ⓓ Ⓔ
71. Ⓐ Ⓑ Ⓒ Ⓓ Ⓔ
72. Ⓐ Ⓑ Ⓒ Ⓓ Ⓔ

73. Ⓐ Ⓑ Ⓒ Ⓓ Ⓔ
74. Ⓐ Ⓑ Ⓒ Ⓓ Ⓔ
75. Ⓐ Ⓑ Ⓒ Ⓓ Ⓔ
76. Ⓐ Ⓑ Ⓒ Ⓓ Ⓔ
77. Ⓐ Ⓑ Ⓒ Ⓓ Ⓔ
78. Ⓐ Ⓑ Ⓒ Ⓓ Ⓔ
79. Ⓐ Ⓑ Ⓒ Ⓓ Ⓔ
80. Ⓐ Ⓑ Ⓒ Ⓓ Ⓔ

81. Ⓐ Ⓑ Ⓒ Ⓓ Ⓔ
82. Ⓐ Ⓑ Ⓒ Ⓓ Ⓔ
83. Ⓐ Ⓑ Ⓒ Ⓓ Ⓔ
84. Ⓐ Ⓑ Ⓒ Ⓓ Ⓔ
85. Ⓐ Ⓑ Ⓒ Ⓓ Ⓔ
86. Ⓐ Ⓑ Ⓒ Ⓓ Ⓔ
87. Ⓐ Ⓑ Ⓒ Ⓓ Ⓔ
88. Ⓐ Ⓑ Ⓒ Ⓓ Ⓔ

COMPLETE PRACTICE EXAM #5
Part B – Address Memory – Segment #4

You have three minutes to answer 88 questions. You must answer from memory. The boxes are not shown. Mark your answers on the sample answer sheet at the bottom of the page. After completing this segment, turn to Segment #5 for further instructions. Begin when you are prepared to time yourself for precisely three minutes.

1. Brady
2. 6300-6499 Lark
3. 9200-9399 Vada
4. Finley
5. 6300-6499 Vada
6. Lamey
7. 6700-6899 Bell
8. 6300-6499 Bell

9. Scott
10. Parker
11. 6700-6899 Lark
12. 6300-6499 Lark
13. 9200-9399 Vada
14. Saratoga
15. 6700-6899 Vada
16. Lamey

17. 8500-8699 Vada
18. 6300-6499 Vada
19. 9600-9799 Lark
20. 9200-9399 Bell
21. 8500-8699 Bell
22. Bethel
23. 9600-9799 Vada
24. Verde

25. 9200-9399 Lark
26. Lamey
27. 9600-9799 Bell
28. Ford
29. Scott
30. 6300-6499 Bell
31. Brady
32. Olivia

33. 9200-9399 Bell
34. 8500-8699 Bell
35. Bethel
36. Brady
37. 6300-6499 Lark
38. Saratoga
39. 8500-8699 Vada
40. Lamey

41. 6700-6899 Bell
42. 9200-9399 Lark
43. 6300-6499 Bell
44. Ford
45. 9600-9799 Vada
46. 6700-6899 Vada
47. 6300-6499 Bell
48. 6300-6499 Vada

1 Ⓐ Ⓑ Ⓒ Ⓓ Ⓔ
2 Ⓐ Ⓑ Ⓒ Ⓓ Ⓔ
3 Ⓐ Ⓑ Ⓒ Ⓓ Ⓔ
4 Ⓐ Ⓑ Ⓒ Ⓓ Ⓔ
5 Ⓐ Ⓑ Ⓒ Ⓓ Ⓔ
6 Ⓐ Ⓑ Ⓒ Ⓓ Ⓔ
7 Ⓐ Ⓑ Ⓒ Ⓓ Ⓔ
8 Ⓐ Ⓑ Ⓒ Ⓓ Ⓔ
9 Ⓐ Ⓑ Ⓒ Ⓓ Ⓔ
10 Ⓐ Ⓑ Ⓒ Ⓓ Ⓔ
11 Ⓐ Ⓑ Ⓒ Ⓓ Ⓔ
12 Ⓐ Ⓑ Ⓒ Ⓓ Ⓔ
13 Ⓐ Ⓑ Ⓒ Ⓓ Ⓔ
14 Ⓐ Ⓑ Ⓒ Ⓓ Ⓔ
15 Ⓐ Ⓑ Ⓒ Ⓓ Ⓔ
16 Ⓐ Ⓑ Ⓒ Ⓓ Ⓔ

17 Ⓐ Ⓑ Ⓒ Ⓓ Ⓔ
18 Ⓐ Ⓑ Ⓒ Ⓓ Ⓔ
19 Ⓐ Ⓑ Ⓒ Ⓓ Ⓔ
20 Ⓐ Ⓑ Ⓒ Ⓓ Ⓔ
21 Ⓐ Ⓑ Ⓒ Ⓓ Ⓔ
22 Ⓐ Ⓑ Ⓒ Ⓓ Ⓔ
23 Ⓐ Ⓑ Ⓒ Ⓓ Ⓔ
24 Ⓐ Ⓑ Ⓒ Ⓓ Ⓔ
25 Ⓐ Ⓑ Ⓒ Ⓓ Ⓔ
26 Ⓐ Ⓑ Ⓒ Ⓓ Ⓔ
27 Ⓐ Ⓑ Ⓒ Ⓓ Ⓔ
28 Ⓐ Ⓑ Ⓒ Ⓓ Ⓔ
29 Ⓐ Ⓑ Ⓒ Ⓓ Ⓔ
30 Ⓐ Ⓑ Ⓒ Ⓓ Ⓔ
31 Ⓐ Ⓑ Ⓒ Ⓓ Ⓔ
32 Ⓐ Ⓑ Ⓒ Ⓓ Ⓔ

33 Ⓐ Ⓑ Ⓒ Ⓓ Ⓔ
34 Ⓐ Ⓑ Ⓒ Ⓓ Ⓔ
35 Ⓐ Ⓑ Ⓒ Ⓓ Ⓔ
36 Ⓐ Ⓑ Ⓒ Ⓓ Ⓔ
37 Ⓐ Ⓑ Ⓒ Ⓓ Ⓔ
38 Ⓐ Ⓑ Ⓒ Ⓓ Ⓔ
39 Ⓐ Ⓑ Ⓒ Ⓓ Ⓔ
40 Ⓐ Ⓑ Ⓒ Ⓓ Ⓔ
41 Ⓐ Ⓑ Ⓒ Ⓓ Ⓔ
42 Ⓐ Ⓑ Ⓒ Ⓓ Ⓔ
43 Ⓐ Ⓑ Ⓒ Ⓓ Ⓔ
44 Ⓐ Ⓑ Ⓒ Ⓓ Ⓔ
45 Ⓐ Ⓑ Ⓒ Ⓓ Ⓔ
46 Ⓐ Ⓑ Ⓒ Ⓓ Ⓔ
47 Ⓐ Ⓑ Ⓒ Ⓓ Ⓔ
48 Ⓐ Ⓑ Ⓒ Ⓓ Ⓔ

49. Finley	65. 9200-9399 Vada
50. 6700-6899 Bell	66. Saratoga
51. Scott	67. Brady
52. 6700-6899 Vada	68. 6700-6899 Vada
53. 8500-8699 Bell	69. Verde
54. 9600-9799 Lark	70. 6700-6899 Bell
55. Olivia	71. 9600-9799 Vada
56. Parker	72. Parker

81. Olivia
82. 6300-6499 Lark
83. Ford
84. 6300-6499 Bell
85. 8500-8699 Bell
86. 9200-9399 Bell
87. 6300-6499 Vada
88. Brady

57. Saratoga
58. 6700-6899 Lark
59. 9200-9399 Vada
60. 6300-6499 Vada
61. 9200-9399 Bell
62. 9600-9799 Bell
63. 8500-8699 Bell
64. Verde

73. 6700-6899 Lark
74. 8500-8699 Vada
75. 9600-9799 Bell
76. Bethel
77. Scott
78. 9200-9399 Lark
79. Finley
80. 9600-9799 Lark

49 Ⓐ Ⓑ Ⓒ Ⓓ Ⓔ
50 Ⓐ Ⓑ Ⓒ Ⓓ Ⓔ
51 Ⓐ Ⓑ Ⓒ Ⓓ Ⓔ
52 Ⓐ Ⓑ Ⓒ Ⓓ Ⓔ
53 Ⓐ Ⓑ Ⓒ Ⓓ Ⓔ
54 Ⓐ Ⓑ Ⓒ Ⓓ Ⓔ
55 Ⓐ Ⓑ Ⓒ Ⓓ Ⓔ
56 Ⓐ Ⓑ Ⓒ Ⓓ Ⓔ

57 Ⓐ Ⓑ Ⓒ Ⓓ Ⓔ
58 Ⓐ Ⓑ Ⓒ Ⓓ Ⓔ
59 Ⓐ Ⓑ Ⓒ Ⓓ Ⓔ
60 Ⓐ Ⓑ Ⓒ Ⓓ Ⓔ
61 Ⓐ Ⓑ Ⓒ Ⓓ Ⓔ
62 Ⓐ Ⓑ Ⓒ Ⓓ Ⓔ
63 Ⓐ Ⓑ Ⓒ Ⓓ Ⓔ
64 Ⓐ Ⓑ Ⓒ Ⓓ Ⓔ

65 Ⓐ Ⓑ Ⓒ Ⓓ Ⓔ
66 Ⓐ Ⓑ Ⓒ Ⓓ Ⓔ
67 Ⓐ Ⓑ Ⓒ Ⓓ Ⓔ
68 Ⓐ Ⓑ Ⓒ Ⓓ Ⓔ
69 Ⓐ Ⓑ Ⓒ Ⓓ Ⓔ
70 Ⓐ Ⓑ Ⓒ Ⓓ Ⓔ
71 Ⓐ Ⓑ Ⓒ Ⓓ Ⓔ
72 Ⓐ Ⓑ Ⓒ Ⓓ Ⓔ

73 Ⓐ Ⓑ Ⓒ Ⓓ Ⓔ
74 Ⓐ Ⓑ Ⓒ Ⓓ Ⓔ
75 Ⓐ Ⓑ Ⓒ Ⓓ Ⓔ
76 Ⓐ Ⓑ Ⓒ Ⓓ Ⓔ
77 Ⓐ Ⓑ Ⓒ Ⓓ Ⓔ
78 Ⓐ Ⓑ Ⓒ Ⓓ Ⓔ
79 Ⓐ Ⓑ Ⓒ Ⓓ Ⓔ
80 Ⓐ Ⓑ Ⓒ Ⓓ Ⓔ

81 Ⓐ Ⓑ Ⓒ Ⓓ Ⓔ
82 Ⓐ Ⓑ Ⓒ Ⓓ Ⓔ
83 Ⓐ Ⓑ Ⓒ Ⓓ Ⓔ
84 Ⓐ Ⓑ Ⓒ Ⓓ Ⓔ
85 Ⓐ Ⓑ Ⓒ Ⓓ Ⓔ
86 Ⓐ Ⓑ Ⓒ Ⓓ Ⓔ
87 Ⓐ Ⓑ Ⓒ Ⓓ Ⓔ
88 Ⓐ Ⓑ Ⓒ Ⓓ Ⓔ

COMPLETE PRACTICE EXAM #5
Part B – Address Memory – Segment #5

Directions

In this segment, you are given five minutes to study the addresses. There are no questions to answer in this segment – it is a study period only. As before, the boxes are not reprinted here for your use. Instead, you are instructed to turn back to Address Memory Segment #1 and to spend five minutes studying the boxes displayed there. After studying for five minutes, turn to Segment #6 for directions on how to continue. Turn back to Segment #1 and begin studying when you are prepared to time yourself for precisely five minutes.

COMPLETE PRACTICE EXAM #5
Part B – Address Memory – Segment #6

You have five minutes to answer 88 questions. Try to answer from memory, but the boxes are shown if you need to refer to them. Mark your answers on the sample answer sheet at the bottom of the page. After completing this segment, turn to Segment #7 for further instructions. Begin when you are prepared to time yourself for precisely five minutes.

A	B	C
9200-9399 Vada Bethel 6700-6899 Bell Ford 9600-9799 Lark	8500-8699 Vada Parker 6300-6499 Bell Finley 9200-9399 Lark	6700-6899 Vada Olivia 9200-9399 Bell Scott 6300-6499 Lark

1. 6700-6899 Lark
2. Verde
3. 9200-9399 Lark
4. Lamey
5. Ford
6. 6700-6899 Bell
7. Saratoga
8. 6300-6499 Lark

9. 9600-9799 Vada
10. 9200-9399 Vada
11. 8500-8699 Bell
12. 6300-6499 Bell
13. Finley
14. 8500-8699 Vada
15. 9600-9799 Bell
16. 6700-6899 Vada

17. Bethel
18. 9200-9399 Bell
19. 6300-6499 Vada
20. Parker
21. 8500-8699 Bell
22. 9600-9799 Bell
23. Ford
24. Brady

25. 6700-6899 Vada
26. 6300-6499 Bell
27. Scott
28. 9200-9399 Vada
29. 9600-9799 Lark
30. Verde
31. 6300-6499 Vada
32. 8500-8699 Lark

33. Finley
34. 6300-6499 Lark
35. 9200-9399 Vada
36. Saratoga
37. 6300-6499 Bell
38. 6700-6899 Lark
39. 8500-8699 Vada
40. Olivia

41. 9200-9399 Lark
42. 6700-6899 Bell
43. 9600-9799 Vada
44. Parker
45. Bethel
46. 6300-6499 Vada
47. 9600-9799 Bell
48. Scott

1 Ⓐ Ⓑ Ⓒ Ⓓ Ⓔ	17 Ⓐ Ⓑ Ⓒ Ⓓ Ⓔ	33 Ⓐ Ⓑ Ⓒ Ⓓ Ⓔ
2 Ⓐ Ⓑ Ⓒ Ⓓ Ⓔ	18 Ⓐ Ⓑ Ⓒ Ⓓ Ⓔ	34 Ⓐ Ⓑ Ⓒ Ⓓ Ⓔ
3 Ⓐ Ⓑ Ⓒ Ⓓ Ⓔ	19 Ⓐ Ⓑ Ⓒ Ⓓ Ⓔ	35 Ⓐ Ⓑ Ⓒ Ⓓ Ⓔ
4 Ⓐ Ⓑ Ⓒ Ⓓ Ⓔ	20 Ⓐ Ⓑ Ⓒ Ⓓ Ⓔ	36 Ⓐ Ⓑ Ⓒ Ⓓ Ⓔ
5 Ⓐ Ⓑ Ⓒ Ⓓ Ⓔ	21 Ⓐ Ⓑ Ⓒ Ⓓ Ⓔ	37 Ⓐ Ⓑ Ⓒ Ⓓ Ⓔ
6 Ⓐ Ⓑ Ⓒ Ⓓ Ⓔ	22 Ⓐ Ⓑ Ⓒ Ⓓ Ⓔ	38 Ⓐ Ⓑ Ⓒ Ⓓ Ⓔ
7 Ⓐ Ⓑ Ⓒ Ⓓ Ⓔ	23 Ⓐ Ⓑ Ⓒ Ⓓ Ⓔ	39 Ⓐ Ⓑ Ⓒ Ⓓ Ⓔ
8 Ⓐ Ⓑ Ⓒ Ⓓ Ⓔ	24 Ⓐ Ⓑ Ⓒ Ⓓ Ⓔ	40 Ⓐ Ⓑ Ⓒ Ⓓ Ⓔ
9 Ⓐ Ⓑ Ⓒ Ⓓ Ⓔ	25 Ⓐ Ⓑ Ⓒ Ⓓ Ⓔ	41 Ⓐ Ⓑ Ⓒ Ⓓ Ⓔ
10 Ⓐ Ⓑ Ⓒ Ⓓ Ⓔ	26 Ⓐ Ⓑ Ⓒ Ⓓ Ⓔ	42 Ⓐ Ⓑ Ⓒ Ⓓ Ⓔ
11 Ⓐ Ⓑ Ⓒ Ⓓ Ⓔ	27 Ⓐ Ⓑ Ⓒ Ⓓ Ⓔ	43 Ⓐ Ⓑ Ⓒ Ⓓ Ⓔ
12 Ⓐ Ⓑ Ⓒ Ⓓ Ⓔ	28 Ⓐ Ⓑ Ⓒ Ⓓ Ⓔ	44 Ⓐ Ⓑ Ⓒ Ⓓ Ⓔ
13 Ⓐ Ⓑ Ⓒ Ⓓ Ⓔ	29 Ⓐ Ⓑ Ⓒ Ⓓ Ⓔ	45 Ⓐ Ⓑ Ⓒ Ⓓ Ⓔ
14 Ⓐ Ⓑ Ⓒ Ⓓ Ⓔ	30 Ⓐ Ⓑ Ⓒ Ⓓ Ⓔ	46 Ⓐ Ⓑ Ⓒ Ⓓ Ⓔ
15 Ⓐ Ⓑ Ⓒ Ⓓ Ⓔ	31 Ⓐ Ⓑ Ⓒ Ⓓ Ⓔ	47 Ⓐ Ⓑ Ⓒ Ⓓ Ⓔ
16 Ⓐ Ⓑ Ⓒ Ⓓ Ⓔ	32 Ⓐ Ⓑ Ⓒ Ⓓ Ⓔ	48 Ⓐ Ⓑ Ⓒ Ⓓ Ⓔ

D	E
9600-9799 Vada Lamey 8500-8699 Bell Saratoga 6700-6899 Lark	6300-6499 Vada Verde 9600-9799 Bell Brady 8500-8699 Lark

49. Olivia
50. 6300-6499 Vada
51. 9600-9799 Lark
52. 8500-8699 Bell
53. 9200-9399 Vada
54. Bethel
55. 6300-6499 Bell
56. 6700-6899 Vada

57. Parker
58. 9600-9799 Vada
59. Lamey
60. 9200-9399 Bell
61. Ford
62. Saratoga
63. Brady
64. Olivia

65. Scott
66. Ford
67. Verde
68. 6300-6499 Lark
69. 6700-6899 Bell
70. 9600-9799 Bell
71. 6300-6499 Vada
72. 8500-8699 Vada

73. 9200-9399 Lark
74. Saratoga
75. 9200-9399 Vada
76. 8500-8699 Bell
77. Finley
78. 6700-6899 Vada
79. 9600-9799 Lark
80. Brady

81. 9200-9399 Bell
82. 6300-6499 Lark
83. Lamey
84. Scott
85. Ford
86. 6700-6899 Lark
87. 6300-6499 Bell
88. 8500-8699 Lark

49 Ⓐ Ⓑ Ⓒ Ⓓ Ⓔ
50 Ⓐ Ⓑ Ⓒ Ⓓ Ⓔ
51 Ⓐ Ⓑ Ⓒ Ⓓ Ⓔ
52 Ⓐ Ⓑ Ⓒ Ⓓ Ⓔ
53 Ⓐ Ⓑ Ⓒ Ⓓ Ⓔ
54 Ⓐ Ⓑ Ⓒ Ⓓ Ⓔ
55 Ⓐ Ⓑ Ⓒ Ⓓ Ⓔ
56 Ⓐ Ⓑ Ⓒ Ⓓ Ⓔ

57 Ⓐ Ⓑ Ⓒ Ⓓ Ⓔ
58 Ⓐ Ⓑ Ⓒ Ⓓ Ⓔ
59 Ⓐ Ⓑ Ⓒ Ⓓ Ⓔ
60 Ⓐ Ⓑ Ⓒ Ⓓ Ⓔ
61 Ⓐ Ⓑ Ⓒ Ⓓ Ⓔ
62 Ⓐ Ⓑ Ⓒ Ⓓ Ⓔ
63 Ⓐ Ⓑ Ⓒ Ⓓ Ⓔ
64 Ⓐ Ⓑ Ⓒ Ⓓ Ⓔ

65 Ⓐ Ⓑ Ⓒ Ⓓ Ⓔ
66 Ⓐ Ⓑ Ⓒ Ⓓ Ⓔ
67 Ⓐ Ⓑ Ⓒ Ⓓ Ⓔ
68 Ⓐ Ⓑ Ⓒ Ⓓ Ⓔ
69 Ⓐ Ⓑ Ⓒ Ⓓ Ⓔ
70 Ⓐ Ⓑ Ⓒ Ⓓ Ⓔ
71 Ⓐ Ⓑ Ⓒ Ⓓ Ⓔ
72 Ⓐ Ⓑ Ⓒ Ⓓ Ⓔ

73 Ⓐ Ⓑ Ⓒ Ⓓ Ⓔ
74 Ⓐ Ⓑ Ⓒ Ⓓ Ⓔ
75 Ⓐ Ⓑ Ⓒ Ⓓ Ⓔ
76 Ⓐ Ⓑ Ⓒ Ⓓ Ⓔ
77 Ⓐ Ⓑ Ⓒ Ⓓ Ⓔ
78 Ⓐ Ⓑ Ⓒ Ⓓ Ⓔ
79 Ⓐ Ⓑ Ⓒ Ⓓ Ⓔ
80 Ⓐ Ⓑ Ⓒ Ⓓ Ⓔ

81 Ⓐ Ⓑ Ⓒ Ⓓ Ⓔ
82 Ⓐ Ⓑ Ⓒ Ⓓ Ⓔ
83 Ⓐ Ⓑ Ⓒ Ⓓ Ⓔ
84 Ⓐ Ⓑ Ⓒ Ⓓ Ⓔ
85 Ⓐ Ⓑ Ⓒ Ⓓ Ⓔ
86 Ⓐ Ⓑ Ⓒ Ⓓ Ⓔ
87 Ⓐ Ⓑ Ⓒ Ⓓ Ⓔ
88 Ⓐ Ⓑ Ⓒ Ⓓ Ⓔ

COMPLETE PRACTICE EXAM #5
Part B – Address Memory – Segment #7

You have five minutes to answer 88 questions. You must answer from memory. The boxes are not shown. Mark your answers on the Complete Practice Exam Answer Sheet. After completing this segment, turn to the Number Series section for instructions on how to continue. Begin when you are prepared to time yourself for precisely five minutes.

1. Brady
2. 6300-6499 Lark
3. 9200-9399 Vada
4. Finley
5. 6300-6499 Vada
6. Lamey
7. 6700-6899 Bell
8. 6300-6499 Bell

9. Scott
10. Parker
11. 6700-6899 Lark
12. 6300-6499 Lark
13. 9200-9399 Vada
14. Saratoga
15. 6700-6899 Vada
16. Lamey

17. 8500-8699 Vada
18. 6300-6499 Vada
19. 9600-9799 Lark
20. 9200-9399 Bell
21. 8500-8699 Bell
22. Bethel
23. 9600-9799 Vada
24. Verde

25. 9200-9399 Lark
26. Lamey
27. 9600-9799 Bell
28. Ford
29. Scott
30. 6300-6499 Bell
31. Brady
32. Olivia

33. 9200-9399 Bell
34. 8500-8699 Bell
35. Bethel
36. Brady
37. 6300-6499 Lark
38. Saratoga
39. 8500-8699 Vada
40. Lamey

41. 6700-6899 Bell
42. 9200-9399 Lark
43. 6300-6499 Bell
44. Ford
45. 9600-9799 Vada
46. 6700-6899 Vada
47. 6300-6499 Bell
48. 6300-6499 Vada

49. Finley
50. 6700-6899 Bell
51. Scott
52. 6700-6899 Vada
53. 8500-8699 Bell
54. 9600-9799 Lark
55. Olivia
56. Parker

57. Saratoga
58. 6700-6899 Lark
59. 9200-9399 Vada
60. 6300-6499 Vada
61. 9200-9399 Bell
62. 9600-9799 Bell
63. 8500-8699 Bell
64. Verde

65. 9200-9399 Vada
66. Saratoga
67. Brady
68. 6700-6899 Vada
69. Verde
70. 6700-6899 Bell
71. 9600-9799 Vada
72. Parker

73. 6700-6899 Lark
74. 8500-8699 Vada
75. 9600-9799 Bell
76. Bethel
77. Scott
78. 9200-9399 Lark
79. Finley
80. 9600-9799 Lark

81. Olivia
82. 6300-6499 Lark
83. Ford
84. 6300-6499 Bell
85. 8500-8699 Bell
86. 9200-9399 Bell
87. 6300-6499 Vada
88. Brady

COMPLETE PRACTICE EXAM #5
Part C – Number Series

You have 20 minutes to answer 24 questions. Each question is a series of numbers followed by two blanks. You are to find which two numbers would logically follow in the series. Mark your answers on the Complete Practice Exam Answer Sheet. After completing this section, turn to the Following Oral Instructions section. Begin when you are prepared to time yourself for precisely 20 minutes.

1. 19 19 20 20 21 21 22 ___ ___   (A) 22,22 (B) 23,24 (C) 22,23 (D) 25,26 (E) 23,26

2. 6 12 18 24 30 ___ ___   (A) 35,41 (B) 38,44 (C) 37,41 (D) 33,40 (E) 36,42

3. 31 28 25 22 19 16 ___ ___   (A) 13,10 (B) 15,14 (C) 14,12 (D) 12,8 (E) 13,9

4. 15 19 16 13 13 10 ___ ___   (A) 10,6 (B) 11,7 (C) 11,9 (D) 12,8 (E) 12,9

5. 8 6 8 7 8 8 ___ ___   (A) 7,8 (B) 9,10 (C) 9,8 (D) 8,9 (E) 9,9

6. 21 29 37 45 53 ___ ___   (A) 60,68 (B) 62,70 (C) 61,70 (D) 60,69 (E) 61,69

7. 8 12 14 10 16 18 12 ___ ___   (A) 20,22 (B) 18,20 (C) 22,24 (D) 20,24 (E) 18,22

8. 7 8 10 9 10 12 11 ___ ___   (A) 10,12 (B) 12,14 (C) 13,15 (D) 14,16 (E) 10,14

9. 9 9 6 9 9 8 9 ___ ___   (A) 8,9 (B) 10,11 (C) 9,10 (D) 9,12 (E) 10,10

10. 25 31 37 43 49 ___ ___   (A) 54,60 (B) 56,62 (C) 55,62 (D) 56,61 (E) 55,61

11. 32 33 35 38 42 47 ___ ___   (A) 53,60 (B) 52,59 (C) 54,62 (D) 54,62 (E) 56,62

12. 3 8 12 6 16 20 9 ___ ___   (A) 22,26 (B) 24,28 (C) 25,29 (D) 26,30 (E) 25,29

13. 3 4 10 5 6 9 7 8 ___ ___   (A) 7,8 (B) 9,11 (C) 10,11 (D) 8,9 (E) 10,12

14. 10 3 20 4 30 5 ___ ___   (A) 40,7 (B) 50,7 (C) 60,8 (D) 50,8 (E) 40,6

15. 5 4 10 8 16 12 ___ ___   (A) 22,15 (B) 24,17 (C) 23,16 (D) 25,17 (E) 21,16

16. 9 14 28 19 24 28 29 ___ ___   (A) 34,28 (B) 35,29 (C) 34,27 (D) 34,29 (E) 35,30

17. 7 8 12 9 10 12 11 ___ ___   (A) 11,12 (B) 13,12 (C) 10,12 (D) 12,11 (E) 12,12

18. 11 12 14 15 17 18 20 ___ ___   (A) 20,22 (B) 21,23 (C) 19,24 (D) 23,21 (E) 22,24

19. 15 8 15 11 15 14 15 ___ ___   (A) 16,14 (B) 18,16 (C) 17,14 (D) 18,15 (E) 17,15

20. 10 9 10 15 8 7 20 25 ___ ___   (A) 7,6 (B) 6,6 (C) 6,5 (D) 7,4 (E) 5,5

21. 26 8 24 10 22 12 ___ ___   (A) 20,16 (B) 22,14 (C) 20,14 (D) 22,16 (E) 18,12

22. 24 25 27 28 30 31 ___ ___   (A) 33,34 (B) 30,32 (C) 34,25 (D) 32,25 (E) 31,34

23. 18 16 18 17 18 18 18 ___ ___   (A) 20,20 (B) 20,16 (C) 16,18 (D) 19,18 (E) 14,18

24. 30 31 33 36 40 ___ ___   (A) 44,52 (B) 45,51 (C) 46,50 (D) 45,52 (E) 46,51

COMPLETE PRACTICE EXAM #5
Part D – Following Oral Instructions

On this section, questions/instructions are presented verbally that lead you to the correct answers. Mark your answers on the Complete Practice Exam Answer Sheet. When you complete the Following Oral Instructions section, you have finished the complete practice exam. Begin when you are prepared to listen to the questions from the author's recording or from someone who will read them to you.

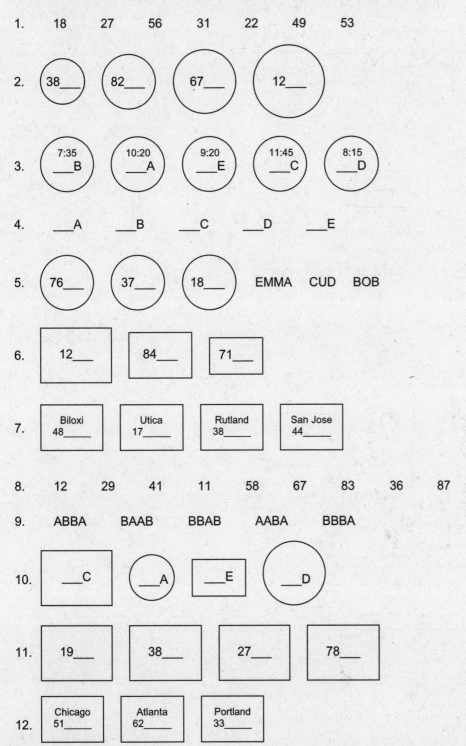

1.   18   27   56   31   22   49   53

2.   38___   82___   67___   12___

3.   7:35 ___B   10:20 ___A   9:20 ___E   11:45 ___C   8:15 ___D

4.   ___A   ___B   ___C   ___D   ___E

5.   76___   37___   18___   EMMA   CUD   BOB

6.   12___   84___   71___

7.   Biloxi 48_____   Utica 17_____   Rutland 38_____   San Jose 44_____

8.   12   29   41   11   58   67   83   36   87

9.   ABBA   BAAB   BBAB   AABA   BBBA

10.   ___C   ___A   ___E   ___D

11.   19___   38___   27___   78___

12.   Chicago 51_____   Atlanta 62_____   Portland 33_____

13. ___A   ___B   ___C   ___D   ___E

14. 3   8   20   32   57   17   14   15

15. [53___]   [81___]   [62___]   [69___]

16. ___D   ___E   ___B   ___C   ___A   ___D

17. [___B]   (17___)   (81___)   [___A]

18. (61___)   (82___)   (43___)   A M O R T I Z A T I O N

19. 72   37   14   4   31   86   17   49

COMPLETE PRACTICE EXAM #6

This complete practice exam contains all four sections of the actual exam. The instructions given are similar to those on the actual exam. The format of this practice exam is identical to the actual exam.

It is imperative that you take the practice exam in as realistic a fashion as possible. **Your practice will have no value unless it is done realistically.** Therefore, you must precisely time yourself on the Address Checking, Address Memory, and Number Series sections. Our Timed Practice Test CD is a convenient way to practice realistically and time yourself precisely. Also, you must listen to the Following Oral Instructions questions on our Oral Instructions Practice Tests CD or have someone read them to you - *do not read the questions yourself!* The Following Oral Instructions questions can be found in the back of your book if someone will be reading them to you.

When taking a practice exam, first turn to the back of your book and tear out one of the **Complete Practice Exam Answer Sheets.** Mark the answers to the scored segments of the exam on this answer sheet. Remember, of the seven segments on the Address Memory Section, only the final one is scored. Accordingly, you should mark answers for only the final Address Memory segment on your Complete Practice Exam Answer Sheet. The other segments of the Address Memory Section that call for answers have their own sample answer sheets where you should mark answers.

Answer keys are provided in the back of your book. Immediately upon completing each section of a practice exam, **it is imperative that you score yourself** using the formulas given in the Scoring Formulas section of the book. Scoring is necessary in order to gauge your progress and to identify your individual areas of weakness that may need extra attention.

After completing and scoring each practice exam, move on to the next. **After finishing all six exams, you should be prepared for the actual exam.** If you feel the need for more practice after completing six practice exams, see page 60 for details on our free extra practice tests.

Do not look over the practice exam questions until you are ready to start - usually meaning either until (1) you have started the Timed Practice Test CD or the Oral Instructions Practice Tests CD or (2) you have set a timer for the allotted period of time. Similarly, after completing one section of the practice test, do not look over the next one until your are ready to start it. Likewise, stop working and put down your pencil immediately when the allotted period of time has expired. As has been emphasized before but cannot be emphasized enough, your practice is of absolutely no value unless it is done realistically. Also, you must train yourself (1) to not open your test booklet or pick up your pencil until instructed to do so and (2) to close your booklet and put down your pencil immediately upon being so instructed. The Postal Service has zero tolerance on these matters. Any variance may be viewed as cheating and may result in your disqualification.

COMPLETE PRACTICE EXAM #6
Part A – Address Checking

Directions

In the Address Checking section, you are to decide whether two addresses are alike or different. You have 6 minutes to answer 95 questions. Each question consists of a pair of addresses. If the two addresses in the pair are exactly alike in every way, darken the oval with the letter "A" for _Alike_. If the two addresses are different in any way, darken the oval with the letter "D" for _Different_. Mark your answers on the Complete Practice Exam Answer Sheet in the section entitled Address Checking. Begin when you are prepared to time yourself for precisely 6 minutes.

Notes:
- *You will notice that the questions on this section of your practice exam are spread across two pages. This is the exact format of the Address Checking section on the real exam. To save printing costs, some study guides condense the two pages of this section down to only one. Other study guides, for reasons we cannot even begin to guess, stretch the Address Checking section out over several pages.*
- *You will also notice that the Address Checking questions are presented in a font, or type of print, that is different from the rest of the book. This font closely matches the type of print used on the real exam, and - as you will see - it makes this section even more challenging.*
- *It is imperative that you practice realistically and that you become acquainted with the actual format of the test. We have therefore formatted the page layout and the font of the Address Checking section on this practice exam realistically for your benefit.*

1.	Muskogee, Okla. 45563-1942	Muskogee, Okla. 45563-1942
2.	Piedras Negras, Tx. 00732-2531	Piedras Negras, Tx. 00132-2531
3.	1517 Waco Way	1517 Waco Bay
4.	Kingsford Rd. NE	Kingsford Rd. NE
5.	Edmund Drive, Hanamaulu, Hawaii	Edmundo Drive, Hanamaulu, Hawaii
6.	1253 Beacon St	1253 Beacon St.
7.	2612 North Ridge Dr.	2612 North Bridge Dr.
8.	Hull, GA 44586-4589	Hull, GA 44586-4589
9.	227 Klondyke Rd.	237 Klondyke Rd.
10.	Jefferson City, MO 68686-4655	Jefferson City, MO 68686-4655
11.	7816 Boulder Drive	7861 Boulder Drive
12.	245 McDonnell Av.	245 McDonnall Av.
13.	Boston, Mass. 33190-1561	Boston, Mass. 33192-1561
14.	Rosalie Blvd. Tippecanoe Ind.	Rosalie Blvd. Tippecanoe Ind.
15.	5179 Washington Ave.	5179 Washington Ave.
16.	Pascagoula, Ms 39567-2792	Pascagoula, MS 38567-2792
17.	897 Pompano Circle	899 Pompano Circle
18.	230 Pointdexter Dr.	230 Pintdexter Dr.
19.	19226 Caron Rd.	19226 Carson Rd
20.	Evanston, Utah 82076-7887	Evanston, Utah 82076-7887
21.	De Los Playera	De Los Playera
22.	110 Wisteria Dr.	110 Wisteria Dr.
23.	1770 Fleetwood Blvd.	1770 Fleetwood Dr.
24.	376 East Beach Blvd.	3760 East Beach Blvd
25.	Chesapeake, VA 46073-5566	Chesapeake, Vir. 46073-5566
26.	3537 Live Oak Ct.	3537 Live Oak Ct.
27.	4932 Ravenwood Terr.	4932 Ravenwood Terr.
28.	19490 Cemetery Lane	19490 Cemetery Lane
29.	918 Courthouse Rd.	819 Courthouse Rd.
30.	Montpelier, Vt. 27100-0001	Montpelier, Vt. 27100-0001
31.	6530 Diamondhead Cir	6530 Diamondlead Cir
32.	Seminole, Fl. 32252-0052	Seminole, Fl. 32252-0052
33.	7600 Lakeridge Ln	7600 Lakeridge Ln
34.	Tacoma, Wash. 18896	Tacoma, Wash. 19688
35.	439 Whispering Pines	439 Whispering Pin
36.	General Pershing Way	General Pershing Lane
37.	Rockville, MD 73232-8286	Rockville, MS 73232-8286
38.	437 18th St. NW	437 18th St. NW
39.	Glendale, Pl.	Glendale, Pl.
40.	1667 Irish Channel Pub	1667 Irish Channel Pub
41.	217 NE Bohn St.	217 NW Bohn St.
42.	Chicago, Ill. 12047	Chicago, Ill. 12047
43.	4614 Maples Lane	4461 Maples Lane
44.	9300 Hardwicke Ct.	9300 Hardwicker Ct.
45.	14 Timber Way	14 Timber Way
46.	22107 Popps Ferry Rd.	22107 Popps Ferry Rd.
47.	Mobile, Al. 84392-5654	Mobile, Ak. 84392-5654
48.	2090 Greenthumb Terr.	2009 Greenthumb Terr.

49.	9973 Catherine Jct.	9973 Catherine Jct.
50.	Magnolia, MS. 38516-8262	Magnolia, MS. 38516-8262
51.	255 Kiln-Delisle Rd.	255 Kiln-Delisle Rd.
52.	Enterprise, Fl. 43150	Enterprize, Fl. 43150
53.	5666 Golf Club Dr.	5666 Gulf Club Dr.
54.	77771 Trailer Ct.	77777 Trailer Ct.
55.	4112 Oaklawn Plaquemines LA	4112 Oaklaun Plaquemines LA
56.	20321 Dedeaux Rd.	20321 Dedeaux Rd.
57.	Fairbanks, AK. 99552-2290	Fairbanks, AK. 99552-2290
58.	1253 Hamilton St.	1253 Hamillton St.
59.	170 Bayridge Bld.	170 Bayridge Bld.
60.	7038 Meadow Bale	7038 Meadow Dale
61.	Phoenix, AZ 18076-8656	Pheonix, AZ 18076-8656
62.	4137 Central Ave.	4137 Central Ave.
63.	11216 Ashford Cir.	11216 Ashford Cir.
64.	6071 Bullock Way	6017 Bullock Way
65.	Fort Smith, Ark., 10132	Ft. Smith, Ark, 10132
66.	875 Strawberry St.	8750 Strawberry St.
67.	12222 Woodhaven Beach	1222 Woodhaven Beach
68.	501 Camille Cir.	501 Camille Ct.
69.	4600 Old Fort Bayou	4600 Old Fort Bayou
70.	Stockton, CA 99989	Sacramento, CA. 99989
71.	Boulder City, Nev. 77852-5252	Boulder City, Neb. 77852-5252
72.	8513 Orchard Av.	8513 Orchard Av.
73.	5417 Beatline Rd.	5417 Beatline Rd.
74.	3207 W Railroad	3207 S Railroad
75.	4713 Alandale St.	4713 Alandale St.
76.	Denever, Colo., 85777-2820	Denver, Colo., 85777-2820
77.	21680 Baywatch Beach	21680 Baywatch Beach
78.	26 Todd Terr., Androscoggin, ME	26 Todd Terr., Androscoggin, ME
79.	4723 Pontiac Dr.	4723 Pontiac Dr.
80.	Hartford, Conn.	Heartford, Conn.
81.	1304 De La Pointe Dr.	1304 De La Point Dr.
82.	179041 Lamney Lane	179041 Lamney Lane
83.	6371 Wooded Acres Rd.	6371 Wood Acres Rd.
84.	007 Dana Cir.	0007 Dana Cir.
85.	Miami, Fl. 67257-8604	Miami, Fl. 67257-8604
86.	5907 Easterbrook Bay	5907 Easterbrook Way
87.	3999 Jody Nelson Dr.	3777 Jody Nelson Dr
88.	3517 Kimberly Lane	3517 Kimberly Lane
89.	7617 Pearlington Pl.	7617 Pearlington Pl.
90.	Atlanta, GA 22127-0054	Atlanta, GA. 22127-0054
91.	15 Eastwood Blvd.	15 Eastwood Bay
92.	4117 Cunningham Point	4117 Cuningham Point
93.	2179 Rhonda Road	2179 Rhonda Road
94.	Honolulu, Hi. 93712-9998	Hilo, Hi. 93712-9998
95.	708 Shields Dr.	708 Shields Dr.

COMPLETE PRACTICE EXAM #6
Part B – Address Memory

Directions

In the Address Memory section, you are to memorize the locations of 25 addresses in five boxes. During this section, you will have several study periods and practice exercises to help you memorize the location of the addresses shown in the five boxes. Answer the questions by darkening the oval containing the letter (A, B, C, D, E) of the box the address came from - Box A, Box B, Box C, Box D, or Box E. At the end of each segment, you will be given instructions on how and where to continue. After completing six preliminary segments, the actual test will be given as segment #7.

Turn the page to begin Segment #1 of the Address Memory section.

Note: You will notice in this practice exam that segments 3, 4, and 6 of the Address Memory section are spread across two pages. The five boxes, the 88 questions, and the sample answer sheet in these segments are spread across two facing pages. This is the exact same format that you will experience on Address Memory segments 3, 4, and 6 of the actual exam. To save printing costs, other study guides frequently condense these segments down from two pages to only one. However, it is imperative that you practice realistically and that you become acquainted with the actual format of the test. We have therefore formatted the Address Memory section on this practice exam realistically for your benefit.

COMPLETE PRACTICE EXAM #6
Part B – Address Memory – Segment #1

The purpose of this small exercise is to acquaint you with the format of the Address Memory section. The first two questions are answered for you. You are to spend three minutes studying this page and answering sample questions 3, 4, and 5. After completing Segment #1, turn to Segment #2 for further instructions. Begin when you are prepared to time yourself for precisely three minutes.

A	B	C	D	E
2100-2199 Micah Hodges 1900-1999 Hilo Wilson 7200-7299 Mose	1400-1499 Micah Doyle 2800-2899 Hilo Lloyd 2100-2199 Mose	1900-1999 Micah Bunker 7200-7299 Hilo Lyman 1400-1499 Mose	7200-7299 Micah Tunica 2100-2199 Hilo Coburn 2800-2899 Mose	2800-2899 Micah Hatch 1400-1499 Hilo Beacon 1900-1999 Mose

1. 2800-2899 Mose   Ⓐ Ⓑ Ⓒ ● Ⓔ
   This address came from Box D, so we sill darken the oval with the letter D.

2. Hatch   Ⓐ Ⓑ Ⓒ Ⓓ ●
   This address came from Box E, so we will darken the oval with the letter E.

3. Lloyd   Ⓐ Ⓑ Ⓒ Ⓓ Ⓔ
   Now that you know how to answer, you do questions 3, 4, and 5.

4. 7200-7299 Micah   Ⓐ Ⓑ Ⓒ Ⓓ Ⓔ

5. Lyman   Ⓐ Ⓑ Ⓒ Ⓓ Ⓔ

The correct answers are D, E, B, D, and C.

187

COMPLETE PRACTICE EXAM #6
Part B – Address Memory – Segment #2

Directions

In this segment, you are given three minutes to study and memorize the addresses. There are no questions to answer in this segment - it is a study period only. However, on the actual exam, the boxes are not reprinted for your use. Instead, you are instructed to turn back to Address Memory Segment #1 and to spend three minutes studying the boxes displayed there. So, we will do the very same on this practice exam. After studying for three minutes, turn to Segment #3 for directions on how to continue the Address Memory Section of the exam. Begin studying when you are prepared to time yourself for precisely three minutes.

COMPLETE PRACTICE EXAM #6
Part B – Address Memory – Segment #3

You have three minutes to answer 88 questions. Try to answer from memory, but the boxes are shown if you need to refer to them. Mark your answers on the sample answer sheet at the bottom of the pages. After completing this segment, turn to Segment #4 for further instructions. Begin when you are prepared to time yourself for precisely three minutes.

A	B	C
2100-2199 Micah Hodges 1900-1999 Hilo Wilson 7200-7299 Mose	1400-1499 Micah Doyle 2800-2899 Hilo Lloyd 2100-2199 Mose	1900-1999 Micah Bunker 7200-7299 Hilo Lyman 1400-1499 Mose

1. Wilson
2. 2800-2899 Micah
3. 7200-7299 Hilo
4. 2100-2199 Mose
5. Doyle
6. Hatch
7. 1900-1999 Hilo
8. 1400-1499 Mose

9. 1400-1499 Micah
10. Coburn
11. 2100-2199 Micah
12. 1900-1999 Micah
13. 7200-7299 Micah
14. Wilson
15. 1400-1499 Hilo
16. 2100-2199 Mose

17. 1900-1999 Mose
18. Bunker
19. 7200-7299 Hilo
20. Tunica
21. Hodges
22. 2100-2199 Hilo
23. 1400-1499 Hilo
24. 2800-2899 Hilo

25. Lyman
26. 2100-2199 Micah
27. 7200-7299 Mose
28. 2800-2899 Micah
29. 2100-2199 Hilo
30. Doyle
31. Lloyd
32. 7200-7299 Micah

33. 2100-2199 Mose
34. 2100-2199 Micah
35. 2800-2899 Mose
36. Beacon
37. 7200-7299 Hilo
38. 1900-1999 Mose
39. Lyman
40. Wilson

41. 1900-1999 Micah
42. 2100-2199 Hilo
43. Coburn
44. 1900-1999 Hilo
45. 1400-1499 Mose
46. 7200-7299 Hilo
47. Hodges
48. 2800-2899 Hilo

1 Ⓐ Ⓑ Ⓒ Ⓓ Ⓔ	17 Ⓐ Ⓑ Ⓒ Ⓓ Ⓔ	33 Ⓐ Ⓑ Ⓒ Ⓓ Ⓔ
2 Ⓐ Ⓑ Ⓒ Ⓓ Ⓔ	18 Ⓐ Ⓑ Ⓒ Ⓓ Ⓔ	34 Ⓐ Ⓑ Ⓒ Ⓓ Ⓔ
3 Ⓐ Ⓑ Ⓒ Ⓓ Ⓔ	19 Ⓐ Ⓑ Ⓒ Ⓓ Ⓔ	35 Ⓐ Ⓑ Ⓒ Ⓓ Ⓔ
4 Ⓐ Ⓑ Ⓒ Ⓓ Ⓔ	20 Ⓐ Ⓑ Ⓒ Ⓓ Ⓔ	36 Ⓐ Ⓑ Ⓒ Ⓓ Ⓔ
5 Ⓐ Ⓑ Ⓒ Ⓓ Ⓔ	21 Ⓐ Ⓑ Ⓒ Ⓓ Ⓔ	37 Ⓐ Ⓑ Ⓒ Ⓓ Ⓔ
6 Ⓐ Ⓑ Ⓒ Ⓓ Ⓔ	22 Ⓐ Ⓑ Ⓒ Ⓓ Ⓔ	38 Ⓐ Ⓑ Ⓒ Ⓓ Ⓔ
7 Ⓐ Ⓑ Ⓒ Ⓓ Ⓔ	23 Ⓐ Ⓑ Ⓒ Ⓓ Ⓔ	39 Ⓐ Ⓑ Ⓒ Ⓓ Ⓔ
8 Ⓐ Ⓑ Ⓒ Ⓓ Ⓔ	24 Ⓐ Ⓑ Ⓒ Ⓓ Ⓔ	40 Ⓐ Ⓑ Ⓒ Ⓓ Ⓔ
9 Ⓐ Ⓑ Ⓒ Ⓓ Ⓔ	25 Ⓐ Ⓑ Ⓒ Ⓓ Ⓔ	41 Ⓐ Ⓑ Ⓒ Ⓓ Ⓔ
10 Ⓐ Ⓑ Ⓒ Ⓓ Ⓔ	26 Ⓐ Ⓑ Ⓒ Ⓓ Ⓔ	42 Ⓐ Ⓑ Ⓒ Ⓓ Ⓔ
11 Ⓐ Ⓑ Ⓒ Ⓓ Ⓔ	27 Ⓐ Ⓑ Ⓒ Ⓓ Ⓔ	43 Ⓐ Ⓑ Ⓒ Ⓓ Ⓔ
12 Ⓐ Ⓑ Ⓒ Ⓓ Ⓔ	28 Ⓐ Ⓑ Ⓒ Ⓓ Ⓔ	44 Ⓐ Ⓑ Ⓒ Ⓓ Ⓔ
13 Ⓐ Ⓑ Ⓒ Ⓓ Ⓔ	29 Ⓐ Ⓑ Ⓒ Ⓓ Ⓔ	45 Ⓐ Ⓑ Ⓒ Ⓓ Ⓔ
14 Ⓐ Ⓑ Ⓒ Ⓓ Ⓔ	30 Ⓐ Ⓑ Ⓒ Ⓓ Ⓔ	46 Ⓐ Ⓑ Ⓒ Ⓓ Ⓔ
15 Ⓐ Ⓑ Ⓒ Ⓓ Ⓔ	31 Ⓐ Ⓑ Ⓒ Ⓓ Ⓔ	47 Ⓐ Ⓑ Ⓒ Ⓓ Ⓔ
16 Ⓐ Ⓑ Ⓒ Ⓓ Ⓔ	32 Ⓐ Ⓑ Ⓒ Ⓓ Ⓔ	48 Ⓐ Ⓑ Ⓒ Ⓓ Ⓔ

D	E
7200-7299 Micah Tunica 2100-2199 Hilo Coburn 2800-2899 Mose	2800-2899 Micah Hatch 1400-1499 Hilo Beacon 1900-1999 Mose

49. Lloyd
50. Tunica
51. Hatch
52. 7200-7299 Mose
53. 1400-1499 Hilo
54. Bunker
55. 2800-2899 Mose
56. 2100-2199 Micah

57. 2100-2199 Mose
58. 7200-7299 Micah
59. Beacon
60. 1400-1499 Micah
61. 2100-2199 Hilo
62. 1400-1499 Mose
63. Wilson
64. 2800-2899 Mose

65. 2100-2199 Mose
66. Beacon
67. 7200-7299 Hilo
68. Coburn
69. Hodges
70. 2100-2199 Hilo
71. 1400-1499 Hilo
72. 2800-2899 Hilo

73. Doyle
74. 1400-1499 Hilo
75. 1900-1999 Hilo
76. Lloyd
77. 7200-7299 Mose
78. Hatch
79. Lyman
80. 2800-2899 Mose

81. 1900-1999 Hilo
82. Bunker
83. 2800-2899 Micah
84. 1400-1499 Micah
85. Tunica
86. 1900-1999 Micah
87. 2100-2199 Mose
88. Coburn

49 Ⓐ Ⓑ Ⓒ Ⓓ Ⓔ
50 Ⓐ Ⓑ Ⓒ Ⓓ Ⓔ
51 Ⓐ Ⓑ Ⓒ Ⓓ Ⓔ
52 Ⓐ Ⓑ Ⓒ Ⓓ Ⓔ
53 Ⓐ Ⓑ Ⓒ Ⓓ Ⓔ
54 Ⓐ Ⓑ Ⓒ Ⓓ Ⓔ
55 Ⓐ Ⓑ Ⓒ Ⓓ Ⓔ
56 Ⓐ Ⓑ Ⓒ Ⓓ Ⓔ
57 Ⓐ Ⓑ Ⓒ Ⓓ Ⓔ
58 Ⓐ Ⓑ Ⓒ Ⓓ Ⓔ
59 Ⓐ Ⓑ Ⓒ Ⓓ Ⓔ
60 Ⓐ Ⓑ Ⓒ Ⓓ Ⓔ
61 Ⓐ Ⓑ Ⓒ Ⓓ Ⓔ
62 Ⓐ Ⓑ Ⓒ Ⓓ Ⓔ
63 Ⓐ Ⓑ Ⓒ Ⓓ Ⓔ
64 Ⓐ Ⓑ Ⓒ Ⓓ Ⓔ

65 Ⓐ Ⓑ Ⓒ Ⓓ Ⓔ
66 Ⓐ Ⓑ Ⓒ Ⓓ Ⓔ
67 Ⓐ Ⓑ Ⓒ Ⓓ Ⓔ
68 Ⓐ Ⓑ Ⓒ Ⓓ Ⓔ
69 Ⓐ Ⓑ Ⓒ Ⓓ Ⓔ
70 Ⓐ Ⓑ Ⓒ Ⓓ Ⓔ
71 Ⓐ Ⓑ Ⓒ Ⓓ Ⓔ
72 Ⓐ Ⓑ Ⓒ Ⓓ Ⓔ
73 Ⓐ Ⓑ Ⓒ Ⓓ Ⓔ
74 Ⓐ Ⓑ Ⓒ Ⓓ Ⓔ
75 Ⓐ Ⓑ Ⓒ Ⓓ Ⓔ
76 Ⓐ Ⓑ Ⓒ Ⓓ Ⓔ
77 Ⓐ Ⓑ Ⓒ Ⓓ Ⓔ
78 Ⓐ Ⓑ Ⓒ Ⓓ Ⓔ
79 Ⓐ Ⓑ Ⓒ Ⓓ Ⓔ
80 Ⓐ Ⓑ Ⓒ Ⓓ Ⓔ

81 Ⓐ Ⓑ Ⓒ Ⓓ Ⓔ
82 Ⓐ Ⓑ Ⓒ Ⓓ Ⓔ
83 Ⓐ Ⓑ Ⓒ Ⓓ Ⓔ
84 Ⓐ Ⓑ Ⓒ Ⓓ Ⓔ
85 Ⓐ Ⓑ Ⓒ Ⓓ Ⓔ
86 Ⓐ Ⓑ Ⓒ Ⓓ Ⓔ
87 Ⓐ Ⓑ Ⓒ Ⓓ Ⓔ
88 Ⓐ Ⓑ Ⓒ Ⓓ Ⓔ

COMPLETE PRACTICE EXAM #6
Part B – Address Memory – Segment #4

You have three minutes to answer 88 questions. You must answer from memory. The boxes are not shown. Mark your answers on the sample answer sheet at the bottom of the page. After completing this segment, turn to Segment #5 for further instructions. Begin when you are prepared to time yourself for precisely three minutes.

1. 2800-2899 Mose	17. 2800-2899 Hilo	33. 1400-1499 Micah
2. Hatch	18. 1900-1999 Mose	34. 1900-1999 Hilo
3. Lloyd	19. Bunker	35. 2100-2199 Mose
4. 7200-7299 Micah	20. Hatch	36. 1400-1499 Mose
5. Lyman	21. Hodges	37. Hatch
6. 2800-2899 Micah	22. 2100-2199 Hilo	38. 2100-2199 Micah
7. 1900-1999 Hilo	23. 2800-2899 Mose	39. 2800-2899 Hilo
8. 1400-1499 Mose	24. Doyle	40. 1900-1999 Micah
9. 1900-1999 Micah	25. 1400-1499 Hilo	41. 2800-2899 Hilo
10. Tunica	26. Wilson	42. Lyman
11. 2100-2199 Micah	27. 7200-7299 Hilo	43. 7200-7299 Mose
12. Coburn	28. Tunica	44. 2800-2899 Micah
13. Beacon	29. 1900-1999 Hilo	45. 7200-7299 Hilo
14. 7200-7299 Mose	30. 7200-7299 Micah	46. Hodges
15. 2100-2199 Hilo	31. 1400-1499 Mose	47. 1900-1999 Mose
16. 1400-1499 Micah	32. Lloyd	48. Doyle

1 Ⓐ Ⓑ Ⓒ Ⓓ Ⓔ
2 Ⓐ Ⓑ Ⓒ Ⓓ Ⓔ
3 Ⓐ Ⓑ Ⓒ Ⓓ Ⓔ
4 Ⓐ Ⓑ Ⓒ Ⓓ Ⓔ
5 Ⓐ Ⓑ Ⓒ Ⓓ Ⓔ
6 Ⓐ Ⓑ Ⓒ Ⓓ Ⓔ
7 Ⓐ Ⓑ Ⓒ Ⓓ Ⓔ
8 Ⓐ Ⓑ Ⓒ Ⓓ Ⓔ

9 Ⓐ Ⓑ Ⓒ Ⓓ Ⓔ
10 Ⓐ Ⓑ Ⓒ Ⓓ Ⓔ
11 Ⓐ Ⓑ Ⓒ Ⓓ Ⓔ
12 Ⓐ Ⓑ Ⓒ Ⓓ Ⓔ
13 Ⓐ Ⓑ Ⓒ Ⓓ Ⓔ
14 Ⓐ Ⓑ Ⓒ Ⓓ Ⓔ
15 Ⓐ Ⓑ Ⓒ Ⓓ Ⓔ
16 Ⓐ Ⓑ Ⓒ Ⓓ Ⓔ

17 Ⓐ Ⓑ Ⓒ Ⓓ Ⓔ
18 Ⓐ Ⓑ Ⓒ Ⓓ Ⓔ
19 Ⓐ Ⓑ Ⓒ Ⓓ Ⓔ
20 Ⓐ Ⓑ Ⓒ Ⓓ Ⓔ
21 Ⓐ Ⓑ Ⓒ Ⓓ Ⓔ
22 Ⓐ Ⓑ Ⓒ Ⓓ Ⓔ
23 Ⓐ Ⓑ Ⓒ Ⓓ Ⓔ
24 Ⓐ Ⓑ Ⓒ Ⓓ Ⓔ

25 Ⓐ Ⓑ Ⓒ Ⓓ Ⓔ
26 Ⓐ Ⓑ Ⓒ Ⓓ Ⓔ
27 Ⓐ Ⓑ Ⓒ Ⓓ Ⓔ
28 Ⓐ Ⓑ Ⓒ Ⓓ Ⓔ
29 Ⓐ Ⓑ Ⓒ Ⓓ Ⓔ
30 Ⓐ Ⓑ Ⓒ Ⓓ Ⓔ
31 Ⓐ Ⓑ Ⓒ Ⓓ Ⓔ
32 Ⓐ Ⓑ Ⓒ Ⓓ Ⓔ

33 Ⓐ Ⓑ Ⓒ Ⓓ Ⓔ
34 Ⓐ Ⓑ Ⓒ Ⓓ Ⓔ
35 Ⓐ Ⓑ Ⓒ Ⓓ Ⓔ
36 Ⓐ Ⓑ Ⓒ Ⓓ Ⓔ
37 Ⓐ Ⓑ Ⓒ Ⓓ Ⓔ
38 Ⓐ Ⓑ Ⓒ Ⓓ Ⓔ
39 Ⓐ Ⓑ Ⓒ Ⓓ Ⓔ
40 Ⓐ Ⓑ Ⓒ Ⓓ Ⓔ

41 Ⓐ Ⓑ Ⓒ Ⓓ Ⓔ
42 Ⓐ Ⓑ Ⓒ Ⓓ Ⓔ
43 Ⓐ Ⓑ Ⓒ Ⓓ Ⓔ
44 Ⓐ Ⓑ Ⓒ Ⓓ Ⓔ
45 Ⓐ Ⓑ Ⓒ Ⓓ Ⓔ
46 Ⓐ Ⓑ Ⓒ Ⓓ Ⓔ
47 Ⓐ Ⓑ Ⓒ Ⓓ Ⓔ
48 Ⓐ Ⓑ Ⓒ Ⓓ Ⓔ

49. Lyman
50. 2100-2199 Hilo
51. Wilson
52. 1900-1999 Mose
53. 2100-2199 Micah
54. Bunker
55. 2800-2899 Micah
56. 1400-1499 Micah

57. 2100-2199 Hilo
58. 2800-2899 Hilo
59. Beacon
60. Hodges
61. 1400-1499 Hilo
62. 2100-2199 Mose
63. Coburn
64. Doyle

65. 7200-7299 Hilo
66. Hodges
67. Beacon
68. Tunica
69. 1900-1999 Hilo
70. 2800-2899 Mose
71. 2100-2199 Mose
72. Bunker

73. Lloyd
74. 7200-7299 Micah
75. 2100-2199 Hilo
76. 2100-2199 Micah
77. Hatch
78. 1900-1999 Micah
79. 1400-1499 Hilo
80. 7200-7299 Mose

81. 2100-2199 Mose
82. 2800-2899 Mose
83. Lyman
84. Beacon
85. 1400-1499 Hilo
86. Wilson
87. Coburn
88. 1400-1499 Mose

49 Ⓐ Ⓑ Ⓒ Ⓓ Ⓔ
50 Ⓐ Ⓑ Ⓒ Ⓓ Ⓔ
51 Ⓐ Ⓑ Ⓒ Ⓓ Ⓔ
52 Ⓐ Ⓑ Ⓒ Ⓓ Ⓔ
53 Ⓐ Ⓑ Ⓒ Ⓓ Ⓔ
54 Ⓐ Ⓑ Ⓒ Ⓓ Ⓔ
55 Ⓐ Ⓑ Ⓒ Ⓓ Ⓔ
56 Ⓐ Ⓑ Ⓒ Ⓓ Ⓔ

57 Ⓐ Ⓑ Ⓒ Ⓓ Ⓔ
58 Ⓐ Ⓑ Ⓒ Ⓓ Ⓔ
59 Ⓐ Ⓑ Ⓒ Ⓓ Ⓔ
60 Ⓐ Ⓑ Ⓒ Ⓓ Ⓔ
61 Ⓐ Ⓑ Ⓒ Ⓓ Ⓔ
62 Ⓐ Ⓑ Ⓒ Ⓓ Ⓔ
63 Ⓐ Ⓑ Ⓒ Ⓓ Ⓔ
64 Ⓐ Ⓑ Ⓒ Ⓓ Ⓔ

65 Ⓐ Ⓑ Ⓒ Ⓓ Ⓔ
66 Ⓐ Ⓑ Ⓒ Ⓓ Ⓔ
67 Ⓐ Ⓑ Ⓒ Ⓓ Ⓔ
68 Ⓐ Ⓑ Ⓒ Ⓓ Ⓔ
69 Ⓐ Ⓑ Ⓒ Ⓓ Ⓔ
70 Ⓐ Ⓑ Ⓒ Ⓓ Ⓔ
71 Ⓐ Ⓑ Ⓒ Ⓓ Ⓔ
72 Ⓐ Ⓑ Ⓒ Ⓓ Ⓔ

73 Ⓐ Ⓑ Ⓒ Ⓓ Ⓔ
74 Ⓐ Ⓑ Ⓒ Ⓓ Ⓔ
75 Ⓐ Ⓑ Ⓒ Ⓓ Ⓔ
76 Ⓐ Ⓑ Ⓒ Ⓓ Ⓔ
77 Ⓐ Ⓑ Ⓒ Ⓓ Ⓔ
78 Ⓐ Ⓑ Ⓒ Ⓓ Ⓔ
79 Ⓐ Ⓑ Ⓒ Ⓓ Ⓔ
80 Ⓐ Ⓑ Ⓒ Ⓓ Ⓔ

81 Ⓐ Ⓑ Ⓒ Ⓓ Ⓔ
82 Ⓐ Ⓑ Ⓒ Ⓓ Ⓔ
83 Ⓐ Ⓑ Ⓒ Ⓓ Ⓔ
84 Ⓐ Ⓑ Ⓒ Ⓓ Ⓔ
85 Ⓐ Ⓑ Ⓒ Ⓓ Ⓔ
86 Ⓐ Ⓑ Ⓒ Ⓓ Ⓔ
87 Ⓐ Ⓑ Ⓒ Ⓓ Ⓔ
88 Ⓐ Ⓑ Ⓒ Ⓓ Ⓔ

COMPLETE PRACTICE EXAM #6
Part B – Address Memory – Segment #5

Directions

In this segment, you are given five minutes to study the addresses. There are no questions to answer in this segment – it is a study period only. As before, the boxes are not reprinted here for your use. Instead, you are instructed to turn back to Address Memory Segment #1 and to spend five minutes studying the boxes displayed there. After studying for five minutes, turn to Segment #6 for directions on how to continue. Turn back to Segment #1 and begin studying when you are prepared to time yourself for precisely five minutes.

COMPLETE PRACTICE EXAM #6
Part B – Address Memory – Segment #6

You have five minutes to answer 88 questions. Try to answer from memory, but the boxes are shown if you need to refer to them. Mark your answers on the sample answer sheet at the bottom of the page. After completing this segment, turn to Segment #7 for further instructions. Begin when you are prepared to time yourself for precisely five minutes.

A	B	C
2100-2199 Micah Hodges 1900-1999 Hilo Wilson 7200-7299 Mose	1400-1499 Micah Doyle 2800-2899 Hilo Lloyd 2100-2199 Mose	1900-1999 Micah Bunker 7200-7299 Hilo Lyman 1400-1499 Mose

1. Wilson
2. 2800-2899 Micah
3. 7200-7299 Hilo
4. 2100-2199 Mose
5. Doyle
6. Hatch
7. 1900-1999 Hilo
8. 1400-1499 Mose

9. 1400-1499 Micah
10. Coburn
11. 2100-2199 Micah
12. 1900-1999 Micah
13. 7200-7299 Micah
14. Wilson
15. 1400-1499 Hilo
16. 2100-2199 Mose

17. 1900-1999 Mose
18. Bunker
19. 7200-7299 Hilo
20. Tunica
21. Hodges
22. 2100-2199 Hilo
23. 1400-1499 Hilo
24. 2800-2899 Hilo

25. Lyman
26. 2100-2199 Micah
27. 7200-7299 Mose
28. 2800-2899 Micah
29. 2100-2199 Hilo
30. Doyle
31. Lloyd
32. 7200-7299 Micah

33. 2100-2199 Mose
34. 2100-2199 Micah
35. 2800-2899 Mose
36. Beacon
37. 7200-7299 Hilo
38. 1900-1999 Mose
39. Lyman
40. Wilson

41. 1900-1999 Micah
42. 2100-2199 Hilo
43. Coburn
44. 1900-1999 Hilo
45. 1400-1499 Mose
46. 7200-7299 Hilo
47. Hodges
48. 2800-2899 Hilo

1 Ⓐ Ⓑ Ⓒ Ⓓ Ⓔ
2 Ⓐ Ⓑ Ⓒ Ⓓ Ⓔ
3 Ⓐ Ⓑ Ⓒ Ⓓ Ⓔ
4 Ⓐ Ⓑ Ⓒ Ⓓ Ⓔ
5 Ⓐ Ⓑ Ⓒ Ⓓ Ⓔ
6 Ⓐ Ⓑ Ⓒ Ⓓ Ⓔ
7 Ⓐ Ⓑ Ⓒ Ⓓ Ⓔ
8 Ⓐ Ⓑ Ⓒ Ⓓ Ⓔ

9 Ⓐ Ⓑ Ⓒ Ⓓ Ⓔ
10 Ⓐ Ⓑ Ⓒ Ⓓ Ⓔ
11 Ⓐ Ⓑ Ⓒ Ⓓ Ⓔ
12 Ⓐ Ⓑ Ⓒ Ⓓ Ⓔ
13 Ⓐ Ⓑ Ⓒ Ⓓ Ⓔ
14 Ⓐ Ⓑ Ⓒ Ⓓ Ⓔ
15 Ⓐ Ⓑ Ⓒ Ⓓ Ⓔ
16 Ⓐ Ⓑ Ⓒ Ⓓ Ⓔ

17 Ⓐ Ⓑ Ⓒ Ⓓ Ⓔ
18 Ⓐ Ⓑ Ⓒ Ⓓ Ⓔ
19 Ⓐ Ⓑ Ⓒ Ⓓ Ⓔ
20 Ⓐ Ⓑ Ⓒ Ⓓ Ⓔ
21 Ⓐ Ⓑ Ⓒ Ⓓ Ⓔ
22 Ⓐ Ⓑ Ⓒ Ⓓ Ⓔ
23 Ⓐ Ⓑ Ⓒ Ⓓ Ⓔ
24 Ⓐ Ⓑ Ⓒ Ⓓ Ⓔ

25 Ⓐ Ⓑ Ⓒ Ⓓ Ⓔ
26 Ⓐ Ⓑ Ⓒ Ⓓ Ⓔ
27 Ⓐ Ⓑ Ⓒ Ⓓ Ⓔ
28 Ⓐ Ⓑ Ⓒ Ⓓ Ⓔ
29 Ⓐ Ⓑ Ⓒ Ⓓ Ⓔ
30 Ⓐ Ⓑ Ⓒ Ⓓ Ⓔ
31 Ⓐ Ⓑ Ⓒ Ⓓ Ⓔ
32 Ⓐ Ⓑ Ⓒ Ⓓ Ⓔ

33 Ⓐ Ⓑ Ⓒ Ⓓ Ⓔ
34 Ⓐ Ⓑ Ⓒ Ⓓ Ⓔ
35 Ⓐ Ⓑ Ⓒ Ⓓ Ⓔ
36 Ⓐ Ⓑ Ⓒ Ⓓ Ⓔ
37 Ⓐ Ⓑ Ⓒ Ⓓ Ⓔ
38 Ⓐ Ⓑ Ⓒ Ⓓ Ⓔ
39 Ⓐ Ⓑ Ⓒ Ⓓ Ⓔ
40 Ⓐ Ⓑ Ⓒ Ⓓ Ⓔ

41 Ⓐ Ⓑ Ⓒ Ⓓ Ⓔ
42 Ⓐ Ⓑ Ⓒ Ⓓ Ⓔ
43 Ⓐ Ⓑ Ⓒ Ⓓ Ⓔ
44 Ⓐ Ⓑ Ⓒ Ⓓ Ⓔ
45 Ⓐ Ⓑ Ⓒ Ⓓ Ⓔ
46 Ⓐ Ⓑ Ⓒ Ⓓ Ⓔ
47 Ⓐ Ⓑ Ⓒ Ⓓ Ⓔ
48 Ⓐ Ⓑ Ⓒ Ⓓ Ⓔ

D

7200-7299 Micah
Tunica
2100-2199 Hilo
Coburn
2800-2899 Mose

E

2800-2899 Micah
Hatch
1400-1499 Hilo
Beacon
1900-1999 Mose

49. Lloyd
50. Tunica
51. Hatch
52. 7200-7299 Mose
53. 1400-1499 Hilo
54. Bunker
55. 2800-2899 Mose
56. 2100-2199 Micah

57. 2100-2199 Mose
58. 7200-7299 Micah
59. Beacon
60. 1400-1499 Micah
61. 2100-2199 Hilo
62. 1400-1499 Mose
63. Wilson
64. 2800-2899 Mose

65. 2100-2199 Mose
66. Beacon
67. 7200-7299 Hilo
68. Coburn
69. Hodges
70. 2100-2199 Hilo
71. 1400-1499 Hilo
72. 2800-2899 Hilo

73. Doyle
74. 1400-1499 Hilo
75. 1900-1999 Hilo
76. Lloyd
77. 7200-7299 Mose
78. Hatch
79. Lyman
80. 2800-2899 Mose

81. 1900-1999 Hilo
82. Bunker
83. 2800-2899 Micah
84. 1400-1499 Micah
85. Tunica
86. 1900-1999 Micah
87. 2100-2199 Mose
88. Coburn

49 Ⓐ Ⓑ Ⓒ Ⓓ Ⓔ
50 Ⓐ Ⓑ Ⓒ Ⓓ Ⓔ
51 Ⓐ Ⓑ Ⓒ Ⓓ Ⓔ
52 Ⓐ Ⓑ Ⓒ Ⓓ Ⓔ
53 Ⓐ Ⓑ Ⓒ Ⓓ Ⓔ
54 Ⓐ Ⓑ Ⓒ Ⓓ Ⓔ
55 Ⓐ Ⓑ Ⓒ Ⓓ Ⓔ
56 Ⓐ Ⓑ Ⓒ Ⓓ Ⓔ

57 Ⓐ Ⓑ Ⓒ Ⓓ Ⓔ
58 Ⓐ Ⓑ Ⓒ Ⓓ Ⓔ
59 Ⓐ Ⓑ Ⓒ Ⓓ Ⓔ
60 Ⓐ Ⓑ Ⓒ Ⓓ Ⓔ
61 Ⓐ Ⓑ Ⓒ Ⓓ Ⓔ
62 Ⓐ Ⓑ Ⓒ Ⓓ Ⓔ
63 Ⓐ Ⓑ Ⓒ Ⓓ Ⓔ
64 Ⓐ Ⓑ Ⓒ Ⓓ Ⓔ

65 Ⓐ Ⓑ Ⓒ Ⓓ Ⓔ
66 Ⓐ Ⓑ Ⓒ Ⓓ Ⓔ
67 Ⓐ Ⓑ Ⓒ Ⓓ Ⓔ
68 Ⓐ Ⓑ Ⓒ Ⓓ Ⓔ
69 Ⓐ Ⓑ Ⓒ Ⓓ Ⓔ
70 Ⓐ Ⓑ Ⓒ Ⓓ Ⓔ
71 Ⓐ Ⓑ Ⓒ Ⓓ Ⓔ
72 Ⓐ Ⓑ Ⓒ Ⓓ Ⓔ

73 Ⓐ Ⓑ Ⓒ Ⓓ Ⓔ
74 Ⓐ Ⓑ Ⓒ Ⓓ Ⓔ
75 Ⓐ Ⓑ Ⓒ Ⓓ Ⓔ
76 Ⓐ Ⓑ Ⓒ Ⓓ Ⓔ
77 Ⓐ Ⓑ Ⓒ Ⓓ Ⓔ
78 Ⓐ Ⓑ Ⓒ Ⓓ Ⓔ
79 Ⓐ Ⓑ Ⓒ Ⓓ Ⓔ
80 Ⓐ Ⓑ Ⓒ Ⓓ Ⓔ

81 Ⓐ Ⓑ Ⓒ Ⓓ Ⓔ
82 Ⓐ Ⓑ Ⓒ Ⓓ Ⓔ
83 Ⓐ Ⓑ Ⓒ Ⓓ Ⓔ
84 Ⓐ Ⓑ Ⓒ Ⓓ Ⓔ
85 Ⓐ Ⓑ Ⓒ Ⓓ Ⓔ
86 Ⓐ Ⓑ Ⓒ Ⓓ Ⓔ
87 Ⓐ Ⓑ Ⓒ Ⓓ Ⓔ
88 Ⓐ Ⓑ Ⓒ Ⓓ Ⓔ

COMPLETE PRACTICE EXAM #6
Part B – Address Memory – Segment #7

You have five minutes to answer 88 questions. You must answer from memory. The boxes are not shown. Mark your answers on the Complete Practice Exam Answer Sheet. After completing this segment, turn to the Number Series section for instructions on how to continue. Begin when you are prepared to time yourself for precisely five minutes.

1. 2800-2899 Mose
2. Hatch
3. Lloyd
4. 7200-7299 Micah
5. Lyman
6. 2800-2899 Micah
7. 1900-1999 Hilo
8. 1400-1499 Mose

9. 1900-1999 Micah
10. Tunica
11. 2100-2199 Micah
12. Coburn
13. Beacon
14. 7200-7299 Mose
15. 2100-2199 Hilo
16. 1400-1499 Micah

17. 2800-2899 Hilo
18. 1900-1999 Mose
19. Bunker
20. Hatch
21. Hodges
22. 2100-2199 Hilo
23. 2800-2899 Mose
24. Doyle

25. 1400-1499 Hilo
26. Wilson
27. 7200-7299 Hilo
28. Tunica
29. 1900-1999 Hilo
30. 7200-7299 Micah
31. 1400-1499 Mose
32. Lloyd

33. 1400-1499 Micah
34. 1900-1999 Hilo
35. 2100-2199 Mose
36. 1400-1499 Mose
37. Hatch
38. 2100-2199 Micah
39. 2800-2899 Hilo
40. 1900-1999 Micah

41. 2800-2899 Hilo
42. Lyman
43. 7200-7299 Mose
44. 2800-2899 Micah
45. 7200-7299 Hilo
46. Hodges
47. 1900-1999 Mose
48. Doyle

49. Lyman
50. 2100-2199 Hilo
51. Wilson
52. 1900-1999 Mose
53. 2100-2199 Micah
54. Bunker
55. 2800-2899 Micah
56. 1400-1499 Micah

57. 2100-2199 Hilo
58. 2800-2899 Hilo
59. Beacon
60. Hodges
61. 1400-1499 Hilo
62. 2100-2199 Mose
63. Coburn
64. Doyle

65. 7200-7299 Hilo
66. Hodges
67. Beacon
68. Tunica
69. 1900-1999 Hilo
70. 2800-2899 Mose
71. 2100-2199 Mose
72. Bunker

73. Lloyd
74. 7200-7299 Micah
75. 2100-2199 Hilo
76. 2100-2199 Micah
77. Hatch
78. 1900-1999 Micah
79. 1400-1499 Hilo
80. 7200-7299 Mose

81. 2100-2199 Mose
82. 2800-2899 Mose
83. Lyman
84. Beacon
85. 1400-1499 Hilo
86. Wilson
87. Coburn
88. 1400-1499 Mose

COMPLETE PRACTICE EXAM #6
Part C – Number Series

You have 20 minutes to answer 24 questions. Each question is a series of numbers followed by two blanks. You are to find which two numbers would logically follow in the series. Mark your answers on the Complete Practice Exam Answer Sheet. After completing this section, turn to the Following Oral Instructions section. Begin when you are prepared to time yourself for precisely 20 minutes.

1. 14 15 16 17 18 19 ___ ___   (A) 20,23 (B) 22,23 (C) 20,21 (D) 19,20 (E) 21,22

2. 26 28 30 32 34 36 ___ ___   (A) 36,38 (B) 37,38 (C) 40,42 (D) 38,42 (E) 38,40

3. 3 6 13 16 23 ___ ___   (A) 26,33 (B) 25,32 (C) 26,35 (D) 27,36 (E) 28,37

4. 3 4 4 6 5 8 6 ___ ___   (A) 10,9 (B) 12,7 (C) 10,8 (D) 10,7 (E) 11,12

5. 29 25 10 12 21 17 14 ___ ___   (A) 15,12 (B) 16,13 (C) 17,14 (D) 18,15 (E) 19,20

6. 15 40 20 30 25 20 ___ ___   (A) 20,20 (B) 20,10 (C) 30,20 (D) 40,10 (E) 30,10

7. 6 12 35 18 24 25 30 ___ ___   (A) 37,16 (B) 35,15 (C) 36,15 (D) 30,10 (E) 34,15

8. 9 9 5 9 9 10 9 ___ ___   (A) 9,15 (B) 10,15 (C) 9,20 (D) 9,17 (E) 15,9

9. 6 7 9 10 12 13 15 ___ ___   (A) 15,17 (B) 16,18 (C) 17,19 (D) 15,16 (E) 16,17

10. 6 5 8 7 10 9 12 ___ ___   (A) 10,13 (B) 12,14 (C) 13,14 (D) 11,14 (E) 11,15

11. 5 5 3 5 5 4 5 5 ___ ___   (A) 5,6 (B) 6,5 (C) 5,5 (D) 5,4 (E) 5,7

12. 20 17 10 10 14 11 10 10 ___ ___   (A) 9,7 (B) 6,7 (C) 9,4 (D) 8,6 (E) 8,5

13. 2 15 28 41 ___ ___   (A) 54,67 (B) 55,68 (C) 53,66 (D) 55,68 (E) 62,71

14. 75 10 65 20 55 30 ___ ___   (A) 45,30 (B) 45,40 (C) 40,45 (D) 55,30 (E) 35,40

15. 90 60 80 70 70 80 ___ ___   (A) 50,90 (B) 40,90 (C) 70,90 (D) 60,90 (E) 50.80

16. 34 32 34 33 34 34 ___ ___   (A) 33,36 (B) 34,34 (C) 34,36 (D) 35,35 (E) 34,35

17. 8 5 7 16 9 11 24 ___ ___   (A) 12,14 (B) 11,14 (C) 13,15 (D) 14,15 (E) 12,13

18. 14 19 16 18 18 17 20 16 ___ ___   (A) 20,13 (B) 22,15 (C) 24,17 (D) 22,16 (E) 23,15

19. 7 3 6 14 9 12 21 15 ___ ___   (A) 20,27 (B) 22,29 (C) 18,27 (D) 18,28 (E) 23,28

20. 8 3 11 8 14 13 17 18 ___ ___   (A) 20,23 (B) 20,24 (C) 21,23 (D) 22,24 (E) 24,26

21. 2 4 0 6 8 0 10 ___ ___   (A) 0,14 (B) 0,10 (C) 12,10 (D) 12,14 (E) 12,0

22. 8 8 10 8 8 9 8 ___ ___   (A) 8,7 (B) 8,8 (C) 8,6 (D) 9,8 (E) 8,9

23. 47 39 31 23 ___ ___   (A) 16,7 (B) 15,8 (C) 15,7 (D) 14,7 (E) 13,6

24. 5 6 8 11 15 20 ___ ___   (A) 25,34 (B) 27,35 (C) 26,35 (D) 25,31 (E) 26,33

COMPLETE PRACTICE EXAM #6
Part D – Following Oral Instructions

On this section, questions/instructions are presented verbally that lead you to the correct answers. Mark your answers on the Complete Practice Exam Answer Sheet. When you complete the Following Oral Instructions section, you have finished the complete practice exam. Begin when you are prepared to listen to the questions from the author's recording or from someone who will read them to you.

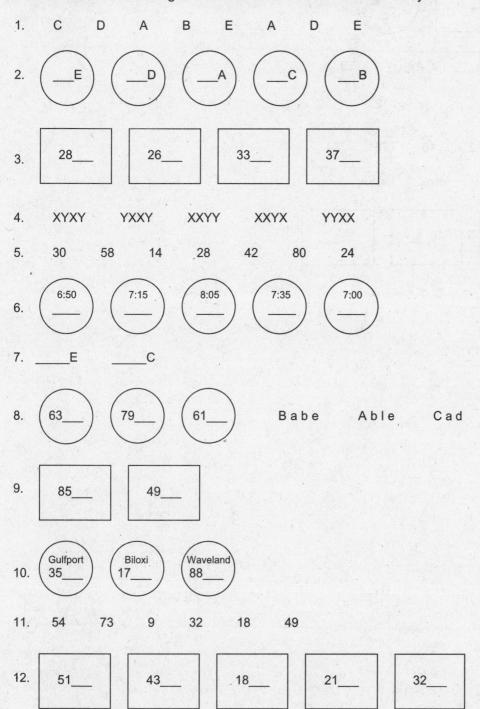

1.   C   D   A   B   E   A   D   E

2.   (__E)   (__D)   (__A)   (__C)   (__B)

3.   [28__]   [26__]   [33__]   [37__]

4.   XYXY   YXXY   XXYY   XXYX   YYXX

5.   30   58   14   28   42   80   24

6.   (6:50 __)   (7:15 __)   (8:05 __)   (7:35 __)   (7:00 __)

7.   ___E   ___C

8.   (63__)   (79__)   (61__)   Babe   Able   Cad

9.   [85__]   [49__]

10.   (Gulfport 35__)   (Biloxi 17__)   (Waveland 88__)

11.   54   73   9   32   18   49

12.   [51__]   [43__]   [18__]   [21__]   [32__]

13.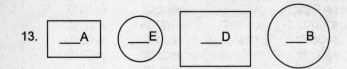
    ___A   ___E   ___D   ___B

14.   51___   32___   78___   12___   29___

15.   A D D I C T E D
        ___   ___   ___   ___

16.   62   64   86   32   16   75   84   81   26

17.   ooxx   xxoo   xoxo   oxox   xxxx

18.   23___   82___   48___   23___

19.   48___   39___   52___

ANSWER SHEET

Address Checking - Part A

1 Ⓐ Ⓓ	13 Ⓐ Ⓓ	25 Ⓐ Ⓓ	37 Ⓐ Ⓓ	49 Ⓐ Ⓓ	61 Ⓐ Ⓓ	73 Ⓐ Ⓓ	85 Ⓐ Ⓓ
2 Ⓐ Ⓓ	14 Ⓐ Ⓓ	26 Ⓐ Ⓓ	38 Ⓐ Ⓓ	50 Ⓐ Ⓓ	62 Ⓐ Ⓓ	74 Ⓐ Ⓓ	86 Ⓐ Ⓓ
3 Ⓐ Ⓓ	15 Ⓐ Ⓓ	27 Ⓐ Ⓓ	39 Ⓐ Ⓓ	51 Ⓐ Ⓓ	63 Ⓐ Ⓓ	75 Ⓐ Ⓓ	87 Ⓐ Ⓓ
4 Ⓐ Ⓓ	16 Ⓐ Ⓓ	28 Ⓐ Ⓓ	40 Ⓐ Ⓓ	52 Ⓐ Ⓓ	64 Ⓐ Ⓓ	76 Ⓐ Ⓓ	88 Ⓐ Ⓓ
5 Ⓐ Ⓓ	17 Ⓐ Ⓓ	29 Ⓐ Ⓓ	41 Ⓐ Ⓓ	53 Ⓐ Ⓓ	65 Ⓐ Ⓓ	77 Ⓐ Ⓓ	89 Ⓐ Ⓓ
6 Ⓐ Ⓓ	18 Ⓐ Ⓓ	30 Ⓐ Ⓓ	42 Ⓐ Ⓓ	54 Ⓐ Ⓓ	66 Ⓐ Ⓓ	78 Ⓐ Ⓓ	90 Ⓐ Ⓓ
7 Ⓐ Ⓓ	19 Ⓐ Ⓓ	31 Ⓐ Ⓓ	43 Ⓐ Ⓓ	55 Ⓐ Ⓓ	67 Ⓐ Ⓓ	79 Ⓐ Ⓓ	91 Ⓐ Ⓓ
8 Ⓐ Ⓓ	20 Ⓐ Ⓓ	32 Ⓐ Ⓓ	44 Ⓐ Ⓓ	56 Ⓐ Ⓓ	68 Ⓐ Ⓓ	80 Ⓐ Ⓓ	92 Ⓐ Ⓓ
9 Ⓐ Ⓓ	21 Ⓐ Ⓓ	33 Ⓐ Ⓓ	45 Ⓐ Ⓓ	57 Ⓐ Ⓓ	69 Ⓐ Ⓓ	81 Ⓐ Ⓓ	93 Ⓐ Ⓓ
10 Ⓐ Ⓓ	22 Ⓐ Ⓓ	34 Ⓐ Ⓓ	46 Ⓐ Ⓓ	58 Ⓐ Ⓓ	70 Ⓐ Ⓓ	82 Ⓐ Ⓓ	94 Ⓐ Ⓓ
11 Ⓐ Ⓓ	23 Ⓐ Ⓓ	35 Ⓐ Ⓓ	47 Ⓐ Ⓓ	59 Ⓐ Ⓓ	71 Ⓐ Ⓓ	83 Ⓐ Ⓓ	95 Ⓐ Ⓓ
12 Ⓐ Ⓓ	24 Ⓐ Ⓓ	36 Ⓐ Ⓓ	48 Ⓐ Ⓓ	60 Ⓐ Ⓓ	72 Ⓐ Ⓓ	84 Ⓐ Ⓓ	

Address Memory - Part B

1 Ⓐ Ⓑ Ⓒ Ⓓ Ⓔ	19 Ⓐ Ⓑ Ⓒ Ⓓ Ⓔ	37 Ⓐ Ⓑ Ⓒ Ⓓ Ⓔ	55 Ⓐ Ⓑ Ⓒ Ⓓ Ⓔ	73 Ⓐ Ⓑ Ⓒ Ⓓ Ⓔ
2 Ⓐ Ⓑ Ⓒ Ⓓ Ⓔ	20 Ⓐ Ⓑ Ⓒ Ⓓ Ⓔ	38 Ⓐ Ⓑ Ⓒ Ⓓ Ⓔ	56 Ⓐ Ⓑ Ⓒ Ⓓ Ⓔ	74 Ⓐ Ⓑ Ⓒ Ⓓ Ⓔ
3 Ⓐ Ⓑ Ⓒ Ⓓ Ⓔ	21 Ⓐ Ⓑ Ⓒ Ⓓ Ⓔ	39 Ⓐ Ⓑ Ⓒ Ⓓ Ⓔ	57 Ⓐ Ⓑ Ⓒ Ⓓ Ⓔ	75 Ⓐ Ⓑ Ⓒ Ⓓ Ⓔ
4 Ⓐ Ⓑ Ⓒ Ⓓ Ⓔ	22 Ⓐ Ⓑ Ⓒ Ⓓ Ⓔ	40 Ⓐ Ⓑ Ⓒ Ⓓ Ⓔ	58 Ⓐ Ⓑ Ⓒ Ⓓ Ⓔ	76 Ⓐ Ⓑ Ⓒ Ⓓ Ⓔ
5 Ⓐ Ⓑ Ⓒ Ⓓ Ⓔ	23 Ⓐ Ⓑ Ⓒ Ⓓ Ⓔ	41 Ⓐ Ⓑ Ⓒ Ⓓ Ⓔ	59 Ⓐ Ⓑ Ⓒ Ⓓ Ⓔ	77 Ⓐ Ⓑ Ⓒ Ⓓ Ⓔ
6 Ⓐ Ⓑ Ⓒ Ⓓ Ⓔ	24 Ⓐ Ⓑ Ⓒ Ⓓ Ⓔ	42 Ⓐ Ⓑ Ⓒ Ⓓ Ⓔ	60 Ⓐ Ⓑ Ⓒ Ⓓ Ⓔ	78 Ⓐ Ⓑ Ⓒ Ⓓ Ⓔ
7 Ⓐ Ⓑ Ⓒ Ⓓ Ⓔ	25 Ⓐ Ⓑ Ⓒ Ⓓ Ⓔ	43 Ⓐ Ⓑ Ⓒ Ⓓ Ⓔ	61 Ⓐ Ⓑ Ⓒ Ⓓ Ⓔ	79 Ⓐ Ⓑ Ⓒ Ⓓ Ⓔ
8 Ⓐ Ⓑ Ⓒ Ⓓ Ⓔ	26 Ⓐ Ⓑ Ⓒ Ⓓ Ⓔ	44 Ⓐ Ⓑ Ⓒ Ⓓ Ⓔ	62 Ⓐ Ⓑ Ⓒ Ⓓ Ⓔ	80 Ⓐ Ⓑ Ⓒ Ⓓ Ⓔ
9 Ⓐ Ⓑ Ⓒ Ⓓ Ⓔ	27 Ⓐ Ⓑ Ⓒ Ⓓ Ⓔ	45 Ⓐ Ⓑ Ⓒ Ⓓ Ⓔ	63 Ⓐ Ⓑ Ⓒ Ⓓ Ⓔ	81 Ⓐ Ⓑ Ⓒ Ⓓ Ⓔ
10 Ⓐ Ⓑ Ⓒ Ⓓ Ⓔ	28 Ⓐ Ⓑ Ⓒ Ⓓ Ⓔ	46 Ⓐ Ⓑ Ⓒ Ⓓ Ⓔ	64 Ⓐ Ⓑ Ⓒ Ⓓ Ⓔ	82 Ⓐ Ⓑ Ⓒ Ⓓ Ⓔ
11 Ⓐ Ⓑ Ⓒ Ⓓ Ⓔ	29 Ⓐ Ⓑ Ⓒ Ⓓ Ⓔ	47 Ⓐ Ⓑ Ⓒ Ⓓ Ⓔ	65 Ⓐ Ⓑ Ⓒ Ⓓ Ⓔ	83 Ⓐ Ⓑ Ⓒ Ⓓ Ⓔ
12 Ⓐ Ⓑ Ⓒ Ⓓ Ⓔ	30 Ⓐ Ⓑ Ⓒ Ⓓ Ⓔ	48 Ⓐ Ⓑ Ⓒ Ⓓ Ⓔ	66 Ⓐ Ⓑ Ⓒ Ⓓ Ⓔ	84 Ⓐ Ⓑ Ⓒ Ⓓ Ⓔ
13 Ⓐ Ⓑ Ⓒ Ⓓ Ⓔ	31 Ⓐ Ⓑ Ⓒ Ⓓ Ⓔ	49 Ⓐ Ⓑ Ⓒ Ⓓ Ⓔ	67 Ⓐ Ⓑ Ⓒ Ⓓ Ⓔ	85 Ⓐ Ⓑ Ⓒ Ⓓ Ⓔ
14 Ⓐ Ⓑ Ⓒ Ⓓ Ⓔ	32 Ⓐ Ⓑ Ⓒ Ⓓ Ⓔ	50 Ⓐ Ⓑ Ⓒ Ⓓ Ⓔ	68 Ⓐ Ⓑ Ⓒ Ⓓ Ⓔ	86 Ⓐ Ⓑ Ⓒ Ⓓ Ⓔ
15 Ⓐ Ⓑ Ⓒ Ⓓ Ⓔ	33 Ⓐ Ⓑ Ⓒ Ⓓ Ⓔ	51 Ⓐ Ⓑ Ⓒ Ⓓ Ⓔ	69 Ⓐ Ⓑ Ⓒ Ⓓ Ⓔ	87 Ⓐ Ⓑ Ⓒ Ⓓ Ⓔ
16 Ⓐ Ⓑ Ⓒ Ⓓ Ⓔ	34 Ⓐ Ⓑ Ⓒ Ⓓ Ⓔ	52 Ⓐ Ⓑ Ⓒ Ⓓ Ⓔ	70 Ⓐ Ⓑ Ⓒ Ⓓ Ⓔ	88 Ⓐ Ⓑ Ⓒ Ⓓ Ⓔ
17 Ⓐ Ⓑ Ⓒ Ⓓ Ⓔ	35 Ⓐ Ⓑ Ⓒ Ⓓ Ⓔ	53 Ⓐ Ⓑ Ⓒ Ⓓ Ⓔ	71 Ⓐ Ⓑ Ⓒ Ⓓ Ⓔ	
18 Ⓐ Ⓑ Ⓒ Ⓓ Ⓔ	36 Ⓐ Ⓑ Ⓒ Ⓓ Ⓔ	54 Ⓐ Ⓑ Ⓒ Ⓓ Ⓔ	72 Ⓐ Ⓑ Ⓒ Ⓓ Ⓔ	

Number Series - Part C

1 Ⓐ Ⓑ Ⓒ Ⓓ Ⓔ	7 Ⓐ Ⓑ Ⓒ Ⓓ Ⓔ	13 Ⓐ Ⓑ Ⓒ Ⓓ Ⓔ	19 Ⓐ Ⓑ Ⓒ Ⓓ Ⓔ
2 Ⓐ Ⓑ Ⓒ Ⓓ Ⓔ	8 Ⓐ Ⓑ Ⓒ Ⓓ Ⓔ	14 Ⓐ Ⓑ Ⓒ Ⓓ Ⓔ	20 Ⓐ Ⓑ Ⓒ Ⓓ Ⓔ
3 Ⓐ Ⓑ Ⓒ Ⓓ Ⓔ	9 Ⓐ Ⓑ Ⓒ Ⓓ Ⓔ	15 Ⓐ Ⓑ Ⓒ Ⓓ Ⓔ	21 Ⓐ Ⓑ Ⓒ Ⓓ Ⓔ
4 Ⓐ Ⓑ Ⓒ Ⓓ Ⓔ	10 Ⓐ Ⓑ Ⓒ Ⓓ Ⓔ	16 Ⓐ Ⓑ Ⓒ Ⓓ Ⓔ	22 Ⓐ Ⓑ Ⓒ Ⓓ Ⓔ
5 Ⓐ Ⓑ Ⓒ Ⓓ Ⓔ	11 Ⓐ Ⓑ Ⓒ Ⓓ Ⓔ	17 Ⓐ Ⓑ Ⓒ Ⓓ Ⓔ	23 Ⓐ Ⓑ Ⓒ Ⓓ Ⓔ
6 Ⓐ Ⓑ Ⓒ Ⓓ Ⓔ	12 Ⓐ Ⓑ Ⓒ Ⓓ Ⓔ	18 Ⓐ Ⓑ Ⓒ Ⓓ Ⓔ	24 Ⓐ Ⓑ Ⓒ Ⓓ Ⓔ

Following Oral Instructions - Part D

1 Ⓐ Ⓑ Ⓒ Ⓓ Ⓔ	19 Ⓐ Ⓑ Ⓒ Ⓓ Ⓔ	37 Ⓐ Ⓑ Ⓒ Ⓓ Ⓔ	55 Ⓐ Ⓑ Ⓒ Ⓓ Ⓔ	73 Ⓐ Ⓑ Ⓒ Ⓓ Ⓔ
2 Ⓐ Ⓑ Ⓒ Ⓓ Ⓔ	20 Ⓐ Ⓑ Ⓒ Ⓓ Ⓔ	38 Ⓐ Ⓑ Ⓒ Ⓓ Ⓔ	56 Ⓐ Ⓑ Ⓒ Ⓓ Ⓔ	74 Ⓐ Ⓑ Ⓒ Ⓓ Ⓔ
3 Ⓐ Ⓑ Ⓒ Ⓓ Ⓔ	21 Ⓐ Ⓑ Ⓒ Ⓓ Ⓔ	39 Ⓐ Ⓑ Ⓒ Ⓓ Ⓔ	57 Ⓐ Ⓑ Ⓒ Ⓓ Ⓔ	75 Ⓐ Ⓑ Ⓒ Ⓓ Ⓔ
4 Ⓐ Ⓑ Ⓒ Ⓓ Ⓔ	22 Ⓐ Ⓑ Ⓒ Ⓓ Ⓔ	40 Ⓐ Ⓑ Ⓒ Ⓓ Ⓔ	58 Ⓐ Ⓑ Ⓒ Ⓓ Ⓔ	76 Ⓐ Ⓑ Ⓒ Ⓓ Ⓔ
5 Ⓐ Ⓑ Ⓒ Ⓓ Ⓔ	23 Ⓐ Ⓑ Ⓒ Ⓓ Ⓔ	41 Ⓐ Ⓑ Ⓒ Ⓓ Ⓔ	59 Ⓐ Ⓑ Ⓒ Ⓓ Ⓔ	77 Ⓐ Ⓑ Ⓒ Ⓓ Ⓔ
6 Ⓐ Ⓑ Ⓒ Ⓓ Ⓔ	24 Ⓐ Ⓑ Ⓒ Ⓓ Ⓔ	42 Ⓐ Ⓑ Ⓒ Ⓓ Ⓔ	60 Ⓐ Ⓑ Ⓒ Ⓓ Ⓔ	78 Ⓐ Ⓑ Ⓒ Ⓓ Ⓔ
7 Ⓐ Ⓑ Ⓒ Ⓓ Ⓔ	25 Ⓐ Ⓑ Ⓒ Ⓓ Ⓔ	43 Ⓐ Ⓑ Ⓒ Ⓓ Ⓔ	61 Ⓐ Ⓑ Ⓒ Ⓓ Ⓔ	79 Ⓐ Ⓑ Ⓒ Ⓓ Ⓔ
8 Ⓐ Ⓑ Ⓒ Ⓓ Ⓔ	26 Ⓐ Ⓑ Ⓒ Ⓓ Ⓔ	44 Ⓐ Ⓑ Ⓒ Ⓓ Ⓔ	62 Ⓐ Ⓑ Ⓒ Ⓓ Ⓔ	80 Ⓐ Ⓑ Ⓒ Ⓓ Ⓔ
9 Ⓐ Ⓑ Ⓒ Ⓓ Ⓔ	27 Ⓐ Ⓑ Ⓒ Ⓓ Ⓔ	45 Ⓐ Ⓑ Ⓒ Ⓓ Ⓔ	63 Ⓐ Ⓑ Ⓒ Ⓓ Ⓔ	81 Ⓐ Ⓑ Ⓒ Ⓓ Ⓔ
10 Ⓐ Ⓑ Ⓒ Ⓓ Ⓔ	28 Ⓐ Ⓑ Ⓒ Ⓓ Ⓔ	46 Ⓐ Ⓑ Ⓒ Ⓓ Ⓔ	64 Ⓐ Ⓑ Ⓒ Ⓓ Ⓔ	82 Ⓐ Ⓑ Ⓒ Ⓓ Ⓔ
11 Ⓐ Ⓑ Ⓒ Ⓓ Ⓔ	29 Ⓐ Ⓑ Ⓒ Ⓓ Ⓔ	47 Ⓐ Ⓑ Ⓒ Ⓓ Ⓔ	65 Ⓐ Ⓑ Ⓒ Ⓓ Ⓔ	83 Ⓐ Ⓑ Ⓒ Ⓓ Ⓔ
12 Ⓐ Ⓑ Ⓒ Ⓓ Ⓔ	30 Ⓐ Ⓑ Ⓒ Ⓓ Ⓔ	48 Ⓐ Ⓑ Ⓒ Ⓓ Ⓔ	66 Ⓐ Ⓑ Ⓒ Ⓓ Ⓔ	84 Ⓐ Ⓑ Ⓒ Ⓓ Ⓔ
13 Ⓐ Ⓑ Ⓒ Ⓓ Ⓔ	31 Ⓐ Ⓑ Ⓒ Ⓓ Ⓔ	49 Ⓐ Ⓑ Ⓒ Ⓓ Ⓔ	67 Ⓐ Ⓑ Ⓒ Ⓓ Ⓔ	85 Ⓐ Ⓑ Ⓒ Ⓓ Ⓔ
14 Ⓐ Ⓑ Ⓒ Ⓓ Ⓔ	32 Ⓐ Ⓑ Ⓒ Ⓓ Ⓔ	50 Ⓐ Ⓑ Ⓒ Ⓓ Ⓔ	68 Ⓐ Ⓑ Ⓒ Ⓓ Ⓔ	86 Ⓐ Ⓑ Ⓒ Ⓓ Ⓔ
15 Ⓐ Ⓑ Ⓒ Ⓓ Ⓔ	33 Ⓐ Ⓑ Ⓒ Ⓓ Ⓔ	51 Ⓐ Ⓑ Ⓒ Ⓓ Ⓔ	69 Ⓐ Ⓑ Ⓒ Ⓓ Ⓔ	87 Ⓐ Ⓑ Ⓒ Ⓓ Ⓔ
16 Ⓐ Ⓑ Ⓒ Ⓓ Ⓔ	34 Ⓐ Ⓑ Ⓒ Ⓓ Ⓔ	52 Ⓐ Ⓑ Ⓒ Ⓓ Ⓔ	70 Ⓐ Ⓑ Ⓒ Ⓓ Ⓔ	88 Ⓐ Ⓑ Ⓒ Ⓓ Ⓔ
17 Ⓐ Ⓑ Ⓒ Ⓓ Ⓔ	35 Ⓐ Ⓑ Ⓒ Ⓓ Ⓔ	53 Ⓐ Ⓑ Ⓒ Ⓓ Ⓔ	71 Ⓐ Ⓑ Ⓒ Ⓓ Ⓔ	
18 Ⓐ Ⓑ Ⓒ Ⓓ Ⓔ	36 Ⓐ Ⓑ Ⓒ Ⓓ Ⓔ	54 Ⓐ Ⓑ Ⓒ Ⓓ Ⓔ	72 Ⓐ Ⓑ Ⓒ Ⓓ Ⓔ	

206

ANSWER SHEET

Address Checking - Part A

1 Ⓐ Ⓓ	13 Ⓐ Ⓓ	25 Ⓐ Ⓓ	37 Ⓐ Ⓓ	49 Ⓐ Ⓓ	61 Ⓐ Ⓓ	73 Ⓐ Ⓓ	85 Ⓐ Ⓓ
2 Ⓐ Ⓓ	14 Ⓐ Ⓓ	26 Ⓐ Ⓓ	38 Ⓐ Ⓓ	50 Ⓐ Ⓓ	62 Ⓐ Ⓓ	74 Ⓐ Ⓓ	86 Ⓐ Ⓓ
3 Ⓐ Ⓓ	15 Ⓐ Ⓓ	27 Ⓐ Ⓓ	39 Ⓐ Ⓓ	51 Ⓐ Ⓓ	63 Ⓐ Ⓓ	75 Ⓐ Ⓓ	87 Ⓐ Ⓓ
4 Ⓐ Ⓓ	16 Ⓐ Ⓓ	28 Ⓐ Ⓓ	40 Ⓐ Ⓓ	52 Ⓐ Ⓓ	64 Ⓐ Ⓓ	76 Ⓐ Ⓓ	88 Ⓐ Ⓓ
5 Ⓐ Ⓓ	17 Ⓐ Ⓓ	29 Ⓐ Ⓓ	41 Ⓐ Ⓓ	53 Ⓐ Ⓓ	65 Ⓐ Ⓓ	77 Ⓐ Ⓓ	89 Ⓐ Ⓓ
6 Ⓐ Ⓓ	18 Ⓐ Ⓓ	30 Ⓐ Ⓓ	42 Ⓐ Ⓓ	54 Ⓐ Ⓓ	66 Ⓐ Ⓓ	78 Ⓐ Ⓓ	90 Ⓐ Ⓓ
7 Ⓐ Ⓓ	19 Ⓐ Ⓓ	31 Ⓐ Ⓓ	43 Ⓐ Ⓓ	55 Ⓐ Ⓓ	67 Ⓐ Ⓓ	79 Ⓐ Ⓓ	91 Ⓐ Ⓓ
8 Ⓐ Ⓓ	20 Ⓐ Ⓓ	32 Ⓐ Ⓓ	44 Ⓐ Ⓓ	56 Ⓐ Ⓓ	68 Ⓐ Ⓓ	80 Ⓐ Ⓓ	92 Ⓐ Ⓓ
9 Ⓐ Ⓓ	21 Ⓐ Ⓓ	33 Ⓐ Ⓓ	45 Ⓐ Ⓓ	57 Ⓐ Ⓓ	69 Ⓐ Ⓓ	81 Ⓐ Ⓓ	93 Ⓐ Ⓓ
10 Ⓐ Ⓓ	22 Ⓐ Ⓓ	34 Ⓐ Ⓓ	46 Ⓐ Ⓓ	58 Ⓐ Ⓓ	70 Ⓐ Ⓓ	82 Ⓐ Ⓓ	94 Ⓐ Ⓓ
11 Ⓐ Ⓓ	23 Ⓐ Ⓓ	35 Ⓐ Ⓓ	47 Ⓐ Ⓓ	59 Ⓐ Ⓓ	71 Ⓐ Ⓓ	83 Ⓐ Ⓓ	95 Ⓐ Ⓓ
12 Ⓐ Ⓓ	24 Ⓐ Ⓓ	36 Ⓐ Ⓓ	48 Ⓐ Ⓓ	60 Ⓐ Ⓓ	72 Ⓐ Ⓓ	84 Ⓐ Ⓓ	

Address Memory - Part B

1 Ⓐ Ⓑ Ⓒ Ⓓ Ⓔ	19 Ⓐ Ⓑ Ⓒ Ⓓ Ⓔ	37 Ⓐ Ⓑ Ⓒ Ⓓ Ⓔ	55 Ⓐ Ⓑ Ⓒ Ⓓ Ⓔ	73 Ⓐ Ⓑ Ⓒ Ⓓ Ⓔ
2 Ⓐ Ⓑ Ⓒ Ⓓ Ⓔ	20 Ⓐ Ⓑ Ⓒ Ⓓ Ⓔ	38 Ⓐ Ⓑ Ⓒ Ⓓ Ⓔ	56 Ⓐ Ⓑ Ⓒ Ⓓ Ⓔ	74 Ⓐ Ⓑ Ⓒ Ⓓ Ⓔ
3 Ⓐ Ⓑ Ⓒ Ⓓ Ⓔ	21 Ⓐ Ⓑ Ⓒ Ⓓ Ⓔ	39 Ⓐ Ⓑ Ⓒ Ⓓ Ⓔ	57 Ⓐ Ⓑ Ⓒ Ⓓ Ⓔ	75 Ⓐ Ⓑ Ⓒ Ⓓ Ⓔ
4 Ⓐ Ⓑ Ⓒ Ⓓ Ⓔ	22 Ⓐ Ⓑ Ⓒ Ⓓ Ⓔ	40 Ⓐ Ⓑ Ⓒ Ⓓ Ⓔ	58 Ⓐ Ⓑ Ⓒ Ⓓ Ⓔ	76 Ⓐ Ⓑ Ⓒ Ⓓ Ⓔ
5 Ⓐ Ⓑ Ⓒ Ⓓ Ⓔ	23 Ⓐ Ⓑ Ⓒ Ⓓ Ⓔ	41 Ⓐ Ⓑ Ⓒ Ⓓ Ⓔ	59 Ⓐ Ⓑ Ⓒ Ⓓ Ⓔ	77 Ⓐ Ⓑ Ⓒ Ⓓ Ⓔ
6 Ⓐ Ⓑ Ⓒ Ⓓ Ⓔ	24 Ⓐ Ⓑ Ⓒ Ⓓ Ⓔ	42 Ⓐ Ⓑ Ⓒ Ⓓ Ⓔ	60 Ⓐ Ⓑ Ⓒ Ⓓ Ⓔ	78 Ⓐ Ⓑ Ⓒ Ⓓ Ⓔ
7 Ⓐ Ⓑ Ⓒ Ⓓ Ⓔ	25 Ⓐ Ⓑ Ⓒ Ⓓ Ⓔ	43 Ⓐ Ⓑ Ⓒ Ⓓ Ⓔ	61 Ⓐ Ⓑ Ⓒ Ⓓ Ⓔ	79 Ⓐ Ⓑ Ⓒ Ⓓ Ⓔ
8 Ⓐ Ⓑ Ⓒ Ⓓ Ⓔ	26 Ⓐ Ⓑ Ⓒ Ⓓ Ⓔ	44 Ⓐ Ⓑ Ⓒ Ⓓ Ⓔ	62 Ⓐ Ⓑ Ⓒ Ⓓ Ⓔ	80 Ⓐ Ⓑ Ⓒ Ⓓ Ⓔ
9 Ⓐ Ⓑ Ⓒ Ⓓ Ⓔ	27 Ⓐ Ⓑ Ⓒ Ⓓ Ⓔ	45 Ⓐ Ⓑ Ⓒ Ⓓ Ⓔ	63 Ⓐ Ⓑ Ⓒ Ⓓ Ⓔ	81 Ⓐ Ⓑ Ⓒ Ⓓ Ⓔ
10 Ⓐ Ⓑ Ⓒ Ⓓ Ⓔ	28 Ⓐ Ⓑ Ⓒ Ⓓ Ⓔ	46 Ⓐ Ⓑ Ⓒ Ⓓ Ⓔ	64 Ⓐ Ⓑ Ⓒ Ⓓ Ⓔ	82 Ⓐ Ⓑ Ⓒ Ⓓ Ⓔ
11 Ⓐ Ⓑ Ⓒ Ⓓ Ⓔ	29 Ⓐ Ⓑ Ⓒ Ⓓ Ⓔ	47 Ⓐ Ⓑ Ⓒ Ⓓ Ⓔ	65 Ⓐ Ⓑ Ⓒ Ⓓ Ⓔ	83 Ⓐ Ⓑ Ⓒ Ⓓ Ⓔ
12 Ⓐ Ⓑ Ⓒ Ⓓ Ⓔ	30 Ⓐ Ⓑ Ⓒ Ⓓ Ⓔ	48 Ⓐ Ⓑ Ⓒ Ⓓ Ⓔ	66 Ⓐ Ⓑ Ⓒ Ⓓ Ⓔ	84 Ⓐ Ⓑ Ⓒ Ⓓ Ⓔ
13 Ⓐ Ⓑ Ⓒ Ⓓ Ⓔ	31 Ⓐ Ⓑ Ⓒ Ⓓ Ⓔ	49 Ⓐ Ⓑ Ⓒ Ⓓ Ⓔ	67 Ⓐ Ⓑ Ⓒ Ⓓ Ⓔ	85 Ⓐ Ⓑ Ⓒ Ⓓ Ⓔ
14 Ⓐ Ⓑ Ⓒ Ⓓ Ⓔ	32 Ⓐ Ⓑ Ⓒ Ⓓ Ⓔ	50 Ⓐ Ⓑ Ⓒ Ⓓ Ⓔ	68 Ⓐ Ⓑ Ⓒ Ⓓ Ⓔ	86 Ⓐ Ⓑ Ⓒ Ⓓ Ⓔ
15 Ⓐ Ⓑ Ⓒ Ⓓ Ⓔ	33 Ⓐ Ⓑ Ⓒ Ⓓ Ⓔ	51 Ⓐ Ⓑ Ⓒ Ⓓ Ⓔ	69 Ⓐ Ⓑ Ⓒ Ⓓ Ⓔ	87 Ⓐ Ⓑ Ⓒ Ⓓ Ⓔ
16 Ⓐ Ⓑ Ⓒ Ⓓ Ⓔ	34 Ⓐ Ⓑ Ⓒ Ⓓ Ⓔ	52 Ⓐ Ⓑ Ⓒ Ⓓ Ⓔ	70 Ⓐ Ⓑ Ⓒ Ⓓ Ⓔ	88 Ⓐ Ⓑ Ⓒ Ⓓ Ⓔ
17 Ⓐ Ⓑ Ⓒ Ⓓ Ⓔ	35 Ⓐ Ⓑ Ⓒ Ⓓ Ⓔ	53 Ⓐ Ⓑ Ⓒ Ⓓ Ⓔ	71 Ⓐ Ⓑ Ⓒ Ⓓ Ⓔ	
18 Ⓐ Ⓑ Ⓒ Ⓓ Ⓔ	36 Ⓐ Ⓑ Ⓒ Ⓓ Ⓔ	54 Ⓐ Ⓑ Ⓒ Ⓓ Ⓔ	72 Ⓐ Ⓑ Ⓒ Ⓓ Ⓔ	

Number Series - Part C

1 Ⓐ Ⓑ Ⓒ Ⓓ Ⓔ	7 Ⓐ Ⓑ Ⓒ Ⓓ Ⓔ	13 Ⓐ Ⓑ Ⓒ Ⓓ Ⓔ	19 Ⓐ Ⓑ Ⓒ Ⓓ Ⓔ
2 Ⓐ Ⓑ Ⓒ Ⓓ Ⓔ	8 Ⓐ Ⓑ Ⓒ Ⓓ Ⓔ	14 Ⓐ Ⓑ Ⓒ Ⓓ Ⓔ	20 Ⓐ Ⓑ Ⓒ Ⓓ Ⓔ
3 Ⓐ Ⓑ Ⓒ Ⓓ Ⓔ	9 Ⓐ Ⓑ Ⓒ Ⓓ Ⓔ	15 Ⓐ Ⓑ Ⓒ Ⓓ Ⓔ	21 Ⓐ Ⓑ Ⓒ Ⓓ Ⓔ
4 Ⓐ Ⓑ Ⓒ Ⓓ Ⓔ	10 Ⓐ Ⓑ Ⓒ Ⓓ Ⓔ	16 Ⓐ Ⓑ Ⓒ Ⓓ Ⓔ	22 Ⓐ Ⓑ Ⓒ Ⓓ Ⓔ
5 Ⓐ Ⓑ Ⓒ Ⓓ Ⓔ	11 Ⓐ Ⓑ Ⓒ Ⓓ Ⓔ	17 Ⓐ Ⓑ Ⓒ Ⓓ Ⓔ	23 Ⓐ Ⓑ Ⓒ Ⓓ Ⓔ
6 Ⓐ Ⓑ Ⓒ Ⓓ Ⓔ	12 Ⓐ Ⓑ Ⓒ Ⓓ Ⓔ	18 Ⓐ Ⓑ Ⓒ Ⓓ Ⓔ	24 Ⓐ Ⓑ Ⓒ Ⓓ Ⓔ

Following Oral Instructions - Part D

1 Ⓐ Ⓑ Ⓒ Ⓓ Ⓔ	19 Ⓐ Ⓑ Ⓒ Ⓓ Ⓔ	37 Ⓐ Ⓑ Ⓒ Ⓓ Ⓔ	55 Ⓐ Ⓑ Ⓒ Ⓓ Ⓔ	73 Ⓐ Ⓑ Ⓒ Ⓓ Ⓔ
2 Ⓐ Ⓑ Ⓒ Ⓓ Ⓔ	20 Ⓐ Ⓑ Ⓒ Ⓓ Ⓔ	38 Ⓐ Ⓑ Ⓒ Ⓓ Ⓔ	56 Ⓐ Ⓑ Ⓒ Ⓓ Ⓔ	74 Ⓐ Ⓑ Ⓒ Ⓓ Ⓔ
3 Ⓐ Ⓑ Ⓒ Ⓓ Ⓔ	21 Ⓐ Ⓑ Ⓒ Ⓓ Ⓔ	39 Ⓐ Ⓑ Ⓒ Ⓓ Ⓔ	57 Ⓐ Ⓑ Ⓒ Ⓓ Ⓔ	75 Ⓐ Ⓑ Ⓒ Ⓓ Ⓔ
4 Ⓐ Ⓑ Ⓒ Ⓓ Ⓔ	22 Ⓐ Ⓑ Ⓒ Ⓓ Ⓔ	40 Ⓐ Ⓑ Ⓒ Ⓓ Ⓔ	58 Ⓐ Ⓑ Ⓒ Ⓓ Ⓔ	76 Ⓐ Ⓑ Ⓒ Ⓓ Ⓔ
5 Ⓐ Ⓑ Ⓒ Ⓓ Ⓔ	23 Ⓐ Ⓑ Ⓒ Ⓓ Ⓔ	41 Ⓐ Ⓑ Ⓒ Ⓓ Ⓔ	59 Ⓐ Ⓑ Ⓒ Ⓓ Ⓔ	77 Ⓐ Ⓑ Ⓒ Ⓓ Ⓔ
6 Ⓐ Ⓑ Ⓒ Ⓓ Ⓔ	24 Ⓐ Ⓑ Ⓒ Ⓓ Ⓔ	42 Ⓐ Ⓑ Ⓒ Ⓓ Ⓔ	60 Ⓐ Ⓑ Ⓒ Ⓓ Ⓔ	78 Ⓐ Ⓑ Ⓒ Ⓓ Ⓔ
7 Ⓐ Ⓑ Ⓒ Ⓓ Ⓔ	25 Ⓐ Ⓑ Ⓒ Ⓓ Ⓔ	43 Ⓐ Ⓑ Ⓒ Ⓓ Ⓔ	61 Ⓐ Ⓑ Ⓒ Ⓓ Ⓔ	79 Ⓐ Ⓑ Ⓒ Ⓓ Ⓔ
8 Ⓐ Ⓑ Ⓒ Ⓓ Ⓔ	26 Ⓐ Ⓑ Ⓒ Ⓓ Ⓔ	44 Ⓐ Ⓑ Ⓒ Ⓓ Ⓔ	62 Ⓐ Ⓑ Ⓒ Ⓓ Ⓔ	80 Ⓐ Ⓑ Ⓒ Ⓓ Ⓔ
9 Ⓐ Ⓑ Ⓒ Ⓓ Ⓔ	27 Ⓐ Ⓑ Ⓒ Ⓓ Ⓔ	45 Ⓐ Ⓑ Ⓒ Ⓓ Ⓔ	63 Ⓐ Ⓑ Ⓒ Ⓓ Ⓔ	81 Ⓐ Ⓑ Ⓒ Ⓓ Ⓔ
10 Ⓐ Ⓑ Ⓒ Ⓓ Ⓔ	28 Ⓐ Ⓑ Ⓒ Ⓓ Ⓔ	46 Ⓐ Ⓑ Ⓒ Ⓓ Ⓔ	64 Ⓐ Ⓑ Ⓒ Ⓓ Ⓔ	82 Ⓐ Ⓑ Ⓒ Ⓓ Ⓔ
11 Ⓐ Ⓑ Ⓒ Ⓓ Ⓔ	29 Ⓐ Ⓑ Ⓒ Ⓓ Ⓔ	47 Ⓐ Ⓑ Ⓒ Ⓓ Ⓔ	65 Ⓐ Ⓑ Ⓒ Ⓓ Ⓔ	83 Ⓐ Ⓑ Ⓒ Ⓓ Ⓔ
12 Ⓐ Ⓑ Ⓒ Ⓓ Ⓔ	30 Ⓐ Ⓑ Ⓒ Ⓓ Ⓔ	48 Ⓐ Ⓑ Ⓒ Ⓓ Ⓔ	66 Ⓐ Ⓑ Ⓒ Ⓓ Ⓔ	84 Ⓐ Ⓑ Ⓒ Ⓓ Ⓔ
13 Ⓐ Ⓑ Ⓒ Ⓓ Ⓔ	31 Ⓐ Ⓑ Ⓒ Ⓓ Ⓔ	49 Ⓐ Ⓑ Ⓒ Ⓓ Ⓔ	67 Ⓐ Ⓑ Ⓒ Ⓓ Ⓔ	85 Ⓐ Ⓑ Ⓒ Ⓓ Ⓔ
14 Ⓐ Ⓑ Ⓒ Ⓓ Ⓔ	32 Ⓐ Ⓑ Ⓒ Ⓓ Ⓔ	50 Ⓐ Ⓑ Ⓒ Ⓓ Ⓔ	68 Ⓐ Ⓑ Ⓒ Ⓓ Ⓔ	86 Ⓐ Ⓑ Ⓒ Ⓓ Ⓔ
15 Ⓐ Ⓑ Ⓒ Ⓓ Ⓔ	33 Ⓐ Ⓑ Ⓒ Ⓓ Ⓔ	51 Ⓐ Ⓑ Ⓒ Ⓓ Ⓔ	69 Ⓐ Ⓑ Ⓒ Ⓓ Ⓔ	87 Ⓐ Ⓑ Ⓒ Ⓓ Ⓔ
16 Ⓐ Ⓑ Ⓒ Ⓓ Ⓔ	34 Ⓐ Ⓑ Ⓒ Ⓓ Ⓔ	52 Ⓐ Ⓑ Ⓒ Ⓓ Ⓔ	70 Ⓐ Ⓑ Ⓒ Ⓓ Ⓔ	88 Ⓐ Ⓑ Ⓒ Ⓓ Ⓔ
17 Ⓐ Ⓑ Ⓒ Ⓓ Ⓔ	35 Ⓐ Ⓑ Ⓒ Ⓓ Ⓔ	53 Ⓐ Ⓑ Ⓒ Ⓓ Ⓔ	71 Ⓐ Ⓑ Ⓒ Ⓓ Ⓔ	
18 Ⓐ Ⓑ Ⓒ Ⓓ Ⓔ	36 Ⓐ Ⓑ Ⓒ Ⓓ Ⓔ	54 Ⓐ Ⓑ Ⓒ Ⓓ Ⓔ	72 Ⓐ Ⓑ Ⓒ Ⓓ Ⓔ	

ANSWER SHEET

Address Checking - Part A

1 Ⓐ Ⓓ	13 Ⓐ Ⓓ	25 Ⓐ Ⓓ	37 Ⓐ Ⓓ	49 Ⓐ Ⓓ	61 Ⓐ Ⓓ	73 Ⓐ Ⓓ	85 Ⓐ Ⓓ
2 Ⓐ Ⓓ	14 Ⓐ Ⓓ	26 Ⓐ Ⓓ	38 Ⓐ Ⓓ	50 Ⓐ Ⓓ	62 Ⓐ Ⓓ	74 Ⓐ Ⓓ	86 Ⓐ Ⓓ
3 Ⓐ Ⓓ	15 Ⓐ Ⓓ	27 Ⓐ Ⓓ	39 Ⓐ Ⓓ	51 Ⓐ Ⓓ	63 Ⓐ Ⓓ	75 Ⓐ Ⓓ	87 Ⓐ Ⓓ
4 Ⓐ Ⓓ	16 Ⓐ Ⓓ	28 Ⓐ Ⓓ	40 Ⓐ Ⓓ	52 Ⓐ Ⓓ	64 Ⓐ Ⓓ	76 Ⓐ Ⓓ	88 Ⓐ Ⓓ
5 Ⓐ Ⓓ	17 Ⓐ Ⓓ	29 Ⓐ Ⓓ	41 Ⓐ Ⓓ	53 Ⓐ Ⓓ	65 Ⓐ Ⓓ	77 Ⓐ Ⓓ	89 Ⓐ Ⓓ
6 Ⓐ Ⓓ	18 Ⓐ Ⓓ	30 Ⓐ Ⓓ	42 Ⓐ Ⓓ	54 Ⓐ Ⓓ	66 Ⓐ Ⓓ	78 Ⓐ Ⓓ	90 Ⓐ Ⓓ
7 Ⓐ Ⓓ	19 Ⓐ Ⓓ	31 Ⓐ Ⓓ	43 Ⓐ Ⓓ	55 Ⓐ Ⓓ	67 Ⓐ Ⓓ	79 Ⓐ Ⓓ	91 Ⓐ Ⓓ
8 Ⓐ Ⓓ	20 Ⓐ Ⓓ	32 Ⓐ Ⓓ	44 Ⓐ Ⓓ	56 Ⓐ Ⓓ	68 Ⓐ Ⓓ	80 Ⓐ Ⓓ	92 Ⓐ Ⓓ
9 Ⓐ Ⓓ	21 Ⓐ Ⓓ	33 Ⓐ Ⓓ	45 Ⓐ Ⓓ	57 Ⓐ Ⓓ	69 Ⓐ Ⓓ	81 Ⓐ Ⓓ	93 Ⓐ Ⓓ
10 Ⓐ Ⓓ	22 Ⓐ Ⓓ	34 Ⓐ Ⓓ	46 Ⓐ Ⓓ	58 Ⓐ Ⓓ	70 Ⓐ Ⓓ	82 Ⓐ Ⓓ	94 Ⓐ Ⓓ
11 Ⓐ Ⓓ	23 Ⓐ Ⓓ	35 Ⓐ Ⓓ	47 Ⓐ Ⓓ	59 Ⓐ Ⓓ	71 Ⓐ Ⓓ	83 Ⓐ Ⓓ	95 Ⓐ Ⓓ
12 Ⓐ Ⓓ	24 Ⓐ Ⓓ	36 Ⓐ Ⓓ	48 Ⓐ Ⓓ	60 Ⓐ Ⓓ	72 Ⓐ Ⓓ	84 Ⓐ Ⓓ	

Address Memory - Part B

1 Ⓐ Ⓑ Ⓒ Ⓓ Ⓔ	19 Ⓐ Ⓑ Ⓒ Ⓓ Ⓔ	37 Ⓐ Ⓑ Ⓒ Ⓓ Ⓔ	55 Ⓐ Ⓑ Ⓒ Ⓓ Ⓔ	73 Ⓐ Ⓑ Ⓒ Ⓓ Ⓔ
2 Ⓐ Ⓑ Ⓒ Ⓓ Ⓔ	20 Ⓐ Ⓑ Ⓒ Ⓓ Ⓔ	38 Ⓐ Ⓑ Ⓒ Ⓓ Ⓔ	56 Ⓐ Ⓑ Ⓒ Ⓓ Ⓔ	74 Ⓐ Ⓑ Ⓒ Ⓓ Ⓔ
3 Ⓐ Ⓑ Ⓒ Ⓓ Ⓔ	21 Ⓐ Ⓑ Ⓒ Ⓓ Ⓔ	39 Ⓐ Ⓑ Ⓒ Ⓓ Ⓔ	57 Ⓐ Ⓑ Ⓒ Ⓓ Ⓔ	75 Ⓐ Ⓑ Ⓒ Ⓓ Ⓔ
4 Ⓐ Ⓑ Ⓒ Ⓓ Ⓔ	22 Ⓐ Ⓑ Ⓒ Ⓓ Ⓔ	40 Ⓐ Ⓑ Ⓒ Ⓓ Ⓔ	58 Ⓐ Ⓑ Ⓒ Ⓓ Ⓔ	76 Ⓐ Ⓑ Ⓒ Ⓓ Ⓔ
5 Ⓐ Ⓑ Ⓒ Ⓓ Ⓔ	23 Ⓐ Ⓑ Ⓒ Ⓓ Ⓔ	41 Ⓐ Ⓑ Ⓒ Ⓓ Ⓔ	59 Ⓐ Ⓑ Ⓒ Ⓓ Ⓔ	77 Ⓐ Ⓑ Ⓒ Ⓓ Ⓔ
6 Ⓐ Ⓑ Ⓒ Ⓓ Ⓔ	24 Ⓐ Ⓑ Ⓒ Ⓓ Ⓔ	42 Ⓐ Ⓑ Ⓒ Ⓓ Ⓔ	60 Ⓐ Ⓑ Ⓒ Ⓓ Ⓔ	78 Ⓐ Ⓑ Ⓒ Ⓓ Ⓔ
7 Ⓐ Ⓑ Ⓒ Ⓓ Ⓔ	25 Ⓐ Ⓑ Ⓒ Ⓓ Ⓔ	43 Ⓐ Ⓑ Ⓒ Ⓓ Ⓔ	61 Ⓐ Ⓑ Ⓒ Ⓓ Ⓔ	79 Ⓐ Ⓑ Ⓒ Ⓓ Ⓔ
8 Ⓐ Ⓑ Ⓒ Ⓓ Ⓔ	26 Ⓐ Ⓑ Ⓒ Ⓓ Ⓔ	44 Ⓐ Ⓑ Ⓒ Ⓓ Ⓔ	62 Ⓐ Ⓑ Ⓒ Ⓓ Ⓔ	80 Ⓐ Ⓑ Ⓒ Ⓓ Ⓔ
9 Ⓐ Ⓑ Ⓒ Ⓓ Ⓔ	27 Ⓐ Ⓑ Ⓒ Ⓓ Ⓔ	45 Ⓐ Ⓑ Ⓒ Ⓓ Ⓔ	63 Ⓐ Ⓑ Ⓒ Ⓓ Ⓔ	81 Ⓐ Ⓑ Ⓒ Ⓓ Ⓔ
10 Ⓐ Ⓑ Ⓒ Ⓓ Ⓔ	28 Ⓐ Ⓑ Ⓒ Ⓓ Ⓔ	46 Ⓐ Ⓑ Ⓒ Ⓓ Ⓔ	64 Ⓐ Ⓑ Ⓒ Ⓓ Ⓔ	82 Ⓐ Ⓑ Ⓒ Ⓓ Ⓔ
11 Ⓐ Ⓑ Ⓒ Ⓓ Ⓔ	29 Ⓐ Ⓑ Ⓒ Ⓓ Ⓔ	47 Ⓐ Ⓑ Ⓒ Ⓓ Ⓔ	65 Ⓐ Ⓑ Ⓒ Ⓓ Ⓔ	83 Ⓐ Ⓑ Ⓒ Ⓓ Ⓔ
12 Ⓐ Ⓑ Ⓒ Ⓓ Ⓔ	30 Ⓐ Ⓑ Ⓒ Ⓓ Ⓔ	48 Ⓐ Ⓑ Ⓒ Ⓓ Ⓔ	66 Ⓐ Ⓑ Ⓒ Ⓓ Ⓔ	84 Ⓐ Ⓑ Ⓒ Ⓓ Ⓔ
13 Ⓐ Ⓑ Ⓒ Ⓓ Ⓔ	31 Ⓐ Ⓑ Ⓒ Ⓓ Ⓔ	49 Ⓐ Ⓑ Ⓒ Ⓓ Ⓔ	67 Ⓐ Ⓑ Ⓒ Ⓓ Ⓔ	85 Ⓐ Ⓑ Ⓒ Ⓓ Ⓔ
14 Ⓐ Ⓑ Ⓒ Ⓓ Ⓔ	32 Ⓐ Ⓑ Ⓒ Ⓓ Ⓔ	50 Ⓐ Ⓑ Ⓒ Ⓓ Ⓔ	68 Ⓐ Ⓑ Ⓒ Ⓓ Ⓔ	86 Ⓐ Ⓑ Ⓒ Ⓓ Ⓔ
15 Ⓐ Ⓑ Ⓒ Ⓓ Ⓔ	33 Ⓐ Ⓑ Ⓒ Ⓓ Ⓔ	51 Ⓐ Ⓑ Ⓒ Ⓓ Ⓔ	69 Ⓐ Ⓑ Ⓒ Ⓓ Ⓔ	87 Ⓐ Ⓑ Ⓒ Ⓓ Ⓔ
16 Ⓐ Ⓑ Ⓒ Ⓓ Ⓔ	34 Ⓐ Ⓑ Ⓒ Ⓓ Ⓔ	52 Ⓐ Ⓑ Ⓒ Ⓓ Ⓔ	70 Ⓐ Ⓑ Ⓒ Ⓓ Ⓔ	88 Ⓐ Ⓑ Ⓒ Ⓓ Ⓔ
17 Ⓐ Ⓑ Ⓒ Ⓓ Ⓔ	35 Ⓐ Ⓑ Ⓒ Ⓓ Ⓔ	53 Ⓐ Ⓑ Ⓒ Ⓓ Ⓔ	71 Ⓐ Ⓑ Ⓒ Ⓓ Ⓔ	
18 Ⓐ Ⓑ Ⓒ Ⓓ Ⓔ	36 Ⓐ Ⓑ Ⓒ Ⓓ Ⓔ	54 Ⓐ Ⓑ Ⓒ Ⓓ Ⓔ	72 Ⓐ Ⓑ Ⓒ Ⓓ Ⓔ	

Number Series - Part C

1 Ⓐ Ⓑ Ⓒ Ⓓ Ⓔ	7 Ⓐ Ⓑ Ⓒ Ⓓ Ⓔ	13 Ⓐ Ⓑ Ⓒ Ⓓ Ⓔ	19 Ⓐ Ⓑ Ⓒ Ⓓ Ⓔ
2 Ⓐ Ⓑ Ⓒ Ⓓ Ⓔ	8 Ⓐ Ⓑ Ⓒ Ⓓ Ⓔ	14 Ⓐ Ⓑ Ⓒ Ⓓ Ⓔ	20 Ⓐ Ⓑ Ⓒ Ⓓ Ⓔ
3 Ⓐ Ⓑ Ⓒ Ⓓ Ⓔ	9 Ⓐ Ⓑ Ⓒ Ⓓ Ⓔ	15 Ⓐ Ⓑ Ⓒ Ⓓ Ⓔ	21 Ⓐ Ⓑ Ⓒ Ⓓ Ⓔ
4 Ⓐ Ⓑ Ⓒ Ⓓ Ⓔ	10 Ⓐ Ⓑ Ⓒ Ⓓ Ⓔ	16 Ⓐ Ⓑ Ⓒ Ⓓ Ⓔ	22 Ⓐ Ⓑ Ⓒ Ⓓ Ⓔ
5 Ⓐ Ⓑ Ⓒ Ⓓ Ⓔ	11 Ⓐ Ⓑ Ⓒ Ⓓ Ⓔ	17 Ⓐ Ⓑ Ⓒ Ⓓ Ⓔ	23 Ⓐ Ⓑ Ⓒ Ⓓ Ⓔ
6 Ⓐ Ⓑ Ⓒ Ⓓ Ⓔ	12 Ⓐ Ⓑ Ⓒ Ⓓ Ⓔ	18 Ⓐ Ⓑ Ⓒ Ⓓ Ⓔ	24 Ⓐ Ⓑ Ⓒ Ⓓ Ⓔ

Following Oral Instructions - Part D

1 Ⓐ Ⓑ Ⓒ Ⓓ Ⓔ	19 Ⓐ Ⓑ Ⓒ Ⓓ Ⓔ	37 Ⓐ Ⓑ Ⓒ Ⓓ Ⓔ	55 Ⓐ Ⓑ Ⓒ Ⓓ Ⓔ	73 Ⓐ Ⓑ Ⓒ Ⓓ Ⓔ
2 Ⓐ Ⓑ Ⓒ Ⓓ Ⓔ	20 Ⓐ Ⓑ Ⓒ Ⓓ Ⓔ	38 Ⓐ Ⓑ Ⓒ Ⓓ Ⓔ	56 Ⓐ Ⓑ Ⓒ Ⓓ Ⓔ	74 Ⓐ Ⓑ Ⓒ Ⓓ Ⓔ
3 Ⓐ Ⓑ Ⓒ Ⓓ Ⓔ	21 Ⓐ Ⓑ Ⓒ Ⓓ Ⓔ	39 Ⓐ Ⓑ Ⓒ Ⓓ Ⓔ	57 Ⓐ Ⓑ Ⓒ Ⓓ Ⓔ	75 Ⓐ Ⓑ Ⓒ Ⓓ Ⓔ
4 Ⓐ Ⓑ Ⓒ Ⓓ Ⓔ	22 Ⓐ Ⓑ Ⓒ Ⓓ Ⓔ	40 Ⓐ Ⓑ Ⓒ Ⓓ Ⓔ	58 Ⓐ Ⓑ Ⓒ Ⓓ Ⓔ	76 Ⓐ Ⓑ Ⓒ Ⓓ Ⓔ
5 Ⓐ Ⓑ Ⓒ Ⓓ Ⓔ	23 Ⓐ Ⓑ Ⓒ Ⓓ Ⓔ	41 Ⓐ Ⓑ Ⓒ Ⓓ Ⓔ	59 Ⓐ Ⓑ Ⓒ Ⓓ Ⓔ	77 Ⓐ Ⓑ Ⓒ Ⓓ Ⓔ
6 Ⓐ Ⓑ Ⓒ Ⓓ Ⓔ	24 Ⓐ Ⓑ Ⓒ Ⓓ Ⓔ	42 Ⓐ Ⓑ Ⓒ Ⓓ Ⓔ	60 Ⓐ Ⓑ Ⓒ Ⓓ Ⓔ	78 Ⓐ Ⓑ Ⓒ Ⓓ Ⓔ
7 Ⓐ Ⓑ Ⓒ Ⓓ Ⓔ	25 Ⓐ Ⓑ Ⓒ Ⓓ Ⓔ	43 Ⓐ Ⓑ Ⓒ Ⓓ Ⓔ	61 Ⓐ Ⓑ Ⓒ Ⓓ Ⓔ	79 Ⓐ Ⓑ Ⓒ Ⓓ Ⓔ
8 Ⓐ Ⓑ Ⓒ Ⓓ Ⓔ	26 Ⓐ Ⓑ Ⓒ Ⓓ Ⓔ	44 Ⓐ Ⓑ Ⓒ Ⓓ Ⓔ	62 Ⓐ Ⓑ Ⓒ Ⓓ Ⓔ	80 Ⓐ Ⓑ Ⓒ Ⓓ Ⓔ
9 Ⓐ Ⓑ Ⓒ Ⓓ Ⓔ	27 Ⓐ Ⓑ Ⓒ Ⓓ Ⓔ	45 Ⓐ Ⓑ Ⓒ Ⓓ Ⓔ	63 Ⓐ Ⓑ Ⓒ Ⓓ Ⓔ	81 Ⓐ Ⓑ Ⓒ Ⓓ Ⓔ
10 Ⓐ Ⓑ Ⓒ Ⓓ Ⓔ	28 Ⓐ Ⓑ Ⓒ Ⓓ Ⓔ	46 Ⓐ Ⓑ Ⓒ Ⓓ Ⓔ	64 Ⓐ Ⓑ Ⓒ Ⓓ Ⓔ	82 Ⓐ Ⓑ Ⓒ Ⓓ Ⓔ
11 Ⓐ Ⓑ Ⓒ Ⓓ Ⓔ	29 Ⓐ Ⓑ Ⓒ Ⓓ Ⓔ	47 Ⓐ Ⓑ Ⓒ Ⓓ Ⓔ	65 Ⓐ Ⓑ Ⓒ Ⓓ Ⓔ	83 Ⓐ Ⓑ Ⓒ Ⓓ Ⓔ
12 Ⓐ Ⓑ Ⓒ Ⓓ Ⓔ	30 Ⓐ Ⓑ Ⓒ Ⓓ Ⓔ	48 Ⓐ Ⓑ Ⓒ Ⓓ Ⓔ	66 Ⓐ Ⓑ Ⓒ Ⓓ Ⓔ	84 Ⓐ Ⓑ Ⓒ Ⓓ Ⓔ
13 Ⓐ Ⓑ Ⓒ Ⓓ Ⓔ	31 Ⓐ Ⓑ Ⓒ Ⓓ Ⓔ	49 Ⓐ Ⓑ Ⓒ Ⓓ Ⓔ	67 Ⓐ Ⓑ Ⓒ Ⓓ Ⓔ	85 Ⓐ Ⓑ Ⓒ Ⓓ Ⓔ
14 Ⓐ Ⓑ Ⓒ Ⓓ Ⓔ	32 Ⓐ Ⓑ Ⓒ Ⓓ Ⓔ	50 Ⓐ Ⓑ Ⓒ Ⓓ Ⓔ	68 Ⓐ Ⓑ Ⓒ Ⓓ Ⓔ	86 Ⓐ Ⓑ Ⓒ Ⓓ Ⓔ
15 Ⓐ Ⓑ Ⓒ Ⓓ Ⓔ	33 Ⓐ Ⓑ Ⓒ Ⓓ Ⓔ	51 Ⓐ Ⓑ Ⓒ Ⓓ Ⓔ	69 Ⓐ Ⓑ Ⓒ Ⓓ Ⓔ	87 Ⓐ Ⓑ Ⓒ Ⓓ Ⓔ
16 Ⓐ Ⓑ Ⓒ Ⓓ Ⓔ	34 Ⓐ Ⓑ Ⓒ Ⓓ Ⓔ	52 Ⓐ Ⓑ Ⓒ Ⓓ Ⓔ	70 Ⓐ Ⓑ Ⓒ Ⓓ Ⓔ	88 Ⓐ Ⓑ Ⓒ Ⓓ Ⓔ
17 Ⓐ Ⓑ Ⓒ Ⓓ Ⓔ	35 Ⓐ Ⓑ Ⓒ Ⓓ Ⓔ	53 Ⓐ Ⓑ Ⓒ Ⓓ Ⓔ	71 Ⓐ Ⓑ Ⓒ Ⓓ Ⓔ	
18 Ⓐ Ⓑ Ⓒ Ⓓ Ⓔ	36 Ⓐ Ⓑ Ⓒ Ⓓ Ⓔ	54 Ⓐ Ⓑ Ⓒ Ⓓ Ⓔ	72 Ⓐ Ⓑ Ⓒ Ⓓ Ⓔ	

ANSWER SHEET

Address Checking - Part A

1 Ⓐ Ⓓ	13 Ⓐ Ⓓ	25 Ⓐ Ⓓ	37 Ⓐ Ⓓ	49 Ⓐ Ⓓ	61 Ⓐ Ⓓ	73 Ⓐ Ⓓ	85 Ⓐ Ⓓ
2 Ⓐ Ⓓ	14 Ⓐ Ⓓ	26 Ⓐ Ⓓ	38 Ⓐ Ⓓ	50 Ⓐ Ⓓ	62 Ⓐ Ⓓ	74 Ⓐ Ⓓ	86 Ⓐ Ⓓ
3 Ⓐ Ⓓ	15 Ⓐ Ⓓ	27 Ⓐ Ⓓ	39 Ⓐ Ⓓ	51 Ⓐ Ⓓ	63 Ⓐ Ⓓ	75 Ⓐ Ⓓ	87 Ⓐ Ⓓ
4 Ⓐ Ⓓ	16 Ⓐ Ⓓ	28 Ⓐ Ⓓ	40 Ⓐ Ⓓ	52 Ⓐ Ⓓ	64 Ⓐ Ⓓ	76 Ⓐ Ⓓ	88 Ⓐ Ⓓ
5 Ⓐ Ⓓ	17 Ⓐ Ⓓ	29 Ⓐ Ⓓ	41 Ⓐ Ⓓ	53 Ⓐ Ⓓ	65 Ⓐ Ⓓ	77 Ⓐ Ⓓ	89 Ⓐ Ⓓ
6 Ⓐ Ⓓ	18 Ⓐ Ⓓ	30 Ⓐ Ⓓ	42 Ⓐ Ⓓ	54 Ⓐ Ⓓ	66 Ⓐ Ⓓ	78 Ⓐ Ⓓ	90 Ⓐ Ⓓ
7 Ⓐ Ⓓ	19 Ⓐ Ⓓ	31 Ⓐ Ⓓ	43 Ⓐ Ⓓ	55 Ⓐ Ⓓ	67 Ⓐ Ⓓ	79 Ⓐ Ⓓ	91 Ⓐ Ⓓ
8 Ⓐ Ⓓ	20 Ⓐ Ⓓ	32 Ⓐ Ⓓ	44 Ⓐ Ⓓ	56 Ⓐ Ⓓ	68 Ⓐ Ⓓ	80 Ⓐ Ⓓ	92 Ⓐ Ⓓ
9 Ⓐ Ⓓ	21 Ⓐ Ⓓ	33 Ⓐ Ⓓ	45 Ⓐ Ⓓ	57 Ⓐ Ⓓ	69 Ⓐ Ⓓ	81 Ⓐ Ⓓ	93 Ⓐ Ⓓ
10 Ⓐ Ⓓ	22 Ⓐ Ⓓ	34 Ⓐ Ⓓ	46 Ⓐ Ⓓ	58 Ⓐ Ⓓ	70 Ⓐ Ⓓ	82 Ⓐ Ⓓ	94 Ⓐ Ⓓ
11 Ⓐ Ⓓ	23 Ⓐ Ⓓ	35 Ⓐ Ⓓ	47 Ⓐ Ⓓ	59 Ⓐ Ⓓ	71 Ⓐ Ⓓ	83 Ⓐ Ⓓ	95 Ⓐ Ⓓ
12 Ⓐ Ⓓ	24 Ⓐ Ⓓ	36 Ⓐ Ⓓ	48 Ⓐ Ⓓ	60 Ⓐ Ⓓ	72 Ⓐ Ⓓ	84 Ⓐ Ⓓ	

Address Memory - Part B

1 Ⓐ Ⓑ Ⓒ Ⓓ Ⓔ	19 Ⓐ Ⓑ Ⓒ Ⓓ Ⓔ	37 Ⓐ Ⓑ Ⓒ Ⓓ Ⓔ	55 Ⓐ Ⓑ Ⓒ Ⓓ Ⓔ	73 Ⓐ Ⓑ Ⓒ Ⓓ Ⓔ
2 Ⓐ Ⓑ Ⓒ Ⓓ Ⓔ	20 Ⓐ Ⓑ Ⓒ Ⓓ Ⓔ	38 Ⓐ Ⓑ Ⓒ Ⓓ Ⓔ	56 Ⓐ Ⓑ Ⓒ Ⓓ Ⓔ	74 Ⓐ Ⓑ Ⓒ Ⓓ Ⓔ
3 Ⓐ Ⓑ Ⓒ Ⓓ Ⓔ	21 Ⓐ Ⓑ Ⓒ Ⓓ Ⓔ	39 Ⓐ Ⓑ Ⓒ Ⓓ Ⓔ	57 Ⓐ Ⓑ Ⓒ Ⓓ Ⓔ	75 Ⓐ Ⓑ Ⓒ Ⓓ Ⓔ
4 Ⓐ Ⓑ Ⓒ Ⓓ Ⓔ	22 Ⓐ Ⓑ Ⓒ Ⓓ Ⓔ	40 Ⓐ Ⓑ Ⓒ Ⓓ Ⓔ	58 Ⓐ Ⓑ Ⓒ Ⓓ Ⓔ	76 Ⓐ Ⓑ Ⓒ Ⓓ Ⓔ
5 Ⓐ Ⓑ Ⓒ Ⓓ Ⓔ	23 Ⓐ Ⓑ Ⓒ Ⓓ Ⓔ	41 Ⓐ Ⓑ Ⓒ Ⓓ Ⓔ	59 Ⓐ Ⓑ Ⓒ Ⓓ Ⓔ	77 Ⓐ Ⓑ Ⓒ Ⓓ Ⓔ
6 Ⓐ Ⓑ Ⓒ Ⓓ Ⓔ	24 Ⓐ Ⓑ Ⓒ Ⓓ Ⓔ	42 Ⓐ Ⓑ Ⓒ Ⓓ Ⓔ	60 Ⓐ Ⓑ Ⓒ Ⓓ Ⓔ	78 Ⓐ Ⓑ Ⓒ Ⓓ Ⓔ
7 Ⓐ Ⓑ Ⓒ Ⓓ Ⓔ	25 Ⓐ Ⓑ Ⓒ Ⓓ Ⓔ	43 Ⓐ Ⓑ Ⓒ Ⓓ Ⓔ	61 Ⓐ Ⓑ Ⓒ Ⓓ Ⓔ	79 Ⓐ Ⓑ Ⓒ Ⓓ Ⓔ
8 Ⓐ Ⓑ Ⓒ Ⓓ Ⓔ	26 Ⓐ Ⓑ Ⓒ Ⓓ Ⓔ	44 Ⓐ Ⓑ Ⓒ Ⓓ Ⓔ	62 Ⓐ Ⓑ Ⓒ Ⓓ Ⓔ	80 Ⓐ Ⓑ Ⓒ Ⓓ Ⓔ
9 Ⓐ Ⓑ Ⓒ Ⓓ Ⓔ	27 Ⓐ Ⓑ Ⓒ Ⓓ Ⓔ	45 Ⓐ Ⓑ Ⓒ Ⓓ Ⓔ	63 Ⓐ Ⓑ Ⓒ Ⓓ Ⓔ	81 Ⓐ Ⓑ Ⓒ Ⓓ Ⓔ
10 Ⓐ Ⓑ Ⓒ Ⓓ Ⓔ	28 Ⓐ Ⓑ Ⓒ Ⓓ Ⓔ	46 Ⓐ Ⓑ Ⓒ Ⓓ Ⓔ	64 Ⓐ Ⓑ Ⓒ Ⓓ Ⓔ	82 Ⓐ Ⓑ Ⓒ Ⓓ Ⓔ
11 Ⓐ Ⓑ Ⓒ Ⓓ Ⓔ	29 Ⓐ Ⓑ Ⓒ Ⓓ Ⓔ	47 Ⓐ Ⓑ Ⓒ Ⓓ Ⓔ	65 Ⓐ Ⓑ Ⓒ Ⓓ Ⓔ	83 Ⓐ Ⓑ Ⓒ Ⓓ Ⓔ
12 Ⓐ Ⓑ Ⓒ Ⓓ Ⓔ	30 Ⓐ Ⓑ Ⓒ Ⓓ Ⓔ	48 Ⓐ Ⓑ Ⓒ Ⓓ Ⓔ	66 Ⓐ Ⓑ Ⓒ Ⓓ Ⓔ	84 Ⓐ Ⓑ Ⓒ Ⓓ Ⓔ
13 Ⓐ Ⓑ Ⓒ Ⓓ Ⓔ	31 Ⓐ Ⓑ Ⓒ Ⓓ Ⓔ	49 Ⓐ Ⓑ Ⓒ Ⓓ Ⓔ	67 Ⓐ Ⓑ Ⓒ Ⓓ Ⓔ	85 Ⓐ Ⓑ Ⓒ Ⓓ Ⓔ
14 Ⓐ Ⓑ Ⓒ Ⓓ Ⓔ	32 Ⓐ Ⓑ Ⓒ Ⓓ Ⓔ	50 Ⓐ Ⓑ Ⓒ Ⓓ Ⓔ	68 Ⓐ Ⓑ Ⓒ Ⓓ Ⓔ	86 Ⓐ Ⓑ Ⓒ Ⓓ Ⓔ
15 Ⓐ Ⓑ Ⓒ Ⓓ Ⓔ	33 Ⓐ Ⓑ Ⓒ Ⓓ Ⓔ	51 Ⓐ Ⓑ Ⓒ Ⓓ Ⓔ	69 Ⓐ Ⓑ Ⓒ Ⓓ Ⓔ	87 Ⓐ Ⓑ Ⓒ Ⓓ Ⓔ
16 Ⓐ Ⓑ Ⓒ Ⓓ Ⓔ	34 Ⓐ Ⓑ Ⓒ Ⓓ Ⓔ	52 Ⓐ Ⓑ Ⓒ Ⓓ Ⓔ	70 Ⓐ Ⓑ Ⓒ Ⓓ Ⓔ	88 Ⓐ Ⓑ Ⓒ Ⓓ Ⓔ
17 Ⓐ Ⓑ Ⓒ Ⓓ Ⓔ	35 Ⓐ Ⓑ Ⓒ Ⓓ Ⓔ	53 Ⓐ Ⓑ Ⓒ Ⓓ Ⓔ	71 Ⓐ Ⓑ Ⓒ Ⓓ Ⓔ	
18 Ⓐ Ⓑ Ⓒ Ⓓ Ⓔ	36 Ⓐ Ⓑ Ⓒ Ⓓ Ⓔ	54 Ⓐ Ⓑ Ⓒ Ⓓ Ⓔ	72 Ⓐ Ⓑ Ⓒ Ⓓ Ⓔ	

Number Series - Part C

1 Ⓐ Ⓑ Ⓒ Ⓓ Ⓔ	7 Ⓐ Ⓑ Ⓒ Ⓓ Ⓔ	13 Ⓐ Ⓑ Ⓒ Ⓓ Ⓔ	19 Ⓐ Ⓑ Ⓒ Ⓓ Ⓔ
2 Ⓐ Ⓑ Ⓒ Ⓓ Ⓔ	8 Ⓐ Ⓑ Ⓒ Ⓓ Ⓔ	14 Ⓐ Ⓑ Ⓒ Ⓓ Ⓔ	20 Ⓐ Ⓑ Ⓒ Ⓓ Ⓔ
3 Ⓐ Ⓑ Ⓒ Ⓓ Ⓔ	9 Ⓐ Ⓑ Ⓒ Ⓓ Ⓔ	15 Ⓐ Ⓑ Ⓒ Ⓓ Ⓔ	21 Ⓐ Ⓑ Ⓒ Ⓓ Ⓔ
4 Ⓐ Ⓑ Ⓒ Ⓓ Ⓔ	10 Ⓐ Ⓑ Ⓒ Ⓓ Ⓔ	16 Ⓐ Ⓑ Ⓒ Ⓓ Ⓔ	22 Ⓐ Ⓑ Ⓒ Ⓓ Ⓔ
5 Ⓐ Ⓑ Ⓒ Ⓓ Ⓔ	11 Ⓐ Ⓑ Ⓒ Ⓓ Ⓔ	17 Ⓐ Ⓑ Ⓒ Ⓓ Ⓔ	23 Ⓐ Ⓑ Ⓒ Ⓓ Ⓔ
6 Ⓐ Ⓑ Ⓒ Ⓓ Ⓔ	12 Ⓐ Ⓑ Ⓒ Ⓓ Ⓔ	18 Ⓐ Ⓑ Ⓒ Ⓓ Ⓔ	24 Ⓐ Ⓑ Ⓒ Ⓓ Ⓔ

Following Oral Instructions - Part D

1 Ⓐ Ⓑ Ⓒ Ⓓ Ⓔ	19 Ⓐ Ⓑ Ⓒ Ⓓ Ⓔ	37 Ⓐ Ⓑ Ⓒ Ⓓ Ⓔ	55 Ⓐ Ⓑ Ⓒ Ⓓ Ⓔ	73 Ⓐ Ⓑ Ⓒ Ⓓ Ⓔ
2 Ⓐ Ⓑ Ⓒ Ⓓ Ⓔ	20 Ⓐ Ⓑ Ⓒ Ⓓ Ⓔ	38 Ⓐ Ⓑ Ⓒ Ⓓ Ⓔ	56 Ⓐ Ⓑ Ⓒ Ⓓ Ⓔ	74 Ⓐ Ⓑ Ⓒ Ⓓ Ⓔ
3 Ⓐ Ⓑ Ⓒ Ⓓ Ⓔ	21 Ⓐ Ⓑ Ⓒ Ⓓ Ⓔ	39 Ⓐ Ⓑ Ⓒ Ⓓ Ⓔ	57 Ⓐ Ⓑ Ⓒ Ⓓ Ⓔ	75 Ⓐ Ⓑ Ⓒ Ⓓ Ⓔ
4 Ⓐ Ⓑ Ⓒ Ⓓ Ⓔ	22 Ⓐ Ⓑ Ⓒ Ⓓ Ⓔ	40 Ⓐ Ⓑ Ⓒ Ⓓ Ⓔ	58 Ⓐ Ⓑ Ⓒ Ⓓ Ⓔ	76 Ⓐ Ⓑ Ⓒ Ⓓ Ⓔ
5 Ⓐ Ⓑ Ⓒ Ⓓ Ⓔ	23 Ⓐ Ⓑ Ⓒ Ⓓ Ⓔ	41 Ⓐ Ⓑ Ⓒ Ⓓ Ⓔ	59 Ⓐ Ⓑ Ⓒ Ⓓ Ⓔ	77 Ⓐ Ⓑ Ⓒ Ⓓ Ⓔ
6 Ⓐ Ⓑ Ⓒ Ⓓ Ⓔ	24 Ⓐ Ⓑ Ⓒ Ⓓ Ⓔ	42 Ⓐ Ⓑ Ⓒ Ⓓ Ⓔ	60 Ⓐ Ⓑ Ⓒ Ⓓ Ⓔ	78 Ⓐ Ⓑ Ⓒ Ⓓ Ⓔ
7 Ⓐ Ⓑ Ⓒ Ⓓ Ⓔ	25 Ⓐ Ⓑ Ⓒ Ⓓ Ⓔ	43 Ⓐ Ⓑ Ⓒ Ⓓ Ⓔ	61 Ⓐ Ⓑ Ⓒ Ⓓ Ⓔ	79 Ⓐ Ⓑ Ⓒ Ⓓ Ⓔ
8 Ⓐ Ⓑ Ⓒ Ⓓ Ⓔ	26 Ⓐ Ⓑ Ⓒ Ⓓ Ⓔ	44 Ⓐ Ⓑ Ⓒ Ⓓ Ⓔ	62 Ⓐ Ⓑ Ⓒ Ⓓ Ⓔ	80 Ⓐ Ⓑ Ⓒ Ⓓ Ⓔ
9 Ⓐ Ⓑ Ⓒ Ⓓ Ⓔ	27 Ⓐ Ⓑ Ⓒ Ⓓ Ⓔ	45 Ⓐ Ⓑ Ⓒ Ⓓ Ⓔ	63 Ⓐ Ⓑ Ⓒ Ⓓ Ⓔ	81 Ⓐ Ⓑ Ⓒ Ⓓ Ⓔ
10 Ⓐ Ⓑ Ⓒ Ⓓ Ⓔ	28 Ⓐ Ⓑ Ⓒ Ⓓ Ⓔ	46 Ⓐ Ⓑ Ⓒ Ⓓ Ⓔ	64 Ⓐ Ⓑ Ⓒ Ⓓ Ⓔ	82 Ⓐ Ⓑ Ⓒ Ⓓ Ⓔ
11 Ⓐ Ⓑ Ⓒ Ⓓ Ⓔ	29 Ⓐ Ⓑ Ⓒ Ⓓ Ⓔ	47 Ⓐ Ⓑ Ⓒ Ⓓ Ⓔ	65 Ⓐ Ⓑ Ⓒ Ⓓ Ⓔ	83 Ⓐ Ⓑ Ⓒ Ⓓ Ⓔ
12 Ⓐ Ⓑ Ⓒ Ⓓ Ⓔ	30 Ⓐ Ⓑ Ⓒ Ⓓ Ⓔ	48 Ⓐ Ⓑ Ⓒ Ⓓ Ⓔ	66 Ⓐ Ⓑ Ⓒ Ⓓ Ⓔ	84 Ⓐ Ⓑ Ⓒ Ⓓ Ⓔ
13 Ⓐ Ⓑ Ⓒ Ⓓ Ⓔ	31 Ⓐ Ⓑ Ⓒ Ⓓ Ⓔ	49 Ⓐ Ⓑ Ⓒ Ⓓ Ⓔ	67 Ⓐ Ⓑ Ⓒ Ⓓ Ⓔ	85 Ⓐ Ⓑ Ⓒ Ⓓ Ⓔ
14 Ⓐ Ⓑ Ⓒ Ⓓ Ⓔ	32 Ⓐ Ⓑ Ⓒ Ⓓ Ⓔ	50 Ⓐ Ⓑ Ⓒ Ⓓ Ⓔ	68 Ⓐ Ⓑ Ⓒ Ⓓ Ⓔ	86 Ⓐ Ⓑ Ⓒ Ⓓ Ⓔ
15 Ⓐ Ⓑ Ⓒ Ⓓ Ⓔ	33 Ⓐ Ⓑ Ⓒ Ⓓ Ⓔ	51 Ⓐ Ⓑ Ⓒ Ⓓ Ⓔ	69 Ⓐ Ⓑ Ⓒ Ⓓ Ⓔ	87 Ⓐ Ⓑ Ⓒ Ⓓ Ⓔ
16 Ⓐ Ⓑ Ⓒ Ⓓ Ⓔ	34 Ⓐ Ⓑ Ⓒ Ⓓ Ⓔ	52 Ⓐ Ⓑ Ⓒ Ⓓ Ⓔ	70 Ⓐ Ⓑ Ⓒ Ⓓ Ⓔ	88 Ⓐ Ⓑ Ⓒ Ⓓ Ⓔ
17 Ⓐ Ⓑ Ⓒ Ⓓ Ⓔ	35 Ⓐ Ⓑ Ⓒ Ⓓ Ⓔ	53 Ⓐ Ⓑ Ⓒ Ⓓ Ⓔ	71 Ⓐ Ⓑ Ⓒ Ⓓ Ⓔ	
18 Ⓐ Ⓑ Ⓒ Ⓓ Ⓔ	36 Ⓐ Ⓑ Ⓒ Ⓓ Ⓔ	54 Ⓐ Ⓑ Ⓒ Ⓓ Ⓔ	72 Ⓐ Ⓑ Ⓒ Ⓓ Ⓔ	

ANSWER SHEET

Address Checking - Part A

1 Ⓐ Ⓓ	13 Ⓐ Ⓓ	25 Ⓐ Ⓓ	37 Ⓐ Ⓓ	49 Ⓐ Ⓓ	61 Ⓐ Ⓓ	73 Ⓐ Ⓓ	85 Ⓐ Ⓓ
2 Ⓐ Ⓓ	14 Ⓐ Ⓓ	26 Ⓐ Ⓓ	38 Ⓐ Ⓓ	50 Ⓐ Ⓓ	62 Ⓐ Ⓓ	74 Ⓐ Ⓓ	86 Ⓐ Ⓓ
3 Ⓐ Ⓓ	15 Ⓐ Ⓓ	27 Ⓐ Ⓓ	39 Ⓐ Ⓓ	51 Ⓐ Ⓓ	63 Ⓐ Ⓓ	75 Ⓐ Ⓓ	87 Ⓐ Ⓓ
4 Ⓐ Ⓓ	16 Ⓐ Ⓓ	28 Ⓐ Ⓓ	40 Ⓐ Ⓓ	52 Ⓐ Ⓓ	64 Ⓐ Ⓓ	76 Ⓐ Ⓓ	88 Ⓐ Ⓓ
5 Ⓐ Ⓓ	17 Ⓐ Ⓓ	29 Ⓐ Ⓓ	41 Ⓐ Ⓓ	53 Ⓐ Ⓓ	65 Ⓐ Ⓓ	77 Ⓐ Ⓓ	89 Ⓐ Ⓓ
6 Ⓐ Ⓓ	18 Ⓐ Ⓓ	30 Ⓐ Ⓓ	42 Ⓐ Ⓓ	54 Ⓐ Ⓓ	66 Ⓐ Ⓓ	78 Ⓐ Ⓓ	90 Ⓐ Ⓓ
7 Ⓐ Ⓓ	19 Ⓐ Ⓓ	31 Ⓐ Ⓓ	43 Ⓐ Ⓓ	55 Ⓐ Ⓓ	67 Ⓐ Ⓓ	79 Ⓐ Ⓓ	91 Ⓐ Ⓓ
8 Ⓐ Ⓓ	20 Ⓐ Ⓓ	32 Ⓐ Ⓓ	44 Ⓐ Ⓓ	56 Ⓐ Ⓓ	68 Ⓐ Ⓓ	80 Ⓐ Ⓓ	92 Ⓐ Ⓓ
9 Ⓐ Ⓓ	21 Ⓐ Ⓓ	33 Ⓐ Ⓓ	45 Ⓐ Ⓓ	57 Ⓐ Ⓓ	69 Ⓐ Ⓓ	81 Ⓐ Ⓓ	93 Ⓐ Ⓓ
10 Ⓐ Ⓓ	22 Ⓐ Ⓓ	34 Ⓐ Ⓓ	46 Ⓐ Ⓓ	58 Ⓐ Ⓓ	70 Ⓐ Ⓓ	82 Ⓐ Ⓓ	94 Ⓐ Ⓓ
11 Ⓐ Ⓓ	23 Ⓐ Ⓓ	35 Ⓐ Ⓓ	47 Ⓐ Ⓓ	59 Ⓐ Ⓓ	71 Ⓐ Ⓓ	83 Ⓐ Ⓓ	95 Ⓐ Ⓓ
12 Ⓐ Ⓓ	24 Ⓐ Ⓓ	36 Ⓐ Ⓓ	48 Ⓐ Ⓓ	60 Ⓐ Ⓓ	72 Ⓐ Ⓓ	84 Ⓐ Ⓓ	

Address Memory - Part B

1 Ⓐ Ⓑ Ⓒ Ⓓ Ⓔ	19 Ⓐ Ⓑ Ⓒ Ⓓ Ⓔ	37 Ⓐ Ⓑ Ⓒ Ⓓ Ⓔ	55 Ⓐ Ⓑ Ⓒ Ⓓ Ⓔ	73 Ⓐ Ⓑ Ⓒ Ⓓ Ⓔ
2 Ⓐ Ⓑ Ⓒ Ⓓ Ⓔ	20 Ⓐ Ⓑ Ⓒ Ⓓ Ⓔ	38 Ⓐ Ⓑ Ⓒ Ⓓ Ⓔ	56 Ⓐ Ⓑ Ⓒ Ⓓ Ⓔ	74 Ⓐ Ⓑ Ⓒ Ⓓ Ⓔ
3 Ⓐ Ⓑ Ⓒ Ⓓ Ⓔ	21 Ⓐ Ⓑ Ⓒ Ⓓ Ⓔ	39 Ⓐ Ⓑ Ⓒ Ⓓ Ⓔ	57 Ⓐ Ⓑ Ⓒ Ⓓ Ⓔ	75 Ⓐ Ⓑ Ⓒ Ⓓ Ⓔ
4 Ⓐ Ⓑ Ⓒ Ⓓ Ⓔ	22 Ⓐ Ⓑ Ⓒ Ⓓ Ⓔ	40 Ⓐ Ⓑ Ⓒ Ⓓ Ⓔ	58 Ⓐ Ⓑ Ⓒ Ⓓ Ⓔ	76 Ⓐ Ⓑ Ⓒ Ⓓ Ⓔ
5 Ⓐ Ⓑ Ⓒ Ⓓ Ⓔ	23 Ⓐ Ⓑ Ⓒ Ⓓ Ⓔ	41 Ⓐ Ⓑ Ⓒ Ⓓ Ⓔ	59 Ⓐ Ⓑ Ⓒ Ⓓ Ⓔ	77 Ⓐ Ⓑ Ⓒ Ⓓ Ⓔ
6 Ⓐ Ⓑ Ⓒ Ⓓ Ⓔ	24 Ⓐ Ⓑ Ⓒ Ⓓ Ⓔ	42 Ⓐ Ⓑ Ⓒ Ⓓ Ⓔ	60 Ⓐ Ⓑ Ⓒ Ⓓ Ⓔ	78 Ⓐ Ⓑ Ⓒ Ⓓ Ⓔ
7 Ⓐ Ⓑ Ⓒ Ⓓ Ⓔ	25 Ⓐ Ⓑ Ⓒ Ⓓ Ⓔ	43 Ⓐ Ⓑ Ⓒ Ⓓ Ⓔ	61 Ⓐ Ⓑ Ⓒ Ⓓ Ⓔ	79 Ⓐ Ⓑ Ⓒ Ⓓ Ⓔ
8 Ⓐ Ⓑ Ⓒ Ⓓ Ⓔ	26 Ⓐ Ⓑ Ⓒ Ⓓ Ⓔ	44 Ⓐ Ⓑ Ⓒ Ⓓ Ⓔ	62 Ⓐ Ⓑ Ⓒ Ⓓ Ⓔ	80 Ⓐ Ⓑ Ⓒ Ⓓ Ⓔ
9 Ⓐ Ⓑ Ⓒ Ⓓ Ⓔ	27 Ⓐ Ⓑ Ⓒ Ⓓ Ⓔ	45 Ⓐ Ⓑ Ⓒ Ⓓ Ⓔ	63 Ⓐ Ⓑ Ⓒ Ⓓ Ⓔ	81 Ⓐ Ⓑ Ⓒ Ⓓ Ⓔ
10 Ⓐ Ⓑ Ⓒ Ⓓ Ⓔ	28 Ⓐ Ⓑ Ⓒ Ⓓ Ⓔ	46 Ⓐ Ⓑ Ⓒ Ⓓ Ⓔ	64 Ⓐ Ⓑ Ⓒ Ⓓ Ⓔ	82 Ⓐ Ⓑ Ⓒ Ⓓ Ⓔ
11 Ⓐ Ⓑ Ⓒ Ⓓ Ⓔ	29 Ⓐ Ⓑ Ⓒ Ⓓ Ⓔ	47 Ⓐ Ⓑ Ⓒ Ⓓ Ⓔ	65 Ⓐ Ⓑ Ⓒ Ⓓ Ⓔ	83 Ⓐ Ⓑ Ⓒ Ⓓ Ⓔ
12 Ⓐ Ⓑ Ⓒ Ⓓ Ⓔ	30 Ⓐ Ⓑ Ⓒ Ⓓ Ⓔ	48 Ⓐ Ⓑ Ⓒ Ⓓ Ⓔ	66 Ⓐ Ⓑ Ⓒ Ⓓ Ⓔ	84 Ⓐ Ⓑ Ⓒ Ⓓ Ⓔ
13 Ⓐ Ⓑ Ⓒ Ⓓ Ⓔ	31 Ⓐ Ⓑ Ⓒ Ⓓ Ⓔ	49 Ⓐ Ⓑ Ⓒ Ⓓ Ⓔ	67 Ⓐ Ⓑ Ⓒ Ⓓ Ⓔ	85 Ⓐ Ⓑ Ⓒ Ⓓ Ⓔ
14 Ⓐ Ⓑ Ⓒ Ⓓ Ⓔ	32 Ⓐ Ⓑ Ⓒ Ⓓ Ⓔ	50 Ⓐ Ⓑ Ⓒ Ⓓ Ⓔ	68 Ⓐ Ⓑ Ⓒ Ⓓ Ⓔ	86 Ⓐ Ⓑ Ⓒ Ⓓ Ⓔ
15 Ⓐ Ⓑ Ⓒ Ⓓ Ⓔ	33 Ⓐ Ⓑ Ⓒ Ⓓ Ⓔ	51 Ⓐ Ⓑ Ⓒ Ⓓ Ⓔ	69 Ⓐ Ⓑ Ⓒ Ⓓ Ⓔ	87 Ⓐ Ⓑ Ⓒ Ⓓ Ⓔ
16 Ⓐ Ⓑ Ⓒ Ⓓ Ⓔ	34 Ⓐ Ⓑ Ⓒ Ⓓ Ⓔ	52 Ⓐ Ⓑ Ⓒ Ⓓ Ⓔ	70 Ⓐ Ⓑ Ⓒ Ⓓ Ⓔ	88 Ⓐ Ⓑ Ⓒ Ⓓ Ⓔ
17 Ⓐ Ⓑ Ⓒ Ⓓ Ⓔ	35 Ⓐ Ⓑ Ⓒ Ⓓ Ⓔ	53 Ⓐ Ⓑ Ⓒ Ⓓ Ⓔ	71 Ⓐ Ⓑ Ⓒ Ⓓ Ⓔ	
18 Ⓐ Ⓑ Ⓒ Ⓓ Ⓔ	36 Ⓐ Ⓑ Ⓒ Ⓓ Ⓔ	54 Ⓐ Ⓑ Ⓒ Ⓓ Ⓔ	72 Ⓐ Ⓑ Ⓒ Ⓓ Ⓔ	

Number Series - Part C

1 Ⓐ Ⓑ Ⓒ Ⓓ Ⓔ	7 Ⓐ Ⓑ Ⓒ Ⓓ Ⓔ	13 Ⓐ Ⓑ Ⓒ Ⓓ Ⓔ	19 Ⓐ Ⓑ Ⓒ Ⓓ Ⓔ
2 Ⓐ Ⓑ Ⓒ Ⓓ Ⓔ	8 Ⓐ Ⓑ Ⓒ Ⓓ Ⓔ	14 Ⓐ Ⓑ Ⓒ Ⓓ Ⓔ	20 Ⓐ Ⓑ Ⓒ Ⓓ Ⓔ
3 Ⓐ Ⓑ Ⓒ Ⓓ Ⓔ	9 Ⓐ Ⓑ Ⓒ Ⓓ Ⓔ	15 Ⓐ Ⓑ Ⓒ Ⓓ Ⓔ	21 Ⓐ Ⓑ Ⓒ Ⓓ Ⓔ
4 Ⓐ Ⓑ Ⓒ Ⓓ Ⓔ	10 Ⓐ Ⓑ Ⓒ Ⓓ Ⓔ	16 Ⓐ Ⓑ Ⓒ Ⓓ Ⓔ	22 Ⓐ Ⓑ Ⓒ Ⓓ Ⓔ
5 Ⓐ Ⓑ Ⓒ Ⓓ Ⓔ	11 Ⓐ Ⓑ Ⓒ Ⓓ Ⓔ	17 Ⓐ Ⓑ Ⓒ Ⓓ Ⓔ	23 Ⓐ Ⓑ Ⓒ Ⓓ Ⓔ
6 Ⓐ Ⓑ Ⓒ Ⓓ Ⓔ	12 Ⓐ Ⓑ Ⓒ Ⓓ Ⓔ	18 Ⓐ Ⓑ Ⓒ Ⓓ Ⓔ	24 Ⓐ Ⓑ Ⓒ Ⓓ Ⓔ

Following Oral Instructions - Part D

1 Ⓐ Ⓑ Ⓒ Ⓓ Ⓔ	19 Ⓐ Ⓑ Ⓒ Ⓓ Ⓔ	37 Ⓐ Ⓑ Ⓒ Ⓓ Ⓔ	55 Ⓐ Ⓑ Ⓒ Ⓓ Ⓔ	73 Ⓐ Ⓑ Ⓒ Ⓓ Ⓔ
2 Ⓐ Ⓑ Ⓒ Ⓓ Ⓔ	20 Ⓐ Ⓑ Ⓒ Ⓓ Ⓔ	38 Ⓐ Ⓑ Ⓒ Ⓓ Ⓔ	56 Ⓐ Ⓑ Ⓒ Ⓓ Ⓔ	74 Ⓐ Ⓑ Ⓒ Ⓓ Ⓔ
3 Ⓐ Ⓑ Ⓒ Ⓓ Ⓔ	21 Ⓐ Ⓑ Ⓒ Ⓓ Ⓔ	39 Ⓐ Ⓑ Ⓒ Ⓓ Ⓔ	57 Ⓐ Ⓑ Ⓒ Ⓓ Ⓔ	75 Ⓐ Ⓑ Ⓒ Ⓓ Ⓔ
4 Ⓐ Ⓑ Ⓒ Ⓓ Ⓔ	22 Ⓐ Ⓑ Ⓒ Ⓓ Ⓔ	40 Ⓐ Ⓑ Ⓒ Ⓓ Ⓔ	58 Ⓐ Ⓑ Ⓒ Ⓓ Ⓔ	76 Ⓐ Ⓑ Ⓒ Ⓓ Ⓔ
5 Ⓐ Ⓑ Ⓒ Ⓓ Ⓔ	23 Ⓐ Ⓑ Ⓒ Ⓓ Ⓔ	41 Ⓐ Ⓑ Ⓒ Ⓓ Ⓔ	59 Ⓐ Ⓑ Ⓒ Ⓓ Ⓔ	77 Ⓐ Ⓑ Ⓒ Ⓓ Ⓔ
6 Ⓐ Ⓑ Ⓒ Ⓓ Ⓔ	24 Ⓐ Ⓑ Ⓒ Ⓓ Ⓔ	42 Ⓐ Ⓑ Ⓒ Ⓓ Ⓔ	60 Ⓐ Ⓑ Ⓒ Ⓓ Ⓔ	78 Ⓐ Ⓑ Ⓒ Ⓓ Ⓔ
7 Ⓐ Ⓑ Ⓒ Ⓓ Ⓔ	25 Ⓐ Ⓑ Ⓒ Ⓓ Ⓔ	43 Ⓐ Ⓑ Ⓒ Ⓓ Ⓔ	61 Ⓐ Ⓑ Ⓒ Ⓓ Ⓔ	79 Ⓐ Ⓑ Ⓒ Ⓓ Ⓔ
8 Ⓐ Ⓑ Ⓒ Ⓓ Ⓔ	26 Ⓐ Ⓑ Ⓒ Ⓓ Ⓔ	44 Ⓐ Ⓑ Ⓒ Ⓓ Ⓔ	62 Ⓐ Ⓑ Ⓒ Ⓓ Ⓔ	80 Ⓐ Ⓑ Ⓒ Ⓓ Ⓔ
9 Ⓐ Ⓑ Ⓒ Ⓓ Ⓔ	27 Ⓐ Ⓑ Ⓒ Ⓓ Ⓔ	45 Ⓐ Ⓑ Ⓒ Ⓓ Ⓔ	63 Ⓐ Ⓑ Ⓒ Ⓓ Ⓔ	81 Ⓐ Ⓑ Ⓒ Ⓓ Ⓔ
10 Ⓐ Ⓑ Ⓒ Ⓓ Ⓔ	28 Ⓐ Ⓑ Ⓒ Ⓓ Ⓔ	46 Ⓐ Ⓑ Ⓒ Ⓓ Ⓔ	64 Ⓐ Ⓑ Ⓒ Ⓓ Ⓔ	82 Ⓐ Ⓑ Ⓒ Ⓓ Ⓔ
11 Ⓐ Ⓑ Ⓒ Ⓓ Ⓔ	29 Ⓐ Ⓑ Ⓒ Ⓓ Ⓔ	47 Ⓐ Ⓑ Ⓒ Ⓓ Ⓔ	65 Ⓐ Ⓑ Ⓒ Ⓓ Ⓔ	83 Ⓐ Ⓑ Ⓒ Ⓓ Ⓔ
12 Ⓐ Ⓑ Ⓒ Ⓓ Ⓔ	30 Ⓐ Ⓑ Ⓒ Ⓓ Ⓔ	48 Ⓐ Ⓑ Ⓒ Ⓓ Ⓔ	66 Ⓐ Ⓑ Ⓒ Ⓓ Ⓔ	84 Ⓐ Ⓑ Ⓒ Ⓓ Ⓔ
13 Ⓐ Ⓑ Ⓒ Ⓓ Ⓔ	31 Ⓐ Ⓑ Ⓒ Ⓓ Ⓔ	49 Ⓐ Ⓑ Ⓒ Ⓓ Ⓔ	67 Ⓐ Ⓑ Ⓒ Ⓓ Ⓔ	85 Ⓐ Ⓑ Ⓒ Ⓓ Ⓔ
14 Ⓐ Ⓑ Ⓒ Ⓓ Ⓔ	32 Ⓐ Ⓑ Ⓒ Ⓓ Ⓔ	50 Ⓐ Ⓑ Ⓒ Ⓓ Ⓔ	68 Ⓐ Ⓑ Ⓒ Ⓓ Ⓔ	86 Ⓐ Ⓑ Ⓒ Ⓓ Ⓔ
15 Ⓐ Ⓑ Ⓒ Ⓓ Ⓔ	33 Ⓐ Ⓑ Ⓒ Ⓓ Ⓔ	51 Ⓐ Ⓑ Ⓒ Ⓓ Ⓔ	69 Ⓐ Ⓑ Ⓒ Ⓓ Ⓔ	87 Ⓐ Ⓑ Ⓒ Ⓓ Ⓔ
16 Ⓐ Ⓑ Ⓒ Ⓓ Ⓔ	34 Ⓐ Ⓑ Ⓒ Ⓓ Ⓔ	52 Ⓐ Ⓑ Ⓒ Ⓓ Ⓔ	70 Ⓐ Ⓑ Ⓒ Ⓓ Ⓔ	88 Ⓐ Ⓑ Ⓒ Ⓓ Ⓔ
17 Ⓐ Ⓑ Ⓒ Ⓓ Ⓔ	35 Ⓐ Ⓑ Ⓒ Ⓓ Ⓔ	53 Ⓐ Ⓑ Ⓒ Ⓓ Ⓔ	71 Ⓐ Ⓑ Ⓒ Ⓓ Ⓔ	
18 Ⓐ Ⓑ Ⓒ Ⓓ Ⓔ	36 Ⓐ Ⓑ Ⓒ Ⓓ Ⓔ	54 Ⓐ Ⓑ Ⓒ Ⓓ Ⓔ	72 Ⓐ Ⓑ Ⓒ Ⓓ Ⓔ	

214

ANSWER SHEET

Address Checking - Part A

1 Ⓐ Ⓓ	13 Ⓐ Ⓓ	25 Ⓐ Ⓓ	37 Ⓐ Ⓓ	49 Ⓐ Ⓓ	61 Ⓐ Ⓓ	73 Ⓐ Ⓓ	85 Ⓐ Ⓓ
2 Ⓐ Ⓓ	14 Ⓐ Ⓓ	26 Ⓐ Ⓓ	38 Ⓐ Ⓓ	50 Ⓐ Ⓓ	62 Ⓐ Ⓓ	74 Ⓐ Ⓓ	86 Ⓐ Ⓓ
3 Ⓐ Ⓓ	15 Ⓐ Ⓓ	27 Ⓐ Ⓓ	39 Ⓐ Ⓓ	51 Ⓐ Ⓓ	63 Ⓐ Ⓓ	75 Ⓐ Ⓓ	87 Ⓐ Ⓓ
4 Ⓐ Ⓓ	16 Ⓐ Ⓓ	28 Ⓐ Ⓓ	40 Ⓐ Ⓓ	52 Ⓐ Ⓓ	64 Ⓐ Ⓓ	76 Ⓐ Ⓓ	88 Ⓐ Ⓓ
5 Ⓐ Ⓓ	17 Ⓐ Ⓓ	29 Ⓐ Ⓓ	41 Ⓐ Ⓓ	53 Ⓐ Ⓓ	65 Ⓐ Ⓓ	77 Ⓐ Ⓓ	89 Ⓐ Ⓓ
6 Ⓐ Ⓓ	18 Ⓐ Ⓓ	30 Ⓐ Ⓓ	42 Ⓐ Ⓓ	54 Ⓐ Ⓓ	66 Ⓐ Ⓓ	78 Ⓐ Ⓓ	90 Ⓐ Ⓓ
7 Ⓐ Ⓓ	19 Ⓐ Ⓓ	31 Ⓐ Ⓓ	43 Ⓐ Ⓓ	55 Ⓐ Ⓓ	67 Ⓐ Ⓓ	79 Ⓐ Ⓓ	91 Ⓐ Ⓓ
8 Ⓐ Ⓓ	20 Ⓐ Ⓓ	32 Ⓐ Ⓓ	44 Ⓐ Ⓓ	56 Ⓐ Ⓓ	68 Ⓐ Ⓓ	80 Ⓐ Ⓓ	92 Ⓐ Ⓓ
9 Ⓐ Ⓓ	21 Ⓐ Ⓓ	33 Ⓐ Ⓓ	45 Ⓐ Ⓓ	57 Ⓐ Ⓓ	69 Ⓐ Ⓓ	81 Ⓐ Ⓓ	93 Ⓐ Ⓓ
10 Ⓐ Ⓓ	22 Ⓐ Ⓓ	34 Ⓐ Ⓓ	46 Ⓐ Ⓓ	58 Ⓐ Ⓓ	70 Ⓐ Ⓓ	82 Ⓐ Ⓓ	94 Ⓐ Ⓓ
11 Ⓐ Ⓓ	23 Ⓐ Ⓓ	35 Ⓐ Ⓓ	47 Ⓐ Ⓓ	59 Ⓐ Ⓓ	71 Ⓐ Ⓓ	83 Ⓐ Ⓓ	95 Ⓐ Ⓓ
12 Ⓐ Ⓓ	24 Ⓐ Ⓓ	36 Ⓐ Ⓓ	48 Ⓐ Ⓓ	60 Ⓐ Ⓓ	72 Ⓐ Ⓓ	84 Ⓐ Ⓓ	

Address Memory - Part B

1 Ⓐ Ⓑ Ⓒ Ⓓ Ⓔ	19 Ⓐ Ⓑ Ⓒ Ⓓ Ⓔ	37 Ⓐ Ⓑ Ⓒ Ⓓ Ⓔ	55 Ⓐ Ⓑ Ⓒ Ⓓ Ⓔ	73 Ⓐ Ⓑ Ⓒ Ⓓ Ⓔ
2 Ⓐ Ⓑ Ⓒ Ⓓ Ⓔ	20 Ⓐ Ⓑ Ⓒ Ⓓ Ⓔ	38 Ⓐ Ⓑ Ⓒ Ⓓ Ⓔ	56 Ⓐ Ⓑ Ⓒ Ⓓ Ⓔ	74 Ⓐ Ⓑ Ⓒ Ⓓ Ⓔ
3 Ⓐ Ⓑ Ⓒ Ⓓ Ⓔ	21 Ⓐ Ⓑ Ⓒ Ⓓ Ⓔ	39 Ⓐ Ⓑ Ⓒ Ⓓ Ⓔ	57 Ⓐ Ⓑ Ⓒ Ⓓ Ⓔ	75 Ⓐ Ⓑ Ⓒ Ⓓ Ⓔ
4 Ⓐ Ⓑ Ⓒ Ⓓ Ⓔ	22 Ⓐ Ⓑ Ⓒ Ⓓ Ⓔ	40 Ⓐ Ⓑ Ⓒ Ⓓ Ⓔ	58 Ⓐ Ⓑ Ⓒ Ⓓ Ⓔ	76 Ⓐ Ⓑ Ⓒ Ⓓ Ⓔ
5 Ⓐ Ⓑ Ⓒ Ⓓ Ⓔ	23 Ⓐ Ⓑ Ⓒ Ⓓ Ⓔ	41 Ⓐ Ⓑ Ⓒ Ⓓ Ⓔ	59 Ⓐ Ⓑ Ⓒ Ⓓ Ⓔ	77 Ⓐ Ⓑ Ⓒ Ⓓ Ⓔ
6 Ⓐ Ⓑ Ⓒ Ⓓ Ⓔ	24 Ⓐ Ⓑ Ⓒ Ⓓ Ⓔ	42 Ⓐ Ⓑ Ⓒ Ⓓ Ⓔ	60 Ⓐ Ⓑ Ⓒ Ⓓ Ⓔ	78 Ⓐ Ⓑ Ⓒ Ⓓ Ⓔ
7 Ⓐ Ⓑ Ⓒ Ⓓ Ⓔ	25 Ⓐ Ⓑ Ⓒ Ⓓ Ⓔ	43 Ⓐ Ⓑ Ⓒ Ⓓ Ⓔ	61 Ⓐ Ⓑ Ⓒ Ⓓ Ⓔ	79 Ⓐ Ⓑ Ⓒ Ⓓ Ⓔ
8 Ⓐ Ⓑ Ⓒ Ⓓ Ⓔ	26 Ⓐ Ⓑ Ⓒ Ⓓ Ⓔ	44 Ⓐ Ⓑ Ⓒ Ⓓ Ⓔ	62 Ⓐ Ⓑ Ⓒ Ⓓ Ⓔ	80 Ⓐ Ⓑ Ⓒ Ⓓ Ⓔ
9 Ⓐ Ⓑ Ⓒ Ⓓ Ⓔ	27 Ⓐ Ⓑ Ⓒ Ⓓ Ⓔ	45 Ⓐ Ⓑ Ⓒ Ⓓ Ⓔ	63 Ⓐ Ⓑ Ⓒ Ⓓ Ⓔ	81 Ⓐ Ⓑ Ⓒ Ⓓ Ⓔ
10 Ⓐ Ⓑ Ⓒ Ⓓ Ⓔ	28 Ⓐ Ⓑ Ⓒ Ⓓ Ⓔ	46 Ⓐ Ⓑ Ⓒ Ⓓ Ⓔ	64 Ⓐ Ⓑ Ⓒ Ⓓ Ⓔ	82 Ⓐ Ⓑ Ⓒ Ⓓ Ⓔ
11 Ⓐ Ⓑ Ⓒ Ⓓ Ⓔ	29 Ⓐ Ⓑ Ⓒ Ⓓ Ⓔ	47 Ⓐ Ⓑ Ⓒ Ⓓ Ⓔ	65 Ⓐ Ⓑ Ⓒ Ⓓ Ⓔ	83 Ⓐ Ⓑ Ⓒ Ⓓ Ⓔ
12 Ⓐ Ⓑ Ⓒ Ⓓ Ⓔ	30 Ⓐ Ⓑ Ⓒ Ⓓ Ⓔ	48 Ⓐ Ⓑ Ⓒ Ⓓ Ⓔ	66 Ⓐ Ⓑ Ⓒ Ⓓ Ⓔ	84 Ⓐ Ⓑ Ⓒ Ⓓ Ⓔ
13 Ⓐ Ⓑ Ⓒ Ⓓ Ⓔ	31 Ⓐ Ⓑ Ⓒ Ⓓ Ⓔ	49 Ⓐ Ⓑ Ⓒ Ⓓ Ⓔ	67 Ⓐ Ⓑ Ⓒ Ⓓ Ⓔ	85 Ⓐ Ⓑ Ⓒ Ⓓ Ⓔ
14 Ⓐ Ⓑ Ⓒ Ⓓ Ⓔ	32 Ⓐ Ⓑ Ⓒ Ⓓ Ⓔ	50 Ⓐ Ⓑ Ⓒ Ⓓ Ⓔ	68 Ⓐ Ⓑ Ⓒ Ⓓ Ⓔ	86 Ⓐ Ⓑ Ⓒ Ⓓ Ⓔ
15 Ⓐ Ⓑ Ⓒ Ⓓ Ⓔ	33 Ⓐ Ⓑ Ⓒ Ⓓ Ⓔ	51 Ⓐ Ⓑ Ⓒ Ⓓ Ⓔ	69 Ⓐ Ⓑ Ⓒ Ⓓ Ⓔ	87 Ⓐ Ⓑ Ⓒ Ⓓ Ⓔ
16 Ⓐ Ⓑ Ⓒ Ⓓ Ⓔ	34 Ⓐ Ⓑ Ⓒ Ⓓ Ⓔ	52 Ⓐ Ⓑ Ⓒ Ⓓ Ⓔ	70 Ⓐ Ⓑ Ⓒ Ⓓ Ⓔ	88 Ⓐ Ⓑ Ⓒ Ⓓ Ⓔ
17 Ⓐ Ⓑ Ⓒ Ⓓ Ⓔ	35 Ⓐ Ⓑ Ⓒ Ⓓ Ⓔ	53 Ⓐ Ⓑ Ⓒ Ⓓ Ⓔ	71 Ⓐ Ⓑ Ⓒ Ⓓ Ⓔ	
18 Ⓐ Ⓑ Ⓒ Ⓓ Ⓔ	36 Ⓐ Ⓑ Ⓒ Ⓓ Ⓔ	54 Ⓐ Ⓑ Ⓒ Ⓓ Ⓔ	72 Ⓐ Ⓑ Ⓒ Ⓓ Ⓔ	

Number Series - Part C

1 Ⓐ Ⓑ Ⓒ Ⓓ Ⓔ	7 Ⓐ Ⓑ Ⓒ Ⓓ Ⓔ	13 Ⓐ Ⓑ Ⓒ Ⓓ Ⓔ	19 Ⓐ Ⓑ Ⓒ Ⓓ Ⓔ
2 Ⓐ Ⓑ Ⓒ Ⓓ Ⓔ	8 Ⓐ Ⓑ Ⓒ Ⓓ Ⓔ	14 Ⓐ Ⓑ Ⓒ Ⓓ Ⓔ	20 Ⓐ Ⓑ Ⓒ Ⓓ Ⓔ
3 Ⓐ Ⓑ Ⓒ Ⓓ Ⓔ	9 Ⓐ Ⓑ Ⓒ Ⓓ Ⓔ	15 Ⓐ Ⓑ Ⓒ Ⓓ Ⓔ	21 Ⓐ Ⓑ Ⓒ Ⓓ Ⓔ
4 Ⓐ Ⓑ Ⓒ Ⓓ Ⓔ	10 Ⓐ Ⓑ Ⓒ Ⓓ Ⓔ	16 Ⓐ Ⓑ Ⓒ Ⓓ Ⓔ	22 Ⓐ Ⓑ Ⓒ Ⓓ Ⓔ
5 Ⓐ Ⓑ Ⓒ Ⓓ Ⓔ	11 Ⓐ Ⓑ Ⓒ Ⓓ Ⓔ	17 Ⓐ Ⓑ Ⓒ Ⓓ Ⓔ	23 Ⓐ Ⓑ Ⓒ Ⓓ Ⓔ
6 Ⓐ Ⓑ Ⓒ Ⓓ Ⓔ	12 Ⓐ Ⓑ Ⓒ Ⓓ Ⓔ	18 Ⓐ Ⓑ Ⓒ Ⓓ Ⓔ	24 Ⓐ Ⓑ Ⓒ Ⓓ Ⓔ

Following Oral Instructions - Part D

1 Ⓐ Ⓑ Ⓒ Ⓓ Ⓔ	19 Ⓐ Ⓑ Ⓒ Ⓓ Ⓔ	37 Ⓐ Ⓑ Ⓒ Ⓓ Ⓔ	55 Ⓐ Ⓑ Ⓒ Ⓓ Ⓔ	73 Ⓐ Ⓑ Ⓒ Ⓓ Ⓔ
2 Ⓐ Ⓑ Ⓒ Ⓓ Ⓔ	20 Ⓐ Ⓑ Ⓒ Ⓓ Ⓔ	38 Ⓐ Ⓑ Ⓒ Ⓓ Ⓔ	56 Ⓐ Ⓑ Ⓒ Ⓓ Ⓔ	74 Ⓐ Ⓑ Ⓒ Ⓓ Ⓔ
3 Ⓐ Ⓑ Ⓒ Ⓓ Ⓔ	21 Ⓐ Ⓑ Ⓒ Ⓓ Ⓔ	39 Ⓐ Ⓑ Ⓒ Ⓓ Ⓔ	57 Ⓐ Ⓑ Ⓒ Ⓓ Ⓔ	75 Ⓐ Ⓑ Ⓒ Ⓓ Ⓔ
4 Ⓐ Ⓑ Ⓒ Ⓓ Ⓔ	22 Ⓐ Ⓑ Ⓒ Ⓓ Ⓔ	40 Ⓐ Ⓑ Ⓒ Ⓓ Ⓔ	58 Ⓐ Ⓑ Ⓒ Ⓓ Ⓔ	76 Ⓐ Ⓑ Ⓒ Ⓓ Ⓔ
5 Ⓐ Ⓑ Ⓒ Ⓓ Ⓔ	23 Ⓐ Ⓑ Ⓒ Ⓓ Ⓔ	41 Ⓐ Ⓑ Ⓒ Ⓓ Ⓔ	59 Ⓐ Ⓑ Ⓒ Ⓓ Ⓔ	77 Ⓐ Ⓑ Ⓒ Ⓓ Ⓔ
6 Ⓐ Ⓑ Ⓒ Ⓓ Ⓔ	24 Ⓐ Ⓑ Ⓒ Ⓓ Ⓔ	42 Ⓐ Ⓑ Ⓒ Ⓓ Ⓔ	60 Ⓐ Ⓑ Ⓒ Ⓓ Ⓔ	78 Ⓐ Ⓑ Ⓒ Ⓓ Ⓔ
7 Ⓐ Ⓑ Ⓒ Ⓓ Ⓔ	25 Ⓐ Ⓑ Ⓒ Ⓓ Ⓔ	43 Ⓐ Ⓑ Ⓒ Ⓓ Ⓔ	61 Ⓐ Ⓑ Ⓒ Ⓓ Ⓔ	79 Ⓐ Ⓑ Ⓒ Ⓓ Ⓔ
8 Ⓐ Ⓑ Ⓒ Ⓓ Ⓔ	26 Ⓐ Ⓑ Ⓒ Ⓓ Ⓔ	44 Ⓐ Ⓑ Ⓒ Ⓓ Ⓔ	62 Ⓐ Ⓑ Ⓒ Ⓓ Ⓔ	80 Ⓐ Ⓑ Ⓒ Ⓓ Ⓔ
9 Ⓐ Ⓑ Ⓒ Ⓓ Ⓔ	27 Ⓐ Ⓑ Ⓒ Ⓓ Ⓔ	45 Ⓐ Ⓑ Ⓒ Ⓓ Ⓔ	63 Ⓐ Ⓑ Ⓒ Ⓓ Ⓔ	81 Ⓐ Ⓑ Ⓒ Ⓓ Ⓔ
10 Ⓐ Ⓑ Ⓒ Ⓓ Ⓔ	28 Ⓐ Ⓑ Ⓒ Ⓓ Ⓔ	46 Ⓐ Ⓑ Ⓒ Ⓓ Ⓔ	64 Ⓐ Ⓑ Ⓒ Ⓓ Ⓔ	82 Ⓐ Ⓑ Ⓒ Ⓓ Ⓔ
11 Ⓐ Ⓑ Ⓒ Ⓓ Ⓔ	29 Ⓐ Ⓑ Ⓒ Ⓓ Ⓔ	47 Ⓐ Ⓑ Ⓒ Ⓓ Ⓔ	65 Ⓐ Ⓑ Ⓒ Ⓓ Ⓔ	83 Ⓐ Ⓑ Ⓒ Ⓓ Ⓔ
12 Ⓐ Ⓑ Ⓒ Ⓓ Ⓔ	30 Ⓐ Ⓑ Ⓒ Ⓓ Ⓔ	48 Ⓐ Ⓑ Ⓒ Ⓓ Ⓔ	66 Ⓐ Ⓑ Ⓒ Ⓓ Ⓔ	84 Ⓐ Ⓑ Ⓒ Ⓓ Ⓔ
13 Ⓐ Ⓑ Ⓒ Ⓓ Ⓔ	31 Ⓐ Ⓑ Ⓒ Ⓓ Ⓔ	49 Ⓐ Ⓑ Ⓒ Ⓓ Ⓔ	67 Ⓐ Ⓑ Ⓒ Ⓓ Ⓔ	85 Ⓐ Ⓑ Ⓒ Ⓓ Ⓔ
14 Ⓐ Ⓑ Ⓒ Ⓓ Ⓔ	32 Ⓐ Ⓑ Ⓒ Ⓓ Ⓔ	50 Ⓐ Ⓑ Ⓒ Ⓓ Ⓔ	68 Ⓐ Ⓑ Ⓒ Ⓓ Ⓔ	86 Ⓐ Ⓑ Ⓒ Ⓓ Ⓔ
15 Ⓐ Ⓑ Ⓒ Ⓓ Ⓔ	33 Ⓐ Ⓑ Ⓒ Ⓓ Ⓔ	51 Ⓐ Ⓑ Ⓒ Ⓓ Ⓔ	69 Ⓐ Ⓑ Ⓒ Ⓓ Ⓔ	87 Ⓐ Ⓑ Ⓒ Ⓓ Ⓔ
16 Ⓐ Ⓑ Ⓒ Ⓓ Ⓔ	34 Ⓐ Ⓑ Ⓒ Ⓓ Ⓔ	52 Ⓐ Ⓑ Ⓒ Ⓓ Ⓔ	70 Ⓐ Ⓑ Ⓒ Ⓓ Ⓔ	88 Ⓐ Ⓑ Ⓒ Ⓓ Ⓔ
17 Ⓐ Ⓑ Ⓒ Ⓓ Ⓔ	35 Ⓐ Ⓑ Ⓒ Ⓓ Ⓔ	53 Ⓐ Ⓑ Ⓒ Ⓓ Ⓔ	71 Ⓐ Ⓑ Ⓒ Ⓓ Ⓔ	
18 Ⓐ Ⓑ Ⓒ Ⓓ Ⓔ	36 Ⓐ Ⓑ Ⓒ Ⓓ Ⓔ	54 Ⓐ Ⓑ Ⓒ Ⓓ Ⓔ	72 Ⓐ Ⓑ Ⓒ Ⓓ Ⓔ	

Answer Key for Complete Practice Exam #1

Address Checking		Address Memory		Number Series	Following Oral Instructions
1. D	49. D	1. D	45. A	1. B	1. 22-E
2. A	50. D	2. D	46. A	2. A	2. 3-C
3. D	51. A	3. A	47. C	3. E	3. 5-E
4. A	52. D	4. D	48. C	4. A	4. 8-A
5. D	53. D	5. C	49. B	5. A	5. 67-D
6. D	54. D	6. D	50. C	6. C	6. 21-E
7. A	55. A	7. E	51. E	7. A	7. 45-A
8. A	56. D	8. B	52. A	8. C	8. 15-D
9. D	57. D	9. C	53. C	9. A	9. 7-D
10. A	58. D	10. A	54. E	10. D	10. 72-E
11. A	59. D	11. C	55. D	11. C	11. 77-A
12. A	60. D	12. D	56. E	12. E	12. 59-A
13. D	61. A	13. D	57. C	13. E	13. 30-C
14. A	62. D	14. E	58. A	14. B	14. 78-C, 88-D, 26-C
15. D	63. D	15. A	59. B	15. B	15. 25-E
16. A	64. A	16. E	60. E	16. C	16. 62-C, 39-D
17. A	65. A	17. A	61. E	17. B	17. 11-B
18. D	66. A	18. A	62. C	18. C	18. 12-C
19. A	67. D	19. B	63. B	19. D	19. 13-A
20. A	68. D	20. C	64. A	20. C	20. 28-A
21. D	69. D	21. B	65. B	21. D	21. 2-D
22. A	70. D	22. B	66. C	22. C	22. 41-A
23. D	71. D	23. E	67. E	23. B	23. 1-E
24. A	72. A	24. A	68. A	24. B	24. 81-A
25. D	73. D	25. B	69. B		25. 33-E
26. A	74. D	26. C	70. B		26. 82-A
27. A	75. A	27. E	71. D		27. 16-A
28. D	76. A	28. D	72. B		
29. A	77. D	29. C	73. D		
30. A	78. D	30. D	74. A		
31. A	79. D	31. C	75. E		
32. D	80. A	32. E	76. C		
33. D	81. A	33. C	77. D		
34. D	82. D	34. A	78. D		
35. A	83. A	35. E	79. A		
36. D	84. A	36. E	80. B		
37. A	85. D	37. C	81. A		
38. A	86. D	38. D	82. E		
39. D	87. A	39. B	83. A		
40. A	88. D	40. E	84. E		
41. D	89. A	41. B	85. E		
42. D	90. A	42. D	86. D		
43. A	91. D	43. A	87. D		
44. A	92. A	44. D	88. C		
45. D	93. D				
46. D	94. A				
47. A	95. D				
48. A					

Answer Key for Complete Practice Exam #2

Address Checking		Address Memory		Number Series	Following Oral Instructions
1. A	49. D	1. E	45. B	1. B	1. 11-A
2. D	50. D	2. E	46. C	2. A	2. 78-B
3. A	51. D	3. C	47. B	3. D	3. 3-A
4. A	52. A	4. B	48. D	4. B	4. 82-B
5. D	53. D	5. C	49. D	5. A	5. 8-A
6. D	54. D	6. E	50. E	6. C	6. 5-B
7. D	55. A	7. E	51. A	7. D	7. 27-A
8. A	56. A	8. C	52. D	8. D	8. 4-C
9. A	57. D	9. C	53. B	9. A	9. 9-D
10. A	58. D	10. A	54. A	10. E	10. 36-E
11. D	59. D	11. B	55. E	11. A	11. 2-B, 33-E
12. D	60. D	12. A	56. B	12. D	12. 62-D
13. D	61. A	13. E	57. C	13. E	13. 54-A
14. D	62. D	14. B	58. D	14. B	14. 10-E
15. A	63. D	15. B	59. E	15. A	15. 44-C
16. A	64. D	16. D	60. E	16. C	16. 64-B
17. D	65. A	17. C	61. E	17. C	17. 17-C, 39-E
18. A	66. D	18. D	62. B	18. C	18. 30-B
19. D	67. A	19. A	63. A	19. E	19. 75-A
20. A	68. D	20. E	64. C	20. A	20. 32-A, 51-E
21. D	69. A	21. D	65. E	21. B	21. 49-C, 1-D
22. A	70. D	22. C	66. C	22. C	22. 22-C
23. A	71. D	23. D	67. A	23. D	23. 12-B
24. D	72. D	24. A	68. E	24. E	24. 71-E
25. A	73. D	25. B	69. B		25. 88-B
26. A	74. D	26. E	70. D		26. 7-C
27. D	75. A	27. B	71. D		
28. D	76. A	28. E	72. D		
29. A	77. D	29. C	73. B		
30. D	78. D	30. A	74. D		
31. D	79. A	31. A	75. C		
32. A	80. D	32. E	76. C		
33. D	81. D	33. D	77. B		
34. A	82. D	34. E	78. B		
35. D	83. D	35. B	79. A		
36. D	84. D	36. D	80. E		
37. A	85. A	37. C	81. E		
38. A	86. D	38. A	82. D		
39. D	87. D	39. D	83. B		
40. A	88. D	40. E	84. A		
41. A	89. D	41. A	85. A		
42. D	90. A	42. A	86. E		
43. A	91. D	43. D	87. A		
44. D	92. D	44. C	88. B		
45. D	93. A				
46. A	94. D				
47. D	95. D				
48. A					

Answer Key for Complete Practice Exam #3

Address Checking		Address Memory		Number Series	Following Oral Instructions
1. D	49. D	1. E	45. B	1. C	1. 42-C
2. D	50. D	2. C	46. D	2. E	2. 11-D
3. A	51. A	3. B	47. B	3. A	3. 35-E
4. D	52. D	4. E	48. E	4. B	4. 73-E, 37-D
5. D	53. A	5. D	49. D	5. D	5. 68-D, 85-A
6. A	54. A	6. C	50. C	6. A	6. 30-D
7. A	55. A	7. A	51. C	7. E	7. 36-E, 83-A
8. D	56. D	8. C	52. C	8. C	8. 79-C
9. A	57. A	9. B	53. A	9. B	9. 38-B
10. D	58. A	10. E	54. E	10. D	10. 7-A, 2-A
11. A	59. D	11. C	55. A	11. A	11. 34-A
12. D	60. D	12. A	56. D	12. E	12. 58-E
13. A	61. A	13. A	57. A	13. E	13. 71-D, 61-E
14. A	62. D	14. D	58. B	14. C	14. 72-E, 22-D
15. A	63. A	15. B	59. D	15. B	15. 15-B
16. D	64. A	16. B	60. B	16. D	16. 1-D
17. A	65. D	17. D	61. E	17. B	17. 17-B
18. A	66. A	18. C	62. C	18. A	18. 4-C
19. D	67. D	19. E	63. A	19. E	19. 20-B
20. A	68. D	20. D	64. A	20. C	20. 56-C
21. D	69. D	21. A	65. C	21. A	21. 41-D
22. A	70. A	22. A	66. E	22. D	22. 14-C
23. A	71. A	23. B	67. B	23. C	23. 5-B
24. A	72. D	24. E	68. D	24. E	24. 6-E
25. D	73. D	25. E	69. E		
26. A	74. A	26. D	70. A		
27. D	75. A	27. C	71. A		
28. D	76. D	28. D	72. D		
29. D	77. D	29. C	73. C		
30. A	78. A	30. B	74. A		
31. A	79. A	31. E	75. E		
32. D	80. A	32. A	76. D		
33. D	81. D	33. A	77. C		
34. D	82. D	34. B	78. B		
35. A	83. A	35. E	79. E		
36. D	84. D	36. D	80. B		
37. D	85. A	37. E	81. E		
38. D	86. D	38. C	82. B		
39. A	87. A	39. C	83. D		
40. D	88. A	40. A	84. A		
41. D	89. D	41. D	85. B		
42. D	90. A	42. B	86. B		
43. A	91. D	43. A	87. E		
44. D	92. A	44. B	88. E		
45. D	93. A				
46. D	94. D				
47. A	95. A				
48. D					

Answer Key for Complete Practice Exam #4

	Address Checking			Address Memory		Number Series		Following Oral Instructions
1.	A	49. D	1. A	45. B		1. B		1. 44-D
2.	A	50. A	2. C	46. E		2. C		2. 23-A
3.	A	51. D	3. E	47. A		3. D		3. 28-B, 3 0-B, 41-B
4.	D	52. A	4. B	48. E		4. B		4. 62-E
5.	A	53. A	5. E	49. B		5. A		5. 19-A
6.	D	54. D	6. D	50. D		6. D		6. 71-D
7.	A	55. A	7. A	51. A		7. E		7. 14-C, 37-B, 21-E
8.	D	56. A	8. E	52. E		8. C		8. 85-B
9.	A	57. D	9. E	53. B		9. E		9. 60-A
10.	D	58. D	10. B	54. C		10. A		10. 18-D, 31-D, 26-D
11.	D	59. D	11. D	55. E		11. B		11. 73-C
12.	A	60. A	12. A	56. A		12. B		12. 64-A, 67-B, 43-E
13.	D	61. D	13. D	57. D		13. D		13. 57-D
14.	A	62. D	14. C	58. C		14. B		14. 54-C
15.	D	63. A	15. B	59. A		15. C		15. 59-B, 12-E, 77-A
16.	A	64. D	16. A	60. E		16. E		16. 13-C, 52D
17.	A	65. A	17. D	61. C		17. A		17. 39-A, 58-A
18.	D	66. D	18. E	62. B		18. E		18. 5-B
19.	A	67. A	19. B	63. B		19. B		19. 35-E
20.	D	68. D	20. C	64. E		20. D		
21.	D	69. A	21. C	65. C		21. E		
22.	A	70. D	22. A	66. D		22. B		
23.	A	71. D	23. C	67. A		23. C		
24.	D	72. A	24. D	68. C		24. A		
25.	D	73. D	25. B	69. E				
26.	A	74. D	26. D	70. B				
27.	D	75. D	27. A	71. D				
28.	D	76. A	28. E	72. B				
29.	A	77. A	29. C	73. E				
30.	A	78. D	30. E	74. A				
31.	A	79. A	31. B	75. C				
32.	D	80. A	32. A	76. D				
33.	A	81. A	33. B	77. B				
34.	D	82. D	34. A	78. D				
35.	A	83. A	35. C	79. B				
36.	A	84. D	36. C	80. D				
37.	D	85. A	37. D	81. A				
38.	A	86. D	38. C	82. D				
39.	A	87. D	39. E	83. C				
40.	D	88. A	40. A	84. D				
41.	A	89. A	41. D	85. A				
42.	A	90. A	42. A	86. E				
43.	D	91. A	43. B	87. C				
44.	D	92. D	44. D	88. E				
45.	A	93. D						
46.	D	94. A						
47.	A	95. A						
48.	A							

Answer Key for Complete Practice Exam #5

Address Checking				Address Memory				Number Series		Following Oral Instructions	

Address Checking		Address Memory		Number Series	Following Oral Instructions
1. A 49. D		1. E 45. D		1. C	1. 56-D
2. A 50. A		2. C 46. C		2. E	2. 82-B
3. D 51. A		3. A 47. B		3. A	3. 11-C
4. D 52. D		4. B 48. E		4. B	4. 42-E
5. A 53. A		5. E 49. B		5. D	5. 37-A, 76-B, 18-D
6. A 54. A		6. D 50. A		6. E	6. 12-E
7. D 55. A		7. A 51. C		7. A	7. 48-C
8. D 56. A		8. B 52. C		8. B	8. 29-B, 41-B, 36-B
9. D 57. D		9. C 53. D		9. C	9. 6-A
10. D 58. D		10. B 54. A		10. E	10. 53-D, 22-E
11. A 59. A		11. D 55. C		11. A	11. 78-C, 27-E
12. A 60. D		12. C 56. B		12. B	12. 51-C
13. A 61. A		13. A 57. D		13. D	13. 71-C
14. A 62. A		14. D 58. D		14. E	14. 8-B, 14-B, 15-B, 32-A, 57-A
15. D 63. D		15. C 59. A		15. C	15. 81-D, 62-D
16. A 64. A		16. D 60. E		16. A	16. 50-B, 60-C
17. D 65. D		17. B 61. C		17. E	17. 88-A
18. D 66. A		18. E 62. E		18. B	18. 61-A
19. A 67. A		19. A 63. D		19. E	19. 4-E
20. D 68. D		20. C 64. E		20. C	
21. A 69. A		21. D 65. A		21. C	
22. D 70. A		22. A 66. D		22. A	
23. D 71. A		23. D 67. E		23. D	
24. A 72. D		24. E 68. C		24. B	
25. A 73. A		25. B 69. E			
26. D 74. D		26. D 70. A			
27. A 75. D		27. E 71. D			
28. D 76. A		28. A 72. B			
29. D 77. A		29. C 73. D			
30. A 78. D		30. B 74. B			
31. A 79. A		31. E 75. E			
32. A 80. D		32. C 76. A			
33. D 81. D		33. C 77. C			
34. A 82. A		34. D 78. B			
35. A 83. D		35. A 79. B			
36. A 84. A		36. E 80. A			
37. A 85. D		37. C 81. C			
38. D 86. D		38. D 82. C			
39. D 87. D		39. B 83. A			
40. A 88. A		40. D 84. B			
41. D 89. A		41. A 85. D			
42. D 90. D		42. B 86. C			
43. A 91. A		43. B 87. E			
44. D 92. A		44. A 88. E			
45. D 93. D					
46. A 94. D					
47. D 95. A					
48. A					

Answer Key for Complete Practice Exam #6

Address Checking				Address Memory				Number Series		Following Oral Instructions	
1. A	49. A			1. D	45. C			1. C		1.	47-E
2. D	50. A			2. E	46. A			2. E		2.	59-B, 21-A, 82-D
3. D	51. A			3. B	47. E			3. A		3.	26-C, 33-C
4. A	52. D			4. D	48. B			4. D		4.	2-D
5. D	53. D			5. C	49. C			5. B		5.	14-A, 24-A, 58-E, 80-E
6. A	54. D			6. E	50. D			6. E		6.	50-B, 70-E
7. D	55. D			7. A	51. A			7. C		7.	65-C
8. A	56. A			8. C	52. E			8. A		8.	79-A, 61-E, 63-C
9. D	57. A			9. C	53. A			9. B		9.	85-D, 49-B
10. A	58. D			10. D	54. C			10. D		10.	88-C
11. D	59. A			11. A	55. E			11. C		11.	73-E, 9-D
12. D	60. D			12. D	56. B			12. E		12.	18-A
13. D	61. D			13. E	57. D			13. A		13.	41-A
14. A	62. A			14. A	58. B			14. B		14.	32-A
15. A	63. A			15. D	59. E			15. D		15.	78-A
16. D	64. D			16. B	60. A			16. E		16.	64-B, 75-B, 81-B
17. D	65. D			17. B	61. E			17. C		17.	20-D
18. D	66. D			18. E	62. B			18. B		18.	23-E
19. D	67. D			19. C	63. D			19. D		19.	39-A
20. A	68. D			20. E	64. B			20. A			
21. A	69. A			21. A	65. C			21. E			
22. A	70. D			22. D	66. A			22. B			
23. D	71. D			23. D	67. E			23. C			
24. D	72. A			24. B	68. D			24. E			
25. D	73. A			25. E	69. A						
26. A	74. D			26. A	70. D						
27. A	75. A			27. C	71. B						
28. A	76. D			28. D	72. C						
29. D	77. A			29. A	73. B						
30. A	78. A			30. D	74. D						
31. D	79. A			31. C	75. D						
32. A	80. D			32. B	76. A						
33. A	81. D			33. B	77. E						
34. D	82. A			34. A	78. C						
35. D	83. D			35. B	79. E						
36. D	84. D			36. C	80. A						
37. D	85. A			37. E	81. B						
38. A	86. D			38. A	82. D						
39. A	87. D			39. B	83. C						
40. A	88. A			40. C	84. E						
41. D	89. A			41. B	85. E						
42. A	90. A			42. C	86. A						
43. D	91. D			43. A	87. D						
44. D	92. D			44. E	88. C						
45. A	93. A										
46. A	94. D										
47. D	95. A										
48. D											

Following Oral Instructions Questions

Provided on the next several pages of the book are the questions for the Following Oral Instructions sections from each of your six complete practice exams. As detailed before, if someone is going to read these questions to you, they should be read at a rather slow and deliberate rate of approximately 75 words per minute and with proper diction. It is important also that the reader pause occasionally according to the specific directions given in the wording of the questions.

Do not look over the questions before taking the practice tests. Once you have completed a practice test, you should then review the questions you missed in order to determine what caused you to miss them. This review should enable you to be more successful on similar questions next time.

Again as previously mentioned, the most effective and convenient way to practice for this section of the exam is to listen to author's Following Oral Instructions Practice Tests CD. See the order form at the back of your book or visit our website _www.PostalExam.com_ for details.

224

Following Oral Instructions Questions
Practice Exam #1

Look at Sample 1. (Pause slightly.) Sample 1 has a number with a line beside it. (Pause slightly.) Write the letter E as in egg on the line. (Pause 2 seconds.) Now, on the Answer Sheet, find number 22 and darken the space for the letter you wrote on the line. (Pause 5 seconds.)

Look at Sample 2. (Pause slightly.) There are four numbers. Circle the smallest number. (Pause 2 seconds.) Now, on the Answer Sheet, find that number, and darken the letter C as in cat. (Pause 5 seconds.)

Look at Sample 3. (Pause slightly.) There are two letters and two numbers. (Pause slightly.) Underline the second number and the last letter. (Pause 3 seconds.) On the Answer Sheet, darken the number-letter combination you just underlined. (Pause 5 seconds.)

Look at Sample 4. (Pause slightly.) There are five numbers. Draw a line under the third number. (Pause 3 seconds.) Now, find the number you underlined on the Answer Sheet, and darken the letter A. (Pause 5 seconds.)

Look at Sample 5. (Pause slightly.) Circle the second letter. (Pause 2 seconds.) Now, on the Answer Sheet, find number 67, and darken the letter you just circled. (Pause 5 seconds.)

Look at the four boxes in Sample 6. (Pause slightly.) Each box has a letter with a line beside it. (Pause slightly.) Find the box with the letter E as in egg, and write the number 21 on the line beside it. (Pause 3 seconds.) On the Answer sheet, darken the number-letter combination you just made. (Pause 5 seconds.)

Look at Sample 7. (Pause slightly.) There are five numbers. (Pause slightly.) If one of the numbers is greater than 42 and less than 57, write an A as in apple on the line beside it. (Pause 5 seconds.) Now find that number on the Answer Sheet, and darken the letter A. (Pause 4 seconds.) If there is not a number greater than 42 and less than 57, darken the letter C on line 23 of the Answer Sheet. (Pause 5 seconds.)

Look at Sample 8. (Pause slightly.) There are two boxes and two circles of different sizes with a number in each. (Pause slightly.) Write the letter D as in dog in the larger box. (Pause 2 seconds.) Now, on the Answer Sheet, darken the number-letter combination in the box. (Pause 5 seconds.)

Look at the letters in Sample 9. (Pause slightly.) Find the letter D as in dog, and write a 7 beside it. (Pause 3 seconds.) On the Answer Sheet, darken the number-letter combination you just made. (Pause 5 seconds.)

Look at Sample 10. (Pause slightly.) There are four different size boxes with a number in each. (Pause slightly.) Write the letter E as in egg on the line in the largest box. (Pause 4 seconds.) On the Answer Sheet, darken the number-letter combination for the box in which you just wrote. (Pause 5 seconds.)

Look at Sample 11. (Pause slightly.) There are two squares and two circles. (Pause slightly.) If 4 is greater than 7 and 6 is less than 9, write the letter D as in dog in the smaller circle. (Pause 5 seconds.) Otherwise, write the letter A as in apple in the larger square. (Pause 4 seconds.) On the answer Sheet, darken the number-letter combination for the circle or square in which you just wrote. (Pause 5 seconds.)

Look at the five letters in Sample 12. (Pause slightly.) If there are two letters that are the same, write the number 59 next to the letter A. (Pause 3 seconds.) Otherwise, write the number 33 by the last letter. (Pause 3 seconds.) On the Answer Sheet, darken the number-letter combination you have made. (Pause 5 seconds.)

Look at Sample 13. (Pause slightly.) There are five circles with a time and a letter in each. On the line in the second circle, write the last two numbers of the time in that circle. (Pause 4 seconds.) On the Answer Sheet, darken the number-letter combination for the circle in which you just wrote. (Pause 5 seconds.)

Look at Sample 14. (Pause slightly.) There are two squares and two circles of different sizes with a letter in each. (Pause 3 seconds.) If 2 is greater than 1 and 9 is less than 11, write the number 78 in the larger square. (Pause 3 seconds.) Otherwise, write the number 32 in the smaller circle. (Pause 3 seconds.) On the Answer Sheet, darken the number-letter combination you have made. (Pause 5 seconds.)

Look at the four letters in Sample 14 again. (Pause slightly.) Draw a line under the first letter if that letter is a B as in boy. (Pause 3 seconds.) Otherwise, draw a line under the last letter. (Pause 3 seconds.) Now, on the Answer Sheet, find the number 88, and darken the letter under which you drew a line. (Pause 5 seconds.)

Look at Sample 14 again. (Pause slightly.) If A comes before B and 7 is greater than 5, draw a line under the third letter. (Pause 3 seconds.) Otherwise, draw a line under the second letter. (Pause 3 seconds.) On the answer Sheet, find the number 26, and darken the letter under which you just drew a line. (Pause 5 seconds.)

Look at Sample 15. (Pause slightly.) There are four boxes with a different time in each. Find the latest time, and write the last two numbers of that time on the line in its box. (Pause 4 seconds.) Now, on the Answer Sheet, find the number you wrote on the line in the box, and darken the letter E as in egg. (Pause 5 seconds.)

Look at Sample 16. (Pause slightly.) The number in each box represents a number of parcels. Find the box with the largest number of parcels. (Pause 3 seconds.) Write the letter C as in cat on the line in that box. (Pause 3 seconds.) On the Answer Sheet, darken the number-letter combination for that box. (Pause 5 seconds.)

Look at the four boxes in Sample 16 again. (Pause slightly.) If the second box has more parcels than the first box, write an E as in egg in the first box. (Pause 4 seconds.) Otherwise, write a D as in dog in the next-to-last box. (Pause 4 seconds.) Now, on the Answer Sheet, darken the number-letter combination for the box in which you just wrote. (Pause 5 seconds.)

Look at sample 17. (Pause slightly.) If the largest circle has the smallest number, write an A as in apple in that circle. (Pause 3 seconds.) Otherwise, write a B as in boy in the second circle. (Pause 3 seconds.) On the Answer Sheet, darken the number-letter combination in the circle in which you just wrote. (Pause 5 seconds.)

Look at Sample 18. (Pause slightly.) If 47 is greater than 33 and less than 49, write the number 12 on the line. (Pause 3 seconds.) If it is not, write the number 72 on the line. (Pause 3 seconds.) On the Answer Sheet, find the number you wrote on the line, and darken the letter C as in cat. (Pause 5 seconds.)

Look at Sample 19. (Pause slightly.) In each of the four boxes is a time that mail is to be collected. Find the earliest collection time, and write the letter E as in egg in that box. (Pause 3 seconds.) On the Answer Sheet, find the number that would be created by using only the first two digits of the time in the box where you wrote the letter E as in egg, and darken the letter A as in Apple. (Pause 5 seconds.)

Look at Sample 20. (Pause slightly.) Draw a line under the next-to-last number. (Pause slightly.) On the Answer Sheet, darken the letter A as in apple for the number you underlined. (Pause 5 seconds.)

Look at Sample 21. (Pause slightly.) Write the letter D as in dog in the box with the city of Chicago. (Pause 3 seconds.) Starting from the right, count the number of boxes stopping at the box in which you wrote. (Pause 3 seconds.) On the Answer Sheet, darken the number-letter combination created by combining the number of boxes you counted with the letter you wrote in the box with the city of Chicago. (Pause 5 seconds.)

Look at Sample 22. (Pause slightly.) There is a letter with a number in front of it. (Pause slightly.) If 2:00 PM is earlier than 3:00 AM, darken the number-letter combination in Sample 22 on the Answer Sheet. (Pause 4 seconds.) Otherwise, darken 41-A on the Answer Sheet. (Pause 5 seconds.)

Look at Sample 23. (Pause slightly.) If the first number is less than the third number, and the last number is greater than the first number, darken the number-letter combination 1-E on the Answer Sheet. (Pause 4 seconds.) Otherwise, darken the number-letter combination 2-A. (Pause 5 seconds.)

Look at Sample 24. (Pause slightly.) If 8 is greater than 10 and 14 is less than 7, write the letter B as in boy in the third box. (Pause 3 seconds.) If not, write the letter A as in apple in the first box. (Pause 3 seconds.) On the Answer Sheet, darken the number-letter combination you have made. (Pause 5 seconds.)

Look at Sample 25. (Pause slightly.) Write the number 33 in front of the first letter. (Pause 2 seconds.) Now, on the Answer Sheet, darken the number-letter combination you have made. (Pause 5 seconds.)

Look at sample 26. (Pause slightly.) If Jefferson was the first President of the United States, write the letter E as in egg in the third circle. (Pause 3 seconds.) If he was not, write the letter A as in apple in the second circle. (Pause 3 seconds.) Now, darken the number-letter combination you have made. (Pause 5 seconds.)

Look at Sample 27. (Pause slightly.) Write the letter A as in apple in the box with the town that has the smallest population. (Pause 3 seconds.) Now, on the Answer Sheet, darken the number-letter combination you have made.

END OF FOLLOWING ORAL INSTRUCTIONS QUESTIONS – PRACTICE EXAM #1

Following Oral Instructions Questions
Practice Exam #2

Look at Sample 1. (Pause slightly.) Draw a line under the second number. (Pause 3 seconds.) On the Answer Sheet, find that number, and darken the letter A as in apple. (Pause 5 seconds.)

Look at Sample 2. (Pause slightly.) Draw a circle around the last letter. (Pause 3 seconds.) On the Answer Sheet, find the number 78 and darken the letter you circled. (Pause 5 seconds.)

Look at Sample 3. (Pause slightly.) There are three letters and three numbers. (Pause slightly.) Underline the first letter and the last number. (Pause 4 seconds.) On the Answer Sheet, darken the number-letter combination you just underlined. (Pause 5 seconds.)

Look at Sample 4. (Pause slightly.) Circle the largest number. (Pause 3 seconds.) Now, find that number on the Answer Sheet, and darken the letter B as in boy. (Pause 5 seconds.)

Look at Sample 5. (Pause slightly.) Find the letter A as in apple, and write the number 8 beside it. (Pause 3 seconds.) On the Answer Sheet, darken the number-letter combination you have made. (Pause 5 seconds.)

Look at Sample 6. (Pause slightly.) There are four different size boxes with a number in each. (Pause slightly.) In the next-to-last box, write the letter B as in boy next to the number. (Pause 3 seconds.) On the Answer Sheet, darken the number-letter combination you have made. (Pause 5 seconds.)

Look at Sample 7. (Pause slightly.) There are four numbers in Sample 7. (Pause slightly.) If 68 is less than 86 and the letter C as in cat comes before the letter D as in dog in the alphabet, underline the first number. (Pause 3 seconds.) Otherwise, underline the last number. (Pause 3 seconds.) On the Answer Sheet, find the number you underlined, and darken the letter A as in apple. (Pause 5 seconds.)

Look at Sample 8. (Pause slightly.) There are two squares and two circles. (Pause slightly.) If 5 is greater than 2 and 9 is less than 12, write the letter C as in cat in the smaller circle. (Pause 3 seconds.) If not, write the letter A as in apple in the larger square. (Pause 3 seconds.) On the Answer Sheet, darken the number-letter combination you have made. (Pause 5 seconds.)

Look at Sample 9. (Pause slightly.) Write the letter D as in dog in the smallest box. (Pause 3 seconds.) On the Answer Sheet, darken the number-letter combination you have made. (Pause 4 seconds.)

Look at Sample 10. (Pause slightly.) There are five letters with a line before each. (Pause slightly.) If the second letter comes before the third letter in the alphabet, write the number 36 on the line before the first letter. (Pause 4 seconds.) Otherwise, write the number 47 on the last line. (Pause 3 seconds.) On the Answer Sheet, darken the number-letter combination you have made. (Pause 5 seconds.)

Look at the boxes and circles in Sample 11. (Pause slightly.) Write the letter B as in boy in the second box. (Pause 4 seconds.) On the Answer Sheet, darken B as in boy for the number in that box. (Pause 5 seconds.)

Look at Sample 11 again. (Pause slightly.) Write the letter C as in cat in the largest box. (Pause 3 seconds.) On the Answer Sheet, find the number 33 and darken the letter E. (Pause 5 seconds.)

Look at Sample 12. (Pause slightly.) There are five numbers in Sample 12. (Pause slightly.) If the second number is larger than the last number, write the letter D as in dog by the last number. (Pause 2 seconds.) Otherwise, write the letter D as in dog by the first number. (Pause 4 seconds.) On the Answer Sheet, darken the number-letter combination you have made. (Pause 5 seconds.)

Sample 13 has a word with four lines under it. (Pause slightly.) On the first line, write the last letter of the word. (Pause 2 seconds.) On the last line, write the second letter of the word. (Pause 3 seconds.) Write the first letter on the second line, and write the third letter on the third line. (Pause 5 seconds.) Find number 54 on the Answer Sheet, darken the letter on the last line. (Pause 5 seconds.)

Look at Sample 14. (Pause slightly.) Listed in the five boxes are various mail delivery times. (Pause slightly.) Write the letter A as in apple in the box with the latest delivery time. (Pause 3 seconds.) On the Answer Sheet, find the number that would be created by using the last two digits of the time in the box in which you wrote the letter A as in apple, and darken the letter E as in egg. (Pause 5 seconds.)

227

Following Oral Instructions Questions
Practice Exam #2 – Continued

In Sample 15, there is a line. (Pause slightly.) If 33 is greater than 22 and 44 is less than 11, write the number 11 on the line. (Pause 4 seconds.) Otherwise, write the number 44 on the line. (Pause 3 seconds.) On the Answer Sheet, find the number you wrote, and darken the letter C as in cat. (Pause 5 seconds.)

Look at Sample 16. (Pause slightly.) Each box has a number of letters to be postmarked. Find the box with the greatest number of letters to be postmarked. (Pause 3 seconds.) Write the letter B as in boy in that box. (Pause 2 seconds.) On the Answer Sheet, darken the number-letter combination you have made. (Pause 5 seconds.)

Look at Sample 17. (Pause slightly.) You will see the names of four cities with a number of parcels going to each city under each city's name. (Pause slightly.) Find the city with the largest number of parcels going to it, and circle the first letter in that city's name. (Pause 4 seconds.) On the Answer Sheet, find the number 17, and darken the letter you just circled. (Pause 5 seconds.)

Look at Sample 17 again. (Pause slightly.) If 56 is greater than 23 but less than 95, underline the second letter in the name of the city with the least number of parcels. (Pause 3 seconds.) Then find the number 39 on the Answer Sheet, and darken the letter you just underlined. (Pause 4 seconds.) Otherwise, darken the letter A as in apple at number 39 on the Answer Sheet. (Pause 5 seconds.)

In Sample 18, there are three boxes with a time of the day in each. (Pause slightly.) Find the box with the latest time in it. (Pause 3 seconds.) On the Answer Sheet, find the number that would be created by using the first two digits of that time, and darken the letter B as in boy. (Pause 5 seconds.)

Look at Sample 19. (Pause slightly.) If the first letter is an R as in rat, look at the last letter. (Pause 2 seconds.) If the last letter is a C as in cat, darken the letter C as in cat at number 75 on the Answer Sheet. (Pause 4 seconds.) Otherwise, darken the letter A as in apple at number 75. (Pause 5 seconds.)

Look at Sample 20. (Pause slightly.) There are two boxes and two circles of different sizes with a number in each. (Pause slightly.) Find the box with the smallest number, and write the letter A as in apple in that box. (Pause 4 seconds.) Find the smallest circle, and write the letter E as in egg in that circle. (Pause 4 seconds.) On the Answer Sheet, darken the number-letter combinations you have made. (Pause 5 seconds.)

Look at Sample 21. (Pause slightly.) There are five different size boxes with a number in each. (Pause slightly.) If the largest box contains the largest number, write the letter C as in cat in that box. (Pause 3 seconds.) Otherwise, write the letter C as in cat in the next-to-largest box. (Pause 3 seconds.) On the Answer Sheet, darken the number-letter combination you have made. (Pause 5 seconds.)

Look at Sample 21 again. (Pause slightly.) In the box with the smallest number, write the letter B as in boy if that number is greater than 5. (Pause 4 seconds.) Otherwise, write the letter D as in dog in that box. (Pause 4 seconds.) Darken the number-letter combination for the box in which you just wrote. (Pause 5 seconds.)

Look at Sample 22. (Pause slightly.) Write the number 22 on the line if A as in apple comes before Z as in zebra in the alphabet. (Pause 4 seconds.) If you wrote the number 22 on the line, find that number on the Answer Sheet, and darken the letter C as in cat. (Pause 4 seconds.) If you did not write the number 22 on the line, darken 63-A on the Answer Sheet. (Pause 5 seconds.)

Look at Sample 23. (Pause slightly.) If 12 is greater than 8 and 25 is less than 32, write the number 12 behind the second letter. (Pause 2 seconds.) If not, write the number 15 behind the fourth letter. (Pause 2 seconds.) On the Answer Sheet, darken the number-letter combination you have made. (Pause 5 seconds.)

Look at Sample 24. (Pause slightly.) Each of the two boxes contains the name of a city. (Pause slightly.) Of the two cities, the city of Gulfport has the earlier delivery time. (Pause slightly.) Write the letter E as in egg beside the number in the box that contains the city with the later delivery time. (Pause 3 seconds.) On the Answer Sheet, darken the number-letter combination you have made. (Pause 5 seconds.)

Look at Sample 25. (Pause slightly.) Write the letter B as in boy below the largest number. (Pause 3 seconds.) On the Answer Sheet, darken the number-letter combination you have made. (Pause 5 seconds.)

Look at Sample 26. (Pause slightly.) Sodas come six cans to a package. (Pause slightly.) How many packages must you buy to have 36 cans of soda? (Pause 3 seconds.) Take this number, and add 1 to it. (Pause 3 seconds.) Find the resulting number on the Answer Sheet, and darken the letter C as in cat.

END OF FOLLOWING ORAL INSTRUCTIONS QUESTIONS – PRACTICE EXAM #2

Following Oral Instructions Questions
Practice Exam #3

Look at Sample 1. (Pause slightly.) Draw a line under the fourth number. (Pause 2 seconds.) Now, on the Answer Sheet, darken the letter C as in cat for the number you underlined. (Pause 5 seconds.)

Look at Sample 2. (Pause slightly.) Write the letter D as in dog in the second box. (Pause 3 seconds.) Now, on the Answer Sheet, darken the number-letter combination you have made. (Pause 5 seconds.)

In Sample 3 there are four letters. (Pause slightly.) Draw a circle around the second letter. (Pause 2 seconds.) Find number 35 on the Answer Sheet, and darken the letter you circled. (Pause 5 seconds.)

In Sample 4 there are four boxes. (Pause slightly.) In each box is a number of parcels to be delivered. (Pause slightly.) In the box with the most parcels to be delivered, write the letter E as in egg. (Pause 3 seconds.) On the Answer Sheet, darken the number-letter combination you have made. (Pause 5 seconds.)

Look at Sample 4 again. (Pause slightly.) If 44 is greater than 48, write the letter A as in apple in the box with the lowest number. (Pause 3 seconds.) Otherwise, write the letter D as in dog in that box. (Pause 3 seconds.) On the Answer Sheet, darken the number-letter combination you have made. (Pause 5 seconds.)

Look at Sample 5. (Pause slightly.) There are four boxes of different sizes with a letter in each. (Pause slightly.) Write the number 68 in the smallest box. (Pause 3 seconds.) On the Answer Sheet, darken the number-letter combination you just made. (Pause 5 seconds.)

Looking at Sample 5 again, find the next-to-smallest box. (Pause slightly.) If 22 is less than 67, write the number 8 in that box. (Pause 4 seconds.) Otherwise, write the number 8 in the last box. (Pause 3 seconds.) Now, on the Answer Sheet, find the number 85, and darken the letter A as in apple. (Pause 5 seconds.)

In Sample 6, there are four circles with a time of day in each. (Pause slightly.) In the circle with the earliest time, write a D as in dog. (Pause 3 seconds.) On the Answer Sheet, find the number that would be created by using the last two digits of earliest time, and darken the letter D as in dog. (Pause 5 seconds.)

In Sample 7, five days of the week listed. If 44 is greater than 39, underline the second letter of the first day listed. (Pause 3 seconds.) If not, underline the seventh letter of the second day listed. (Pause 3 seconds.) On the Answer Sheet, find the number 36, and darken the letter you underlined. (Pause 5 seconds.)

Look at Sample 7 again. (Pause slightly.) If the name of the last day of the week listed begins with the letter R as in rat, draw a line under the last letter of the first day listed. (Pause 5 seconds.) Otherwise, darken the letter A as in apple at number 83 on the Answer Sheet. (Pause 5 seconds.)

Look at Sample 8. (Pause slightly.) There are four boxes with a number in each. (Pause slightly.) Write the letter C as in cat in the box that has the number closest to 77. (Pause 4 seconds.) On the Answer Sheet, darken the number-letter combination you have made. (Pause 5 seconds.)

Look at Sample 9. (Pause slightly.) Each box contains a mail delivery time. (Pause slightly.) If any of the mail delivery times is after 5:55 PM, darken the letter E as in egg at number 38 on the Answer Sheet. (Pause 4 seconds.) Otherwise, darken the letter B as in boy at that number. (Pause 5 seconds.)

Look at Sample 10. (Pause slightly.) There are three boxes and two circles of different sizes. (Pause slightly.) If B as in boy comes before D as in dog in the alphabet, and if 23 is less than 34, darken the letter A as in apple on the Answer Sheet at the number found in the smallest box. (Pause 4 seconds.) Otherwise, darken the letter E as in egg at the number found in the smaller circle. (Pause 5 seconds.)

Look at Sample 10 again. (Pause slightly.) If the number in the largest box is smaller than the number in the largest circle, darken the letter B as in boy on the Answer Sheet at the number found in the largest circle. (Pause 5 seconds.) Otherwise, darken the letter A as in apple on the Answer Sheet at the number found in the smaller circle. (Pause 5 second.)

Look at Sample 11. (Pause slightly.) If the second number is an odd number and the first number is an even number, underline the first number. (Pause 4 seconds.) Then, on the Answer Sheet, find the number you underlined, and darken the letter A as in apple. (Pause 4 seconds.) Otherwise, find the second number on the Answer Sheet, and darken the letter B as in boy. (Pause 5 seconds.)

Look at the letters in Sample 12. (Pause slightly.) There are five lines, one for each letter. Circle the E as in egg, and write the number 58 under the fourth letter. (Pause 3 seconds.) If the number you just wrote is under the letter you circled, darken that number-letter combination on the Answer Sheet. (Pause 5 seconds.) Otherwise, at number 58 on the Answer Sheet, darken the letter above the number 58. (Pause 5 seconds.)

Look at Sample 13. (Pause slightly.) Draw a circle around the second number. (Pause 2 seconds.) Draw a circle around the last number. (Pause 2 seconds.) Draw a circle around the first number. (Pause 2 seconds.) On the Answer Sheet, find the second number you circled, and darken the letter D as in dog. (Pause 5 seconds.)

Look at Sample 13 again. (Pause slightly.) If the number you did not circle is larger than 78, darken the letter A as in apple on the Answer Sheet at the number you did not circle. (Pause 3 seconds.) Otherwise, darken the letter E as in egg on the Answer Sheet at the number you did not circle. (Pause 5 seconds.)

Look at Sample 14. (Pause slightly.) There are two squares and two lines. (Pause slightly.) Write the letter E as in egg in the smaller square. (Pause 3 seconds.) Write the number 72 on the first line. (Pause 2 seconds.) Darken this number-letter combination on the Answer Sheet. (Pause 5 seconds.)

Look at Sample 14 again. (Pause slightly.) If 12 is less than 15, write the letter D as in dog in the largest square, and write the number 22 on the last line. (Pause 3 seconds.) Then, on the Answer Sheet, darken this number-letter combination. (Pause 4 seconds.) Otherwise, darken 64-C. (Pause 5 seconds.)

Look at Sample 15. (Pause slightly.) There are four boxes, each containing the name of a city with a mail collection time. (Pause slightly.) Write the letter B as in boy in the box that contains the city with the latest collection time. (Pause 4 seconds.) On the Answer Sheet, find the number that would be created by using the last two digits of the time in that box, and darken the letter you wrote in that box. (Pause 5 seconds.)

Look at Sample 16. (Pause slightly.) Each circle contains a mail delivery time. Find the earliest time. (Pause 2 seconds.) On the line in the circle with the earliest time, write the first digit of that time. (Pause 2 seconds.) On the Answer Sheet, darken the letter D as in dog for the number you just wrote. (Pause 5 seconds.)

Look at the five circles in Sample 17. (Pause slightly.) Each circle has a time and a letter in it. (Pause slightly.) On the line in the last circle, write the last two digits of the time in that circle. (Pause 2 seconds.) On the Answer Sheet, darken the number-letter combination you have made. (Pause 5 seconds.)

Look at the letters in Sample 18. (Pause slightly.) Draw a line under the second letter. (Pause 2 seconds.) Find the number 4 on the Answer Sheet, and darken the letter under which you drew a line. (Pause 5 seconds.)

Look at Sample 19. (Pause slightly.) Each box contains a number of sacks of mail. Find the box with the smallest number of sacks. (Pause 2 seconds.) On the line in that box, write the letter B as in boy. (Pause 2 seconds.) On the Answer Sheet, darken the number-letter combination in that box. (Pause 5 seconds.)

Look at Sample 20. (Pause slightly.) Each number has a line under it. (Pause slightly.) If the first number is the largest, write the letter A as in apple under the second number. (Pause 2 seconds.) Otherwise, write the letter C as in cat under the third number. (Pause 2 seconds.) On the Answer Sheet, darken the number-letter combination you have made. (Pause 5 seconds.)

Look at Sample 21. (Pause slightly.) Each box contains a number. (Pause slightly.) Write the letter D as in dog by the middle number. (Pause 3 seconds.) On the Answer Sheet, darken the number-letter combination you have made. (Pause 5 seconds.)

Look at Sample 22. (Pause slightly.) If P as in puddle comes before R as in rain in the alphabet, write the number 14 in the first circle. (Pause 2 seconds.) If not, write the number 27 in the last circle. (Pause 2 seconds.) On the Answer Sheet, darken the number-letter combination you have made. (Pause 5 seconds.)

Look at sample 23. (Pause slightly.) Write the letter B as in boy in the smallest box. (Pause 3 seconds.) On the Answer Sheet, darken the number-letter combination you have made. (Pause 5 seconds.)

Look at Sample 24. (Pause slightly.) If 15 is less than 12, write the letter D as in dog in the first circle. (Pause 2 seconds.) If not, write the letter E as in egg in the last circle. (Pause 2 seconds.) On the Answer Sheet, darken the number-letter combination you have made.

END OF FOLLOWING ORAL INSTRUCTIONS QUESTIONS – PRACTICE EXAM #3

Following Oral Instructions Questions
Practice Exam #4

Look at Sample 1. (Pause slightly.) Underline the fifth letter in the sequence. (Pause 3 seconds.) On the Answer Sheet, find the number 44, and darken the letter that you underlined. (Pause 5 seconds.)

Look at Sample 2. (Pause slightly.) There are four different size circles with a letter in each. (Pause slightly.) In the smallest circle, do nothing. (Pause slightly.) In the largest circle, write the number 23. (Pause 3 seconds.) On the Answer Sheet, darken the number-letter combination you have made. (Pause 5 seconds.)

Look at the numbers in Sample 3. (Pause slightly.) Draw a line under the numbers greater than 27 but less than 43. (Pause 4 seconds.) On the Answer Sheet, darken the letter B as in boy for the numbers you underlined. (Pause 5 seconds.)

Look at Sample 4. (Pause slightly.) If 21 is greater than 27, draw a line under the last letter. (Pause 2 seconds.) Otherwise, draw a line under the third letter. (Pause 2 seconds.) On the Answer Sheet, find the number 62, and darken the letter you underlined. (Pause 5 seconds.)

Look at Sample 5. (Pause slightly.) There are two circles and two boxes of different sizes with a number in each. (Pause 2 seconds.) If 6 is greater than 5 and 8 is less than 7, write the letter C as in cat in the larger box. (Pause 3 seconds.) Otherwise, write the letter A as in apple in the larger circle. (Pause 3 seconds.) On the Answer Sheet, darken the number-letter combination you have made. (Pause 5 seconds.)

Look at the five circles in Sample 6. (Pause slightly.) The circles contain different mail delivery times. (Pause slightly.) Write the letter D as in dog in the circle that has the latest delivery time. (Pause 3 seconds.) On the Answer Sheet, find the number that would be created by using the first two numbers of the time in that circle, and darken the letter D as in dog. (Pause 5 seconds.)

Look at the circles and words in Sample 7. (Pause slightly.) Write the first letter of the last word in the first circle. (Pause 3 seconds.) Write the middle letter of the first word in the second circle. (Pause 3 seconds.) Write the last letter of the second word in the last circle. (Pause 3 seconds.) On the Answer Sheet, darken the number-letter combinations you have made. (Pause 5 seconds.)

Look at Sample 8. (Pause slightly.) If March comes before April in the calendar year, write the letter B as in boy in the first box. (Pause 4 seconds.) Otherwise, write the letter C as in cat in the second box. (Pause 4 seconds.) Now, on the Answer Sheet, darken the number-letter combination you have made. (Pause 5 seconds.)

Look at the X's and O's in Sample 9. (Pause slightly.) Draw a line under all of the X's. (Pause 3 seconds.) Count the number of X's you underlined, and write that number at the end of the series of X's and O's. (Pause 3 seconds.) Now, add 52 to that number. (Pause 3 seconds.) Find the resulting number on the Answer Sheet, and darken the letter A as in apple. (Pause 5 seconds.)

Look at Sample 10. (Pause slightly.) Write the letter D as in dog next to the numbers that are greater than 12 but less than 32. (Pause 4 seconds.) Now, on the Answer Sheet, darken the number-letter combinations you have made. (Pause 5 seconds.)

Look at Sample 11. (Pause slightly.) Draw a line under the sixth number. (Pause 3 seconds.) Draw two lines under the third number. (Pause 3 seconds.) Now, on the Answer Sheet, find the number you underlined twice and darken the letter C as in cat. (Pause 5 seconds.)

Look at Sample 12. (Pause slightly.) There are three boxes with a number in each. (Pause slightly.) The first box has mail for Portland and Seattle. (Pause slightly.) The second box has mail for Fargo and Butte. (Pause slightly.) On the line in the third box, write the letter A. (Pause 3 seconds.) On the Answer Sheet, darken the number-letter combination you have made. (Pause 5 seconds.)

Look at Sample 12 again. (Pause slightly.) Write the letter E as in egg in the box that has mail for Fargo and Butte. (Pause 3 seconds.) Write the letter B as in boy in the box that has mail for Portland and Seattle. (Pause 3 seconds.) Now, on the Answer Sheet, darken the number-letter combinations you have just made. (Pause 5 seconds.)

Look at Sample 13. (Pause slightly.) Write the letter D as in dog next to the number on the left side. (Pause 3 seconds.) On the Answer Sheet, darken the number-letter combination you have made. (Pause 5 seconds.)

Look at Sample 14. (Pause slightly.) In each box is a number of sacks of mail to be delivered. (Pause slightly.) Write the letter C as in cat in the box with the second highest number of sacks to be delivered. (Pause 3 seconds.) On the Answer Sheet, darken the number-letter combination you have made. (Pause 5 seconds.)

Look at Sample 15. (Pause slightly.) On the fourth line, write the smallest of the following numbers: 31, 12, 15, 27, 20. (Pause 3 seconds.) Write the number 59 on the first line. (Pause 2 seconds.) Write the largest of the following numbers on the fifth line: 51, 67, 77, 28, 49. (Pause 3 seconds.) Now, on the Answer Sheet, darken the number-letter combinations you have made. (Pause 5 seconds)

Look at Sample 16. (Pause slightly.) Draw one line under the third letter. (Pause 3 seconds.) Draw two lines under the last letter. (Pause 3 seconds.) On the Answer Sheet, find the number 13, and darken the letter under which you drew one line. (Pause 5 seconds.) Then, on the Answer Sheet, find the number 52, and darken the letter under which you drew two lines. (Pause 5 seconds.)

Look at Sample 17. (Pause slightly.) Of the cities listed in the three boxes, Baton Rouge has the earliest delivery time. (Pause slightly.) Write the letter A as in apple on the lines in the other two boxes. (Pause 3 seconds.) On the Answer Sheet, darken the number-letter combinations you have made. (Pause 5 seconds.)

Look at Sample 18. (Pause slightly.) Draw a line under each letter B as in boy that you see in the sequence. (Pause 3 seconds.) Count the number of B's you underlined, and write that number at the end of the sequence. (Pause 3 seconds.) Then, subtract 3 from that number. (Pause 3 seconds.) Now, find the resulting number on the Answer Sheet, and darken the letter B as in boy. (Pause 5 seconds.)

Look at Sample 19. (Pause slightly.) Draw a line under the odd number in the sequence. (Pause 3 seconds.) Find that number on the Answer Sheet, and darken the letter E as in egg.

END OF FOLLOWING ORAL INSTRUCTIONS QUESTIONS – PRACTICE EXAM #4

Following Oral Instructions Questions
Practice Exam #5

Look at Sample 1. (Pause slightly.) Draw a circle around the largest number. (Pause 3 seconds.) On the Answer Sheet, find the number you circled, and darken the letter D as in dog. (Pause 5 seconds.)

Look at Sample 2. (Pause slightly.) There are four different size circles with a number in each. (Pause slightly.) Counting from the right, write the letter B as in boy in the third circle. (Pause 4 seconds.) Now, on the Answer Sheet, darken the number-letter combination you have made. (Pause 5 seconds.)

Look at the five circles in Sample 3. (Pause slightly.) Each circle contains a mail delivery time. (Pause slightly.) On the line in the box with the latest delivery time, write the number that would be created by using the first two digits of that time. (Pause 4 seconds.) On the Answer Sheet, darken the number-letter combination you have made. (Pause 5 seconds.)

Look at Sample 4. (Pause slightly.) If 42 is greater than 28 but less than 67, write the number 42 in front of the last letter. (Pause 3 seconds.) If not, write the number 42 in front of the first letter. (Pause 3 seconds.) On the Answer Sheet, darken the number-letter combination you have made. (Pause 5 seconds.)

Look at the circles and words in Sample 5. (Pause slightly.) Write the last letter of the first word in the second circle. (Pause 3 seconds.) Write the first letter of the last word in the first circle. (Pause 3 seconds.) Write the third letter of the second word in the last circle. (Pause 3 seconds.) On the Answer Sheet, darken the number-letter combinations you have made. (Pause 5 seconds.)

Look at the three boxes in Sample 6. (Pause slightly.) If the smallest box has the largest number, write the letter B as in boy in that box. (Pause 3 seconds.) Otherwise, write the letter E as in egg in the largest box. (Pause 3 seconds.) On the Answer Sheet, darken the number-letter combination you have made. (Pause 5 seconds.)

Look at Sample 7. (Pause slightly.) Each of the four boxes contains the name of a city and the number of parcels to be delivered to that city. (Pause slightly.) If the last box has the largest number of parcels to be delivered, write the letter A as in apple next to the number in that box. (Pause 3 seconds.) Otherwise, write the letter C as in cat on the line next to the number in the first box. (Pause 3 seconds.) On the Answer Sheet, darken the number-letter combination you have made. (Pause 5 seconds.)

Look at Sample 8. (Pause slightly.) Draw a line under the numbers that are greater than 12 but less than 42. (Pause 4 seconds.) On the Answer Sheet, darken the letter B as in boy for the numbers you underlined. (Pause 5 seconds.)

Look at Sample 9. (Pause slightly.) Draw a line under each letter A as in apple that you see in the sequence. (Pause 3 seconds.) Count the number of A's you underlined, and write that number at the front of the sequence. (Pause 3 seconds.) Subtract 3 from that number. (Pause 3 seconds.) Find the resulting number on the Answer Sheet, and darken the letter A as in apple. (Pause 5 seconds.)

Look at Sample 10. (Pause slightly.) There are two boxes and two circles of different sizes. (Pause slightly.) Write the number 22 next to the letter in the smaller box. (Pause 3 seconds.) Write the number 53 next to the letter in the larger circle. (Pause 3 seconds.) On the Answer Sheet, darken the number-letter combinations you have made. (Pause 5 seconds.)

Look at Sample 11. (Pause slightly.) Write the letter C as in cat in the last box. (Pause 3 seconds.) In the first box, do nothing. (Pause slightly.) In the third box, write the letter E as in egg. (Pause 3 seconds.) On the Answer Sheet, darken the number-letter combinations you have made.

Look at Sample 12. (Pause slightly.) Each of the three boxes contains the name of a city and the number of express parcels to be delivered to that city. (Pause slightly.) Find the city with the second highest number of express parcels, and write the first letter of that city's name on the line in its box. (Pause 3 seconds.) On the Answer Sheet, darken the number-letter combination you have made. (Pause 5 seconds.)

Following Oral Instructions Questions
Practice Exam #5 – Continued

Look at Sample 13. (Pause slightly.) If 8 is greater than 6 and 15 is less than 23, write the number 71 in front of the third letter. (Pause 3 seconds.) Otherwise, write the number 34 in front of the fourth letter. (Pause 3 seconds.) On the Answer Sheet, darken the number-letter combination you have made. (Pause 5 seconds.)

Look at Sample 14. (Pause slightly.) Draw a line under the numbers greater than 3 but less than 17. (Pause 4 seconds.) On the Answer Sheet, find the numbers you underlined, and darken the letter B as in boy for each. (Pause 5 seconds.)

Look at Sample 14 again. (Pause slightly.) Draw two lines under the numbers greater than 31 but less than 58. (Pause 3 seconds.) On the Answer Sheet, find the numbers under which you drew two lines, and darken the letter A as in apple for each. (Pause 5 seconds.)

Look at Sample 15. (Pause slightly.) There are four different size boxes. (Pause slightly.) Write the letter D as in dog in the middle-sized boxes. (Pause 3 seconds.) On the Answer Sheet, darken the number-letter combinations you have made. (Pause 5 seconds.)

Look at Sample 16. (Pause slightly.) Write the numbers 50 and 60 in front of the third and fourth letters respectively. (Pause 4 seconds.) On the Answer Sheet, darken the number-letter combinations you have made. (Pause 5 seconds.)

Look at Sample 17. (Pause slightly.) If February comes before January in the calendar year, write the letter C as in cat in the smaller circle. (Pause 3 seconds.) If not, write the number 88 in the smaller box. (Pause 3 seconds.) Now, on the Answer Sheet, darken the number-letter combination you have made. (Pause 5 seconds.)

Look at Sample 18. (Pause slightly.) You will find three circles followed by the word "AMORTIZATION". (Pause slightly.) Write the eighth letter in the word "AMORTIZATION" on the line in the first circle. (Pause 3 seconds.) On the Answer Sheet, darken the number letter combination you have made. (Pause 5 seconds.)

Look at Sample 19. (Pause slightly.) Draw a line under the smallest number in the sequence. (Pause 3 seconds.) On the Answer Sheet, find the number you underlined and darken the letter E as in egg.

END OF FOLLOWING ORAL INSTRUCTIONS QUESTIONS – PRACTICE EXAM #5

Following Oral Instructions Questions
Practice Exam #6

Look at Sample 1. (Pause slightly.) Draw a line under the fifth letter from the left. (Pause 3 seconds.) On the Answer Sheet, find the number 47, and darken the letter you underlined. (Pause 5 seconds.)

Look at Sample 2. Pause slightly.) There are five circles, each containing a letter with a line beside it. (Pause slightly.) On the line in the last circle, write the smallest of the following numbers: 82, 78, 59, 64, 69. (Pause 3 seconds.) On the line in the third circle, write the number 21. (Pause 3 seconds.) On the line in the first circle, do nothing. (Pause slightly.) On the line in the second circle, write the largest of the following numbers: 80, 78, 56, 82, 79. (Pause 3 seconds.) On the Answer Sheet, darken the number-letter combinations you have made. (Pause 5 seconds.)

Look at Sample 3. (Pause slightly.) If there are 365 days in the calendar year and if Ronald Reagan is the current president of the United States, write a D as in dog on the line in the fourth box. (Pause 3 seconds.) Otherwise, write a C as in cat on the lines in the second and third boxes. (Pause 3 seconds.) On the Answer Sheet, darken the number-letter combination or combinations you have made. (Pause 5 seconds.)

Look at the X's and Y's in Sample 4. (Pause slightly.) Count the number of X's, and write the number of X's at the end of the line X's and Y's. (Pause 4 seconds.) Count the number of Y's, and write the number of Y's under the number of X's at the end of the line. (Pause 4 seconds.) Then subtract the number of Y's from the number of X's. (Pause 3 seconds.) Find the resulting number on the Answer Sheet, and darken the letter D as in dog. (Pause 5 seconds.)

Look at the numbers in Sample 5. (Pause slightly.) Draw a line under all the even numbers that are less than 27. (Pause 3 seconds.) On the Answer Sheet, find the numbers you underlined, and darken the letter A as in apple for each. (Pause 5 seconds.)

Look at Sample 5 again. (Pause slightly.) Circle the even numbers that are greater than 56. (Pause 3 seconds.) On the Answer Sheet, find the numbers you circled, and darken the letter E as in egg for each. (Pause 5 seconds.)

Look at the circles in Sample 6. (Pause slightly.) Each circle contains a mail collection time. (Pause slightly.) Write the letter B as in boy on the line in the circle with the earliest collection time. (Pause 3 seconds.) On the same line in the same circle, write the number that would be created by using the last two digits of the time in that circle. (Pause 3 seconds.) On your Answer Sheet, darken the number-letter combination you have made. (Pause 5 seconds.)

Look at Sample 6 again. (Pause slightly.) If 5 is greater than 3 and 13 is less than 15, write the letter E as in egg in the last circle. (Pause 3 seconds.) If not, write the letter B as in boy in the third circle. (Pause 3 seconds.) On the line beside the letter in the circle in which you just wrote, write the number that would be created by using the first two digits of the time in that circle. (Pause 3 seconds.) On the Answer Sheet, darken the number-letter combination you have made. (Pause 5 seconds.)

Look at Sample 7. (Pause slightly.) Write the number 65 by the letter on the right. (Pause 3 seconds.) Now, on the Answer Sheet, darken the number-letter combination you have made. (Pause 5 seconds.)

Look at Sample 8. (Pause slightly.) There are three circles and three words. (Pause slightly.) Write the first letter of the second word in the second circle. (Pause 3 seconds.) Write the last letter of the first word in the last circle. (Pause 3 seconds.) Write the first letter of the third word in the first circle. (Pause 3 seconds.) On the Answer Sheet, darken the number-letter combinations you have made. (Pause 5 seconds.)

Look at the two boxes in Sample 9. (Pause slightly.) In the first box is the number of Priority Mail packages in route to the Jacksonville Post Offices. (Pause slightly.) In the second box is the number of Priority Mail packages in route to the Boston Post Office. (Pause slightly.) Write the letter D as in dog in the box that has the number of Priority Mail packages in route to the Jacksonville Post Office. (Pause 3 seconds.) Now, on the Answer Sheet, darken the number-letter combination you have made. (Pause 5 seconds.)

Look at Sample 9 again. (Pause slightly.) Write the letter B as in boy in the box with the smaller number of Priority Mail packages. (Pause 3 seconds.) On the Answer Sheet, darken the number-letter combination you have made. (Pause 5 seconds.)

Following Oral Instructions Questions
Practice Exam #6 – Continued

Look at Sample 10. (Pause slightly.) There are three circles, each containing the name of a city. (Pause slightly.) The city of Gulfport has the latest mail delivery time. (Pause slightly.) The city of Waveland has the earliest delivery time. (Pause slightly.) The city of Biloxi has the middle delivery time. (Pause slightly.) Write the letter C as in cat in the circle with the city that has the earliest delivery time. (Pause 3 seconds.) On your Answer Sheet, darken the number-letter combination you have made. (Pause 5 seconds.)

Look at Sample 11. (Pause slightly.) Write the letter E as in egg above the largest number. (Pause 3 seconds.) Write the letter D as in dog below the smallest number. (Pause 3 seconds.) On the Answer Sheet, darken the number-letter combinations you have made. (Pause 5 seconds.)

Look at Sample 12. (Pause slightly.) Each of the five boxes contains a number of sacks of mail to be delivered. (Pause slightly.) Write the letter A as in apple in the box with the smallest number of sacks of mail to be delivered. (Pause 3 seconds.) On the Answer Sheet, darken the number-letter combination you have made. (Pause 5 seconds.)

Look at Sample 13. (Pause slightly.) If 42 is larger than 39 and 12 is less than 10, write the number 41 in the larger box. (Pause 3 seconds.) If not, write the number 41 in the smaller box. (Pause 3 seconds.) On the Answer Sheet, darken the number-letter combination you have made. (Pause 5 seconds.)

Look at Sample 14. (Pause slightly.) If the letter D as in dog comes before the letter B as in boy in the alphabet, write the letter C as in cat on the line after the third number. (Pause 3 seconds.) If not, write the letter A as in apple on the line after the second number. (Pause 3 seconds.) On the Answer Sheet, darken the number-letter combination you have made. (Pause 5 seconds.)

Look at Sample 15. (Pause slightly.) In Sample 15, there is a word with four lines below it. (Pause slightly.) Write the last letter of the word on the first line. (Pause 3 seconds.) Write the first letter of the word on the last line. (Pause 3 seconds.) Write the number 78 on the third line. (Pause 3 seconds.) On the Answer Sheet, darken the number-letter combination you have made. (Pause 5 seconds.)

Look at Sample 16. (Pause slightly.) Draw a line under each of the listed numbers that are greater than 62 but less than 83. (Pause 4 seconds.) On the Answer Sheet, find the number or numbers you underlined, and darken the letter B as in boy for each. (Pause 5 seconds.)

Look at Sample 17. (Pause slightly.) Draw a line over each of the X's in the sequence. (Pause 3 seconds.) Count the number of X's, and write that number at the end of the sequence. (Pause 3 seconds.) Now, count the number of O's in the sequence, and add the number of O's to the number of X's. (Pause 3 seconds.) Write the total at the end of the sequence. (Pause 3 seconds.) On the Answer Sheet, find that total number, and darken the letter D as in dog. (Pause 5 seconds.)

Look at Sample 18. (Pause slightly.) There are four boxes, each containing a number of sacks of mail to be delivered. (Pause slightly.) Write the letter E as in egg in the boxes that have the same number of sacks of mail to be delivered. (Pause 3 seconds.) On the Answer Sheet, darken the number-letter combination you have made. (Pause 5 seconds.)

Look at Sample 19. (Pause slightly.) If 8 is greater than 5 and 3 is less than 4, write the letter A as in apple on the middle line. (Pause 3 seconds.) Otherwise, write the letter D as in dog on the last line. (Pause 3 seconds.) On the Answer Sheet, darken the number-letter combination you have made.

END OF FOLLOWING ORAL INSTRUCTIONS QUESTIONS – PRACTICE EXAM #6

Number Series Solutions – Practice Exam #1

1. 31 32 33 34 35 36 37 38
Series increases by 1.

2. 5 5 5   5 5 5   5 5 5
      10   10   10
Upper series is the number 5 repeating. Lower series is the number 10 repeating.

3. 22   22   22   22   22
      10   9   8   7   6
Upper series is the number 22 repeating. Lower series decreases by 1.

4. 1   4   7   10   13
     2   5   8   11
Upper series increases by 3. Lower series increases by 3.

5. 1 2   3 4   5 6   7 8
    0   0   0   0
Upper series increases by 1. Lower series is the number 0 repeating.

6. 2   9   16   23   30
    5   12   19   26
Upper series increases by 7. Lower series increases by 7.

7. 2 4 6 10 16 26 42 68
Each number is added to the number before it to create the number that follows it.

8. 89 88 87 86 85 84 83
Series decreases by 1.

9. 2 4 8 16 32 64
Each number is added to itself to create the following number.

10. 2 17 32 47 62 77
Series increases by 15.

11. 16 16   16 16   16
     33 33   33 33
Upper series is the number 16 repeating. Lower series is the number 33 repeating.

12. 65   55   45   35   25
    20   30   40   50
Upper series decreases by 10. Lower series increases by 10.

13. 18 18   12 12   6
     15 15   9 9
Each number repeats once and then decreases by 3. Then the resulting number repeats once before again decreasing by 3, and so on.

14. 1 14 27 40 53 66
Series increases by 13.

15. 8 11 14 17 20 23
   29 26 23 20 17
Upper series increases by 3. Lower series decreases by 3.

16. 2 8 14 20 26
   4 10 16 22
Upper series increases by 6. Lower series increases by 6.

17. 3 6 9 15 18 21 27 30 33 39
  (+3) (+3) (+6) (+3) (+3) (+6) (+3) (+3) (+6)
This is an addition series with an alternating addition factor. The series increases by 3 twice, then by 6 once, then again by 3 twice, and then again by 6 once, and so on.

18. 80 70 60 50 40
   50 60 70 80
Upper series decreases by 10. Lower series increases by 10.

19. 83 63 43 23
  13 23 33 43
Upper series decreases by 20. Lower series increases by 10.

20. 31 31 31 31 31
   3 4 5 6
Upper series is the number 31 repeating. Lower series increases by 1.

21. 8 16 24 32 40 48 56
Series increases by 8.

22. 1 25 49 73
   5 15 25 35
Upper series increases by 24. Lower series increases by 10.

23. 21 18   15 12   9
    10 8   6 4
Upper series decreases by 3. Lower series decreases by 2.

24. 10 12 14 16 18
   6 5 4 3
Upper series increases by 2. Lower series decreases by 1.

Number Series Solutions – Practice Exam #2

1. 12   10   8   6   4
    11   9   7   5
Upper series decreases by 2. Lower series decreases by 2.

2. 14 16 18 20 22 24 26 28
Series increases by 2.

3. 4   14   24   34
   9   19   29
Upper series increases by 10. Lower series increases by 10.

4. 2   3   4   5
   5   11   17   23
Upper series increases by 1. Lower series increases by 6.

5. 3   11   19   27
   8   13   18   23
Upper series increases by 8. Lower series increases by 5.

6. 28 25   22 19   16
   10 12   14 16
Upper series decreases by 3. Lower series increases by 2.

7. 33   44   55   66
   66   55   44   33
Upper series increases by 11. Lower series decreases by 11.

8. 21   24   27   30
   87   85   83   81
Upper series increases by 3. Lower series decreases by 2.

9. 10   15 20   25 30   35
   30   35   40
Upper series increases by 5. Lower series increases by 5.

10. 75   75   75   75
   8   15   22   29
Upper series is the number 75 repeating. Lower series increases by 7.

11. 1 9 8   1 9
   1 9 8
Series is the numbers 1, 9, and 8 repeating over and over again in order. (1 9 8, 1 9 8, 1 9 8, etc.)

12. 13 15   35 37   57 59
   90   87
Upper series is an addition series where the addition factor alternates between 2 and 20. (13 + 2 = 15, 15 + 20 = 35, 35 + 2 = 37, 37 + 20 = 57, 57 + 2 = 59) Lower series decreases by 3.

13. 1   4   7   10   13
   2   5   8   11
Upper series increases by 3. Lower series increases by 3.

14. <u>41 36   31 26   21</u>
      63 68   73 78
Upper series decreases by 5. Lower series increases by 5.

15. <u>7 12   17 22   27 32</u>
    37   40   43
Upper series increases by 5. Lower series increases by 3.

16. <u>14 14 14   17 17 17   20 20 20</u>
      26   40
In the upper series, each number repeats twice and then increases by 3. Then the resulting number repeats twice before again increasing by 3, and so on. Lower series increases by 14.

17. <u>   22 21   20 19   18 17</u>
  24   34   44
Upper series decreases by 1. Lower series increases by 10.

18. 1 3 4 7 11 18 29 47
Each number is added to the number before it to create the number that follows it.

19. 2 7 12 17 22 27
Series increases by 5.

20. <u>   44 42 40   38 36 34</u>
  13 14   15 16
Upper series decreases by 2. Lower series increases by 1.

21. <u>9 10   11 12</u>
    30 28   26 24
Upper series increases by 1. Lower series decreases by 2.

22. <u> 32   31   30   29</u>
  33   31   29   27   25
Upper series decreases by 1. Lower series decreases by 2.

23. <u> 30 29 28   27 26 25   24 23</u>
  10   9   8
Upper series decreases by 1. Lower series decreases by 1.

24. <u> 45 40   35 30   25 20</u>
  8   28   48
Upper series decreases by 5. Lower series increases by 20.

Number Series Solutions – Practice Exam #3

1. 3 5 7 9 11 13 15 17 19
Series increases by 2.

2. 1 7 13 19 25 31 37 43 49
Series increases by 6.

3. 12 15 18 21 24 27 30 33 36
Series increases by 3.

4. 21 28 35 42 49 56 63 70 77
Series increases by 7.

5. 62 60 58 56 54 52 50 48 46
Series decreases by 2.

6. 82 71 60 49 38 27 16 5
Series decreases by 11.

7. 16 20 24 28 32 36 40 44 48
Series increases by 4.

8. 58 55 52 49 46 43 40 37 34
Series decreases by 3.

9. 4 5 6 7 8 9 ____
    8   11   14
Upper series increases by 1. Lower Series increases by 3.

10. 19 21 23 25 27 29 ____
    50   47   44
Upper series increases by 2. Lower series decreases by 3.

11. 3 9 15 21 27 33 39 45 51
Series increases by 6.

12. 12 11 10 9 8 7 6 5 ____
    37   36
Upper series decreases by 1. Lower series decreases by 1.

13. 42 37 32 27 22 ____
    64 69   74 79
Upper series decreases by 5. Lower series increases by 5.

14. 71 76 81 86 91 ____
    31 29   27 25
Upper series increases by 5. Lower series decreases by 2.

15. 1 7 13 19 25 ____
    13 19 25 31
Upper series increases by 6. Lower series increases by 6.

16. 21 21 18 18 15 15 ____
    14   52   90
In the upper series, each number repeats once and then decreases by 3. Then the resulting number repeats once before again decreasing by 3, and so on. Lower series increases by 38.

241

17. <u>36   39 39   42 42   </u>
     7 5   3 1

In the upper series, each number repeats once and then increases by 3. Then the resulting number repeats once before again increasing by 3, and so on. Lower series decreases by 2.

18. <u> 37 61   85 109   133 157 </u>
  27   21   15

Upper series increases by 24. Lower series decreases by 6.

19. <u>11   7 7 7   3 3 3 </u>
   17   .   23   29

In the upper series, each number repeats twice and then decreases by 4. Then the resulting number repeats twice before again decreasing by 4, and so on. Lower series increases by 6.

20. <u> 14   17   20   </u>
    32   35   38
<u>80   65   50   </u>
  69   54   39

This question is usually viewed as mind-blowing problem containing four separate sequences. Starting from the top, the first series increases by 3. The second series from the top also increases by 3. The third series from the top decreases by 15. And, finally, the bottom series decreases by 15 as well.

Question 20 could also be solved as only two sequences, albeit unusual sequences, as outlined below:

<u> 14 32   17 35   20 38 </u>
 80   ·69 65   54 50·   39

The upper series consists of pairs of numbers grouped like this – 14 & 32, 17 & 35, 20 & 38. To find the first number of the pair, add 3 to the first number in the preceding pair. (14 + 3 = 17, 17 + 3 = 20) To find the second number of each pair, add 18 to its first number. (14 + 18 = 32, 17 + 18 = 35, 20 + 18 = 38) The lower series consists of a similar subtraction sequence grouped into pairs like this – 80 & 69, 65 & 54, 50 & 39. To find the first number of each pair, subtract 15 from the first number in the preceding pair. (80 – 15 = 65, 65 – 15 = 50) To find the second number of each pair, subtract 11 from its first number. (80 – 11 = 69, 65 – 11 = 54, 50 – 11 = 39)

---

21. <u>15   25   35   45   55   </u>
   22   32   42   52

Upper series increases by 10. Lower series increases by 10.

22. <u>96 96   75 75   54 54   </u>
    11   14   17

In the upper series, each number repeats once and then decreases by 21. Then the resulting number repeats once before again decreasing by 21, and so on. Lower series increases by 3.

23. <u>27   57   87   117   </u>
   42   72   102

Upper series increases by 30. Lower series increases by 30.

24. <u>6 7   '10 11   15 16   </u>
    21   26   31

The upper series is an addition sequence that alternates between a constant addition factor of 1 and a graduating addition factor that begins as a 3 and then increases by 1 each time it is used. (6 + 1 = 7, 7 + 3 = 10, 10 + 1 = 11, 11 + 4 = 15, 15 + 1 = 16) Lower series increases by 5.

Number Series Solutions – Practice Exam #4

1. <u>   6 8   10 12   14 16 </u>
    5   10   15
Upper series increases by 2. Lower series increases by 5.

2. 21 24 27 30 33 36 39
Series increase by 3.

3. <u>   3 5   7 9   11 13 </u>
    1   5   9
Upper series increases by 2. Lower series increases by 4.

4. <u>11 11   9 9   7 </u>
        10 10   8 8
Each number repeats once and then decreases by 1. Then the resulting number repeats once before again decreasing by 1, and so on.

5. <u>1   1   1   1   1 </u>
    31   32   33   34
Upper series is the number 1 repeating. Lower series increases by 1.

6. <u>14   14   14   14 </u>
     12   13   14   15
Upper series is the number 14 repeating. Lower series increases by 1.

7. <u>   1 3   5 7   9 11 </u>
    11   15   19
Upper series increases by 2. Lower series increases by 4.

8. <u>11 12 14 17 21 26 32 39 47 </u>
   (+1) (+2) (+3) (+4) (+5) (+6) (+7) (+8)
This is a graduated addition series where the addition factor begins as a 1 and then increases by 1 each time it is used. (11 + 1 = 12, 12 + 2 = 14, 14 + 3 = 17, 17 + 4 = 21, etc.)

9. <u>8 8   12 12   16 </u>
    10 10   14 14
Each number repeats once and then increases by 2. Then the resulting number repeats once before again increasing by 2, and so on.

10. <u>3 4   8 9   13 14 </u>
     13   13   13
The upper series alternately increases by 1, then by 4, then by 1 again, then by 4 again, and so on. (3 + 1 = 4, 4 + 4 = 8, 8 + 1 = 9, 9 + 4 = 13, 13 + 1 = 14) The lower series is the number 13 repeating.

11. <u>   31   32   33   34 </u>
    2   2   2   2   2
Upper series increases by 1. Lower series is the number 2 repeating.

12. <u>3   7   11   15   19 </u>
    2   5   8   11
Upper series increases by 4. Lower series increases by 3.

13. <u>16   16   16   16   16</u>
    15   16   17   18
Upper series is the number 16 repeating. Lower series increases by 1.

14. <u>2   4   6   8   10</u>
    4   4   . 4   4
Upper series increases by 2. Lower series is the number 4 repeating.

15. <u> 6 6   12 12   18 18</u>
  18   18   18
Upper series repeats once and then increases by 6. Then, the resulting number repeats once before again increasing by 6, and so on. Lower series is the number 18 repeating.

16. <u>15   16   17   18</u>
  1   2   3   4
Upper series increases by 1. Lower series increases by 1.

17. <u>2   4   6   8   10</u>
   1   3   5   7
Upper series increases by 2. Lower series increases by 2.

18. <u>1   2   3   4   5</u>
   12   12   12   12
Upper series increases by 1. Lower series is the number 12 repeating.

19. <u>26   24   22 20</u>
   2   4   6   8
Upper series decreases by 2. Lower series increases by 2.

20. <u> 13 15   17 19   21 23</u>
  6   7   8
Upper series increases by 2. Lower series increases by 1.

21. <u>9 10   11 12   13 14</u>
    15   15   15
Upper series increases by 1. Lower series is the number 15 repeating.

22. <u> 16 18   20 22   24 26</u>
  23   18   13
Upper series increases by 2. Lower series decreases by 5.

23. <u>10 11 13 16 20 25 31 38</u>
  (+1) (+2) (+3) (+4) (+5) (+6) (+7)
This is a graduated addition series where the addition factor begins as a 1 and then increases by 1 each time it is used.
(10 + 1 = 11, 11 + 2 = 13, 13 + 3 = 16, 16 + 4 = 20, etc.)

24. <u>9   12   15   18   21</u>
   10   13   16   19
Upper series increases by 3. Lower series increases by 3.

Number Series Solutions – Practice Exam #5

1. 19 19   21 21   23
      20 20   22 22

Each number repeats once and then increases by 1. Then, the resulting number repeats once before again increasing by 1, and so on.

2. 6 12 18 24 30 36 42
Series increases by 6.

3. 31 28 25 22 19 16 13 10
Series decreases by 3.

4.   19 16   13 10   7
    15   13   11

Upper series decreases by 3. Lower series decreases by 2.

5.   6   7   8   9
    8   8   8   8

Upper series increases by 1. Lower series is the number 8 repeating.

6. 21 29 37 45 53 61 69
Series increases by 8.

7.   12 14   16 18   20 22
    8   10   12

Upper series increases by 2. Lower series increases by 2.

8. 7 8   9 10   11 12
     10   12   14

Upper series increases by 1. Lower series increases by 2.

9. 9 9   9 9   9 9
     6   8   10

Upper series is the number 9 repeating. Lower series increases by 2.

10. 25 31 37 43 49 55 61
Series increases by 6.

11. 32 33 35 38 42 47 53 60
This is a graduating addition sequence where the factor begins as a 1 and increases by 1 each time it is used. (32 + 1 = 33, 33 + 2 = 35, 35 + 3 = 38, 38 + 4 = 42, etc.)

12.   8 12   16 20   24 28
    3   6   9

Upper series increases by 4. Lower series increases by 3.

13. 3 4   5 6   7 8   9
     10   9   8

Upper series increases by 1. Lower series decreases by 1.

Number Series Solutions – Practice Exam #5
Continued

14. 10   20   30   40
    3   4   5   6

Upper series increases by 10. Lower series increases by 1.

15.   4   8   12   16
   5 10 16 23

Upper series increases by 4. Lower series is a graduating addition sequence where the factor begins as a 5 and increases by 1 each time it is used. (5 + 5 = 10, 10 + 6 = 16, 16 + 7 = 23)

16. 9 14   19 24   29 34
     28   28   28

Upper series increases by 5. Lower series is the number 28 repeating.

17. 7 8   9 10   11 12
    12   12   12

Upper series increases by 1. Lower series is the number 12 repeating.

18. 11   14   17   20   23
    12   15   18   21

Upper series increases by 3. Lower series increases by 3.

19. 15   15   15   15   15
    8   11   14   17

Upper series is the number 15 repeating. Lower series increases by 3.

20. 10 9   8 7   6 5
    10 15   20 25

Upper series decreases by 1. Lower series increases by 5.

21. 26   24   22   20
    8   10   12   14

Upper series decreases by 2. Lower series increases by 2.

22. 24 25 27 28 30 31 33 34
Series is an addition sequence where the addition factor alternates between 1 and 2. (24+ 1 = 25, 25 + 2 = 27, 27 + 1 = 28, 28 + 2 = 30, etc.)

23. 18   18   18   18   18
    16   17   18   19

Upper series is the number 18 repeating. Lower series increases by 1.

24. 30 31 33 36 40 45 51
Series is a graduating addition sequence where the factor begins as a 1 and increases by 1 each time it is used. (30 + 1 = 31, 31 + 2 = 33, 33 + 3 = 36, 36 + 4 = 40, 40 + 5 = 45, 45 + 6 = 51)

Number Series Solutions – Practice Exam #6

1. 14 15 16 17 18 19 20 21
Series increases by 1.

2. 26 28 30 32 34 36 38 40
Series increases by 2.

3. <u>3   13   23   33</u>
    6   16   26
Upper series increases by 10. Lower series increases by 10.

4. <u>3   4   5   6   7</u>
   4   6   8   10
Upper series increases by 1. Lower series increases by 2.

5. <u>29 25   21 17   13</u>
     10 12   14 16
Upper series decreases by 4. Lower series increases by 2.

6. <u>15   20   25   30</u>
   40   30   20   10
Upper series increases by 5. Lower series decreases by 10.

7. <u>6 12   18 24   30 36</u>
    35   25   15
Upper series increases by 6. Lower series decreases by 10.

8. <u>9 9   9 9   9 9</u>
   5   10   15
Upper series is the number 9 repeating. Lower series increases by 5.

9. <u>6   9   12   15   18</u>
   7   10   13   16
Upper series increases by 3. Lower series increases by 3.

10. <u>6   8   10   12   14</u>
   5   7   9   11
Upper series increases by 2. Lower series increases by 2.

11. <u>5 5   5 5   5 5   5</u>
   3   4   5
Upper series is the number 5 repeating. Lower series increases by 1.

12. <u>20 17   14 11   8 5</u>
    10 10   10 10
Upper series decreases by 3. Lower series is the number 10 repeating.

13. 2 15 28 41 54 67
Series increases by 13.

14. <u>75   65   55   45</u>
     10   20   30   40

Upper series decreases by 10. Lower series increases by 10.

15. <u>90   80   70   60</u>
     60   70   80   90

Upper series decreases by 10. Lower series increases by 10.

16. <u> 32   33   34   35</u>
  34   34   34   34

Upper series increases by 1. Lower series is the number 34 repeating.

17. <u> 5 7   9 11   13 15</u>
  8   16   24

Upper series increases by 2. Lower series increases by 8.

18. <u> 19   18   17   16   15</u>
  14   16   18   20   22

Upper series decreases by 1. Lower series increases by 2.

19. <u> 3 6   9 12   15 18</u>
  7   14   21   28

Upper series increases by 3. Lower series increases by 7.

20. <u>8   11   14   17   20</u>
   3   8   13   18   23

Upper series increases by 3. Lower series increases by 5.

21. <u>2 4   6 8   10 12</u>
    0   0   0

Upper series increases by 2. Lower series is the number 0 repeating.

22. <u>8 8   8 8   8 8</u>
   10   9   8

Upper series is the number 8 repeating. Lower series decreases by 1.

23. 47 39 31 23 15 7
Series decreases by 8.

24. 5 6 8 11 15 20 26 33
Series is a graduating addition sequence where the factor begins as a 1 and increases by 1 each time it is used. (5 + 1 = 6, 6 + 2 = 8, 8 + 3 = 11, 11 + 4 = 15, 15 + 5 = 20, 20 + 6 = 26, 26 + 7 = 33)

Postal Phone Directory

The below phone numbers were confirmed to be valid as of the publish date of this book. However, it is possible that some of these numbers may change from time to time. If one of these numbers does not work when you try it, call another nearby location and ask for the updated number.

As of this book's publish date, the Postal Service was in the midst of consolidating some district offices. In such cases, other nearby district offices assume responsibility for the office that was closed. As additional consolidations occur, phone numbers for the closed offices will become invalid.

The "HOTLINE" column contains "Hiring & Testing Hotline" numbers that can be called 24/7 to hear recorded announcements of open employment and testing opportunities. The 1-800, 1-866, 1-877, and 1-888 numbers are all toll free calls.

The "EXAM OFFICE" numbers ring into exam and human resources offices where you can speak to a person to ask specific questions.

STATE, ETC.	CITY	HOTLINE	EXAM OFFICE
Alabama	Birmingham (District Office)	205-521-0214	205-521-0272
Alabama	Huntsville		256-461-6640
Alabama	Mobile	251-694-5921	251-694-5920
Alabama	Montgomery	334-244-7551	334-244-7553
Alaska	Anchorage (District Office)	907-564-2964	907-564-2962
Arizona	Phoenix (District Office)	602-223-3624	602-223-3633
Arizona	Tucson	520-388-5191	520-388-5103
Arkansas	Little Rock (District Office)	501-945-6665	501-945-6664
California	Anaheim	714-662-6375	
California	Bakersfield	661-392-6261	661-392-6251
California	Fresno	559-497-7636	559-497-7770
California	Long Beach (District Office)	562-435-4529	562-983-3010
California	Los Angeles (District Office)	323-586-1351	323-586-1392
California	Oakland (District Office)	510-251-3040	510-251-3041
California	Sacramento (District Office)	916-373-8448	916-373-8679
California	San Bernardino	909-335-4339	909-335-4329
California	San Diego (District Office)	858-674-0577	858-674-2626
California	San Francisco (District Office)	415-550-5534	415-550-5330
California	San Jose (District Office)	408-437-6986	408-437-6989
California	San Mateo	650-377-1124	
California	Santa Ana (District Office)	626-855-6339	626-855-6355
California	Santa Barbara	805-278-7668	805-278-7648
California	Stockton	209-983-6490	
California	Van Nuys (District Office)	661-775-7014	661-775-7030
Colorado	Colorado Springs	719-570-5316	719-570-5443
Colorado	Denver (District Office)	1-877-482-3238	303-853-6132
Connecticut	Hartford (District Office)	860-524-6120	860-524-6259
Delaware	See Bellmawr, NJ District Office		
District of Columbia	Washington (District Office)	301-324-5837	202-523-2949
Florida	Fort Myers	1-800-533-9097	239-768-8025

STATE, ETC.	CITY	HOTLINE	EXAM OFFICE
Florida	Jacksonville (District Office)	904-359-2737	904-359-2979
Florida	Lake Mary (District Office)	1-888-771-9056	407-444-2014
Florida	Miami (District Office)	1-888-725-7295	305-470-0782
Florida	Orlando	1-888-771-9056	407-850-6314
Florida	Pensacola	850-434-9167	850-434-9136
Florida	Tallahassee	850-216-4248	
Florida	Tampa (District Office)	1-800-533-9097	813-872-3501
Georgia	Atlanta (District Office)	770-717-3500	770-717-3500
Georgia	Macon (District Office)	478-752-8465	478-752-8473
Georgia	Savannah	912-235-4629	912-235-4628
Hawaii	Honolulu (District Office)	808-423-3690	808-423-3613
Idaho	Boise	208-433-4415	
Illinois	Bedford Park (District Office)	708-563-7496	708-563-7494
Illinois	Carol Stream (District Office)	630-260-5200	630-260-5633
Illinois	Chicago (District Office)		312-983-8522
Illinois	Peoria	309-671-8835	309-671-8865
Illinois	Rockford	815-229-4824	815-229-4752
Illinois	Springfield	217-788-7437	217-788-7480
Indiana	Indianapolis (District Office)	317-870-8500	317-870-8564
Iowa	Cedar Rapids		319-399-2965
Iowa	Des Moines (District Office)	515-251-2061	515-251-2214
Kansas	See Omaha, NE District Office		
Kansas	Topeka	785-295-9164	785-295-9145
Kansas	Wichita	316-946-4596	316-946-4594
Kentucky	Lexington	859-231-6755	859-231-6851
Kentucky	Louisville (District Office)	502-454-1625	502-454-1641
Louisiana	Baton Rouge	1-888-421-4887	225-763-3788
Louisiana	New Orleans (District Office)	1-888-421-4887	504-589-1187
Louisiana	Shreveport	1-888-421-4887	
Maine	Bangor	207-941-2064	207-941-2084
Maine	Portland (District Office)	207-828-8520	207-828-8576
Maryland	Baltimore (District Office)	410-347-4320	410-347-4473
Massachusetts	Boston (District Office)	617-654-5569	617-654-5608
Massachusetts	North Reading (District Office)	978-664-7665	978-664-7711
Massachusetts	Springfield (District Office)	413-731-0425	
Massachusetts	Worcester		508-795-3676
Michigan	Detroit (District Office)	1-888-442-5361	313-226-8007
Michigan	Grand Rapids (District Office)		616-336-5323
Michigan	Royal Oak (District Office)	248-546-7104	248-546-7157
Minnesota	Duluth (Remote Encoding Center)		218-624-9599
Minnesota	St Paul (District Office)	1-877-293-3364	651-293-3009
Mississippi	Gulfport	228-831-5438	228-831-5419
Mississippi	Jackson (District Office)	601-351-7099	601-351-7269
Missouri	Kansas City (District Office)	816-374-9346	816-374-9163
Missouri	St Louis (District Office)	314-436-3855	314-436-4489
Montana	Billings (District Office)	406-657-5763	406-657-5765
Montana	Missoula	406-657-5763	406-329-2227

STATE, ETC.	CITY	HOTLINE	EXAM OFFICE
Nebraska	Lincoln	402-473-1669	402-473-1665
Nebraska	Omaha (District Office)	402-348-2523	402-255-3989
Nevada	Las Vegas (District Office)	702-361-9564	702-361-9326
Nevada	Reno	775-788-0656	775-788-0699
New Hampshire	Manchester (District Office)	603-644-4065	603-644-4061
New Jersey	Bellmawr (District Office)	856-933-4314	856-933-4288
New Jersey	Edison (District Office)	732-819-4334	732-819-3832
New Jersey	Elizabeth	908-820-8454	
New Jersey	Newark (District Office)	866-665-3562	973-693-5153
New Mexico	Albuquerque (District Office)	505-346-8780	505-346-8793
New York	Albany (District Office)	518-452-2445	518-452-2450
New York	Binghamton		607-773-2152
New York	Buffalo (District Office)	716-846-2478	716-846-2472
New York	Long Island (District Office)	631-582-7530	516-582-7543
New York	New York (District Office)	212-330-3633	212-330-3641
New York	Queens (Triboro District Office)	718-529-7000	718-529-7011
New York	Rochester		716-272-5705
New York	Syracuse	315-452-3616	315-452-3436
New York	White Plains (District Office)	914-697-5400	914-697-7190
North Carolina	Charlotte (District Office)	704-393-4490	704-393-4557
North Carolina	Greensboro (District Office)	1-866-839-7826	336-668-1258
North Carolina	Raleigh	919-420-5284	919-420-5282
North Dakota	Fargo	1-888-725-7854	701-241-6161
Ohio	Akron (District Office)	330-996-9530	330-996-9532
Ohio	Canton	330-438-6425	330-438-6427
Ohio	Cincinnati (District Office)	513-684-5449	513-684-5481
Ohio	Cleveland (District Office)	216-443-4210	216-443-4241
Ohio	Columbus (District Office)	614-469-4356	614-469-4322
Ohio	Dayton	937-227-1146	937-227-1144
Ohio	Toledo	419-245-6834	419-245-6823
Ohio	Youngstown		330-740-8932
Oklahoma	Oklahoma City (District Office)	405-553-6159	405-553-6173
Oklahoma	Tulsa		918-732-6742
Oregon	Eugene	541-341-3625	541-341-3625
Oregon	Portland (District Office)	503-294-2270	503-294-2283
Pennsylvania	Devon	610-964-6462	610-964-6464
Pennsylvania	Erie (District Office)	1-800-868-6835	814-898-7310
Pennsylvania	Harrisburg (District Office)	717-257-2191	717-257-2173
Pennsylvania	Johnstown	814-533-4926	814-533-4923
Pennsylvania	Lancaster (District Office)	1-866-271-4711	717-390-7468
Pennsylvania	Lehigh Valley		610-882-3290
Pennsylvania	Philadelphia (District Office)	215-895-8830	215-895-8869
Pennsylvania	Pittsburgh (District Office)	412-359-7516	412-359-7974
Pennsylvania	Scranton		570-969-5156
Puerto Rico	San Juan (District Office)	787-767-3351	787-767-2374
Rhode Island	Providence (District Office)	1-800-755-2397	401-276-5044
South Carolina	Charleston	843-760-5343	843-760-5344

STATE, ETC.	CITY	HOTLINE	EXAM OFFICE
South Carolina	Columbia (District Office)	803-926-6400	803-926-6437
South Carolina	Greenville	864-282-8374	864-282-8320
South Dakota	Sioux Falls (District Office)	1-888-725-7854	605-333-2694
Tennessee	Chattanooga	423-499-8348	423-499-8355
Tennessee	Knoxville	865-558-4540	865-558-4596
Tennessee	Memphis	901-521-2550	901-521-2227
Tennessee	Nashville (District Office)	615-885-9190	615-885-9306
Texas	Abilene		915-738-2110
Texas	Austin	512-342-1139	512-342-1150
Texas	Beaumont (Remote Encoding Center)		409-654-2600
Texas	Corpus Christi	361-886-2281	361-886-2288
Texas	Dallas (District Office)	214-760-4531	972-393-6714
Texas	El Paso		915-780-7534
Texas	Fort Worth (District Office)	817-317-3366	817-317-3356
Texas	Houston (District Office)	713-226-3872	713-226-3968
Texas	Lubbock	806-799-6547	806-799-1756
Texas	Midland		915-560-5108
Texas	San Angelo		915-659-7710
Texas	San Antonio (District Office)	210-368-8400	210-368-8401
Texas	Waco		254-399-2244
Utah	Salt Lake City (District Office)	801-974-2209	801-974-2219
Vermont	See Springfield, MA District Office		
Virgin Islands	See San Juan, Puerto Rico District Office		
Virginia	Merrifield (District Office)	703-698-6561	703-698-6342
Virginia	Norfolk	757-629-2225	757-629-2208
Virginia	Richmond (District Office)	804-775-6290	804-775-6196
Washington	Seattle (District Office)	206-442-6240	206-442-6199
Washington	Spokane (District Office)	509-626-6896	509-626-6820
Washington	Tacoma	253-471-6148	
West Virginia	Charleston (District Office)	304-561-1266	304-561-1256
Wisconsin	Milwaukee (District Office)	414-287-1835	414-287-1815

Postal Test Prep Tools & Accessories by T. W. Parnell

Postal Exam Quick Course Book

Exams 470 & 460 • Copyright 2004 • Only $15.95 + S/H

Complete test preparation in less that 12 hours ... 256 power packed pages featuring ...
- Free Live Support ... Test prep answers & advice by phone or e-mail.
- Fully Up-to-Date ... Details on new hiring program and for online job & exam announcements.
- Six Complete Practice Exams ... Practice is the key to a high score and to getting a job.
- Free Bonus ... Free extra online practice tests.

Postal Exam Quick Course Book with CD-ROM

Exams 470 & 460 • Copyright 2004 • Only $24.95 + S/H

Includes a copy of the Postal Exam Quick Course book plus a test prep CD-ROM featuring ...
- Series of Six Self-Paced Test Prep Classes ... Complete instruction on every detail of the exam.
- Timed Practice Tests ... Just like the real exam ... The most convenient and realistic way to practice.
- Following Oral Instructions Practice Tests ... Presentation of all 6 oral practice tests in the book.
- Compatible with any internet ready version of Windows®. (You do not have to be hooked up to internet.)

Postal Exam Quick Course Book with 3 Audio CD's

Exams 470 & 460 • Copyright 2004 • Only $29.95 + S/H

Includes a copy of the Postal Exam Quick Course book plus 3 audio CD's featuring ...
- Postal Exam Training Course CD ... Your own personal test prep class.
- Postal Exam Timed Practice Test CD ... The most convenient and realistic way to practice.
- Following Oral Instructions Practice Tests CD ... Presentation of all 6 oral practice tests in the book.
- The only way we could make it easier would be to take the test for you!

Extra Address Checking & Address Memory Practice Tests

Exams 470 & 460 • Only $9.95 + S/H

For applicants committed to achieving the highest possible score ...
- Ten Extra Address Checking Tests ... Master the incredible speed demanded on this section.
- Six Extra Address Memory Tests ... Master the memorization skills & speed needed to succeed.
- Practice Equals Performance ... Practice is the one and only key to improving performance.
- For truly motivated applicants willing to invest the extra effort needed to assure success!

Postal Test Prep CD-ROM

Exams 470 & 460 • Only $14.95 + S/H

The ultimate test prep technology assures maximum performance ...
- Series of Six Self-Paced Test Prep Classes ... Complete instruction on every detail of the exam.
- Timed Practice Tests ... Just like the real exam ... The most convenient and realistic way to practice.
- Following Oral Instructions Practice Tests ... Presentation of all 6 oral practice tests in the book.
- Compatible with any internet ready version of Windows®. (You do not have to be hooked up to internet.)

Continued on next page ...

Postal Test Prep Tools & Accessories by T. W. Parnell

3 Audio CD Test Prep Combo
Exams 470 & 460 • Only $19.95 + S/H

Package includes all 3 audio CD's at a special combo price ...
- Postal Exam Training Course CD ... Your own personal test prep class.
- Postal Exam Timed Practice Test CD ... The most convenient and realistic way to practice.
- Following Oral Instructions Practice Tests CD ... Presentation of all 6 oral practice tests in the book.
- The only way we could make it easier would be to take the test for you!

Postal Exam Training Course Audio CD
Exams 470 & 460 • Only $9.95 + S/H

Your own personal test prep class featuring ...
- Complete up-to-date facts ... What's on the exam, how to prepare, and much more.
- Step-by-step instructions for all four sections of the exam ... Follows exact exam format.
- Simple explanations for the all-important test taking strategies.
- Master the skills and speed needed to achieve your highest possible score.

Postal Exam Timed Practice Test Audio CD
Exams 470 & 460 • Only $9.95 + S/H

The most convenient way to practice realistically and time yourself precisely ...
- Accurately timing yourself is the most important part of practicing realistically.
- Finding someone to time you day after day for extended periods can be very difficult.
- Timing yourself is distracting, and you simply cannot afford to be distracted.
- The Postal Exam Timed Practice Test CD does the timing for you conveniently and precisely.

Following Oral Instructions Practice Tests Audio CD
Exams 470 & 460 • Only $9.95 + S/H

A professional presentation of all 6 Following Oral Instructions practice tests in the book ...
- Finding someone to read all the questions for you is difficult ... and on 6 different occasions yet.
- With this CD, you are no longer dependent on someone else's schedule or whims.
- Practice at your own convenience ... anytime and anywhere you choose.
- Do not cheat yourself out of the realistic practice you so desperately need!

Postal Exam Speed Marking System
Only $9.95 + S/H

Science and common sense combine to elevate test taking technology to a new level ...
- Features a set of Speed Marking Pencils with ergonomic design and oversized marking surface.
- Also includes a booklet of unique speed building strategies for maximum performance.
- More than doubles your marking speed ... Less time marking equals more questions answered.
- Answer more questions ... Capture more points ... Achieve your highest possible score!

Continued on next page ...

254

Postal Test Prep Tools & Accessories by T. W. Parnell

CD-ROM Upgrade Kit with Speed Marking System
Exams 470 & 460 • Only $19.95 + S/H

Upgrade your Quick Course book with a CD-ROM and Speed Marking System combo kit ...

- Series of Six Self-Paced Test Prep Classes ... Complete instruction on every detail of the exam.
- Timed Practice Tests ... Just like the real exam ... The most convenient and realistic way to practice.
- Following Oral Instructions Practice Tests ... Presentation of all 6 oral practice tests in the book.
- Postal Exam Speed Marking System ... Double your marking speed ... Capture more points!

3 Audio CD Upgrade Kit with Speed Marking System
Exams 470 & 460 • Only $24.95 + S/H

Upgrade your book with all 3 audio CD's plus the Speed Marking System ...

- Postal Exam Training Course CD ... Your own personal test prep class.
- Postal Exam Timed Practice Test CD ... The most convenient and realistic way to practice.
- Following Oral Instructions Practice Tests CD ... Presentation of all 6 oral practice tests in the book.
- Postal Exam Speed Marking System ... Double your marking speed ... Capture more points!

How to Order

Order Online
Visit our website *www.PostalExam.com* to order Pathfinder products online using a credit card. Online orders are usually shipped within 24 hours.

Order by Phone
Call 1-800-748-1819 to order by phone using a credit card. Phone orders are usually shipped within 24 hours. This toll free number is answered by Customer Service Representatives prepared to assist you with orders, but they are not trained to provide test prep support, and they cannot connect you to the Test Prep Support Group. For test prep support, you must call the Support Line phone number given on page 60.

Order by Mail
To order by mail, send a check or money order for the proper amount to the below address along with the order form found on the next page. It is important that you send the completed order form to assure we understand exactly which item or items you wish to order. Mail orders are usually shipped within 24 hours once your payment is received at our office.

Pathfinder Distributing Co.
P.O. Box 1368
Pinehurst, TX 77362-1368

Shipping & Handling Charges
For fast, accurate, traceable, and economical delivery, Pathfinder ships via Priority Mail. Typical delivery time is 2 - 3 Postal working days. This delivery time does not include the shipping date and is not guaranteed. However, in our experience, Priority Mail is almost always delivered within this time frame. For your benefit, Pathfinder charges a flat $5.00 shipping and handling fee for Priority Mail. Depending on weight and address, our cost can exceed $5.00, but Pathfinder absorbs any shipping costs over this amount. For even faster delivery, Express Mail is available for a flat fee of $15.00. Express Mail offers guaranteed next day delivery to metropolitan addresses and second day delivery to rural addresses. Call for details.

Continued on next page ...

Order Form

Mail to:

Pathfinder Distributing Co.
P.O. Box 1368
Pinehurst, TX 77362-1368

Item	Price Each		Shipping & Handling		Sub Total	Quantity	Total
Postal Exam Quick Course	$15.95	+	$5.00	=	$20.95	X	=
Postal Exam Quick Course with CD-ROM	$24.95	+	$5.00	=	$29.95	X	=
Postal Exam Quick Course with 3 Audio CD's	$29.95	+	$5.00	=	$34.95	X	=
Extra Address Checking & Address Memory Practice Tests	$ 9.95	+	$5.00	=	$14.95	X	=
Postal Test Prep CD-ROM	$14.95	+	$5.00	=	$19.95	X	=
3 Audio CD Test Prep Combo	$19.95	+	$5.00	=	$24.95	X	=
Postal Exam Training Course Audio CD	$ 9.95	+	$5.00	=	$14.95	X	=
Postal Exam Timed Practice Test Audio CD	$ 9.95	+	$5.00	=	$14.95	X	=
Following Oral Instructions Practice Tests Audio CD	$ 9.95	+	$5.00	=	$14.95	X	=
Postal Exam Speed Marking System	$ 9.95	+	$5.00	=	$14.95	X	=
CD-ROM Upgrade Kit with Speed Marking System	$19.95	+	$5.00	=	$24.95	X	=
3 Audio CD Upgrade Kit with Speed Marking System	$24.95	+	$5.00	=	$29.95	X	=

Don't forget to enclose a check or money order for this amount …... Grand Total:

Please print the below information carefully to assure correct shipment.

Name	
Mailing Address	
City / State / Zip Code	
Phone Number (with area code)	